Living Generously

Women mentoring women

"The world is made of stories not of atoms." – Muriel Rukeyser.

Also in the "Women's Voices, Women's Lives" series:

BREAKING THROUGH – WOMEN, WORK AND CAREERS
AS A WOMAN – WRITING WOMEN'S LIVES
GLORIOUS AGE – GROWING OLDER GLORIOUSLY
NO FEAR OF FLYING – WOMEN AT HOME AND ABROAD
TAKING A STAND – WOMEN IN POLITICS AND SOCIETY
CITY WOMEN COUNTRY WOMEN – CROSSING THE BOUNDARIES
SINGULAR WOMEN – RECLAIMING SPINSTERHOOD
SISTERS – SIBLING RIVALRY, SISTERLY LOVE *(forthcoming)*
MY MOTHER, MY DAUGHTER *(forthcoming)*
GROWING UP FEMINIST –
    THE NEW GENERATION OF AUSTRALIAN WOMEN
GROWING UP FEMINIST TOO –
    RAISING WOMEN, RAISING CONSCIOUSNESS
FORCE OF CIRCUMSTANCE –
    WOMEN, PLACE, POWER AND SURVIVAL *(forthcoming)*

Living Generously
Women mentoring women

Edited by Jocelynne A Scutt

Artemis

Artemis Publishing Pty Ltd
PO Box 151
Market Street Post Office
Melbourne 8007 Victoria
Tel: (03) 9614 3920
Fax: (03) 9670 1252

First published 1996
Copyright © Jocelynne A Scutt 1996
Copyright in individual written contributions remains
with the contributors.

Interviews: Joyce Apap, Carmel Guerra, Donna Justo, Joan
Kirner, Daphne Milward, Edith Morgan, Christine
Ramsay, Edel Suede copyright © Jocelynne A. Scutt 1996

All rights reserved. No part of this publication may be
reproduced in a retrieval system, or transmitted in any
form or by any means, electronic, mechanical, photo-
copying, recording or otherwise, without prior written
permission of the publisher.

National Library of Australia
Cataloguing-in-Publication entry:

Living generously : women mentoring women.
   Includes index.
   ISBN 1 875658 09 2

   1. Women in business – Australia. 2. Women – Social
networks. 3. Mentors in business – Australia. 4. Women
in the professions – Australia. 5. Mentors in the
professions – Australia. I. Scutt, Jocelynne A., 1947– .
(Series : Women's voices, women's lives ; no. 8).

658.409082

Typeset in Janson by Claire Warren
Printed in Australia by Australian Print Group

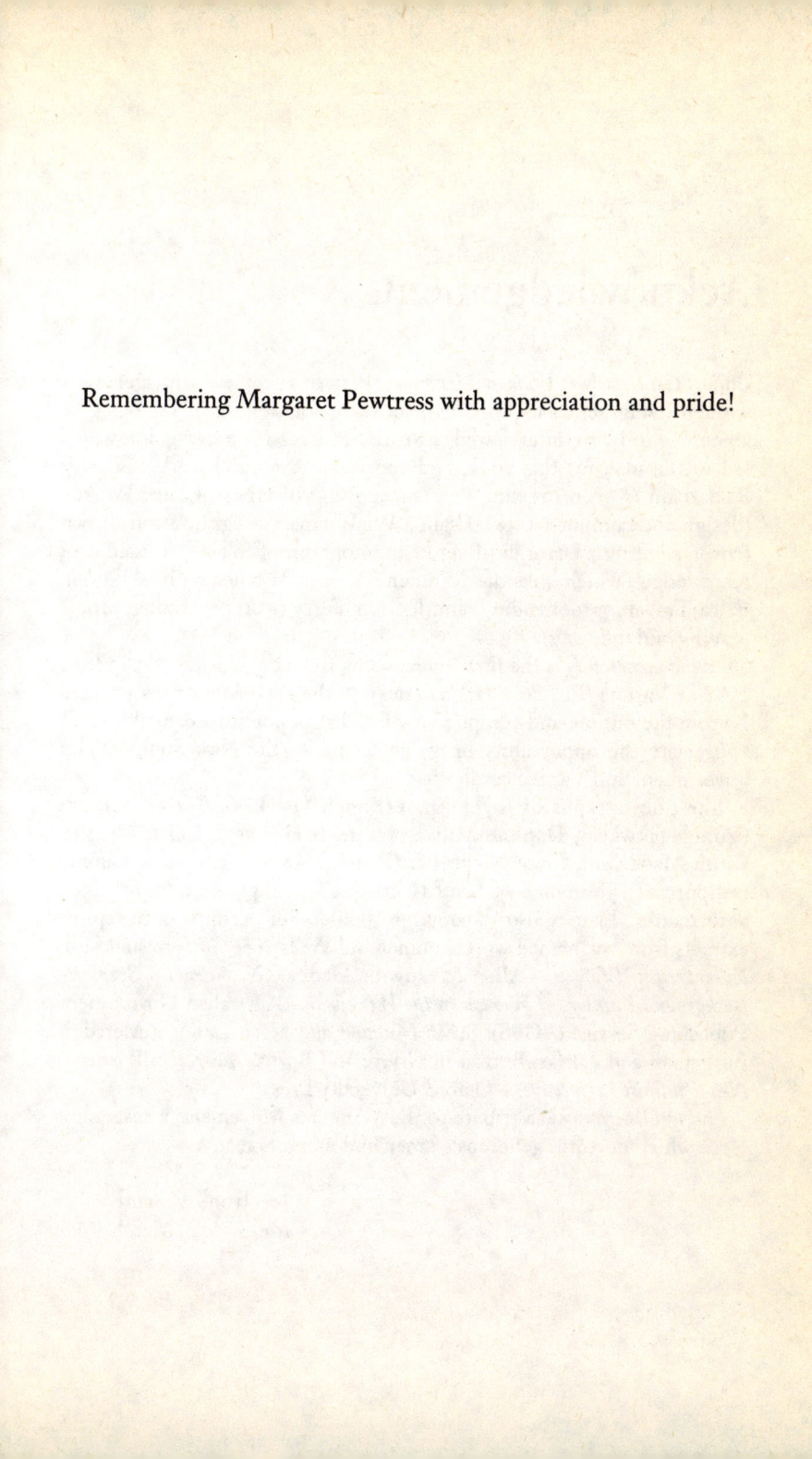

Remembering Margaret Pewtress with appreciation and pride!

Acknowledgements

Living Generously – Women Mentoring Women is replete with generous women living generous lives. I thank them for writing or for being so amenable to being interviewed. I thank Agi Racz for a discussion which led to the idea for this book, and appreciate the good work of Lesley Robertson (wordprocessing and transcribing of tapes); Claire Warren (design and computerwork); Dianna Wells (cover design); Alison Brown (cover painting); Diarmuid Piggott (photograph of 'The Five Lamps of Knowledge', which links the 'Women's Voices, Women's Lives' books), Erica Travers (proofreading) and Jocelyn Terry (wordprocessing, proofreading and indexing).

Living Generously is the fifth book arising from my ten-day stay in June 1992 at Varuna, Eleanor Dark's cottage in the Blue Mountains – where I wrote the outline and compiled my first list of potential contributors. I appreciate the opportunity provided to me by the New South Wales government and Varuna committee.

The photographs of Joyce Apap (Ponch Hawkes), Carmel Guerra (Ponch Hawkes), Daphne Milward (Ponch Hawkes), Edith Morgan (Ruth Maddison), Joyce Nicholson (Ponch Hawkes), Christine Ramsay (selfportrait), Jocelynne A. Scutt (Christine Ramsay), are acknowledged with thanks. Thanks also to copyright holders for permission to reprint extracts from the named works: Poiner and Wills, *The Gifthorse* and Still, *Enterprising Women* – Allen & Unwin; Alcorso, *Non-English Speaking Background Immigrant Women in the Workforce* – Australian Government Publishing Service (AGPS); Susan Mitchell and News Limited; Meredith Burgmann and Fairfax; Burton in Grieve and Burns, *Australian Women – New Feminist Perspectives* – Oxford University Press.

Living Generously is a tribute to the Women's Movement, a sustaining force which nurtures generous women and mentors many.

Jocelynne A. Scutt
Melbourne, March 1996

Contents

INTRODUCTION
    Jocelynne A Scutt *Mentoring Women* 1

PART I
So Strong My Family
    Lillian Holt *Soaring with Eagles* 21
    Donna Justo *Something Special – Womentoring* 31
    Wendy Weeks *Critical Reflection and Action: A Mutual Sharing* 45
    Marge Oke *Standing on a Table-top and Learning to Lead* 57
    June Benson *How Brave You Can Be* 79
    Daphne Milward *Descended from a Matriarch* 88
    Joan Kirner *To Do Something Good* 100

PART II
Darkness into Light
    Susan Kelly *Much More than Tea and Sympathy* 119
    Val Marsden *White Knuckles and Strong Women* 130
    Kay Saunders *Neither Singularly Saints Nor Sinners* 144
    Edith Morgan *A Strong Commitment* 154
    Joyce Apap *A Smile Speaks any Language* 167

PART III
Contradictions
    Joyce Nicholson *Women Must Keep Talking* 187
    Natasha Stott Despoja *Gorgeous Girls, Great Women* 199
    Melinda McPherson *An Empowering Journey* 208
    Carmel Guerra *Life and Belonging* 219
    Christine Ramsay *As One Door Shuts, Another Opens* 233
    Mary Owen *The Women in My Life* 243

PART IV
Good Fortune, My Company

Jill Lennon *A Traveller, Not a Tourist* 259
Ruth Lechte *Unseen Energy* 267
Audrey McDonald *Raised 'Living Generously'* 274
Edna Chamberlain *Women – Mentors and Models* 284
Edel Suede *Living My Beliefs* 294
Margaret Pewtress *The Wisdom of Keeping Options Open* . . . 305
Lenore Coltheart *Thank you, Women, and Whitlam Too* . . . 317

EPILOGUE

Jocelynne A Scutt *Generous Women, Generous Lives* 325

INDEX 340

COVER ILLUSTRATION – ACKNOWLEDGEMENT 360

INTRODUCTION

Mentoring Women

Jocelynne A Scutt

Mary Cunningham was, in her own words, a woman 'in the right place at the right time'. A graduate of Harvard Business School, she had been inundated with job offers before she graduated, and was planning a career in investment banking. Then came an offer to work for Bendix, a Fortune 500 company – one of the top 500 companies in the United States. Not only was Mary Cunningham to work for Bendix, but she was to be executive assistant to Bill Agee, the head man and himself a highly-esteemed graduate of Harvard Business School. Yet before joining the company, she had qualms. Interviews with the four vice-chairmen (indeed, all *were* men) went badly: one was a bully, the second terrified of her, the third a 'hey, look at me, I'm great' type, whilst the fourth was addicted to jokes that fell flat. She decided to turn down Bendix and take up an offer from investment bank Morgan Stanley.

'Most investment bankers are whores,' exploded Bill Agee when she told him of her decision. Anyway, he went on, you've already had a stint in both commercial and investment banking: 'You've been on the service side long enough. What you need now is to be mentored.'

Cunningham needed, Agee told her, someone to show her 'the inside, the real guts, of corporate life'. 'Look at the case studies of every successful chief executive,' he said, 'and in nine out of 10 cases they've been mentored. That's how I got ahead. Not by sitting at some desk dotting the i's and crossing the t's on other people's deals. If you go to Morgan Stanley, you'll be doing the paperwork on Bendix deals. At Bendix you have a chance to make those deals, to design them, to do the creative work.'

Confronted, now, with a dilemma: what should she do? Mary Cunningham talked with her closest advisors and several professors. *All were in Agee's camp*: investment banking was something she could do 'any time', but an opportunity to work for a 'distinguished alumnus' like Bill Agee 'was rare'. *Mentorship was a favourite route to the top around Harvard, and who could be a better mentor than Bill Agee.* When *he* was 28 (Mary Cunningham's age) he had been mentored by a high flier at the Fortune 500 company. Her Harvard professors were adamant: *no better mentor could be found.*

In *Powerplay – What Really Happened at Bendix*, Mary Cunningham writes of the outcome of her decision to take the mentoring route. In Australia in the late 1970s and 1980s, the buzz word for women working their way into male power structures was 'networking'. In the late 1980s and 1990s, 'mentoring' took its place alongside. Neither concept is new for the Women's Movement, and networking amongst and between women for mutual support and political action certainly has a long and sustained history.

> *... networking amongst and between women for mutual support and political action has a long and sustained history.*

In the late nineteenth century, when local school boards were established in the United Kingdom with the passage of the *Education Act* of 1870 (which made all children eligible for elementary school education), women networked with other women to ensure women gained board positions. Where a woman retired from a board, women networked to ensure that the vacancy was filled by another woman. In Australia, women's trade unions – like the Tailoresses Union (the first official Australian women's union, founded in 1874 by 300 Melbourne women) and the Laundresses Union – provided opportunities for women to network with others in their industries. Women's organisations such as the Karrakatta Club (in Western Australia), the National Council of Women (founded in 1896) and the South Australian Women's Suffrage League extended local and Australia-wide networking opportunities to women. This was a practice building on past practices of women, and continued into the twentieth century. Women used networking for political ends, through lobbying and securing support for political goals, and for personal support. Mentoring was more difficult.

Traditionally, mentoring is seen as involving a person in a position of power in the 'public sphere' (the world of paidwork and public office) encouraging one further down the hierarchy, 'showing the ropes' to the person positioned at a lower status. Traditionally, the concept relates to men. Overwhelmingly it is men who hold positions of power in the public service and in public and private sector corporations, industries and businesses, and who hold powerful public offices. Rarely do women hold positions 'at the top'. Overwhelmingly it is men holding lower posts in the hierarchy who are mentored by the men at the top. The 'cloning effect' operates so that 'like support like'. Men in positions of power seek to encourage those 'below' them whom they see as their mirror image when young or younger. Men on selection panels tend to hire candidates who most closely resemble themselves. Men with the power to hire tend to employ jobseekers who look, act, think, speak like themselves. After all, if a man has confidence in his own abilities and approves of his own approach to the job, he is likely to see admirable qualities and potential in those *who appear to be most like himself.*

In *Australian Women – New Feminist Perspectives*, Clare Burton extends this into the learning process within organisations. 'How are relevant occupational organizational experiences passed on?' she asks, replying:

> It is probable that highly informal situations, on and off the job, are the most important training contexts. We need to reflect on the idea of homosociability, the idea that senior men will feel more comfortable imparting such knowledge to junior male colleagues, in a host of informal ways, taking them under their wing, introducing them to other people, than they would with female staff.

'I have heard female staff complain,' she writes, 'of their relative invisibility in processes such as these.' Rather than a *conscious intent* to discriminate, this problem can arise from 'perceptual maps':

> The idea of the male-as-breadwinner affects people's perceptions, so that a male is more likely than a female to be seen as disadvantaged by the lack of a career structure and therefore given more consideration when opportunities arise. Very different processes of work allocation occur in apparently identical jobs.

Where few women are at the apex of hierarchies, few women are able to mentor others in the traditional sense – be they women or men. Where few women network in the upper echelons of power, few women will be in a position to recommend or employ women who are lower in the hierarchy. When women are absent from the upper layers of business and powerful organisations and institutions, women cannot 'learn the ropes' or divine the 'inner secrets' of the boardroom. They cannot then hand on knowledge to other women, for the knowledge is not there – or theirs – to give.

For Mary Cunningham at Bendix, the quickest way to learn about the corporate culture of the company was from the man who had become her mentor, Bill Agee. The best way she could learn about the issues and activities of Bendix which were most important from the perspective of those at the top was from *men* at the top: all chief posts were held by men. The fastest way she could learn about the projects which were most important to the company (so far as the company head was concerned) was from the head of the company – a man.

Mary Cunningham learned Bendix operations from 'top down' and 'bottom up': top down, because she initially accompanied Bill Agee on his daily rounds, involving meetings, more meetings, then 'debriefing' sessions afterwards; bottom up, because (amongst other projects) she took on an assignment looking into pensions – 'negotiations with the United Automobile Workers union were coming up and pensions promised to be a crucial issue' – talking to people in accounting and 'anyone at Bendix who had anything to do with pensions'.

Mentoring need not begin at the very top, of course. Women and men further down the hierarchy can be encouraged and assisted by those in middle-management. People on 'the bottom rungs' need mentoring to enable them to learn about the levels of business immediately above them, then several rungs further on, in order to move onward and upward. Yet for many years, laws, regulations, rules and customs maintained a system where no woman could find any woman in middle-management to promote and encourage her career. Even if she could find a man prepared to act as mentor, his faith in her qualifications and ability was irrelevant: the system was organised so that it was impossible for her to 'move up', even if she learned the ropes.

The public service was founded on the notion that if women were to 'serve' then they should do so in support roles only.

Although the public service might be expected to be organised so as to fulfil its aim: public service, since its inception this has been far from the truth. The public service was founded on the notion that if women were to 'serve' then they should do so in support roles only. No places at the tier of secretary, deputy secretary, or assistant secretary for women.

When allowed into the service, women held positions as stenographic secretary, cleaner, clerical assistant, typist and tealady. Even this narrowing of career opportunities for women was not enough so far as those running the public service and those making the laws were concerned. Further restrictions were deliberately built-in to the system. As if the limitations imposed upon women were not enough, if a woman married, until the late 1960s her status within the public service dropped even more dramatically. She was no longer entitled to remain on the 'permanent' establishment; she was automatically transferred to the category labelled 'temporary'. This eliminated her from access to many industrial entitlements, such as longservice leave and superannuation. It severely interfered with any prospects of promotion, whether she was an officer of the public service for the federal government or for state governments. As for women generally, in the federal public service, the third division was until the early 1970s 'out of bounds' for women. Women were relegated to the fourth division and thus to the non-promotional support roles. The first and second divisions were automatically out of the range of any women, for promotion into those divisions came from the third division – from which women were outlawed. 'Bright' men in the third division were cultivated by their superiors in the second and first divisions. 'Bright' men were mentored and leapt up the ladder. The mentoring of a bright woman meant only that she could become private secretary to a powerful man, or go to the top of the clerical division. The divisions within state public service operated similarly.

Affirmative action and equal opportunity in paid employment are designed to redress the balance. Women are no longer precluded overtly by laws, regulations or rules from being appointed to any position in the public service, state or federal. Yet customs continue to prevail, the effects of discriminatory laws remain, and past discrimination operates so that, at most, only 10 percent or so of positions in the senior executive service are held by women in any public service. The criterion for advancement (in private or public sectors) is now required to be 'merit'. But what does merit mean?

The kinds of standards used to select on merit are 'culture bound' – and the culture is that of 'dominant, white, male, urbanised, industrialised, ethnics'.

In 'Culture and Merit', a paper delivered to a Macquarie University conference, 'Defining Merit', in 1985, M. Kalantzis, M. Issaris and B. Cope suggest that the kinds of standards used to select on merit are 'culture bound' – and the culture is that of 'dominant, white, male, urbanised, industrialised, ethnics':

> Words such as 'resourcefulness', 'leadership', 'initiative' are used again and again in the Public Service Notices and job advertisements, all projecting a very accurate image of the person required rather than abilities or potential. It is of course possible, as has been done, to fit certain women and certain 'ethnics' into these same criteria, but this is simply a refinement of the pre-existing system. No real change has occurred which would alter the criteria selecting an elite group of 'anglo' and 'ethnic' males and females. The composition of the group may change, but the nature of it doesn't, nor does the structure which gave rise to it in the first place. Using the merit principle well, all middle class people are given equal opportunity for middle class jobs regardless of sex or ethnicity.

Gaining promotion by merit is said, amongst other claims, to overcome discrimination against women and ethnic and racial minorities inherent in the old 'promotion by seniority' rule. Yet in addition to criticism of the so-called merit principle, as Robin Jackson points out in 'A City Person', in *City Women Country Women – Crossing the Boundaries*, the seniority principle did not always militate against promotion for women and minorities:

Much has been said about the inequity of the seniority system in the public service. In hindsight, it does seem ridiculous and totally unfair to give someone a promotion only because they have been in the place longer than another person. And yet, another point of view is that this system assisted many women to reach fairly high levels in the public service. It meant that women such as myself and most of my friends, who had never sat down and thought about a career path, ended up after many years in well-paid secure positions. We didn't have to make decisions about jobs, we were just pulled up the ladder as the positions above us became vacant. I have never seen analysis of the way this aspect of the public service actually helped women. Now the system has been modernised and is based on merit. But the old way enabled many of my female friends in the service, who were single, to buy their own homes and often travel extensively overseas.

Ironically, with many more women, married and single, now in a position to claim promotion by reason of seniority (and, with every year, more becoming likely to do so), that rule has been abandoned and a new rule, which has its own drawbacks (favouring the already 'favoured group'), has been introduced!

In their book *The Gifthorse – A critical look at Equal Employment Opportunity in Australia*, published in 1991, Gretchen Poiner and Sue Wills discuss the phenomenon of women going into middle- and upper-management (the latter at an even slower pace than the former). In their observation, two groups of women have become visible through affirmative action and the operation of equal employment opportunity legislation and programs: women entering middle-management and 'networking feverishly with each other', and 'the lone pioneer intrepidly entering the world of traditional men's work – the first woman jockey, the first woman railway fettler, the first woman commercial airline pilot'. Media coverage of the first group, they say (at least so far as concerns the print media) is 'fairly constant':

> This is no doubt partly because of the suspicion that attaches to any formerly disadvantaged brokers who determine the allocation of advantages.

As for the second group, 'who are good visual media material':

> ... coverage is sporadic and peters out very quickly. After all ... who is interested in the 'second woman to' or the 'fifteenth woman to'?

Poiner and Wills conclude that women entering management 'are by far the most visible, the most studied and counted and their rising salaries the most sought after by advertisers'. Does this make a difference to the position of women generally?

A problem for women in the mentoring stakes in today's business world is that the 'cloning effect' does not operate for women as it does for men. Some men (a few) may renounce the cloning effect when it comes to mentoring others. Like Bill Agee at Bendix, they are prepared to mentor women, or at least some women. Yet most men in a position to mentor concentrate their efforts wholly on their own kind. Contrarily, women *may* mentor women – or they may very well mentor young (or younger) men. Women may even mentor older men, and men more powerful than they – although in the world of the dominant ethos, this is not called 'mentoring' but 'mothering'.

Women on interview panels are far more likely to select a man over a woman, as a man is likely to select a woman over a man. Women may select men for positions because they (the women) are persuaded to do so by men on the panel. Women may select men for positions because they (the women) have to guard their own positions against attacks (overt or covert) by their male co-panellists or colleagues. Women may select men over women, because they (the women) lack the courage to align themselves with other women – for choosing a woman candidate may well be seen in this light. Women may select a man over a woman, because they (the women) are threatened by the quality of a woman candidate. The choice of a man may arise from a meanness of not wanting a (or another) woman to succeed, or fear that the woman outshines *them*. Or women may select men for positions *because they (the candidates) are men*. Women have been colonised by the dominant ethos to elevate the abilities and capabilities of men above those of women. Many women resist, or do their best to resist, this colonisation. But it can be no surprise that other women do not resist: colonisation can be so strong that it creates a barrier to any recognition by a woman that it exists.

In her analysis of staffing levels at Broughton psychiatric hospital in Melbourne, Victoria, in the 1950s, Zelda D'Aprano observed this dynamic. In *Zelda – The Becoming of a Woman*, published in 1977 and 1995, she concluded that a major factor causing a serious shortage of staff was, without doubt, 'the attitude of senior staff towards those below them'. When, some years later, she became a part the Women's Liberation Movement, Zelda D'Aprano came to understand that all power structures 'have been created by men'. When women occasionally, 'by the grace of men', gain positions of power, 'they feel the need to prove themselves capable of carrying out this authority'. This need, she says, often makes the women 'more ruthless than men'. They can rule the roost with a vengeance.

And it can go one step further: to mentoring *male* subordinates – for this is what they see their male counterparts doing.

Yet the mentoring by women of men may be done under silent protest, because it is required and the woman has no choice, or 'willingly' – until the woman realises the trick that has been played upon her. In a 1993 interview 'Not According to the Calendar' in *Glorious Age – Growing Older Gloriously*, Ethel Kirsop spoke of how she was unwilling mentor of a man who knew far less than she about the business of the firm where she worked:

> I was secretary to a 'top man' for 25 years. Then as often happened in large organisations there were changes, and he left, together with three of the four 'top men'. That left me holding the cards. I was not holding the power, but I had the information, quite a lot of information. I inherited my former boss' successor, whom I had loathed for 20 years. He was as nice as could be to me for about six months, then he thought he knew the job. I saw the writing on the wall. One day I decided I could stand it no longer, so I packed my belongings in a paper bag and walked out of a job of 25 years without any recognition or reward. There was no golden handshake for the secretary.

In her subsequent career as a temporary secretary, then a teacher of shorthand (initially at business colleges, subsequently to cadet journalists with Australian Consolidated Press (ACP), then with News Limited), Ethel Kirsop played a considerable role as mentor. She was never in a position of formal power within a business or public sector hierarchy. She worked as 'backroom gal' and campaign manager to have women elected into local government, succeeding when Joan Pilone was elected to North Sydney Council and, later, Sydney City Council in the 1970s.

At Bendix, Mary Cunningham had no support network; her sole support was her mentor, Bill Agee. At 5.00 pm on Friday nights, the office emptied rapidly:

> 'Goodnight,' the secretaries would sing out. 'Goodnight,' I would respond in my cheerful, businesslike voice. 'Are you sure you wouldn't like to come out for a drink with us?' a few would ask. 'No, thank you,' I'd say. Usually, the only stragglers were Agee and me, but even he left by seven. Sometimes I worked late to avoid going home. Where was I going? To an apartment stockpiled with Campbell's Chunky Soups and unopened cartons [from my interstate move]? It was hardly a home...

But she did have a mentor. And the way the mentorship began was not unusual: in the way of many mentorships, it came about through a network. J. Leslie Rollins was a recruiter for several Fortune 500 companies, as well as having been assistant dean at Harvard Business School. Some of Mary Cunningham's professors told him she was one of their best students. One of the deans said she had 'the best chance of being the first female graduate of the Harvard Business School to become the chairman of a non-cosmetics company'. Mary Cunningham had no doctors or lawyers, or 'successful professionals in business', in her family tree, nor bank presidents or engineers. But she had worked at a New York law firm and on Wall Street in Chase Manhattan Bank, and during vacation whilst at Harvard Business School was an intern at Salomon Brothers, New York, a 'blue-ribbon investment banking house'. She had also met a Bendix executive, Karen Walker, at a Women Students' Association meeting and gone to dinner with her and other students later. It was Karen Walker who had 'hounded Agee' to get Mary Cunningham 'out to Bendix as quickly as possible'. Les Rollins knew Bill Agee personally: it was Les Rollins who had 'brought Agee to Harvard', from which he had graduated 16 years previously.

Being in a network is a first step. And networks are not confined to the business elite. The networks to which a person gains access can dictate many aspects of the individual's life. Networks, at whatever part of the socio-economic spectrum a person stands, can have a determinative effect. In *Blue collar and beyond – the experiences of non-english speaking background women in the Australian labour force*, published in 1993, Caroline Alcorso and Graham Harrison write of networks and the way women of non-English speaking background or birth gain access to paidwork. 'There appears to be,' they say, 'a reliance' by non-English speaking background women 'on informal networks, rather than formal channels, as a means of finding [paid]work'. This, they say, can have a conservative effect. In 1991 in her report *Non-English Speaking Background Immigrant Women in the Workforce*, Caroline Alcorso commented upon this aspect of networks:

> Migrant workers know the jobs that migrant men and women from different countries perform in Australia and use this knowledge to help friends and compatriots to get work. Despite the existence of . . . the [Commonwealth Employment Service], migrant women today, as in past years, are more likely to find a job through a friend or relative; often in the same factory or company as the latter.

. . . *in a world where money, profit, status and prestige attach to clearly defined occupations, mentors may well be 'more valuable' in career-terms in some fields than in others.*

In their survey of large employers, written up in the 1990 report *EEO in Thirteen Organisations*, Carmel Niland and Rafe Champion found that reliance on unsolicited applications and word-of-mouth recruiting 'was widespread for labouring jobs in the construction and manufacturing industries, and was indeed favoured by these employers, despite the obvious implications of inequity'.

The effect of reliance on networks is twofold: people get jobs (a good, except that certain people may be favoured over others, whatever their respective abilities), and people in particular networks who get jobs, get them in fields related to those networks (a good or a bad – depending upon what network a person is in, and what job she or he might *really* want or be suited to). A person in the 'high flyer' networks – professionals, entrepreneurs, 'top' businesspeople, holders of 'high' public office and the like – will be most likely to succeed in the fields related to those networks. People in less salubrious networks will be likely to remain outside the realm of 'the elite'. There will be mentors in all fields – but in a world where money, profit, status and prestige attach to clearly defined occupations, mentors may well be 'more valuable' in career-terms in some fields than in others.

Yet even if one takes the conventional approach to careerpaths, success and achievement, elevating those in areas seen as prestigious according to the dominant ethos, networking and mentoring are not always positive experiences. As Mary Cunningham discovered, there are drawbacks to mentoring:

> I was becoming increasingly indispensable to Agee, but at my own expense. And I started to resent it. I was too busy to live. My entire life was devoted to Agee. I got messages from my mother warning me I wasn't living a balanced life, and she was right. But I found it difficult to extricate myself either from Bendix or from Agee. The demands of the job [were] insatiable. I'd try to round out my life, to make plans to see someone for dinner, and then Agee would say, 'Mare, I really need you for this one, could you please just cancel that?' That was the flip side of mentorship they never told you about at Business School. Once you were mentored, how did you get unmentored?

... the notion that it 'is not unknown for a woman to sleep her way to the top' has no validity in the real world, despite poorly conceived statements to the contrary.

There is another drawback for women, which was voiced in 1994 without apology by Justice Spender of the Federal Court of Australia in the course of argument in *Chambers v. James Cook University*, where the plaintiff had been dismissed from James Cook University as a consequence of his engaging in sexual activity with women students, which they (and the university) subsequently said was sexual harassment.

'It is not unknown for a woman to sleep her way to the top,' said the judge. Had he said: 'It is *alleged* that it is not unknown for a woman to sleep her way to the top,' or 'Some people say, without regard to whether the statement is factual or not, that it is not unknown for a woman to sleep her way to the top', or 'There is no research substantiating it, but some people say it is not unknown for a woman to sleep her way to the top', or even (most accurately): 'The available research and authorities overwhelmingly indicate otherwise, but nonetheless some people assert that it is not unknown for a woman to sleep her way to the top,' there could have been no complaint. But the notion that it 'is not unknown for a woman to sleep her way to the top' has no validity in the real world, despite poorly conceived statements to the contrary.

How many women *are there* 'at the top'? In Australia, so few that most activists in the Women's Movement could name the lot. Joan Kirner, former Premier of Victoria and now head of the Employment Services Regulatory Authority; Carmen Lawrence, former Premier of Western Australia and now federal minister for health; Rosemary Follett, former Chief Minister of the Australian Capital Territory, then leader of the opposition; Kate Carnell, Chief Minister of the Australian Capital Territory; Pamela O'Neil, former deputy leader of the opposition in the Northern Territory; Rosemary Foot, former deputy leader of the New South Wales opposition; Mary Gaudron of the High Court of Australia; Lois O'Donoghue, head of the Australian and Torres Strait Islander Commissioner (ATSIC); Elizabeth Evatt, formerly Chief Judge of the Family Court of Australia, then President of the Australian Law Reform Commission; Roma Mitchell, former judge of the Supreme Court of South Australia and now governor; Leneen Forde, who holds the office of governor in Queensland; Janet Holmes a Court and Anna Booth of the Reserve Bank board; Eve Mahlab of the board of Westpac; Margaret Jackson, Cathy Walters and a very few other women members of corporate boards; Jean Blackburn, former chancellor of Canberra University; Pat O'Shane, chancellor of the University of New England; Leonie Kramer, chancellor of the University of Sydney; Di Yerbury and Faye Gale, vice chancellors of, respectively, Macquarie University and the University of Western Australia; the five women judges of the Federal Court of Australia; the very few women judges of Supreme Courts of Queensland, the Northern Territory and New South Wales and of the County and District Courts of some states, and of the Family Court; the few women who hold chief executive or town clerk positions in local government around Australia; the very few women who hold ministerial positions in state and federal governments; the very few women heads of government departments. Who else is there? And is anyone sufficiently foolish to attempt to assert that any one of these women claimed her post by any means other than brains, tenacity and the work of the Women's Movement over the ages? Hardly.

What of all those cases of which we know, whether through the media or, more frequently now, through the courts, equal opportunity boards and tribunals, the Human Rights and Equal Opportunity Commission, or industrial tribunals (and sometimes through the criminal courts), where women have been discriminated against by sexual harassment or have suffered non-consensual sexual imposition amounting to rape, sexual assault or indecent assault? If a woman engages in *consensual* sexual activity with her boss or a paidwork superior, the research indicates that she is likely to be relieved of her services – both paidwork and sexual – at a date in the future by being fired or forced to 'resign'; that she is likely to be demoted, moved sideways, or have a 'nothing' job created for her so that she is the subject of derision and 'knowing' looks and eventually resigns. If the sexual activity is imposed upon her and she refuses, the woman will far from arrive 'at the top'; if she submits, the ultimate result will be (whether sooner or later) termination of her services. If some suggest that women engage in consensual sexual activity – then *marry* 'the boss', this is hardly 'sleeping one's way to the top'! After all, *she* isn't the boss, *he* is – and marrying him don't change it – however many facile jokes may be made about 'who wears the pants'.

> *... the notion that mentoring is a very different relationship for a subordinate, if the subordinate happens to be a woman, is all too real.*

Despite the lack of reality so far as women 'sleeping their way to the top' is concerned, as Mary Cunningham discovered, the notion that mentoring is a very different relationship for a subordinate, if the subordinate happens to be a woman, is all too real. Into her second year at Bendix, and in the middle of a restructure which involved relieving some of the existing middle-management of their positions, Bill Agee approached her:

'Mary, we need to talk ... I've been getting some troubling calls recently from Harry Cunningham and a few of the other members of the board. They want to know if there's something going on between you and me.' ... 'Now, it's not that they think there is anything,' he said, before I could feel the full weight of the accusation sink in. 'In fact, they've each reassured me that they don't believe there's anything really wrong. It's just that they've been getting a few anonymous letters ...'

Yet ultimately it was not the converting, by mischievous co-workers, of a mentor relationship into a sexual one that brought down Mary Cunningham. The gameplan was far more important. The target was Bill Agee and Bendix.

Powerplay is a salutary tale of the deficiencies of mentoring, male-style. Mary Cunningham's loss of position came about not so much because of her mentor relationship with Bill Agee, but because of a 'destruct factor' which appears to be built-in to male-style mentoring itself.

The president of Bendix in 1972, when Bill Agee was 'headhunted', was W. Michael Blumenthal. Blumenthal built up the company, was 'on his way to becoming chairman' and was 'looking for a chief financial officer' to fill the number-two position. He fixed on Agee. They had a paradigm mentoring relationship – 'like father and son'. Then in 1977, when Blumenthal was officially sworn in as secretary of the treasury in the Carter administration, Agee was made head of Bendix. So far, everything was fine: the mentor had promoted his 'son' into the role he had vacated. The mentor had risen to a position of power which meant he could 'pass on' the position he no longer needed and which had now been eclipsed by his own rise.

Blumenthal's stated approach was to let Agee run the company, and not to interfere. 'Don't keep the seat warm for me,' he said. Yet he subsequently lost his post with the Carter administration. Why would Agee not ensure him a place on the Bendix board? Then came a massive falling out, involving plans to merge Bendix and Burroughs (a computer company). Put bluntly, Blumenthal organised a position on the Bendix board, created his own 'faction' within it, and ultimately brought down Agee. A sideline of the powerplay was forcing Mary Cunningham's resignation as a preliminary to forcing Agee's.

Male mentoring is like this. It is about the mentor *always* remaining in the more powerful position. It is about the mentored *always* remaining in a 'beholden' position to the mentor. It is about the mentor *never* being eclipsed by the mentored.

Powerful old *men are inevitably eclipsed, eventually, by powerful* young *(or younger) men.*

Yet, as we know, men grow old. Powerful *old* men are inevitably eclipsed, eventually, by powerful *young* (or younger) men. And, not liking it – for who, in the world of men as it is, would? – they strike back. The striking back is necessary, for they wish to regain their sense of being all-powerful (as they once were). Invariably it is directed against those who threaten them most: the very men they have mentored. In a world built on hierarchy, in a system where power and prestige breathe life into those who depend upon having them, mentoring is a necessary – and a dangerous – business.

The notion that all a woman needs is a (male) mentor, and she will 'make it' to the top in a flash, or that men 'make it' through mentoring and women need to emulate them, fails to address the problems that are built-in to hierarchies, the abuses of power and position for corporate and personal gain, and structural deficiencies within existing institutions. Few would deny that it is important to provide useful mechanisms for learning on the job. Nor would anyone seriously dispute the value of older, more experienced people sharing their knowledge and learning with others who do not have them, or have less of them. Learning on the job and gaining wisdom and knowledge from those who *have* wisdom and knowledge are essential. Yet to elevate as *the* answer a system of mentoring that has developed through power structures devised and developed by powerful men is hardly illuminating.

Networking has its negative aspects too. Clare Burton comments that 'increasing numbers' of women:

> ... are sharing [in] the emergence of women's networks or groups within occupations and organizations. Apart from those who might be familiar with collectives and collective modes of decision making in the women's movement, more women are discovering the value of sharing experiences, particularly across occupational divisions (where we realize that apparently different circumstances share important characteristics) and learning the value of compromise and negotiation so that a minimum negative impact is felt by any one category of people.

But networks can develop into cliques of women exchanging business cards with an eye to the main chance, rather than being inclusionary groupings aimed at encouraging, supporting and advancing the position of *as many women as possible*. Networking can be about being 'included in' to the male hierarchy, rather than about challenging it.

Networking can be about being 'included in' to the male hierarchy, rather than about challenging it.

An article by Deborah Hope in the *Weekend Australian* of 2–3 December 1995 commented on the 'make it work for (only) *me*' approach. She quotes Susan Mitchell who contrasts 1980s and 1990s networking with the consciousness-raising that was a hallmark of the Women's Movement in the 1960s and 1970s:

> The aim [of consciousness-raising] was to swap the real stories of our lives. In the bland politeness of network dinners the only things women swap are their business cards . . . It's yuppie feminism. When was the last time one of those trendy, high-profile gatherings raised money for a women's cause. What has networking ever achieved for those women who live below the poverty line?

Sisterhood is far more than just 'succeeding' in the corporate world or in public office or powerful institutions, or linking with others for the sole purpose of advancing one's own career without regard to others. Mentoring, too, can be more than this.

There is a woman's way of mentoring, that can bring to each one of us strength and support, the will to go on and keep on going on, in our quest for making the world a different place. In the world of women's mentoring, self-aggrandisement and power for power's sake are not the aim. Rather, the goal is to build up each other. In aiming for this, we strive to provide to others the knowledge and learning we have. We strive to develop the wisdom to seek out learning and knowledge from those who have it, despite their not being recognised in the present world as having it, for the dominant ideology sees them as unimportant and what they know is ignored or decried. We come to appreciate the value of what is known and understood by those who are not 'at the top' of a male hierarchy. We are learning to accept that *our* knowledge and experience has a real value, that *our* encouragement and support have worth.

Living Generously – Women Mentoring Women is about just this: the way so many women mentor one another both generously and positively. It is not a mentoring that contains the destructive seeds of 'you owe me' or 'ignore my advice at your peril'. Nor is it a mentoring that requires the mentored always to remain 'the junior', the mentor always 'on top'. Nor is it one where superiority and hierarchy dictate the relationship, or where the mentoring relationship is only 'one on one'. It is far broader and more generous than that, for it is not about 'you scratch my back, I'll scratch yours' – and if you don't scratch mine, I'll never pay yours the slightest bit of attention, whatever the itch!

The mentoring of women, by women, comes often in the encouragement of groups of women by one or a number of women, collectively. It comes often through collective action and reciprocation. It is not a mentoring that leads to an inexorable 'falling out' if (when) the junior party – the mentored – rises to a position of power greater than that of the one who has been the mentor.

It is also one that recognises the tenuous nature of women's grasp upon the power which is 'allowed' to us by those who truly hold the power in the world the way it is. It recognises, too, that the position of individual women in the present power structure can vary significantly over time – by day, by week, by month, by year. Today one woman may be able to promote another or others into a stronger position; tomorrow that very same woman may well need the mentoring of the women she mentored.

> ... *the tenuous nature of women's grasp upon power which is 'allowed' to us by those who truly hold the power in the world the way it is.*

Women mentoring women begins with family, with the sense of ourselves as encouraged, supported, celebrated for the girls and the women we are and are to become. 'So Strong, My Family.' Lillian Holt, Donna Justo, Wendy Weeks, June Benson, Daphne Milward, Marj Oke and Joan Kirner are amongst the truly blessed ones. They learned from the start, through the words and the actions of mothers, fathers, aunts, grandmothers, caring relations who took on these central roles, relatives in distant lands, siblings and childhood friends, that who they were was important, just as who they were to become was worthwhile. And it was this strong, unerring sense of self that provided a foundation for creating strong ties with friends, partners, colleagues, fellow activists, children, siblings in the future. It was this, too, that developed in them a desire and will to support and acknowledge the valid and valuable existence of others to whom they might give a hand, whom they could assist and encourage as they had been encouraged and assisted.

For Susan Kelly, Val Marsden, Kay Saunders, Edith Morgan and Joyce Apap, a struggle arose within the conundrum of family life. Many women come from 'Darkness into Light'. For some, a brother or brothers are elevated above them, taking precedence in a struggle for appreciation and being recognised as worthy. For others, poverty, separation from family, a mother's personal torment or battle with her own demons, intrude. Yet mentors appear, who understand and bolster where the child or woman's sense of herself would otherwise have been lost or damaged. For some, the mentors appear early. For others, mentoring is unknown until much, much later. But whenever it comes, this positive response – of mentors outside the family, or 'standing in' for family members, or in adulthood adults supporting and mentoring one another – in turn enables women to encourage and support.

For many women, there are always the 'Contradictions': positive messages from within the family circle or outside it, combined with contradictory experiences. For Joyce Nicholson, Natasha Stott Despoja, Melinda McPherson, Carmel Guerra, Christine Ramsay and Mary Owen there were contradictions in everyday life. A father who applauded his daughter's brains and skills, yet did not see the immediate wisdom of having her take over the family business. Carrying two cultural inheritances, and not feeling 'at home' in either of them. Encouragement to strive educationally, from women who had no formal education. A remote parent and a loving one; a sense of distance within family, yet a knowledge, too, that family members cared; anger at a restrictive childhood, yet a recognition, also, of the caring and love underlying each edict. But where there are contradictions, there are always possibilities. Women who are faced with such contradictions in their childhood years are not bereft of mentoring, and they in turn repay, passing on to others what they have learned.

Women who have been mentored, and who in turn mentor, are blessed with good fortune. 'Good Fortune, My Company.' Edna Chamberlain, Ruth Lechte, Audrey McDonald, Jill Lennon, Edel Suede, Margaret

Pewtress and Lenore Coltheart recognise well their blessings. For some, mentoring by women was not so usual in their earlier years, for men were more likely to be in a position to mentor them. Many had strong support in childhood, then grew up into a world where it was easy (or simply 'a matter of course') to repay trust and confidence they had received by responding positively to others in need of it. All came to develop vital links in the community and with women – some younger, some older, some of like-age, in the country and the city, in foreign lands and interstate, and in the local, national and international Women's Movement.

So many women live generous lives. All have setbacks to overcome, whether in childhood, youth or adulthood. All have confronted sexism and discrimination. Many have faced up to racism and ethnophobia. Many have confronted other hurdles that exist to be overcome. Most will have found themselves, at times, despairing of the way the world is and of women's place within it. And yes, sadly, most will have encountered the worst times, of women's unfriendliness to women, even lack of caring and betrayal.

So many women live generous lives.

Despite all this, women have a deep capacity for generosity. This generosity shows itself in a way of mentoring which is not dictated to by patriarchal orthodoxies. Despite (or perhaps because of) women's lack of (male) power, women so often recognise and use the power we have to benefit other women. In the doing, we benefit ourselves. Women recognise generosity and repay it. And so women live generous lives.

PART I
So Strong, My Family

Soaring with Eagles

Lillian Holt

Lillian Holt is principal of Tauondi (formerly Aboriginal Community College), Port Adelaide, in South Australia, where she has worked for the past 15 years. She enjoys people, reading, writing, travel.

Born on 17 February 1945 at Cherbourg Aboriginal Settlement in Queensland, Lillian Holt was educated at Aramac Primary School, Aramac, Queensland; at the University of Queensland – where she graduated with a bachelor of arts; and the University of Northern Colorado in the United States of America, where she graduated with a master of arts.

Two days before my fiftieth birthday I received a confidential fax, first thing on arrival at work, to be a contributor to *Living Generously*. I was feeling furious, feisty and feral as I prepared to trudge – but not begrudge – my next half century. Not that I was worried about turning fifty. Hell no. You can't 'live generously' if you don't honour your god-given age.

I was heavily laden with a cold (in mid-summer), when the temperature in Adelaide had remained static and stagnated in the high thirties for the past few days and there was a 'big mamma' full moon that night (sure to have an effect on 'lunar-tics' like me). My star sign Aquarius was heavily aligned with my companion sign, neurosis. I was in a mood to run with wild wolves and soar with the eagles whilst simultaneously catering to, and contemptuous of, the pervading presence of the patriarchal pygmies who 'steer' the stultifying ship called the 'system'.

Fifteenth of February – comes the fax. A generous offer. Living Generously? Hell, I'm more fit to write about living dangerously, I reckon. Which is what I have done for the past 49 years, 364 days.

Nevertheless, there is danger in generosity and generosity in danger, I thought to myself.

And most of the women who have affirmed, allowed and given and striven of their generosity, have been 'dangerous' as well as generous. My life has been peppered with such women. Not prominent in numbers but most definitely in impact.

The Dollys, The Muriels, The Ritas, The Dianas, The Katies. They deserve to be honoured in an ode. Gracious, generous gals, all of them. All of them have made indelible footprints on my heart and soul, not just through love but through conflict, on occasions. Hence, the richness of the whole gamut of emotions. They steered and guided whilst I sometimes ranted and raved. All of them came along in durations of decades, just when I needed to be monitored and nurtured.

They were divining gifts, though I didn't really recognise them as that, at the time. Some were there, all of the time, some were there most of the time. Physically we may have been apart but not mentally and emotionally. They nurtured me through dark nights of the soul, the wounds of racism, they humoured the seriousness out of me and coaxed and cajoled my talent within. Like angels watching over the mosaic of me, they were there in one form or another. When I went berserk on automatic pilot, they rectified the deviation.

> *They nurtured me through dark nights of the soul, the wounds of racism, they humoured the seriousness out of me and coaxed and cajoled my talent within.*

My Mum deserves the first accolade. She loved me in the most wonderful way – to the core and bone and depth of her being. I knew that supremely right through my childhood and adulthood. No analysis paralysis about the tensions of dysfunctional mother/daughter relationships so prevalent in today's era. My Mum stood bold and firm within my firmament. I loved cuddling up to her and sleeping in the same bed – even up to my late twenties – during my university days when I went home to see her! On cold, wintry nights, during my semester break, when I returned, wounded, scarred and jarred by life, I went home to Mum, cuddled up next to her and knew all would be well. Somehow the frumpiness of her bed was a little like being back in the womb. It was an old, scraggy, well-used and worn bed, a bit like Mum. Dad was deceased, by then, for a couple of years. She'd weathered the storms of life and was awash with welcome that one of her daughters had returned.

Oh sure, she pissed me off at times, as she cautioned me against this and that. That I needed to relax, was still too highly strung, needed to slow down, stop impressing 'the snows' (which is what she called whitefellas) and told me to believe in God. At the time, this was a bit too much for me, especially the remarks about God, as I was a card-carrying

Marxist and hell bent on changing the world. When I did object, she'd tell me I was getting a bit too big for my boots and would cut the conversation short by saying: 'I don't know what they teach you at uni, Lillian, but it certainly isn't manners!'

It was her sobriety and dignity, both reflected in her demeanour, I have come to admire. I suppose, in a sense, her world was much different from mine. But I can reap the benefits in hindsight.

I was part of her blessed brood of three – an older sister and a younger brother. She didn't know her own birthdate nor any of her relations – including her mother and father – as she was taken from her parents in the 'olden days' of assimilationist policy and put on an Aboriginal settlement in Queensland.

You could call my Mum one of those older Aboriginal women of the matriarch type. I once asked her why she never touched alcohol (as my Dad did) and she philosophically replied: 'Somebody had to be in control.' End of matter. No whingeing, whining, moralising, nor analysis. Just matter of fact. She loved gardening and growing our own vegetables and flowers, tilling and tending the garden in the same way with her kids. My Mum was one of those women you could 'go home to'.

When the tough got going, Mum got going. She was a 'flash' dresser and once told me, when I was a teenager, that all one needed to stop the wrinkles or crows feet under eyes was a dose of your own saliva, run elegantly outwardly to inwardly with one of your fingers. She never wore an ounce of make-up (said it was no good for you, besides it gave her a 'headache' on the one occasion she had donned lipstick and powder in her life!). She, along with my Dad, went to bed with the birds and got up with them.

At a time when White Australia rejected and made you feel dejected about your Aboriginal features, my Mum would say: 'That's a strong, intelligent forehead you've got. Use it.' So I went through life thinking I was pretty damned smart, having such a prominent Aboriginal forehead.

One of the biggest impacts my Mum made on me along with my other many older Aboriginal relatives – including men – was never describing people in terms of being attractive, beautiful, good looking, handsome, which is such a whitefella tendency in our image-ridden society of today. It was usually a comment such as: 'They are a fine stamp of a person' or 'a good/decent humanbeing'. Mum and those older relatives all judged by the inner rather than the outer. Mum encouraged me to look after my good teeth, hair and skin, which she said I had been 'blessed with'.

Yes, she scrubbed us up as well as scrubbing floors for the local hotel and/or bank manager's wife. She cooked, cleaned and ironed for others, to bring in a few shillings in order for us to survive and revive – all of which I didn't appreciate when I was much, much, younger. No, I never appreciated the vegies and flowers she grew for our consumption and delight. No, I never appreciated the fact that I was raised in a loving, non-violent household. I only ever heard Mum and Dad raising their voices to each other – ONCE! Sounds incredible, but it is true. I distinctly remember it, as it shook my world, momentarily, at the time. Hush, I thought, as I ceased my activity, to listen further. My Mum and Dad arguing! Shock, horror. But then it was all forgotten as we sat down for our evening meal. That was something else I took for granted – sitting down as a family for the evening meal. And, in the 1950s, wow, chicken for Sunday dinner when we could afford it! Mum and I had big fights about eating my pumpkin, which I just HATED with a vengeance, as a child. I'd get the usual lecture from her about the need to eat it, along with my other vegies, in order to build strong bones, and so on. At the time it sounded like a dribbling diatribe to me and, indeed, I won out, because I sulked and refused to eat. As with all lessons in life, later I came to appreciate pumpkin, but not until I was in my early twenties. Today, I love it and whenever I eat pumpkin think of Mum and the fights we had over it.

> *As with all lessons in life, later I came to appreciate pumpkin, but not until I was in my early twenties. Today, I love it . . .*

At 17, my restlessness and risk-taking meant I was determined to see the bright lights and big cities. I did just that. Beginning with Brisbane, in the next 30 years I boomeranged all over the world: London, Denver, Rio De Janeiro, Madrid, New Delhi, Manila, Gothenburg. Ironically, at 50, I have come full circle and yearn to go back to Mum. But she isn't there any more, the Mum I could go home to! The Mum who so generously shielded, guided, loved, cajoled, scolded, nurtured, directed and loved me. My first and generous female encounter who gave me my spiritual values of today through her homespun wisdom and plain commonsense.

I can still see her round, brown, button face today, before she died in 1987. She had silken, brown, smooth skin crowned on top with a graceful and energetic crop of silvery grey hair. Perhaps the greatest accolade I can offer her is imitation and emulation. So if she is listening and looking afar from the firmament, I want her to know that I have a generous crop of foxy black and white peppered hair, which I can't wait to go grey, just like hers. That she never dyed her hair was, I suppose, her way of honouring life rather than trying to control it. She just accepted, honoured and let go – and let the grey roots come through.

Right to the end, everybody commented on her brilliant, healthy, youthful-looking hair, slick and silver. I have another 20 or more years to achieve her crowning glory, which complemented her dignity and generosity. So, thanks Mum, too, for your genes, which I hope will age me into the ranks of the elders.

In 1962, on flying the coop at age 17, wanting to explore and implore the bright lights, big cities, big living, I went to Brisbane to work for the Australian Broadcasting Commission (ABC), which was my first job. Lillian Roth once said her life was never her own, it was charted before she was born. Boy, you'd better believe it. Within a month or two I met an Englishwoman who had lived in India for 11 years and had vowed, after the spirit and vivacity of India, never to return to her homeland. She was looking to fill the void and found it through working voluntarily with fledgling Aboriginal organisations and people. At the time I didn't really know this, it is only in retrospect, but on first encounter she hugged me like a daughter and I was to become like a daughter, for she became my second Mum, my 'migloo Mum' for want of a better word. ('Migloo' is a Queensland Aboriginal term for 'whitefella'.) I can still remember meeting her, in 1962, in the office of the state director of Aboriginal affairs in Brisbane. She was and still is an incredibly tactile person, embracing me and owning me like one of her own brood. From there on in, we became 'attached'. That was 33 years ago. Little did I know that this bold, tactile encounter, which (not being a very tactile person myself) I shrank from, was the beginning of a beguiling bond lasting to this day.

I don't think either of us knew what we were getting into. As with all 'families', the arguments began, mostly over the fact that she thought I was wasting my life, being a wage slave, and that I should develop 'that brilliant, absorbent brain' and DO SOMETHING with my life. So, after a few years, and being the 'people pleaser' I was then, I went back to do my matriculation. She 'hustled' a rich woman she knew to pay my fees, so I could do so. Not that I knew about this surreptitious activity on her part, so when I kept saying I couldn't afford to become a 'mature' student at the age of 22, she replied: 'Oh yes, you can, I have arranged it all.' So off I trotted. Did my matric in one year and then signed up for university.

She said she was sent to Australia to be my 'hair-coat'.

She said she was sent to Australia to be my 'hair-coat'. How true! She fired me up and shot me down! She was a feminist before it became fashionable and remonstrated at me about the 'need to have a man on my arm' instead of developing my mental capacities, saying that I could do anything I wanted to, if I set myself to the task. She believed violently and passionately in my capabilities and capacities, at a time when I wasn't even aware of them.

She introduced me to a different world. So many cosmopolitan, 'very educated' (in my view, at the time) diverse people, from all walks of life and from all over the world, visited and she entertained them with her generosity. I was always included. But there was nothing snobbish about it, for her circle of people was diverse, with many worldly, yet unlettered, unfettered and uncluttered people traversing her premises, also. I met many, many, interesting people through her, from diplomats to dreamers to derelicts (the latter word is not meant to be derogatory).

She had a magnetic and energetic personality and was, most assuredly, a 'people person'.

Little did I know it, but as she introduced me to others and their thoughts and values, I was also being introduced to myself. The discussions were homely and vigorous, particularly between her and me. She was a Shakespeare fanatic and explained away my confusion in that area. She'd throw quotes and words my way and I'd ask her what it meant. She'd explain so that I never felt dumb – just enlightened. She encouraged and inspired me, with my university assignments, as we sipped tea and discussed the ins and outs, pros and cons of my assignment.

Twenty and more years ago I had a most vile fight with her in her loungeroom where she sat, legs folded, sipping a cup of tea whilst she dropped a clanger in my lap by saying: 'I think you will need to examine seriously the proposition that you hate women.' I frothed frenetically, denied, reviled and cursed her then left. Went away wounded, bent on revenge and 'sulked' as she stayed on my mental hit list.

But not for long; her delicious curries brought me back. They were as scintillating as her conversation and concern. I have conceded, given time, that she was right about my being a women hater. Ouch! That truth hurt along with the many other things said to me, in the form of tough love. Well, today, I still love that woman. We keep in touch by telephone.

> ... *her forgiveness when I was just plain, downright rude, vulgar, scornful, manipulating. You name it.*

I loved her generosity in the form of her forgiveness when I was just plain, downright rude, vulgar, scornful, manipulating. You name it. I've often said to her, in retrospect, I wondered how she put up with me. Her reply is that she wouldn't have missed it all for quids, and that her life has been enriched by knowing me. What an affirmation! They don't come much more generously than that. So thanks, Mrs L as I always called her. We still joke about her being sent as a 'hair-coat' via India to meet up with me, prickle me and point me in the right direction.

Another women was high in the ascendant, at the same time as Mrs L. This was my Aunty Rita. She was another who was to make indelible footprints on my heart. A blood relation, a woman of passion and compassion, she took me under her wing and into her household the moment I planted my feet in the 'big city' (to me at the time!) of

Brisbane, 1962. I was 17, fresh, raw, naive and frisky, exploring this new found world of mine. So where else do you go when, as a young Aboriginal woman, you also want to 'belong'? To your relations, of course. My Aunty Rita filled that void. She welcomed me with open arms, into her often hectic and chaotic household, where all were welcome, including all our other relations. Vivacious, dynamic, raising four children on her own (her husband had died four years before) she didn't ever stint on her generosity. I could turn up unannounced, day or night, and there would always be a welcome, a bed, food and love meted out to me, unconditionally.

She provided more than a home for me. She provided her heart. She felt, she cried, she laughed, she danced. Many a time, we did this together, sometimes just through sitting around and yarning (which was an activity rather than a boredom). Aunty Rita was earthy, uncluttered and classy. She was my role model for style. Someone once said that style and class are a bit like humility and spirituality – either you've got it or you haven't and if you have, you don't have to go around broadcasting it. Well, Aunty Rita had 'IT'. An indefinable essence which came from just being herself. She could adorn herself with clothes of many colours that would either clash or look insipid on others. But not on her! Oh no, they became alive and alert, just as she was. She brought colour and personality to her clothes and to those she met.

More importantly, Aunty Rita was a dreamer. She always had plans for life and was always about to embark on something exotic. As with all of us, they often did not materialise, but I loved and partook of that zest for life. She shared it and passed it on to me.

> *She always had plans for life and was always about to embark on something exotic.*

Later, in my travels in and out of Brisbane, there was always a bed and a feed for me awaiting at Aunty Rita's, often without ritual of writing – just turning up. If there wasn't room, she'd MAKE room. To try to pinpoint exactly her generosity is like trying to describe the taste of icecream to someone who has not tasted it. Her generosity was just THERE. Encompassing, pervasive, loving. To me, she was one of those older, Aboriginal maturates, who cared and shared. To say more would be to denude the essence.

Then came Diana. Slim, blue-eyed, blonde, erudite, articulate. She, of all women, particularly encouraged me in my own search for my creativity and further study. It was SHE who arranged for me to do postgraduate studies in the United States of America. SHE listened to my drunken raves when I thrashed and lashed out about NOT being 'blue-eyed and blonde haired and conventionally good looking like SHE was'. SHE admired and affirmed my Aboriginal beauty in its own right. She caressed and cajoled me, as the case may be. More importantly, she had faith in me and my ability. She sent me packing at a time I couldn't decide for myself. Yes, it is true: she literally packed my bags to go to the States to study. I ranted and raved upon my arrival through letters – to her. She calmly wrote back and acknowledged my feelings.

On arrival home in Australia, in 1980, she presented me with a meticulously bound bundle of letters and said: 'Here is your story or novel, now write!' Yes, she had kept all the letters I had written from afar and which she felt held great promise as the premise for my writing.

The time our paths crossed was relatively short, which does not detract from its impact. She encouraged me in literary, creative pursuits. Oh, and she was so fiercely loyal to me. I bunked into her place, on many an occasion. She, like the others, shared generously of her belongings and herself. She was my 'amanuensis'.

My geographical journeying took me to many places before I arrived in Adelaide, where I now reside and where I met up with Katie. Free spirited, Irish Catholic, from County Cork. Lilting, lyrical personality, which was reflected in her voice. The gift of the gab, flowing generously in her voice. A woman of the universe, we clicked on first meeting. There are just some women, indeed people, with whom one has, upon meeting, immediate rapport. As a result, I shared intimately with her, often on a daily basis, speaking of the depths of my doubts and baring my soul to her. She pulled me through, on all occasions, by sharing her own experience, strength and hope. We fought, sought, talked, baulked. Sometimes I would resile or reel from something which she said and thought to myself: 'I won't ring that bossy Irish bitch, today.' Katie, not being the silent type, nor a woman of half measures, would always be communicative.

She was somewhat like a Celtic sister. Mad, zany, with a lilting laugh. She shared generously of the depths of her feelings. We talked about topics like our own spiritual growth, relationships, emotions. To the depth and core. Uncovering, discovering, recovering. She was placed in my path and fate, at a time when I needed to stand naked, in a metaphorical sense, and bare my soul to another humanbeing. As we journeyed together, much was revealed about me and to me through her as the instrument. She was always there, and gave of her generosity, graciously, willingly. You can't describe it in words, except to say that every woman needs a Celtic sister like Katie.

My Mum, Aunty Rita, Mrs L (Muriel is her real name), Diana and Katie were instrumental in playing a big role in my own growth, by sharing their generosity. No, I can't pinpoint one action, one direction, which they gave me and thus 'saved' me. It was more the warmth of their smile, the greeting in their voice, the security – even in silence. Their generosity was often reflected in tough love. They turned up at the time they were meant to and we journeyed together as they motivated and nurtured me, in their own distinctive manner.

They were all older women, but their spirit was ageless whilst at the same time it had depth and experience, precisely because they had 'walked the walk' and thus could 'talk the talk'. I was introduced to myself, through their sharing, caring and generosity. This in turn allowed me to be introduced to a further spectrum of women of all colours, hues, ages and experience. The Hilarys, The Trishes, The Heathers, The Jackies, The Annes.

They were all older women, but their spirit was ageless...

I've never been one to make a whole lot of friends. Many acquaintances, yes. But not a glittering array or range of women (or indeed, men) with whom I have been able to lay bare my soul as I did with my five mentors. They dug the deep channels within and helped me exorcise the demons inside, which is why they reign supreme in the firmament of my psyche. I could never forget these women. They aligned rather than maligned me, and for that I shall be eternally grateful. I keep in touch with all of them. The turf we trod together provided much of the ground I continue to tread.

Whilst writing and procrastinating over (the latter is my usual form) this essay, I had a 'fallout' with Katie over her not honouring her age. My clinical version of the whole incident would say that she is in 'denial'. My passionate version was to tell her she 'gave me shits' over refusing to acknowledge her age and subsequently I feel really peeved with her (to say nothing of my self-righteousness!). My immediate reaction was to put her on my 'eternal mental list' and cross/smudge her out of my life and this article, because of my grudge.

But no, Katie, in her generosity, persisted with me, left messages in her lilting, Irish accent on my answering machine (which I never answered) and communicated with me by letter. Then the universe took over – I was thrown into her company unexpectedly, at a talk on meditation which I went to hear. Then all was well! This woman I was avoiding (in a small town like Adelaide) greeted me generously on encounter. Now that is what I call generosity. Sheer, pure, unadulterated, generosity. One could never refuse it. I have much to learn from that.

The generosity of all these women has consisted of persistence, spontaneity, understanding, listening and sharing. Ah, how could I not feel blessed!

On Saturday night I rang Katie on being hurt by a 'smart' remark from a 'clever dick' (yeah, white male, real-estate jerk) who made an ungenerous remark about Aboriginal people. She listened, replied and suggested how I could handle such incidents in future. In doing so, she accorded me a strength I had forgotten I had. More importantly she shared her strength and generosity and in doing so, engendered that which was ebbing within it.

Ah, that is what I call generosity!

I had a similar incident with a younger women, Hilary, my friend in Healesville, who pulled me through another recent racist incident. Neither of these women is Aboriginal, but in the world of the spirit – where generosity emanates – colour is of no importance.

... she accorded me a strength I had forgotten I had.

In many ways, not just of colour, these women were disparate in their dispositions. A couple, unlike me, were extremely methodical and disciplined. One or two were a bit more mad, zany and passionate. Whatever. They all made indelible footprints on my heart, in their own way and contributed to my own encounter, with me.

Oh sure, others have contributed, in other, even lesser ways. And, no doubt, I have done the same for others. It can't be any other way, as we are all interconnected.

I return to the words of Lillian Roth: 'My life was never my own, it was charted before I was born.' Hence, these women have been placed in my path and fate. Always have been and always will be. They come, they go, but they are always there.

Something Special: Womentoring

Donna Justo

Born on 18 September 1959 in a bayside suburb of Brisbane, Donna Justo spent her early years on the Darling Downs, west of Toowoomba, in Queensland. She went to Wynnum State High School and undertook further studies at Griffith University in Brisbane. Since 1979 she has worked extensively in women's services, confronting the issues of domestic violence, substance abuse, 'women in the too-hard basket', rape and incest.

Donna Justo lives to travel and travels to live. On her tombstone she would like to see written, as she once read: 'A big troublemaker and a good writer.'

The original Guistos came from Gibraltar and Italy, then intermarried with the Spanish. Justo is a Spanish name, pronounced 'Hoosto' and originally spelt 'Guisto'. The name then evolved to 'Justo'. In all its versions, it means 'justice'. I grew up knowing this, and am sure it affected and continues to affect the way I think and what I believe is important. For as long as I can remember, too, I have been conscious that 'Donna' means 'woman' or 'lady'. I prefer 'woman', so identify my name as meaning 'woman's justice'. This fits well with my vision and my demands for women in the world.

I was my mother's first child and she decided to travel to 'the big smoke' – Brisbane – to have expert medical care for my birth. In those first days, she recalls, I kicked and thrashed constantly. After some time she realised something was not quite right, but she had to seek long and hard for support. It was not until I was six years old that a woman doctor in a clinic agreed with her. One paediatrician dealt with what he said was her 'imagination', by saying she had dropped me on my head or off the bed, and that was the cause of the problem. Over the period she battled for medical recognition of my disability, she had to endure many judgemental statements about her caring capacity. When it became clear that my mother was right, and they found a label for my disability – 'muscular dystrophy' – she received no apologies.

By the time I was four, I could read. One of the finest joys for a child with muscular dystrophy – me in the 1960s – was the great companionship I found in reading. I lived my adventures through the pages of prescribed writers such as Louisa May Alcott, Margaret Mitchell and many more. They later gave way to Christina Stead, Doris Lessing and other women writers of my own choice.

When I was 10 years old, my neighbours, two young women, Joan and Margaret Lockie, decided to travel overseas indefinitely to find work and to stay for as long as the money lasted and the challenge endured. This left a lasting impression on me. When they set off to explore the world, I could not have been more excited than if it were me! They wrote constantly and their example took up a permanent place in my psyche. The effort they made to motivate a young girl from a working-class suburb in Brisbane left me with traveller's feet and an adventurous soul. It meant that later I could say to the younger women members of my family: 'Yes! Single women can travel alone, and to the most remote outposts on earth.' Amongst other journeys, I travelled to the Amazon, and saw the snows of Mount Kilimanjaro. Adventure is not the sole domain of the male sex.

The effort they made to motivate a young girl from a workingclass suburb in Brisbane left me with traveller's feet and an adventurous soul.

Now, when I see my children, Luke and Kahl, immersed in good books and excited about travel, I feel a sense of continuity, of the flow of life and life's dreams from one generation to another. Travel and reading may seem small things to some, but for me they have been life changing.

I have clear memories of life in the country. We lived on a wheat and cotton property. Many times I sat on the huge harvester with my father, often at night time, with the spotlight burning and foxes darting through the paddocks. In the farm house a shelf ran behind the wood stoves; an adult could lie there in comfort. Often, I lay on that shelf reading to my heart's content. In those early years we had no radio, but there were always books.

One of my grandmothers looked and acted just like Aunty Mame. She was great fun and loved me unconditionally. The other was immensely career-orientated. She had been matron of a hospital, involved daily with supporting, caring and the nurturing of others. From the time my sisters and I were six and seven years old, we had to tell her what we wanted to be when we grew up. At the time I felt some need to conform. My father's was a medical family. Later, however, we stood out against this tradition.

I spent my first year at university studying Australian environmental science and political science. I experienced great support in my immediate family for the path I had chosen. There was an understanding that whatever any of us did, it was embraced whole-heartedly. 'All you can do is give the best you can possibly give,' was a constant refrain.

I grew up, too, with a strong sense of loyalty. Loyalty was probably the strongest character trait encouraged in our home, together with support, love and kindness. My parents were socially-minded and were dedicated to helping others. This brought me to recognise the importance of being involved. If changes were to be made, an injustice to be ended, then involvement was essential. My parents did battle for their children and we knew it was worth the fight. We knew too that it was worth the fight to see things happen for other people.

I was a conservative child, who was always excited about life. I went through the stage of wanting to be a nun like Audrey Hepburn in *The Nun's Story*. Despite not being overtly religious, I believed that to be a nun was my destiny. I was a little concerned, however, about the bowing and scraping, and particularly the effect it would have on my knees.

The trade union movement was all-important in our household. Pat Mackey and the strikes at Mount Isa were the main topic of conversation at the celebrations for my sixth birthday. My birthday party was in progress when a huge debate took place between a number of my relatives, until finally my mother said: 'Remember that this is a child's party.' I can still recall that name, Pat Mackey, being yelled out, and loud voices arguing back and forth.

My father was a staunch unionist. He believed strongly in the Australian Labor Party (ALP) and particularly in the Labor left. This brought my first identification with politics and humanrights and today I make a point of firmly impressing on my children that they are from a workingclass family, and that it is something to be proud of. For me it means a person works for everything she or he gets. That is what life is about – working for a living and working for change.

I make a point of firmly impressing on my children that they are from a workingclass family, and that it is something to be proud of.

There were, however, some contradictions in our family ethos. On some issues there was not a lot of choice. For my mother, there were no options so far as developing a career was concerned. My father was the wage-earner in our family. He was in paidwork. My mother was in unpaidwork. Nonetheless, the concept that all things are possible steeped itself in my brain. The work ethic was there, too, engrained through the personalities of my father and mother who were loyal and hardworking.

I grew up also with a strong sense of my family's history. It spans Spain, Australia, Argentina, England and Germany. My greatgrandfather came to Australia via the Alaskan goldmines, where he made his fortune. He was the eldest child and, possibly, a troublemaker (a good thing in my eyes!), for he was asked to leave the family home. He ended up on the Gympie goldfields in Queensland, where he again struck it rich and purchased a huge property, 'Cootharraba', on the Sunshine Coast.

The Argentine family began with Francisco Justo travelling from Spain to Buenos Aires. In the 1930s, Agustin Justo rose to the ranks of general and as General Justo became President of Argentina through a military coup: it appears he was a corrupt character, yet revered by some. Nonetheless other members of the family lived up to their name. One, Juan B Justo ('John the Baptist'), a doctor, founded the Socialist Party of Argentina. General Justo's son, Liborio, was a writer and agitator, and was a member of the Communist Party at the time his father was President of Argentina. This was of considerable concern to the general, but of great joy to the family.

Dr Sarah Justo was a dentist. Alicia Moreau de Justo was a politician. Many of the Justo women were directly involved in the development of the Women's Movement in Argentina. Sarah Justo and Alicia Moreau de Justo were driving forces behind 'feminismo' – the introduction of feminist ideology into Argentinean culture. They were not alone. They worked beside their sisters to challenge the patriarchal proprieties of Argentinean life. It was not an easy task.

Feminismo, a book written by Mary Jane Carlsen, talks about the women of my family and other women who stood up to the entrenched macho culture – a mixture of Italian, Spanish and English. Alicia Moreau de Justo advocated for women and was a humanrights activist for much of her life. She gave her farewell speech to parliament in 1986 at the age of ninety-two. It was a two-hour address to the Argentine Assembly on humanrights issues for Argentines and people throughout the world. She challenged what the authorities were doing for the women of the Argentine and flagged the many issues fundamental to the rights of women and children, in particular, domestic violence and health issues, which had been her lifelong work. She also railed against the disparity of wealth in Argentina. For some 10 years prior to her retirement she sat on humanrights committees. Her work was proactive, particularly in relation to finding displaced persons and getting them back, safely, to their homes. Sadly, many people have been murdered as a consequence of political upheavals, and it is impossible to find them – not even their bodies.

She challenged what the authorities were doing for the women of the Argentine . . .

At the end of the 1980s I travelled to Argentina to meet with family members. Sadly, Alicia Moreau de Justo died in 1986, before I travelled there, and before we could meet. I was also unable to meet many of the

Justos aged about 45 years and under, because they were missing. People could show me family photographs of wedding celebrations, where of 10 or 12 people only two or three members remained.

Argentina was no 'foreign country' to me. I recall discussions about our family history, held when I was a child. Through them, I gained some understanding of the men's history, but the women in the family talked more of what they knew. There were letters and visits to Australia from some members of the Spanish and Argentinean sides of the family. All the women were hardworking and they often gave birth at home.

Yet to a young girl growing up in Brisbane in the 1960s and 1970s, multiculturalism was unheard of, and Aboriginal or Torres Strait Islander people were kept in the background and seldom seen. I saw only one Aboriginal child throughout the entire time of my primary and highschool education. Through that 12-year period only one first generation family from another country came into contact with me and my family: they were from Holland. There was a great deal of cruelty directed at 'difference'. At one time, triplets came to our school, and no one loved or cared for them. They smelt, their hair was never combed, and some children called them terrible names.

There was a great deal of cruelty directed at 'difference'.

My upbringing meant that I was fascinated rather than repelled by the accents and habits of the family from the Netherlands. As for the triplets, they scared me a little because they were so different and it was difficult to comprehend the cruelty with which they were treated at home, on top of the cruelties meted out to them at school. Despite my fear, I gave one of them my new shoes. The contrast with what would happen today is vivid: children these days would be likely to take some of their own clothes to school to share with the children, rather than almost everyone in the classroom shunning them. At the time, I wanted to take these children home to mother them. Today, with the benefit of hindsight and an adult understanding, I realise that life was difficult for the family altogether. The children's mother was a single parent who was coping alone, with many issues. Although it is difficult for single parents today, there is a great relaxation in attitudes and many resources, never available then, exist.

There were other cruelties. One child was made to stand on a seat all day because he was unable to calculate a lengthy sum. Even then it was obvious to me that he had learning difficulties. (Perhaps it was dyslexia.) When the headmaster finally left the room for a short break, I gave the boy the answer. When my deed was discovered, I was the one in trouble! I went home furious at the injustice of it all, but proud of myself for what I had done. It was at times like this that I knew how fortunate I was: my parents supported me.

Apart from these incidents, I have wonderful memories of school. In the early years we had several wonderful older women as teachers. In Year 1 Miss Hishon, probably in her early sixties, was my teacher. She went on to live to a ripe old age, but even at the time she taught me she was a sweet, grandmotherly person, full of kindness and inspiration. She judged each child as an individual, but did not distinguish between us as girls and boys when it came to punishment. Unlike some of the other teachers, she did not invent special punishments for girls, others for boys. This brought home to me clearly the need to treat boys and girls equally, rather than making distinctions on grounds of sex.

As a child growing up in the 1960s, I seemed to be surrounded by Amazons of virtue and wisdom, and valued women's energies. My sister Jo and I were taught music by the nuns at St John Vianney's. We had women Sunday School teachers, women Brownie and Guide leaders, women art of speech teachers, and were taught ballet and jazz by a wonderful woman who later died as a consequence of the HIV/AIDS virus. Each of these women brought her own brand of individualism and a cooperative spirit to these voluntary jobs and this in turn has had an important impact on me throughout my life.

Initially I attended Manly State School, in a bayside suburb of Brisbane. Purple jacarandas bloomed each year in the schoolyard. I was then sent to Wynnum High School to receive an equal education.

Being a child with a disability was difficult. Suddenly there was a large number of girls. At primaryschool no one had ever bothered to look at the way I walked. No one paid attention in an obtrusive or unkind way to difficulties I confronted, and which I taught myself to overcome. But many of the older boys were cruel, and teenage years are not easy for most young people. It was a struggle for me.

Nevertheless, at highschool many of the teachers were inspirational. The senior mistresses were characters. Mrs Bonner (Del) and Miss Bunn (Felda) were unforgettable. Del Bonner was a self-contained woman who encouraged lots of younger women into sport as well as into professions they may not have considered otherwise, such as physics, chemistry and biology. Miss Bunn was equally passionate about careers for women. She promoted the teaching of languages at the school and on one occasion I was absent from school for 18 months having a series of muscle transplants and other operations. As the German teacher, she sent homework to me, so that I could 'keep up'.

Miss Bunn had an excellent understanding of the need to follow-up. She was a strict disciplinarian, but showed no sex or gender bias in her discipline. Miss Bunn's personal and professional commitment meant she followed up issues out of hours. She looked to see if there were problems and searched for workable resolutions, particularly for the young women students who confronted difficult times.

In Year 12, Judy Walker came as a teacher. She was at school for a short time only. She had been travelling for two years with her partner, she came to the school to teach, then she went off again, travelling. Her free-spiritedness influenced me a great deal, as did the fact that she was a woman capable of taking on the establishment and challenging antiquated ideas. Then there were the women teachers who supported us students when we advocated with the principal for the right to hold a form dinner, which was eventually held. It was during these highschool years that a special friendship was formed with Peta Koch. We share a similar life philosophy and the valuable friendship established at school continues today.

Her free-spiritedness influenced me a great deal...

After completing highschool I went immediately to Griffith University, commencing my degree in Australian environmental science, and together with other undergraduates was one of the first students who attended that university. There were many teething problems. What was the role of the environmental science faculty? What knowledge was to be imparted to the students? There was a crisis, and many of the lecturers took sabbatical leave. This meant our first year was extremely disjointed. Nonetheless it was interesting. However, during the latter years of my schooling, I had been working in parttime jobs at chemist shops, 'fast food joints', and serving in bars. After completing first year I dropped out, ostensibly to put together more monetary resources. However the confusion in the faculty was an incentive to step back.

I had given some thought to environmental law as my field. But I was already working on the fringes of the Women's Movement. Women in Brisbane were active, getting things done, and women of all ages were involved. The older women, in particular, impressed many of us with their activism and commitment. In the 1970s, too, it was women from other cultures, in other countries, who inspired me. Golda Meir, India's Indira Ghandi, Mother Theresa, Bernadette Devlin of Ireland, and South Africa's Winnie Mandela. Politics and women's politics became a priority for me. I felt (and hoped, perhaps) that women would choose to come to the negotiating table instead of declaring war or dropping bombs at random.

Refuges were springing up to give shelter to women and their children who were victims of male violence in the home. Women's House was established in West End, Madonna House was set up, then Jebb House. I began working voluntarily at some of the refuges.

Anne Foley, Alison Green, Cherryl Levinge and other women whose friendships are of the everlasting kind, became my friends during these years. In the early days there was no money for refuge work and other issues of concern to women. Much of our work and lobbying related to philosophy and fundraising; it was about finding second-hand beds and anything and everything we could lay hands on to pass to the women and their children. Women like Anne, Alison, Cheryl and Peta Koch were invaluable. To help, they were prepared to put in money, they had energy, they had time and were willing to make a practical commitment to support those of us who were working directly with the women. These friendships continue to inspire and sustain me.

The women were a cross-representation of women from all walks of life, and from all cultures. When I first met them, I was still only 17 or eighteen. Germaine Greer's *The Female Eunuch* was an inspiration, and her ideas were still influential in what was written and spoken about. I had read Betty Friedan's *The Feminine Mystique*. At Griffith University, I joined with other women in discussing the issues raised in both books, although they had been published some time before.

The ideas and intellectual sustenance I had gained from books throughout my childhood and early teenage years continued into my time at university and formed a strong base for my activism in the Women's Movement. Actors such as Katherine Hepburn, Vanessa Redgrave and Lynne Redgrave impressed me; I watched Jane Fonda trying to break out of the 'dollybird' mould. I admired their pizzazz and that of a number of fledgling Australian actors as well. This meant I spent a great deal of time hanging about at the theatre. My sisters and I were encouraged to pursue speech and drama, music and fine arts, and did. Beverley Kruck, a senior lecturer in drama at the Queensland University of Technology (QUT), Kelvin Grove campus, made a big impact on me through these years. I attended her speech and drama classes. She was well-travelled and had risen to senior ranks within the university sector. She was gutsy and, for me, this counted.

I spent much of the 1980s overseas or working in social justice areas in Queensland. Kay Cottee, Wendy Harmer, Jean Kitson and Gillian Armstrong reinforced my understanding that creative and adventurous spirits ought never to be allowed to die and that all careerpaths are open to be explored. I recognised more and more that I was surrounded by strong women – the Beverley Krucks, the actors on stage and screen, the writers like Germaine Greer, the activists at Women's House, the women in the refuge movement, the women of my family. There were women's stories and women sharing and I developed an awareness of belonging to a huge family of women. Men were there, too, but it was the women who were the carriers of herstory.

I recognised more and more that I was surrounded by strong women ...

A closet ambition was to be a writer. In the mid-1970s I had applied for cadetships and desperately wanted one that was advertised at the Australian Broadcasting Commission (ABC). What became clear in the interviews was that the school I'd attended was central to whether or not the job was available. I was proud of my education, of myself and my achievements. The attitude of 'what school?' disillusioned me. Yet, next to my ambition to write came an ambition to travel. So, when I decided I had better do something other than apply unsuccessfully for cadetships, I began saving my fare.

My family encouraged me to travel and live out my dreams. No blocks were put in my path. No one ever said (even though I had a disability): 'You wouldn't be able to do that.' When at 21 I announced I had a one-way ticket for Athens, the response was to join in with my excitement. At about 5.15 am one February morning in 1980 a huge farewell took place at Brisbane airport. It was sad to say goodbye to my sisters Jo and Sherrin, both younger than I am. 'Who knows,' I thought, 'I might not be home for 10 years.' But I knew we'd keep in touch. Then suddenly I saw all my friends coming towards me, through the terminal. I was so moved that so many people, my friends and family, would rise so early in the morning to come out to say goodbye. I was off to Greece!

At that time, I had a walking stick and zero balance. On landing in Athens, I needed the stick for support. When studying at Griffith, walking had become very difficult. Sometimes it would take me hours to get from one location to the next. I wasn't in a wheelchair, but exhaustion levels had an enormous impact on my studying habits. Now, travel had become an obsession. I had grand visions of myself being in a turret or a tent, on the coast of Spain or Greece, writing furiously. As I stepped onto the plane, I had thought: 'Where am I going!' But I knew I would be fine. I was embarking on a wonderful journey. As it was, I didn't stay away for 10 years. After two years I wanted to return home – but only for two weeks!

In Greece I travelled to the islands and during the summer months spent some time writing. I travelled throughout Europe and lived in London, where I was involved with Brixton Housing Group and the Marie Stopes Clinic. I found that women's services had not developed further than in Australia, and this surprised me. The only difference was that the numbers of women on the ground were so much greater. There were many creative ideas flowing about, and this was enormously energising. I was exposed to so many different women from so many different cultures. I listened and heard their ideas and saw what had been put into practice. I went to public forums and talks given by women who had been only names on the spine of a book to me, like Erin Pizzey who wrote *Scream Quietly or the Neighbours Will Hear*. Working with women in London validated the work I had done in Australia and it was at this time I met Mary Smart, a feminist from New Zealand who has a wonderful laugh – a great sense of humour and a sharp wit. I began to develop a strong urge to return to that work in Queensland and I developed ideas about what I would do when I returned.

I met Sou Haila in Greece, then we met again in Sweden. A Palestinian woman, Sou Haila had been displaced twice. She and her family moved first to Jordan, then were displaced to Egypt. They were then obliged to remove from Egypt, so she moved to Stockholm. She was a marvellous career woman with a fantastic attitude to travel. She took her two children somewhere every year – to a different place on the world map, to expose them to cultures and ways of life they had not known. She was supportive of women and a practical example of feminism at its best. Whenever we went out, it was to visit with women, to engage in discussions on women's issues. We travelled for a time through Greece. Women flocked to hear her talk. She was a great storyteller. It was from her and many other women I learned that there do not have to be endings and beginnings. There are experiences that can occur throughout a person's life, that add on to one another and become part of a continuum.

I returned to Australia. Refuges were my focus and I undertook relief work. Meanwhile I was thinking about what to do next. I did counselling courses and social welfare courses so that I could match the theory with practice. Dawn Rowan (then with Christie's Beach Women's Shelter in Adelaide) was one of the many women around Australia who were working in the refuge movement from the beginning. Judy Taylor and Pauline Woodbridge were working in the north of Queensland. So many of these women provided inspiration not only to me, but to hundreds and thousands of women workers, and to hundreds and thousands of women seeking refuge and support.

Anne Foley introduced me to Elaine Dixon, a Mercy nun, who gave me one of the biggest boosts in this area. She encouraged me to become actively involved in lobbying for and establishing a special needs refuge for women, working together with Jennifer Snow, a scientist from Tasmania. The special needs refuge, Coolock House, ran for 11 years but at the end of 1994 closed. The Mercy nuns moved their attention to another project. The refuge served an important need: we focused on issues such as illiteracy, childhood sexual abuse and how to practically assist the mother of the children, for many were children themselves. We dealt with young women's lack of direction or ambition, their lack of desire for achievement and the sense of hopelessness that develops where a child has grown to teenage and young adulthood with abuse, sexual exploitation and violence at the very core of her life.

Refuge work is hard work.

Jennifer Snow is a great feminist. She is involved with the disability area and exposed me to aspects of feminism I hadn't looked at, or looked at closely, before she drew them to my attention. She helped me to see the value of more militant approaches. These were a daily source of discussion. She, Robyn Morris, Elaine Dixon and Else Franks played an enormously important part in my development. I like hard work and believe in it. Refuge work is hard work. It is particularly difficult to undertake the intensive work that is necessary where young women seek help. But whatever the cultural or ethnic background, whatever the age group, Jennifer, Robyn, Else and Elaine were hard workers. They were a practical inspiration to me.

Before Coolock House was established, I had been travelling in Africa, where I attended the non-government organisations forum which accompanied the United Nations Women's Forum in Nairobi, Kenya. I had been thinking of returning overseas, but when Elaine (after suffering a stroke – perhaps work-related) became incapacitated and reliant on a wheelchair for mobility, I developed a strong commitment to stay to see the project, which had initially been a pilot, become a reality. Many great women came through that service, including Else Franks, Fran Tankred and many more. They were influential in the development of my work practice and my private philosophy. I was the youngest woman at the service, and they took me under their wing and guided me, more by peer modelling and support than by any specific directions.

I didn't feel pressured to conform to their way of dealing with issues. I was allowed my scope to be both young and creative and to try innovative projects. But in discussions or analysis of their own situations, I gleaned the message that patience and willingness to spend time and commitment is essential. I learned how important it was to see a family, a woman, or a woman and child self-determining their life's directions and outcomes. Being alongside Else and Fran meant I developed my appreciation of what is important so much more rapidly than might have been the case had they not been there to be my role models. They gave me the opportunity to formulate my own work practices and to select from their practices those I felt were most appropriate for me and my work, and to make a genuinely practical and useful application of theory work in the refuge context.

Further along the track, in 1985, the Sunshine Coast Women's Rape Crisis Service was established. Marg O'Donnell, Jackie Byrne and others such as Helen Day and Marg Stevens began a voluntary 24-hour rape crisis telephone line. At the same time, on the Gold Coast a similar push was emerging. Women were coming together to support the establishment of rape crisis and incest services in addition to the now traditional feminist-orientated refuges. That the workers constantly came together was invaluable. There were opportunities to network and, almost every year, a major conference was held. Women came from around the state – from the north and central areas of Queensland, and from Brisbane. They had had experience on the ground, and many had years and years of direct involvement with refuges, women's services, and the process of securing these services. This interaction was invaluable and sometimes far more valuable than formalised training or courses.

At the Sunshine Coast Women's Rape and Incest Counselling and Advocacy Service, we believe it is vital that sharing take place. We share with women who have come through the service, those who have become involved with research projects, younger women, older women, women in the community who are not directly involved with our service but are a part of other community agencies. The knowledge and information and herstory of what has gone before is equally as valuable as working with the knowledge of the here and now. It is in my work with Gay Sheldon, Bev Innes and Else Franks that I saw the strength of teamwork and solidarity. Annie Roberts from Cairns and Di McLeod from the Gold Coast have been great 'womentors' through the development of rape services.

Services come into being at different times. It is important for women working in all of them to be able to learn of what has gone before, as well as bringing new ideas, commitment, energies and enthusiasm to their service and sharing them with already existing services. I have been fortunate to work with women who are committed to sharing knowledge, and share an appreciation of other women's talents. This 'womentoring' is not only about someone putting down a hand from above. It is about mutual support, which is invaluable in itself. It can operate alongside support that comes from people who are in different positions of power. For example, in June 1992 tenders were called for a research project to be conducted under the auspices of the Women's Policy Unit in the department of premier and cabinet. The Sunshine Coast Inter-Agency Research Group was invited to tender for the project alongside many other individuals and groups from around Australia. The subject was the economic cost of violence against women, and we won the tender. Dawn Wilson, Beverly Innes, myself, Leah Gibbs and Debbie Blummet worked on the project. Carolyn Mason and Anna Bligh from the Women's Policy Unit, Cathy Munro who had worked previously at Ruby Gaea House in Darwin, and Janet Ramsay of the Women's Health Policy Unit made the assessment and the decision. I believe that a significant factor in the award of the tender was that our approach built in an awareness of the importance of consulting with the grassroots. Not only did we see it as important to *consult* in this way. Our proposal saw it as vital that those doing the work understand and work directly with and at a grassroots level. The project could not be completed successfully, in our view, without direct contact with women, and as women, at a grassroots level. As with all consultancies, we no doubt did 10 times the work.

Our proposal saw it as vital that those doing the work understand and work directly with and at a grassroots level.

When the state Labor government came to power in Queensland in 1988, a transition took place, with movement of women from the community sector to the government sector. Many of the women with whom we had worked closely in the community sector were now very much involved in the bureaucracy, holding bureaucratic positions. This meant we had to go further afield to find women who could support and advise us from a practical level of involvement in services. It was important that women move into the government sector. At the same time, we needed to retain links with women working in community and women's services at the grassroots level. This has meant that we are more likely, now, to have women from interstate attending and speaking at our conferences. Kate Gilmour, of the Royal Women's Hospital and Centre Against Sexual Assault in Melbourne, is one of a number whose expertise we appreciate. It is important to tap into the creative energy of these women.

The move into bureaucracy can cut off the possibility of women being womentors or giving guidance, for it becomes difficult for them to participate in an informal way with grassroots services. The bureaucracy has an enormous ability to silence people who become bureaucrats. But there are women who retain an ability to work practically and helpfully with women outside the bureaucracy. Lizzie Mulder, who was one of the early policy workers in the Women's Health Policy Unit in the Queensland Department of Health, is such a person. Lizzie made the transition into the bureaucracy, but was able to maintain a balance – retaining the professionalism and confidentiality of working with the bureaucracy, whilst being practical and professional in her support to the women's services sector. There are very few who are able to take this practical and professional approach.

It was at this time that superintendent Jill Bolen chose to leave the Queensland Police Service – a great loss to the women's and community sector, for Jill was ever-willing to 'go out on a limb' and to constantly challenge the criminal justice system. She had done much in her work to bridge the gap between the police service and the community.

> ... ever-willing to 'go out on a limb' and to constantly challenge the criminal justice system.

The women with whom I have travelled and worked are important to me and my development. So is my family, and my story is centred there. It begins when, as a child, I had only a vague awareness of the history of my family. I knew we had relatives in Argentina. We had written information about Argentina. One of my great uncles kept documents in a box. Yet it was only a throwaway line, the precise words of which I cannot now recall, that suddenly brought me up short: we had a family connection with another country. In another country, there were Justos going about their business, working for goals, struggling for what they believed in. Then, in 1988, I read Sally Morgan's book My Place. *I too felt compelled to seek out my roots. That was the year I went to Argentina for the first time. I returned in 1992. Landing in Buenos Aires was like coming home.*

This journey, the discovery of Justos in another country across the world, has made me feel more complete. It has given me a different sense of purpose. It makes me feel proud to know that there is a parallel activism occurring across the world. There are Justos in the Argentine seeking change, agitating for social justice. They are not sitting back, hoping someone else will do it, but are actively involved.

That is one of the biggest challenges women face in working for change. It is the commitment of other women, the inspiration of other women, that keeps us all going. It helps, too, to bring to our work in Australia, or in whichever country we live, an international perspective. All over the world, women are working, fighting, agitating, lobbying – even dying – to see our hopes for fairness and justice realised.

It was not long after I returned from that first trip to Argentina that I met Mark, my partner. The greatest attraction for me in establishing the partnership I have with him was his generosity of spirit. That, a mutual desire for social justice for all, and his pro-feminist stance has continued to strengthen our relationship.

Critical Reflection and Action: A Mutual Sharing

Wendy Weeks

Born in Melbourne, Victoria in 1943, Wendy Weeks studied socialwork at the University of Melbourne in the early 1960s. In the 1970s she became actively involved in the Women's Movement in Canada, where she lived and worked for 11 years. More recently, her books include *Women Working Together – Lessons from Feminist Women's Services* (1994) and *Issues Facing Australian Families – Human Services Respond* (1993, 1995, with Robyn Batten and John Wilson).

Wendy Weeks is committed to feminist theory development arising from practice and collaboration with women in the community. Her present understanding of the future of gender relations has been influenced by Aboriginal traditions, which respect women's business, men's business and common, shared business. She adores her two sons and is sustained by friends and kindred spirits in Australia and Canada, and by her love of art and the natural environment.

What has brought me to celebrate the tradition of womanhood and to grapple with the daily demands of trying to 'live generously' in a world of patriarchal practices and ideas which belittle and harm many women each day? I felt uneasy at the thought of writing about mentoring. But 'so often I don't' shrieked the girl inside me who never feels she has 'done or been enough'. Subsequently, in the year of turning 50, it seemed to be a good opportunity to reflect on and write about the people and experiences which have enriched my life, and to contemplate the lessons learned. In particular it allows me to celebrate being 'born woman', and the sea of generosity and support which women, and some men, provide.

I was a war-time baby born to Edith Philipson and Clem Davenport who had married in 1942. Clem was a navigator in the Royal Australian Airforce (RAAF), and Edith had already served several years as an apprentice schoolteacher. Like many women of her time, she did not complete her evening studies (taken while working), but went to live near the airforce camp. Later she lived with her parents and young baby when her husband went to New Guinea. My mother, Edith, has been a powerful influence in my life in her valuing of women as wonderful and capable people. Loyalty and generosity of spirit are two of her outstanding characteristics. She has known one of her best friends, Margaret (to whom I owe my first name) since she was six years old. Some of my mother's edicts have become part of my social philosophy: 'There is good in everybody.' 'Do your best in any situation.' 'Look on the positive side.' Others have proven more difficult to implement: 'Wendy, you should not argue with men.' Or: 'You can do anything you try.' Alas, wealth redistribution and abolishing violence require more than individual effort!

Atypical of women in the eastern suburbs of her time, Edith entered the paid labourforce as a teacher when each of her children went to school. A legacy of the juggling act of her generation was a model of 'supermum' – always busy; vacuuming and tidying before she went to work; cooking casseroles for sick neighbours; playing the piano or doing the flowers for the Church; listening to women at her kitchentable; and being a good wife and mother. She was the first pre-school teacher for physically disabled children in Victoria at what was then called the Victorian Society for Crippled Children. She taught a remedial class at the Salvation Army Boys Home, taught at Travencore and later at Alkira. At the age of 54 she went back to school herself and qualified as a special education teacher. Since her retirement from paidwork she has enjoyed devoting more time to community work and to her crafts and music.

> ... when I was something of a 'tomboy', he taught me to fish and to shoot holes in tins lined up on a tree – I drew the line at learning to shoot rabbits!

My father is a shy man, who has been a quiet rock of Gibraltar in our family, and has a good sense of humour and fun. Originally a country boy from Dunolly, my father was employed in a bank and in addition has a range of practical talents. While earning a steady income in a job which I think he often found boring, it seemed he gained his greatest pleasures from being a handyman at home; from his family; from sport; and his lovely pottery in the last 20 years. In my childhood, when I was something of a 'tomboy', he taught me to fish and to shoot holes in tins lined up on a tree – I drew the line at learning to shoot rabbits! Clem has always been well-liked and I remember once when he was approached to stand for the local council. The decision was not to do so. My mother explained: 'We're little people.' 'We do not have the money to buy the sort of clothes and do the entertaining' that such positions were seen to require. Of course, neither did they have much spare time – families with two adults in the paid labourforce faced even more constraints then than now. Their community involvement was through the Church and neighbourhood.

My brother, Christopher, was born in 1953. Having a loving and loved father and brother provided the ground for my views that women and men could be different but equal.

In the lower-middleclass suburbs in the 1950s most of the adult women's lives seemed thoroughly boring. My mother's life made more sense, but it seemed pretty hard work and she had a terrible struggle getting me to help with the housework. I recall being impressed by two independent women, who were family friends. Bessie Ridgeway, a 'war widow' and neighbour who taught art, and Gwen Outhred, a hospital matron. Both seemed to be pretty happy and to laugh more than most women I knew. I began to search for adventurous women's lives through reading. Along with many others, Louisa M Alcott's character Jo (in *Little Women*) was an early heroine – in retrospect a model of vicarious social contribution: supposedly 'doing good' through adopting children and marrying a non-conformist professor. There was 'Wendy at Winterton' and 'Nora of Billabong' who were later replaced by the novels and other writings of Simone de Beauvoir and Doris Lessing.

My parents made considerable sacrifice to give me an education at Methodist Ladies College (MLC), though a scholarship helped in part. At an all-girls school it was possible to stretch myself academically, without fear of the conflict between femininity and competence. But when I did well it was a secret not to be shared at the youth club, in case the boys were threatened and rejected me. I also learned the mixed blessings of formal leadership positions through being form captain, a prefect, house captain and a leader of the debating team. This education resourced me well for adult life, and I enjoyed it. We students knew nothing, then, of the personal struggles of our women teachers. They were 'spinsters' and were seen as 'maiden aunts' to be pitied, as apparently they had been 'left on the shelf' (as the saying was) and not been chosen to marry. It did not occur to me then that they might have chosen independence. Dorothea Cerutty, with her sensuous love of literature, and smartly-dressed, fun-loving Betty Jackson, inspired some hope in youthful souls seeking to combine womanhood with competence.

I studied socialwork at the University of Melbourne in the early 1960s. As the first member of our extended family to enter a university, this was new territory. I recall an interview at enrolment, when a young man in the registrar's office told me that with my matriculation results I really should do honours. But, as it was, four years seemed a long time to perpetuate being a student (women were meant to be married, not have careers) and so I felt affirmed, but nevertheless enroled for a BA and diploma of social studies.

The course thoroughly engaged me, and a lifelong friendship with Helen Friday and Frank Pavlin began. I edited *Electra*, the socialwork student newsletter (the year after David Green and the year before David Hall), and I was active in university and socialwork student affairs. My final two placements were at Winlaton Girls Training Centre in the youth welfare division of the Social Welfare Department, Victoria. This sparked a commitment to women whose lives had been damaging and hurtful to them – the form of 'sisterhood' which Dorothy Smith describes as an identification with other women in their oppression.

Kathleen Crisp, from the Commonwealth Department of Social Services, recruited me – I received a Commonwealth cadetship. On graduation I began to serve it out, but when I married I received what I often call the one benefit I have obtained from sexism. At that time (1965) there was a marriage bar in place. When I married, they had to resign me from the permanent to the temporary service, and I was free of my bond. I still felt morally bound, but, gradually disgusted by the trivial role socialworkers had in the department of social services at that time, I took my freedom and joined the non-government sector.

> ... *when I married I received what I often call the one benefit I have obtained from sexism. When I married, they had to resign me from the permanent to the temporary service, and I was free of my bond.*

In retrospect, I realise how unfortunate it was that no one could help me find a 'career' in that department, or that I did not have the confidence or know-how to forge one. No one talked about the difficulties of women having careers and traditional marriages; or took any steps to help me think longterm – rather than simply having a desperate feeling that I had to make my social contribution before I had children, which in my era could be postponed for a few years with contraception. Lyra Taylor, Kathleen Crisp, Francis Donovon and Joan Scratton were models in that they were 'mothers' of Australian socialwork – but were all single women. Without advice and help on how to manage dual careers, children's needs and domestic management, or a wider social understanding of democratic work and family life, neither I nor many other women of my generation could envisage emulating them. Our 'lot' was to be the 'juggling act' of home, family and career. Connie Benn was significant for many women socialworkers in my generation precisely for this reason. Although she set us high standards and challenges, she modelled a democratic marriage. She also passed out helpful hints, such as: 'You need a good childcare arrangement, and two lines of back-up childcare as well.'

When I try to identify 'a few' key women who helped me along the way, I recall instead literally hundreds of individuals in groups and networks, studying or working together on common life issues, supporting each other's solutions and efforts to change things for women – and for children and men. The tradition of women's lives – doing the caring work, supporting the personal and social processes of family and community life – was transformed by many women in this era into conscious and political 'collectivity'. Actively trying to make sense of our lives as women – in relation to the political economy, our children, men and each other – we talked and shared, read, wrote and acted together. We rejected hierarchical male-dominated structures of power and decision-making. We wanted to learn and act in more democratic groups, where we had our own voices, where leadership was shared. We wanted to define the issues and problems of life through our own eyes and experiences.

At Citizens Welfare Service (CWS) in Melbourne in the mid-1960s I was involved in developing one of Connie Benn's 'brain child' projects: the first secular hostel for young women who were wards of state or in conflict with their families and/or the law. The couple-based assessment categories used in marriage counselling at CWS did not, we found, explain or address women's experience. When Betty Friedan's book *The Feminine Mystique* was published, Joan Walters, our intake worker, began to use 'feminine mystique problem' (the 'problem which has no name') as an informal intake category. Women whose lives were unfulfilled, deeply unhappy, and sometimes endangered by domestic violence, came to the agency. We tried to support them in fulfilling their dreams that they might have meaningful lives. We made some bad mistakes in supporting young pregnant women to relinquish, rather than fight to keep, their babies, in those years before supporting parents' benefits were available. Many years later I learned from people in the Adoption Reform Movement – David, Tricia, Marie, Gillian and others – about the pain and difficulties such professional practices had supported.

In 1970, in New Haven, Connecticut, in the United States of America, where I had gone with my husband for him to study, I recall going to hear Kate Millett speak. Joining a standing ovation at the end was, in retrospect, a turning point in my life. I knew as I stood there, lonely among the still-sitting group with whom I had come, that I had just heard the naming of my life issues: being a woman in a sexist society. What was to be done? A year later, in Canada where my husband had taken a job, I obtained a scholarship to do my MA. There was a lot for women to think through, and I had better set my mind to the task.

I had just heard the naming of my life issues: being a woman in a sexist society. What was to be done?

My first son, Dion, had been born in 1969, just before Ian Weeks and I had left Australia. Karl was born in Canada in 1972. Beautiful, curious and enchanting children, it was easy to love them and celebrate motherhood. At the same time there was no choice but to grapple with the obligation for which my education had groomed me to make a social contribution – as though high quality childcare grew on trees, and women had wives to help out in the home! I was arrogantly determined that our generation could work this out, preferably without using other women's labour to free us on the basis of our 'class privilege', as had previously been the case for educated women. There were many times when this vision of full citizenship for women seemed daunting. When I was writing my MA thesis, on the implications of parttime work for women, Dion put a photograph of himself in front of the typewriter and announced: 'This is so you won't forget me!' Later I recall Karl stopping me at the frontdoor and asking: 'Is there really any need for more committee meetings?' So, rather than cringe too long with guilt, it all had to be talked out and worked out together.

From 1973 to 1975 I worked parttime. Linda Siegal, a neighbour also working parttime as a psychologist, and I developed a cooperative childcare group, for Dion, Laura and some other children. Five families pooled funds and employed a woman with childcare qualifications from Belgium. She was the wife of a graduate student, and would otherwise have been unable to engage in paidwork. Car-pools and cooperative lunch arrangements supplemented this. From when Karl was two years until he was six (the age for starting school fulltime), he was in a wonderfully warm and stable family daycare arrangement with Millie Selman – either part or full days. Fred, her husband, was a union organiser and worker at Westinghouse. Millie and other union women pioneered a cooperative family daycare group around a childcare centre in Hamilton.

However, 1975, International Women's Year (IWY), marked my marital separation, with lots of associated guilt and pain for us all. Subsequently we lived family life differently, with a carefully worked out and cooperative joint custody arrangement. Doing things differently has a cost. Sole parenthood meant I went to work fulltime, and I was grateful my rent was low enough to manage. Buying a house then was out of the question.

The 1970s at McMaster University in Ontario, Canada – as a graduate student in sociology and then eight and a half years working halftime, then fulltime, in the school of socialwork – were intellectually exhilarating years. A year of reading social theory – Hegel, Marx and many women writers (between the dishes, the diapers and playing in the park) gave me a way to locate socialwork practice in an analysis of the state, power and social inequality. Having read Freud and the neo-Freudians in the 1960s, I at last began to see an intellectual canvas broad and deep enough to refine clearer questions and tentative answers which were less ideological than the popular theoretical explanations of people's lives.

In 1973, at the local women's centre, Ann Duffy and I ran a discussion group on women and social class while Karl sat in his babyseat. Ann has been a kindred spirit on the journey to transform women's experience ever since. In the same year, Linda Graff, Cathy Coady and I brought together a group of women from the mental health services. All of us thought our mothers' lives had been too hard and hurtful. The outcome was Phyllis Chesler, author of *Women and Madness*, Tina Mandell, a feminist therapist from New York, and 800 women from across Ontario spending a weekend discussing women and mental health, from women's points of view. McMaster security service was not pleased that we had exceeded by 300 people the fire regulations limit for the main lecture theatre. The school of nursing officials were a little amazed at the content of the conference they had helped to fund. Eight hundred and three women went away exhilarated. The videotapes of the weekend flew freely around the country for several years, in spite of Phyllis and her publisher Doubleday trying to make a commercial profit from them.

The school of socialwork at McMaster, under the leadership of Harry Penny, was an unusual place. It had begun in 1968 and people there had a strong commitment to social justice; to socialworkers, community service workers and service users working together for better social conditions; and staff/student parity in decision-making. Being a junior staff member in a school of experienced, ethical and practical theorists, I was privileged to participate in years of well-informed debate about what should be taught and how; about field education; and about the school's responsibility in education and research in the wider community. A wonderful apprenticeship! By teaching one night a week I was able to adamantly refuse to attend late afternoon meetings, and living five minutes away from my work was a great help to parenthood.

Harry Penny taught me a lot about management. He believed himself to be among equals and encouraged staff to follow their social values and to develop their ideas and practice. He always asked first: 'What needs to be done?' and only then considered whether the existing rules could handle it, or whether the rules should be changed. In this climate it was possible to innovate: to take socialwork students on field visits to the steel company (the largest employer in town); to place and work with students in politicians' offices, with the council of advocates, the native women's centre, the white women's centre, and so on. Later it was possible to run women's groups at the Red Hill daycare centre, and involve students on placement.

In preparation for International Women's Year, Helen Levine, from Ottawa, involved me as a regional representative on the planning committee for the first 'Women in Social Work' conference in 1975. This began a long association with Helen, who has been an inspiration for me as a feminist activist, and who now works as a feminist therapist. Her partner, Gil Levine, was the research director at Canadian Union of

Public Employees for 30 years. He contributed to making sure that the union movement used my parttime work research, as well as alerting me to support the industrial action of parttime cleaners in the Hamilton-Wentworth Schools.

We were pioneering new ideas and practices and that is never easy, even in a relatively supportive environment.

In 1978, some students and I initiated our first class on women in socialwork which then became instituted as a regular elective. Maureen Orton was also involved with students and me in editing *Connections*, the newsletter of the Women's Caucus of the Canadian Schools of Social Work, as well as developing a framework to put feminist content throughout the curriculum. Telling it like this makes it sound too simple. We were pioneering new ideas and practices and that is never easy, even in a relatively supportive environment. During these years Mary Lee Stephenson, editor of the first sociology of *Women in Canada*, was denied tenure. She obtained an open hearing for her appeal, and we local women daily attended the hearing in which feminist epistemology was on trial.

In the 1970s, feminists of various traditions in Hamilton, Ontario, worked together across our differences. Had we not done so, there would have been no collective women's analysis or voice. There are many women who could be named, and many wonderful stories from that era. There were hard times and sad times. There were 'Persons Campaigns' to encourage women to use their vote; 'Reclaim the Night' marches to bring safety on the streets; women's dinners for building a community of support. Much of this was around the Hamilton Women's Centre. At the Social Planning and Research Council in 1976 we developed proposals on income security for single parents which involved a combination of parttime work and state assistance. This was based on my research into parttime work, and was part of a series of efforts to improve the situation of sole parents in Ontario. At the Elizabeth Fry Society volunteers worked with women in prison and after. I convened the social action committee comprised largely of women who knew the flaws of the system from having 'done time' inside. Nancy Adamson, Linda Brisken and Margaret McPhail much later theorised the practice of the Canadian Women's Movement in 'making change'. It was a privilege, as an 'immigrant' woman, to have been part of it.

My personal and political 'struggles' (a word used advisedly, because that is how it felt!) were sustained by wonderful friendships and mutual support: Ann, Elena, Sheila, and our children, Linda, Anna, Donna, Liz Mordue and others. Peta Tancred (Sheriff) was at McMaster in the 1970s, and her intellectual rigour and personal dignity came to symbolise for me excellent and accountable scholarship. Michael Wheeler proved to be both a loving friend and my toughest intellectual critic. Over subsequent years I learned much about myself from him, not least of which were lessons about the importance of independence of mind and spirit.

The year 1982 began with the boys and me returning to Australia. The re-entry was very rocky because the other adults in the family network did not join us as soon as we all had planned and expected. Moving to a new job on the opposite side of the world is no fun for either a single parent or her children, in spite of the support of extended family and old friends, such as Rae Mathew. My brother Chris and his family were then, and have been since, wonderful friends to the boys and me.

The social backdrop to what could obviously be a much longer personal story of returning to my homeland, was the nature of the rather polarised and 'tough' public and organisational politics in Australia. The intellectual and personal freedom and support which I had glimpsed and experienced in Canada, seemed thwarted in a society where citizenship is about mateship and fraternity, and where conceptions of equality contain too little respect for sex, racial or ethnic differences. Whereas in Toronto, in 1979, a street poll reported that 54 percent of women and men were 'feminists', feminists in Australia appeared to be viewed as 'man-hating lesbians', whatever their sexual preference. Australian society is one where too many women are cowed into apologetic manner and polite, angry or frustrated silence. The 'masculinist' 'cut and thrust' culture of public life appears to me to be destructive, unknowing of women's 'lived experience', and unwilling to learn from women's ways of doing things. Rather, women who enter public life are expected to 'toughen up', 'take it like a man', while dressing like a *Vogue* magazine model. There are, of course, some notable women who have displayed great courage and strength in public life in the 1980s and 1990s in Australia, and have kept close to their communities and 'done it like women'. Carmen Lawrence, Joan Kirner, Kay Setches and Kate Gilmore stand out for me. They have my great respect.

> ... *women who enter public life are expected to 'toughen up', 'take it like a man', while dressing like a* Vogue *magazine model.*

I found myself, in the 1980s, continuing to most strongly identify with community groups and the 'creatively marginal' possibilities of community cooperation and action and education. I had become committed to a process of social transformation. The means cannot be sacrificed for the end goals. As a woman, I had to focus first on what this might mean for women, and restructuring work and family life appear necessary to achieve equality. I had learned 'the personal is political', that 'everyday life' and personal and social practices were as relevant as 'public life'. At best these are social processes which can contribute to a stronger and more just and equal social fabric, even if indirectly and slowly. If education can survive the assaults of the economic rationalists, it may be possible for us in that location to follow Hugh Stretton's suggestion that its prime purpose is to stimulate debate about social values and purposes.

From 1982 to 1991 I was employed as principal lecturer in socialwork at Phillip Institute (PIT, now part of RMIT). Building on the strong foundation of Frances Donovon and her staff in the 1970s, a team of people in the 1980s worked together around a commitment to social justice and learning structural, developmental and feminist approaches to socialwork, welfare and community work theory and practice. My personal educational philosophy is that teaching is not possible, but that education is about resources and opportunities for learning. 'Teachers' can pose only the most relevant social questions they have learned, systematically share their learning, and develop resources, structures and processes to support people learning, working and acting together. Staff and students at 'PIT' in the 1980s worked together to do this in a dynamic and challenging educational community.

Time spent as a sexual harassment adviser on academic board and PIT council taught me more than I ever wanted to know about being among the 'token' women ...

This community was no 'ivory tower'. People worked hard and were active in community and social issues. Internally we tried to transform social relationships to be democratic, cooperative and mutually respectful. We did not always succeed, and individual 'egos' sometimes thwarted community. In the wider institution school staff and students were involved in the development of many important workplace and student policies and practices. All staff were union members, and I enjoyed working with and learned much from Jaccie Adie and Faye Gravenall who were active in the staff union, and from Teresa Ewinska, the equal opportunity officer. Time spent as a sexual harassment adviser on academic board and PIT council taught me more than I ever wanted to know about being among the 'token' women representatives in a climate of patriarchal practices and economic rationalism. Externally the staff group was engaged in social criticism, advocacy and community development.

Some of the happiest memories of what felt like 'socially useful work' at 'PIT' were the social policy classes 'co-taught' with John Wiseman, and our success in offering socialwork and community development in northern Victoria. The development of Women's Studies in both socialwork and community development courses was exciting. This was complemented by Bob Pease's work in developing pro-feminist men's studies. New models of community-based field education were developed in the Western Region, involving Sharon Moore, and in Broadmeadows, with Marjorie Quinn (who both subsequently joined the staff). Learning together about shared management and leadership with Valerie Gerrand was an unusual and excellent experience in a bureaucratic organisation. We all spent many hours talking and working things out in the staff group, with many others than those whom I have named making their contribution. The MA in social policy was crafted in many hours of work, and finally offered in 1991.

We developed our theory and practice with a wide range of people outside the institution. The first 'Socialwork Education' conference was in Beijing in 1988. Bob Pease and I were proud to be two of the 10 Australians. Subsequently, after Tian An Mien Square, we hosted a moving visit from Hong Kong socialwork educators committed to social democracy in the future of China. In 1984, when I was a visiting scholar at the University of Queensland, I met and began to learn from Aboriginal elder, Lilla Watson, by her generosity in allowing me to sit in her classes. In 1988, Lilla came to PIT/RMIT as the first Aboriginal visiting scholar and launched Aboriginal studies in the socialwork program. Glenn Alderson, from Commonground Cooperative in Seymour, worked with us in expanding the Summer School for the Human Services. Subsequently several staff developed an on-going association with them. Yoland Wadsworth taught research in the program and concurrently several of us continued to be involved with her in ARIA, the Action Research Issues Association.

Another highlight, which has allowed me to write and theorise, was the collaborative writing about the community services. First came the book on *Issues Facing Australian Families*, co-edited with Robyn Batten and John Wilson, which includes case studies of Australian programs and practice, and more recently the collaboration with feminist women's services to write about lessons from their pioneering efforts, *Women Working Together*.

Several of the school's loyal group of administrative staff took up studying Women's Studies and other tertiary subjects, and then moved on to become independent businesswomen. After a long, slow process we introduced a permanent job-sharing position for two administrative staff with family responsibilities. The students who shared in learning became colleagues in the local community services. Working together at the Centre Against Sexual Assault (CASA) at the Royal Women's Hospital, where we developed the first feminist field education centre, and at the Victorian Council of Social Service (VCOSS) are two examples.

Sometimes the younger ones insist that the elders learn!

So, in my experience, learning, mutual support, and taking action all seem to happen concurrently, with people working together. Sometimes one receives from one, and then gives to another, in an individualised 'mentoring' progression based on the model of elder and child. Mostly what strikes me about social action or practice is its shared, mutual and dynamic process of critical reflection and action. Sometimes the younger ones insist that the elders learn! In 1991, after three years as head of department, I stepped 'out and down'. My analysis of organisational gender politics suggests to me that shared and rotating leadership is essential, especially for those who cannot or will not learn to do it 'like a man'. In my experience, 'earth mothers' are particularly prone to being seen and treated as stronger than they feel, and receive their unfair share of cultural 'mother blaming', while getting pretty tired doing the organisational housekeeping!

In 1991 I took up a teaching post at the University of Melbourne, very much enjoying further developing Women's Studies and its potential contribution to women's personal and social liberation. There are many women at the university and in the community working together on this important agenda, and again I feel privileged to work among them.

Standing on a Table-top and Learning to Lead

Marjorie Oke

Born on 18 December 1911 in the Melbourne suburb of Richmond, Victoria, Marjorie (Marj) Oke has long been active in the Women's Movement, particularly as a member of the Union of Australian Women (UAW). Amongst many other activities, she was for a number of years UAW delegate to the National Council of Women (NCW). In 1988, she was the Mary Owen Dinner speaker.

In the 1980s Marj Oke was instrumental in establishing the Northcote Self-help Hydrotherapy and Massage Group which grew out of the Northcote Community Health Centre's physiotherapy and warm water exercise sessions. The number of women participating grew from eight to more than 40, continuing to expand yearly. Inspired by this example, other groups began similar activities throughout Melbourne and in other parts of Australia.

I was born in the bedroom of a little wooden house at the Richmond swimmingbaths. At that time, homebirths were the norm. Hospitals were only just being built on any large scale, and it was not long after that hospital births became more common. My two younger sisters were born at Bethesda Hospital, which was completed after I was born.

My mother, Elizabeth Grace Weston, was one of seven children. She was 12 or 13 when she left school, having reached Grade 8, the highest grade in primaryschool. From the way she talked, it was evident that she was a good student. She would have liked to have had the opportunity to continue with her schooling. Not a lot of young people did. The only highschool in existence was 'the Continuation School'. It later became Melbourne High School, situated in Spring or Nicholson Street, not far from Parliament House.

After leaving school, my mother spent several weeks working at Bedggoods' boot factory, but when her younger brother Alex was born

STANDING ON A TABLE-TOP AND LEARNING TO LEAD

she left to look after him and help run the house. Alex was referred to, always, as 'her' baby, for she cared for him as if he was her own. For many years, she was a slave in the household, doing the washing and ironing and other housework, whilst Grandma (her mother) did the cooking.

Grandma worked in the little bootshop she and her husband ran between them, repairing boots as well as making them. It was their business, and the shop was known as 'Westons'.

Dad was a Richmondite, too. William Bennett (known as 'Bill' Bennett) was one of five – two girls and three boys. As far as I know he left school at 12 or 13, too. Almost everyone did, in those days. He didn't talk about his schooling, but I know he went to work in Bedggoods' bootfactory, learning the boot trade. It was before complicated machinery came in, and there was a great deal to learn. At about the time he married Mum, he opened a boot repairing shop in Hawthorn.

Mum and Dad worked in the shop, until Dad saw an advertisement for the job of running the Richmond Baths. He had done a lot of physical education and had read many of the physical culture books coming from America in those days. He was good at swimming and good at teaching people to box and wrestle, as well as doing everything else acrobatic and gymnastic. Richmond council had built a big swimmingpool for the citizens of Richmond. At the end of the pool was a gymnasium, a big tin shed containing all the gymnasium equipment possible in those days: bolting horses, horizontal bars, parallel bars, Roman rings, trapezes and wrestling mats, a punchingball in one corner and dumbbells for weightlifting in another. A chap by the name of Lamb had been employed by the Richmond council to teach gymnastics. Then the job fell vacant. Dad applied.

That is how Bill Bennett started off working professionally in the field: he supervised the running of the baths as well as running the gymnasium and teaching swimming. I grew up as Marj Bennett, living at the Richmond Baths.

I was placed in the brand new infants' room. It was built as the 'new' model for young children.

I attended the same school as Mum had, Central School, Richmond. It became an all-girls school several years ago, and now has changed its character again. When I attended, I was placed in the brand new infants' room. It was built as the 'new' model for young children. There was a large hall in the middle, with rooms set all around it, on the periphery. Later I moved into the old two-storey brick building; it was the one where Mum had been taught. There were long stools for the children to sit on, with no backs to rest against. The desks ran in a long line in front of the stool, with eight children seated at each desk. We wrote on slate with slate pencils. A dirt rag was tied to the top of each slate; if the pencil didn't work properly, the children spat on their slates, then rubbed them with the rag to clean off the pencil and start again. No one was given a lead pencil until Grade 2.

In the bubs' grade, one teacher, Mrs Murphy, told us stories. I realise now it was history – the Greek and Roman myths and legends. There was Horatius at the bridge, Leonidas at Thermopylae and Alexander the Great with his horse Bucephalus. There was nothing about Diana or Hera, or even Athena. But I loved horses, so was particularly taken with Alexander the Great and when I was in Grade 6 did a special project on Bucephalus.

We had a horse, so I identified with Alexander. I was also looking for brave heroes, for this that attracted me. Probably it fitted my father's aspirations for me.

Central School, Richmond, was used as a hospital when the pneumonic plague broke out, after the 1914–18 war. The soldiers had come home, bringing it with them. All the schools were shut down by the authorities, with many then being used for hospitals. To control the outbreak, inoculations were given out to people at the swimming baths. In those days, few had baths in their own homes. In the Richmond area, people used the six hot baths at the Richmond pool.

At Richmond Baths, we had a boiler for making the hot water for people to wash in, and for washing our clothes and the hundreds of towels used at the baths. Technically, the washing of clothes and towels was Mum's job, as was dealing with the togs. Togs – bathing costumes – were hired in those days, too. When they were handed in after an afternoon's swimming, they had to be washed.

Running the baths and the gymnasium was a real husband-and-wife job. Dad was supposed to clean up the place while Mum did the washing, but Mum and I often swept the sheds and did other tasks about the place.

When, at the time of the pneumonic plague scare, the schools were closed, people came to the window at the baths where the money was passed over for swimming. They'd make their appointments for injections, then move over to the area where the six hot water baths stood, and the doctors and nurses (many of them voluntary aid detachments – VADs) administered the needles. There was a side effect: people were too scared to visit us, in case we had the disease and passed it on to them.

My mother's sisters were part of the VAD in those days. Later, when the first world war was over, they went to Austin Hospital to train to be 'proper' nurses. (To learn nursing at Austin Hospital was to have the best training in Melbourne in those days.) For the first year of training the nurse worked for no pay at all, while her family provided the uniforms. In the second year, nurses received about 2/6d per week. Austin was a general hospital, so after completing their courses there, Mum's sisters were off to the Women's Hospital in Carlton to do 'women's nursing', then they went to the Children's Hospital in Flemington Road, where they trained in children's illnesses and diseases. Next came Fairfield Hospital, for training in infectious diseases. They had an all-round training.

In my family there was constant talk about helping people and caring for them, and action followed the words. My family was extremely conscious of our responsibilities to the community. This, and the impression my aunts made upon me as a young child, meant I wanted to be a nurse. Then I began reading girls' books where everyone went to boardingschool and had sportsmistresses. I immediately wanted to be a sportsmistress. The job appealed because I was keen on swimming and athletics, and was in the gymnasium daily, trying out the equipment. So it was a 'toss up' between nursing or being a sportsmistress. Either would have suited me, for both involved helping people and looking after them.

> *I was keen on swimming and athletics, and was in the gymnasium daily, trying out the equipment.*

I was an avid reader. The family gave us children books for presents for our birthdays and at Christmas. I built up a good library of books containing information and pictures of Australian wildlife – both flowers and animals. We had a block of land at Warrandyte. (Now it is the suburbs; then it was the country.) We visited it each weekend, and that was how my love of Australia and the land developed.

I was an environmentalist in the early days, before it gained general support. I constantly saved this and saved the other, and took care of the land and our natural surroundings. I knew a great deal about the wildflowers growing on our land and around about, and about many of the animals. I knew their names. Later in life, when I was working as a school teacher in Moe, I took the kids out regularly into the bush to show them the wonders of the country. I wanted them to learn, as I had learned, of the beauty and importance of the flowers, the plants and the animals.

When I returned from Moe to Melbourne, I had the school hire a bus to take the children as close to the bush as we could. There was a wild reservation near Pound Bend Road, along the road to Warrandyte, near the place where the River Yarra was dammed. Warrandyte was a gold mining area and the damming was done to assist the miners in sluicing the alluvial gold. Our own block of land was covered in hundreds of tiny holes where miners had dug, and we stayed in what was an old miners' hut: it was square, with huge tarantulas climbing up the walls. (Now I know they were really grass spiders.) I was brought up not to be frightened of spiders.

There were beautiful patches of orchard at Pound Bend. The area had that name, because lost and stray horses or dogs were impounded there in the old days. It is now known as Yarra Bend, and is a picnic ground.

Books were important in our family and influenced the way I grew up.

Seven Little Australians impressed me greatly. As in the Billabong books, the children were sent away to boardingschool. Everyone went from the country or the outback to colleges in the city. At school I read both those books known as 'girls' books', and those classed as 'boys' books'. I read more boys' books than girls' books, because Dad was doing his best to bring me up as a boy. There were no boys in our family and I was the first-born, so he was making me into a boy! I was reared with all the advantages of learning boys' skills as well as having the girls' skills through working with Mum. I had the advantage of being brought up with many of the freedoms that in other families were extended only to boy children. I wore romper pants. My hair was cut in an 'American bob'; it was never long. I did boxing and everything else boys did, as well as sewing and cooking. Dad always said girls were 'sissy'. You didn't howl – you were a sissy girl if you howled! You had to be brave and strong like a boy and not howl when you fell over. I don't know whether I thought I was a boy or a girl, but I knew what I wasn't – a 'sissy girl'.

Dad was doing his best to bring me up as a boy.

I read the Edward S Ellis Indian books. A native American, he wrote about the Red Indians in the United States of America. After reading every one of those books, I read *Seven Little Australians*, which Grandma gave to me as a reward for doing 'good' writing. I was savage that I received what I thought was as 'sissy' girl book, and not a boy book, although there were some boys in it. We often bought *Boys' Own Magazine* to read.

I enjoyed school. I began late – at seven and a quarter years of age – because of the school being used as a hospital. Until the schools reopened, I spent every day swimming at the Richmond Baths. Friday was the only official day for ladies, but I swam with the boys and men from Saturday through to Thursday, then on Fridays I swam with the boys and men too. I wore the same sort of togs as the boys: we call them bikinis now. Mine were made from gold velvet, for I was known as a goldfish.

I gave swimming demonstrations in the gold togs, which were made up of tiny pants and a square top like a jacket. Most of the boys and men didn't worry about wearing anything on the days set aside exclusively for them. They swam in nothing. I was always dressed up in my pants, because it was the rule that girls were not supposed to let the men see their unclothed bodies. But it was evidently all right for me to see men!

On Friday, ladies' day, everyone wore neck-to-knee togs. It became fashionable for those in swimming races to wear the cotton one-piece costume. I grew up owning one, and Mum wore the cotton one-piece, too. I can't recall ever seeing Mum in neck-to-knees: her one-piece came about halfway down the thigh, with the armholes free.

I have been a swimmer all my life. I swam before I was four years old.

Dad encouraged me in my swimming and rescue lessons; he was always keen on it. But it was Mum who walked me up and down the pool and set me off on learning how to swim. I was giving swimming demonstrations for the Royal Lifesaving Society by the time I was four, and recall swimming across the Brunswick Baths at the deep end for a carnival for the Royal Lifesaving men. I went around saying: 'If this little girl can do these things – see how easy it is for you grownups to do it.'

I was active in the 'learn to swim' campaign, and taught others how to rescue people. A policeman named Uren swam in the demonstrations, too. I used to pull him out as the first rescue demonstration. A photograph of me doing my lifesaving demonstrations showed me with my little fingers correctly placed on his head, near his face, with me kicking and him floating; I was pulling him along, showing everybody how easy it was.

At 18 and a half years of age I left University High School. University High had been educating students since 1912 and was a training school for student teachers. It was initially called the University Practising School, because students from Melbourne University were sent to practise on the students. When highschools came into being, it became known as University High School. It retained its position as a training school, and the principal could choose teachers with the best qualifications, as the aim was to teach the students well. There was also a strong belief that the school children shouldn't be damaged by being practised on, so this gave an additional incentive to having the best teachers.

Before they entered the school as pupils, children had to sit for a test. There was comprehension, maths, grammar and spelling. The goal was to ensure that pupils would be able to cope well. The aim was to select pupils who would not be lost in what was, in some ways, an experimental atmosphere. If the test indicated that a child might not adapt, then the child was not accepted.

After attending Richmond Central I had gone to Mentone Primary School. We had moved to Mentone when my father was appointed to the Mentone Baths. Mordialloc High School had just opened when I completed primaryschool, and the head teacher came around to our school to talk about our going on to highschool. I went home all excited, convincing the family I should go. I was 14 years old by then, and it meant that I would not be going out to get a job. My parents would have to keep me. *It was a huge struggle for people to keep their children at school, and particularly for my parents.* Not much money was made at the Mentone Swimming Baths. If it rains at the weekend, no one comes to swim. This means that not only is the entry fee not paid, but sweets and icecreams are not sold. If the Christmas holidays are damp, that ruins everything:

no swimming, and no income. The whole system operates on the idea that a lot of money will be made over the summer, to tide the family over the winter. But if there is little or no money in summer, then it's a matter of scratching to get by all year long.

Anyway, my parents decided I would go to Mordialloc High School. I did well in the first term, but then became a nuisance in the classroom. I discovered I could put on a performance with everyone looking at me, saying: 'Oh! Look what Marj is doing!' I jumped out of my seat when I should be sitting. I skited and skylarked, and made strange and terrible noises. I attached a piece of chalk to elastic, so that it bounced about the classroom, appearing on someone's head wherever I aimed it. I had seen other children doing such things before, but I had never aped them until I got into highschool.

The hall had three rows of classrooms, each separated by dark green curtains. Our class was up on the platform. It was not a good way to start a highschool education, for it was extremely makeshift. The growth in school numbers and expansion of education meant this was happening all around Victoria. Church halls and other buildings, not purpose built, were being used. Teachers were not properly trained, or had no training at all. I was not being stretched.

The following year, we moved over to the Presbyterian Sunday School hall. I took to hiding in cupboards then jumping out and shouting: 'Booo' at the teachers when they entered. I was up to all sorts of silly tricks and was extremely cheeky to the teachers. I look back upon it now with shame. Still, it did teach me how to deal with disruptive students when I became a teacher. I knew that the best approach was to take no notice, and the children would give up. I often said to the pupils I had at school in Moe: 'If you take no notice of so-and-so – I won't, and you won't – then they'll give up.' I'd tell the children that if they all behaved themselves they could have peanuts to eat as they went home, and I kept a jar of peanuts handy, giving them to the students for good work.

I took to hiding in cupboards then jumping out and shouting: 'Booo' at the teachers when they entered.

Next, the education department decided it had insufficient money and everyone should pay to attend school. The charge was 2/- a term. Our family decided that that was more than they could afford. The decision was taken that I should stay at home, play on the sand and swim when the summer came, and could help serve in the shop attached to the baths, and in the café. But I was torn between staying on at school or giving up. I changed my mind about a dozen times – would I go to school, or wouldn't I? It was tempting to stay at home, playing on the sand, swimming, and going out in a canoe. Finally I made up my mind. I went to the school to tell them I had decided to continue. But all the way there I was wishing I had made a different decision, so I turned around and came home.

So, there I was, at home doing nothing. I worked around the baths, did a lot of fancywork from transfers impressed onto cloth, and was pretty good at drawing. At Black Rock a factory made materials for fancywork – transfers and designs. It was not far from Mentone and I could walk there from home. I decided I could get a job at the factory, designing patterns. In our family ignorance, we didn't realise it was necessary to be trained for such a job. I sailed over, with Dad in tow. There was no job advertised. We simply went in and said that this is what I had come to do for them. They looked somewhat staggered, and asked about my training. Then they explained it wasn't possible just to sit down to draw whatever came into your head. Still, because I was keen to have a job, they said they would give me one. They sent me back into another room where two metal bars stood straight up in the air. They gave me threads and strands. These had to be put over the bar and the woollen skeins stretched, then a piece of paper had to be put in the correct place, tying the skeins. One piece of paper bore the number for the ball of wool; another piece, tied at the other end, carried the name of the manufacturer and the colours in the ball. I did this until lunchtime, when I got the stitch. Instead of eating my lunch, then going back into the workroom, I ate my lunch then went home saying: 'Not doing that!'

I discovered a friend from my Richmond Central School days was to attend University High School. We had been friends since we were children, and her mother and my mother had become friends in the mothers' club. No fees were paid at University High School: because the children were used for training, the school considered it couldn't charge them; they were practising on you! Immediately I approached my parents and said: 'Look, I could go back to school again and be a nurse or *something!*' I had just finished reading L M Montgomery's *Anne of Green Gables*. She had struggled hard to get to university, and I thought: 'Well, if Anne can do it, so can I.' That gave me the inspiration to struggle hard to get into the school, and then to work hard like Anne. I will always be grateful to Anne of Green Gables and to L M Montgomery.

I will always be grateful to Anne of Green Gables and to L M Montgomery.

I wasn't certain what I should do in order to be accepted into University High School; also, school was already in full-swing for that year. I went to the education department to see the assistant inspector, Mr Seitz (later, he became chief inspector). I'd met him at primaryschool swimming-carnivals. May Cox, who was in charge of the swimming and knew of my ability, introduced me to Mr Seitz at the carnivals, saying: 'Marj will become one of our outstanding teachers for swimming when she completes her education.' So, off I went to Mr Seitz.

Mr Seitz telephoned University High School, after warning me that as it was halfway through the year, the school was probably full. I didn't hear all the conversation, but could hear Mr Seitz say to Mr Shalin, the principal: 'Look, you don't have to worry that you haven't enough room. She can be a goldfish in a pool. That's all you need – a pool of water, and she'll be alright.' But it didn't work! There was no pool of water, and I was out. But I didn't leave it there.

I was mad keen to go, so my dad hunted out the address. University High School was in Lygon Street, Carlton, a little triangular block of land at the end of the cemetery, opposite what is now the building where people go to get a car licence. Off dad went to see Mr Shalin. 'Yes, he'll take you for a trial for six weeks, because you haven't done the test,' he said, when he returned home. 'Mr Shalin doesn't know whether you're suitable for the school, so they'll put you on trial.' He added: 'You mightn't be material for them. You might be more suitable for dishwashing.' Well, that was fair enough.

I trotted along. After being there for about two days, I decided it was time to play up. I skited and got people looking. That was my first and only endeavour at those tricks. The teacher simply looked at me and said: 'Marj, if that's how you feel, you can go out with the clothes pegs. We don't do that in this school. We don't know what you did at the other school, but it won't happen here. We're not interested one little bit.' No one in the class laughed or commented. Later, at playtime, they said: 'You were a stupid nut, weren't you.'

It was Miss Guest, the English teacher, who brought me into line. I am very appreciative of her. That form of discipline flattened me properly. So that was that.

At the end of the six weeks, they kept me at the school. The only subject in which I couldn't perform well was German: I had never studied it before. But I could do some French, for I had studied it at Mordialloc High School. Because I'd missed an entire year, one way or the other, between leaving Mordialloc High School, then beginning in the middle of the next, so they put me back a grade. That was June 1927, so I was doing what I would have done in 1926, had I gone straight through. Still, I excelled at swimming and took up hockey. I began with basketball, but it was a dangerous game: too many people jumped on the feet of other players. I couldn't bear people crowding around and jumping on my feet, so I took up hockey instead. Players could be hit with the ball, but there was more space to get out of the way. I received the sports award for hockey, which meant I had a green and white stripe to put at the top of my blazer pocket.

I was proud of my prowess, and gained a swimming award as well. By the time I reached what we called 'Leaving Pass' (Year 11), rather than gaining attention through being a naughty girl, I had become a hero. My house, Duff, chose me as house captain. I went on to do 'Leaving Honours' (matriculation), and became Form 6 captain.

Under the system at University High School prefects were not used as 'police people'; we assisted in the organisation of the school. The staff chose four girls and four boys, and the school chose two girls and two boys – the boys voting for their candidates, the girls voting for the two they wanted. I was nominated, and Cath Mills, a fellow student, and I were chosen. Cath then went off to do clerical and business college work. I stayed on and was chosen as senior prefect.

I had so many opportunities to learn how to organise in the classrooms and at phys ed, and had other prefect responsibilities. For phys ed, the school was divided into squads. When the bell went, each of us went out to whichever squad we were taking for that period. This meant we learnt to handle pupils. We were seen as teachers. Because I had swimming ability and lifesaving training, I took special lessons. As well, I was hockey captain and swimming captain. The school held classes to train us students to take on these administrative and leadership roles.

Conducting swimming lessons had also been my role at the first school I attended, in Richmond, as a primary student. The school was nextdoor to the swimmingbaths, which meant all the teachers knew me. They brought their pupils to swim. When the swimming season began, they did 'land drill' which was teaching the pupils how to swim, standing on dry land. They did the movements necessary to move in the water, before jumping in! The teachers asked me if I would demonstrate for the pupils, and do the lessons. (At the time, I was seven and a bit.) 'Yes,' I said, 'but you'll have to keep the kids in order. You'll have to put me on a table so that they can hear me and see me.' They obligingly put me on a table and helped keep order. This training has been useful all my life. It stood me in good stead at University High School.

Still, I had some harrowing experiences. At Richmond, Dad had a bath attendant who worked with him, and whom he had to tell what to do. I was a bit cheeky to him several times. On one occasion he made as if to 'dong' me, which I probably deserved. In getting out of his way, I lost my balance and went into the water. My arm caught between the rail and the pool. Mum had to rescue me. 'How did you get in there?' she asked. I said I just didn't know, for I wasn't brave enough to tell her I'd been rude to him and he'd pushed me. I didn't want to dob him in, either; I had been brought up according to the principle that you *don't* 'dob'. Anyway, I knew it was my fault, not his. That was another lesson learned. On another occasion a little girl wouldn't do what I wanted her to do. 'Look,' I said, 'you do as I tell you or I'll have my

> *I had been brought up according to the principle that you* don't *'dob'.*

father throw you out.' What Dad would have said, had I asked him to do this, I don't know, but the girl went off and did what I was wanting her to do.

I had so many opportunities to gain leadership experience. I also had my mother and father in positions where they were in charge, and saw how they went about it. I learnt at a very early age that sometimes it was necessary to take someone by the collar and seat of their pants, and remove them from places where they are disruptive. I did that with big, 16-year-old school kids at a primaryschool where I was teaching. I'd been taught wrestling, and I used that training to remove another disruptive student. I gave him a half-Nelson, holding his arm firmly up his back. He yelped and under my direction came out of the classroom.

I was the junior teacher in charge of 48 pupils. The head teacher was absent at his father's funeral. I knew I couldn't let the noisy students beat me, or I'd have the whole school acting up. I used my physical prowess and what I had been taught in the boxing ring and gymnasium. I told the boys they could return when the head teacher did. That afternoon, he was back. I had a pink fit wondering what he would say. His wife told him what had happened, because I told her. (The whole district knew, anyway!) His wife had supported me, saying it was the right action to take. The head teacher came into the classroom. As soon as he walked in, he asked where the two boys were. The other pupils were looking at me. From my corner, and shivering in my boots, I said: 'Please, sir, I sent them home.' He replied: 'Well, I'll deal with them when they come back.' 'I told them they had to stay away until you came,' I said. To the room in general he announced: 'Tell them they can come back tomorrow morning. I'll be here.' The following morning, when they appeared, he gave them a good talking to.

It was a little country school at Scoresby, which would have completely disappeared today. At that time, the children were kept there by their families until they were educated. Most of the people in the district were dairy farmers who grew fruit trees, particularly lemons. That was the industry in Scoresby in those days. Out of that experience, all the students at the school recognised that they couldn't put anything over me.

I had support and a good example all the way through my student days. Mum's mother was keen that I become a good writer. She was concerned that I couldn't rule with red ink without making a mess everywhere, and offered me book prizes if I could keep an exercise book without red blotches, and if I could improve my writing. Mum and dad gave little prizes for a good performance. They'd arrive home saying: 'I have a surprise for you – because you did "x" so well.' I received so many prizes for my abilities in swimming and gymnasium. I

Mum's mother was keen that I become a good writer.

was trained to win an Olympic gold medal, and although I didn't get near it, I was brought up knowing I could win prizes. Boy Charlton came from Sydney to swim in Melbourne races. He trained at Richmond Baths and I trained with him. I was impressed that I was swimming with an outstanding swimmer. This was another incentive.

Aunty Eva, Mum's sister, impressed on me that listening hard and doing well at what you could do was important. My relatives had qualifications, particularly nursing, and Aunty Sarah worked in a bookbinding shop as well as being the organist at the Methodist Church in Brunswick Street, Fitzroy. (The building is still there, but it is no longer a church.) Dad's father, Steve (Stephanos) Bennett, was a foundation member of the Labour Council. Dad and Mum were in the Labor Party (ALP) and Mum made the supper for the Richmond branch. It met in the band hall, opposite the baths. So I grew up with political discussions going on around me. Members of parliament and councillors attended the Richmond branch meetings. I got to know all of them. There had not been many prime ministers way back in 1911, nor even when I was 18 years of age, but I met those (on the Labor side) there were, growing up in a situation where I was 'rubbing shoulders' with them. They didn't impress me greatly, but they were there and they were Labor people, so we automatically knew they must be good. We were very one-eyed!

I grew up with political discussions going on around me.

From Grade 3 at school we studied civics. I was eight or nine when I was taught about parliament. We learned that there were two houses, a lower and an upper, and why. We knew that poor people couldn't get into parliament because it was necessary to have a lot of money in the bank and to own property of some sort. That was drummed into us very early. Dad was very cross because when he was a young man he'd paid threepence per week from his meagre wages to have Billy Hughes taught to be a lawyer – then Hughes ratted on the Labor Party. My father said that was a dreadful thing to do after all the work and support of ALP members. But when the Labor Party was formed and began sending members into parliament, they saw it was necessary to have people with legal knowledge, or the Labor Party would be sunk. I have no idea how Billy Hughes was chosen, but he was. After he deserted the Labor Party, I waited eagerly for the *Labor Call* to arrive every week, to see the regular cartoon featuring Billy Hughes, 'the rat'. I grew up knowing that what you never did was rat.

Dad told me another story about ratting. It influenced me for life. We were not brought up in church theories or mythologies, and the day before I went to school for the first time, Dad said to me respectfully: 'Now, when you go to school, you will learn about a person called *God*.

Well, there is no such thing as that. It's just a fairytale. But this fairy is supposed to live up in the sky. You can forget all about that.' There was more: 'Then they say there was a man called *Jesus Christ*, who was his son. Well, he wasn't. He was born the same as every other man, with a man and a woman. Christ was a very good man, as was his whole family. They were always looking to do what they could for the poor people and the people who were sick, and those who couldn't get work or were distressed. He was a wonderful person in the way he went out, looking after people.' Then he went into his conclusion: 'Now,' he said, very seriously and *never* laughing, 'he and his father and brothers were all members of the Carpenters Trade Union. It is because he didn't ever rat on the workers that the bosses hung him up on the cross.' So I decided I would *never* rat, and would have to be like Christ, getting out to help as many people as I could, particularly poor people. That talk of my father's probably influenced me a lot, but not in a religious or mystical way. That was the foundation I gained when I was seven.

> *I decided I would never rat, and would have to be like Christ, getting out to help as many people as I could...*

From the word 'go' I was involved in the Women's Movement. Both my paternal and my maternal grandmother moaned and groaned about working in the bootshop with their husbands and never receiving any money from them. They had housekeeping money, but if they wanted to spend anything on themselves, they had to scrabble it out of that. As a little girl, I thought: 'I'm always going to have my own money. No man will dominate me with the money. When I'm working, I'll have my own bank account, and I'll spend it how I want. If I share it with anybody else, I'll do it only on the basis that I know what I am getting before I start.' I would say to Mum: 'Why is it that Grandma didn't ever stand up to Grandfather over that?' Mum replied: 'Oh, you can't stand up to them over money.' She was in the same situation. She and Dad had a joint job and he wasn't any better than the others at handing over money. He was very good at spending it!

At about 26, in 1937, I joined the Union of Australian Women (UAW). Then I joined the Labor Party, which had its own women's group; I was a member, going to quarterly councils, conferences and committee meetings. I was also in the peace movement, and met many other women for peace. I learned about the Women's International League for Peace and Freedom (WILPF), but didn't join because the UAW was for peace too. That impressed me greatly.

I had heard about the National Council of Women (NCW). I was proud that there were women's groups fighting for women. Two of my mother's cousins were members of the NCW. An aunt was a member of the Travellers Aid Society. They met people at railway stations, giving out addresses of good, safe accommodation, and serving tea. Grandma and some cousins were members of the Women's Christian Temperance Union (WCTU), fighting against drinking and for women's rights. They visited the pubs, saying to the men: 'Come out and go home. You should be looking after your wife and kids, not standing in here drinking.' They took their umbrellas with them, because men bashed them with walking sticks. The umbrellas were necessary protection.

> *They took their umbrellas with them, because men bashed them with walking sticks.*

I recall a photograph of Grandma and other women, with their hands across their chests and holding their umbrellas, which were unfurled. My mother was very proud of her mother, because she stood up for her principles. When a woman turned 40 she was supposed to go into a special kind of hat, with a high crown, which meant 'I am 40', to let everyone know. Grandma refused. The hats were not attractive, and she was determined to stay in fashion. Until she died, at 90-something, she wore the latest hat.

For a long time I longed for the UAW to send me off as delegate to the NCW. When Joan Curlewis died, I said I'd go. I was keen to be where my relatives had been. I wanted to meet with women who had been working and fighting for women for years. There were all sorts of groups in the NCW, with varying points of view and ways of working. I said to the UAW: 'If you're going to win votes, you've got to be there. How will you get people to understand your ideas if you don't work with them?' Once, I was told I was a good evangelist, and that is the approach I take. What is the use of having theories, if you are not prepared to go out to explain them to others? I thought I could stand up at the NCW, talk and persuade them of the need for various actions. I had been there for less than nine months when Diane Alley nominated me for the executive. (It was she who had originally nominated the UAW as a member of the NCW.)

It was the late 1960s and early 1970s. Many women encouraged me to speak out. Standing at the washbasin at the toilets they said: 'I liked what you said today.' After one meeting, a woman said: 'Oh, that was *good*. I like to come to hear what you have to say.' However, it was necessary to be nominated to the executive every year. The following year I was nominated but didn't get a place; not liking what I had to say, a group had organised against me. Other members were amazed. The next year they organised to ensure I was back on the executive.

Back in my schooldays, nursing and teaching were the only possibilities for a girl who finished highschool. Clerical work was coming in for those who left after completing five years of highschool rather than six. I trained as a teacher, doing most of my teaching in the country. As a student teacher, after teaching at Scoresby I was transferred to Bentleigh East. I rode a pushbike back and forth from Mentone. Then I graduated to a motorbike. It was light enough to lift off the ground. Its piston was as big as a small teacup, and the bike did 25 miles per hour downhill. They let me go out of the shop with it on the condition that I left my Malvern Star as a deposit. They didn't know I hadn't finished paying for it!

I taught as a junior teacher for eight years. Then, from Elwood Central School, which was nextdoor to St Kilda where we were then living, I went to teachers college. A student teacher could do exams and gradually work her way up. But to go to teachers college meant having money: you had to pay and be able to support yourself. We couldn't do that. Then there was a change: a shortage of teachers meant that the department had to adopt a policy of lending teachers £40 (from future wages), to enable them to attend teachers college. When that happened, I applied.

The first year, I couldn't get in. My head teacher was antagonistic toward me. I had been teaching nature study. The timetable said maths. Not to do what was on the timetable was a terrible transgression. Immediately after the lunchbreak, the head teacher heard a loud noise in my room. The mosquito wrigglers had come to the top and were splitting their skins, then extricating themselves and walking across the water. I had the class around the table watching what was happening. The head teacher came in to see what was going on: 'You don't do nature study at this time of the day,' he said. 'What's on your timetable.' Maths. 'Well, you get down to do that,' he said. I said: 'Look, these wrigglers aren't going to wait for us to do maths. We'll never have the opportunity again. They're walking across the water!' To the students he said: 'Go and sit down, then get your maths out.' Turning to me he said: 'And you do as you're told, Miss Bennett. Get the maths *out!*' As soon as he was out of the room, I said to the children: 'Now, come out quietly and forget about maths.' He returned to find them all around the table again. I had defied him. So I knew he wouldn't give me a good report to go to the teachers college.

The following year, I applied again. He gave me a good report, apologising for not doing so the year before. The inspector may have said something to him: inspectors have their useful purposes. As well, the inspectors were aware of my work. I'd found the money to take myself to a 'New Education Fellowship' conference, held in 1934. I learned of books that were useful to read and discovered there were different ways of teaching geography, having the pupils do projects rather than participate passively. Grade 5 was the principal's class, but I had been teaching it, so charts and posters from the projects were around the room. When the inspectors came, I was left outside the classroom and the principal took over. Later, the inspectors spoke with me. I had the nous to say: 'All that material around the walls is mine. That is what I have been doing with the class.' 'Yes,' they said, 'don't worry. We know what you're doing.' I am confident they would have given me a good report, which also helped me in my efforts to go to teachers college.

In 1939 I married, which meant I had to give up teaching: married women were banned from the education department and the public service. The rule extended to women working in some factories. I was angry about it. I had anticipated it happening to me, and had been fighting through the union to abolish the rule. As soon as I became a junior teacher I had joined the teachers union, and when in teachers college I was the college representative on the Victorian Teachers Education Council. Having been brought up on unions, I joined as soon as I could. I became a member of the executive. When I was thrown out of the profession, I was told: 'You're no longer a teacher, so you can't be in the union.'

> *Having been brought up on unions, I joined as soon as I could.*

At conferences, I argued on women's equality, one issue being equal wages for women and men. 'Why should you men get more money than I do, when I teach Grade 3 in the room nextdoor to where you are teaching Grade 3?' I would say. 'You get so much more money than I do. Why?' The men unionists simply sat looking at me.

At one conference, during the 1940s or 1950s, I stood up and said: 'Now, look, because I have what I have, and you have a penis, doesn't mean there has to be a difference in our wages.' I argued that an entitlement to a residence attached to the school, and the right for a teacher to take the family with them, should not be limited to the men. 'Think of all the women who look after their fathers and mothers, nephews and nieces. They have just as much responsibility as anyone else and should have the same rights as men who happen to be married with children.' If a teacher living in Melbourne was caring for members of her extended family, I could see she needed to be able to take them with her if transferred to the country. Or what if it was a sister with children? They should be able to go too. Yet – again the looks, with no comment. Then it was on to the next item.

Through the 1940s, I worked in the Jam Factory (AJC) in South Yarra. After being thrown out of teaching I was stuck at home for ages, doing nothing. It bored me stiff. Then one of the women in the St Kilda Labor Party branch, Mrs Davies, whose husband was a chemist, told me she was tired of being home, too. 'Let's go to the AJC,' she said. 'They want anyone who'll work in their factory, for even one or two hours a day.' They had such a bad reputation that no one would go there to work if they had any other choice. The Jam Factory was short of people for war work, as all the food that was canned had to go overseas and there was a big demand. I didn't know whether I would like working in a jam factory, but said I'd give it a go. We went there just as the peach season was beginning. We had to cut the peaches in half and stone them. That had to be done all morning and all afternoon. We agreed graciously that we'd go in for an afternoon. We returned for several afternoons, then one of the supervisors (she clicked our tickets when the food came in to the bins) asked: 'Would you come in in the mornings, starting at 8 o'clock?' I said I'd think about it. I talked with my husband. Brian agreed, and I rode from Blessington Street, up Chapel Street to the Australian Jam Factory each day to save fares. I ended up as a fulltime worker.

I wasn't as worried about the housework – polishing up brass, cleaning the cutlery – as some others. I say women do that only because you've got to do *something* and there's nothing else to do so a woman goes around the house thinking up jobs for herself. During the war years, the government used me to go about talking with women about how to look after the housework while going out and getting a job! It was part of the war effort, and I was involved in the war effort for the Food Preservers Union.

At a Food Preservers Union meeting one night I moved that we shouldn't always send Percy Cleary and others off to represent the union. People off the factory floor, who knew what was going on there, should attend. That idea was accepted. Then came a war organisation conference The union was asked for representatives to attend. Because I had said what I did and was always up talking about what we should do for the war effort and on other industrial topics, the union decided to send me.

'Look,' they said to me at the factory, when they knew I was to attend. 'If you're going, see if you can get us better spoons to cut the peaches. The Carmichael comes from America. Let's see if we can get them.' 'You'll have to give me one to take to show them what to get,' I replied. So they looked for their best Carmichael. Ma Brown gave me hers, saying she'd cut my throat if I lost it! It was a spoon with a sharp edge on each side, and a point at the tip was made for easy scooping out of fruit. It was very dangerous if not used properly; people ripped themselves open with it.

After handing me the Carmichael they said: 'We want to see you dressed before you go. You've got to represent us properly. You've got to look right!' 'Alright,' I said, coming in in my Greta Garbo hat and coat. They approved of that, but asked: 'Where's your engagement ring?' I had never had one. 'But you're married, aren't you?' 'Brian knew I didn't have a watch,' I replied, 'and he thought I was a girl who wouldn't want an engagement ring. He gave me a watch instead.' 'Well,' they said, 'you can't go letting them see a workingclass girl and trade union representative hasn't a ring!' They went around the factory, finding the best engagement ring and giving it to me to wear. Then the manageress who looked after the girls and their problems, and who helped hire and fire, said she was going to the conference, representing management. She asked would I like to

'Where's your engagement ring?' I had never had one. 'But you're married, aren't you?'

go together with her. The workers were agreeable to that, so they farewelled us at lunchtime and off Mrs Barter and I went.

When we arrived and the topic of production arose, I produced the Carmichael spoon, telling the conference the difference it made, and the speed with which fruit could be de-stoned. I said: 'You want a lot of fruit produced, tinned stuff, particularly peaches. It can be done quicker with these spoons.' So they put them on a list, and the spoons came!

I was a delegate to another war organisation conference. This time Massey Green from Sunshine Harvesters was chairing. They were talking away and I said: 'Look, when the war is at end, and it's almost over now, what are we going to do about jobs for the blokes? What are we going to do with the women who are in the jobs? You've got to discuss this. It's part of the war program.' I was also outspoken about the need to look to markets in Asia when the produce was no longer needed on such a large scale in Europe. 'They'll be interested in buying,' I said. 'They've seen our tinned fruit – the Americans have it where they are, our men have it over there. We should be planning that now.' Massey Green's eyes looked at me. He said: 'Oh. You think that, do you?' 'Well, don't you?' I said. He stared at me again, and blushed.

> He said: 'Oh. You think that, do you?' 'Well, don't you?' I said.

They were interested in a little woman from the factory floor standing up and speaking out, and looking ahead to planning. I had been brought up thinking about forward planning. It wasn't that anyone had to go to special classes to develop this way of thinking. They had gone to the 'best' schools, they were the 'top dogs', but they weren't thinking about these issues, for all that they were the 'top dogs'.

At AJC a lot of food was being wasted: parsnips and other vegetables that weren't the right size were being put in a heater, mushed, and sent down the drains into the River Yarra. The Americans wanted carrots canned, but they didn't want a carrot that was green inside. Such carrots were melted down, and straight out into the river. We weren't allowed to give the rejects to hospitals or to the poor. All was wasted. The pricing structure meant the factory didn't lose: they were allowed to charge 10 percent more than the product cost. This meant all our taxes were going down the River Yarra. So we had campaigns on that too.

One day, suddenly there were workers with hoses cleaning the walls and floors and all the machinery. Someone said: 'There's going to be an inspection. Look at how they're cleaning us up.' Sure enough, there was. And the day before the inspecting group came we were told to throw nothing away. I guessed that our carrot and parsnip wastage was to be looked at. We should have had everyone agree not to do as the management said. But we didn't have much time to organise a protest.

There were industrial as well as production issues at AJC. Workers weren't allowed to sit. But when the schoolteachers came in over the Christmas holidays to work they refused to work without chairs to sit on. Then AJC brought stools in. I joined after the holidays, when the teachers were no longer there. 'We might need to sit down,' I said. Some of the girls pointed: 'There's all the stools they got for the teachers.' 'Well, you've got to do the same,' I said. 'Protest like they did.' We weren't able to achieve that, but did have a victory with the toilet paper! I argued with management over that. 'Oh, they'll just take it home.' 'No they won't. I'll guarantee they won't,' I said, bravely. (I *believed* the workers wouldn't, but was taking it on trust.) 'Look,' I said, 'you give me a roll we can tie at the stairs going up to the toilet. I'll talk to the women at lunchtime, telling them they're on their honour not to take it home.' I was given a roll, and went out to talk with the workers. We hooked it on a string, and it was never taken. In the end, the management put proper toilet paper in every toilet.

I returned to teaching in 1956. Initially, after being thrown out, I had no desire to return to it. Being able to see people grow and develop is a wonderful thing. It's like watching mushrooms grow, and plants and seeds. I had seen children grow, but in the years immediately before 1939 the economic and political situation meant I hadn't been able to gain any such satisfaction. The Depression brought with it the premiers' plan. Everything was cut to pieces, and it was very similar to the situation at present, with people being tossed out of jobs, government services slashed, every program orientated toward people and the community destroyed.

> ... *people being tossed out of jobs, government services slashed.*

I had attended Melbourne Teachers College – all the others had been shut down, because they didn't want to pay the wages. But by going to the New Education Fellowship conferences I regained my enthusiasm. I went regularly to Cheshire's bookshop. I found a wonderful journal on children's art. It was what they were teaching in English schools: not just a flowerpot or a plant growing in a pot, or wool with knitting needles stuck in it; the children had free access, painting and drawing what they liked. *If they are doing that in England*, I thought, *we should be doing it here.* To the people at Cheshire's I said: 'I haven't any money to buy this magazine, but will you give me "tick". Here's my record number at the education department. You can check. If you let me have the subscription for the year, I'll pay you when I finish teachers college.' They accepted the offer, so back I went to school with my magazines: I had the four they gave me that day, the current issue and three back numbers.

Mr White was in charge. Mr Montgomery was the other art teacher. I went up to them, taking the journal and talking about it to both of them. 'Look,' I said, 'this is what we should be doing.' They'd never seen the magazine or heard of it. 'Oh,' they said.

At the following lecture, Mr White stood up, saying the class would do something new. He showed them the magazines: 'We'll start on this next week.' When he'd finished he said: 'Did I do right, Miss Bennett?' I could have gone through the floor! But it began there: my going to New Education Fellowship conferences, and looking in Cheshire's bookshops, and Cheshire's letting me have the journal. Later, Montgomery gained a special job at Geelong Grammar, teaching new art ideas. He went from strength to strength.

Teaching should begin with rainbow writing, big rows with reds and pinks and purple.

At Cheshire's on another occasion I saw a book on writing. Writing's a bugbear to teach, but Marianne Anderson, the author, said writing is only an art. It is the movement of the whole arm, and should be practised that way. Teaching should begin with rainbow writing, big rows with reds and pinks and purple. Then teachers should move on to other shapes, C's and O's, then N's and M's and W's all together, then H and K. The letters and words should grow out of the patterns children begin drawing. Only then should pupils arrive at straight lines.

I was in training school at Princes Hill. The headmistress gave me permission to teach writing in this way. Then the inspector arrived. He saw the work I was doing and was interested, although none of the other teachers was. I had evolved a way of talking about education, saying it is the same as learning to be an Olympic champion. You have to get in and do it every day to develop the expertise. If you do that, and the students become good at writing, they'll become good at maths. But it is essential that pupils do a bit each day, and to be observed and helped.

One day the inspector brought a whole raft of inspectors to see what I was doing. I was at Princes Hill the year after polio hit Melbourne and many of the schools had been closed. I was there when they were restarting, and had 100 children through prep grade that year. With the brand new pupils, I used the Marianne Anderson approach to writing. The inspectors came to talk with other teachers about the handwriting of the pupils coming from my prep grade. All agreed that the handwriting was much better than that of children in prep grades who were not learning in the same way. This was back in 1942.

When I returned to teaching in 1956, in Moe, the entire education department was doing Marianne Anderson writing. But sadly, the teaching had declined. Teachers didn't practise the method properly. They didn't read the books which said it is necessary to do it every day. Writing got out of hand again, with children being required to write on straight lines: red lines going that way, blue lines this, and letters having to be fitted into each block. There were no blank sheets of paper anymore, with children using their whole arm to write. Teachers simply wrote on the blackboard, in the old way. I was staggered what had happened when, many years later, I returned to Errol Street Primary School teaching puppetry as a voluntary effort to the North Melbourne community. No wonder the children weren't writing well!

My return to teaching came about because my husband, Brian Oke, had always wanted to work on the land. I had a cousin at Moe who was a dairy farmer. Her cousin, my aunt, went to live with her, helping to raise her two children. We were invited to visit for the weekend, then an invitation arrived for the Christmas holidays. A short time later, another letter appeared (it was a week before Christmas), saying: 'A pity you're not coming now. Eric's man has gone to run his own farm, and Eric has been left high and dry. Brian could have hopped in and helped. Eric is looking for a man who doesn't know anything about farming, so that he can train him to do it his way.'

When I read the letter, it seemed the answer to Brian's prayer. When I gave him the letter, he read it then sat looking at me. 'Would you like to apply?' I asked. 'Oh! Would you come down?' 'Of course I would,' I said. 'Wouldn't be suggesting it otherwise.' We thought it would be good for the children to live on the land, so we asked them how they'd like it. 'Yes,' they said. 'We could still travel to Melbourne or Geelong for the football premiership, and we'd come up for the Royal Show.' That suited them.

I knew that one of the local schools had too few teachers, so I saw this as a way of getting back into teaching. The works at Yallourn were expanding, and people were building in Morwell as well as Newborough and Moe. All at once, six schools were built. The schools were simply bursting. The education department said I could take the job, 'but you'll have to be there by 25 January'. There were 10 days to pack.

The schools were simply bursting.

Down we went. The school hadn't begun. Only the building was there. We rounded up the children, who had commenced in neighbouring schools. On the first day, there were no steps at the entrance. To get into the schoolrooms, we had the wheelbarrows stood to one side and the gang-planks were used for the children. We held the children up as they went in, so that they didn't fall and break their necks! So that was my return to teaching.

By this time, I had read a great deal more and had concentrated on helping slow learners. The bright ones get ahead without the teachers. A teacher can steer them a little, show them where to look up subjects and direct them to sources that will make them think, but those who are not in the 'bright' category need patience and labour to bring them up to average. Once they become average, they can go ahead and be brilliant too. It's simply a matter of giving them confidence that they are alright, and giving the families that same confidence. If a family doesn't think the children are alright, the kids never get anywhere.

> *Through the years, I have talked a number of women into recognising their skills.*

Through the years, I have talked a number of women into recognising their skills. Some (like Thelma Prior of the Iron Workers Union, a wonderful activist and speaker) would say: 'Oh, I haven't any brains. I have no skills. I'm no good.' Then they would get up to speak, and be wonderful. I have been able to talk a number out of saying and thinking: 'I'm no good.' Now, they tackle jobs, go to conferences, travel to international meetings. My policy has been to tell women they should try. It's not necessary to sit there, being squashed. Women have to get up, speak, do their own thinking and their own thing.

How Brave You Can Be

June Benson

A Western Australian, June Benson holds a bachelor of arts degree and a postgraduate diploma in business, both of which she gained through parttime studies. She is also completing a master of commerce degree parttime.

After working in the public service, June Benson took up a position at Edith Cowan University, where she was closely involved with the equal opportunity and women in leadership programs, as well as the mentoring scheme. She was an organiser of the first Women and Leadership conference at Edith Cowan University in the early 1990s.

I was born into a generous family. To them, the fact that money and generosity of spirit didn't coincide was irrelevant. The most important thing was that the children of the family were clothed, fed and loved. My Grandmother, Ellen Benson, was the head of a large family she raised single-handedly following my Grandfather's early death. She was a single mother, back when single parenthood wasn't a statement about attitudes – and when there wasn't adequate provision for social security (indeed any social security) to help her face single parenthood on a single, low income.

Ellen Benson steadfastly refused to let her situation make her a victim, or to let her children be taken from her. She was the first women I was ever conscious of not conforming to what the stereotypes expected from her. Stories of her life and of her achievements were told to me from a very early age by all members of our family. She had many sons, and many more grandsons, yet she was a woman who obtained a respect from her family when any sort of emancipation or independence of action or thought by women was not well regarded by the 'average person'. All the men in her family held her almost in awe, with a great deal of respect, immeasurable admiration and definitely a great deal of love. It was from her that the very small number of women born into the family were afforded equality of respect, and that our opinions were counted and meant something.

My cousin Lydia was ordained in 1994 as one of Britain's first female Anglican priests. I know that if my Grandmother were alive, she would be so proud of Lydia, as we all are. I can't help but wonder how much influence my Grandmother was to Lydia, as she was to all her children and grandchildren. A hallmark of my Grandmother's approach to life was identified in her fair treatment of every member of her family regardless of their age or their sex. This fairness extended to our opinions being given a fair and equal hearing, our being consistently encouraged by her and by our parents to 'do our best' – and we were all given the same presents at Christmas (always slippers)!

> *One factor was a constant: my Grandmother was always 'there'!*

I retain strong recollections of the family congregating at my Grandmother's house. At times we were almost on top of one another, talking and arguing, everyone having an opinion – but no one person's views dominating. One factor was a constant: my Grandmother was always 'there'! She was ever ready to provide a cuppa for members of her large extended family, her many children and grandchildren and her friends.

Concerned about the wellbeing of all her family and friends, my Grandmother had the most generous of spirits. She continued to look after her elder brother, my Great Uncle Ted, into the last years of her life. There was a spare meal for him at all times, and he was always included in family affairs. This would have been important to him as he had no family of his own. When my Grandmother died, this care was continued by my two Aunts, Linda and Alice.

My Grandmother is still missed. She is talked about, fondly and often with a great deal of emotion, by her family. She left me a legacy of compassion and understanding for which I am and always will be grateful. She passed on her generosity of spirit to her children – and particularly to her two daughters.

Since my Grandmother's death my Aunt Linda has assumed the role of the family matriarch. She is there to listen to the problems of her large extended family and to offer assistance where it is required or requested. Linda has shown me the difficult duality of being able to be sentimental (she would call it 'soft'), yet tough when it is needed. She is the most caring and sensitive person I have ever met – yet the most unswerving, and unyielding. She, for me, epitomises the challenges for womanhood in the 1990s.

My mother, Irene Benson, is a significant influence in my life. Irene is an extremely generous woman, both in terms of her time and her funds. When I was very young, my father was in a serious accident and was hospitalised and off work for almost a year. Due to the insolvency of the insurance company with which he was insured, there was no provision for the payment of insurance or sickness benefits. My mother had two small children and no formal income support. Yet she managed to 'hold body and soul together' and kept going, mainly by putting her children before herself.

Irene Benson looks out for both the members of her family and the people she worked with, particularly the younger members at her office. My mother was forever 'adopting' someone at her work, nurturing and mentoring them – often it seemed she was acting as a surrogate mother. This was to be the cause of resentment for many years – until I realised I was the lucky one having her for my mother. The women she mentored were not competitors, and I wasn't deprived through my mother's generosity, I benefited from it.

> *My mother was forever 'adopting' someone at her work, nurturing and mentoring them ...*

Irene inspires generosity in those around her. She has forever had a strong belief in me and what I can do. She and my father have encouraged me to be whatever makes me the happiest – and to do whatever it takes to most significantly contribute to this wellbeing.

We moved around a great deal when I was younger. I attended six primaryschools in seven years, in three countries. The very nature of mobility precluded any one person providing me with any extended influence in my primary education. My highschool education was completed at one of Western Australia's state schools – North Lake Senior High School. The school no longer exists as a highschool, but serves as a teaching avenue for people to complete their studies to matriculation level.

One of the most significant and important memories of highschool are those associated with my Year 8 English teacher – Jillian Mercer. Jillian was the first person in my life to use the title 'Ms'! I remember going home to exclaim to my mother: 'We've got a Ms at school – can you imagine!' The whole concept of 'Msdom' was so alien to me.

Jillian proceeded to teach me, over the next two years, the importance of being independent, and of being true to yourself (and the relevance of the title Ms). She was a wonderful teacher. She questioned the hierarchy of our school, she demanded answers to questions that previously nobody had cared enough to ask. She cared passionately about her students, and we knew it. She was, and is, a firm and favourite memory of highschool for a great many of us who have maintained contact.

Jillian Mercer was the first and only teacher in highschool to care enough about our futures to take us to a university. She showed us what universities were like and she showed us just how broad our career options could be. She was the first teacher (and the last for a great many years) who asked us what we thought, then took the time to listen.

Jillian made her students believe we could do anything. She taught us life was an adventure – and continually demonstrated her commitment to this philosophy. We all remember clearly her commitment to go to Iceland to work – in a fish factory was the story circulating at the time – simply for the life experience and the sheer enjoyment of travel. Jillian Mercer was a source of inspiration to us – and particularly to me. Her inspiration remains strong.

I renewed my link with Jillian Mercer when she began working with the Western Australian Public Service. She not only remembered me, but placed me in the correct context – no mean feat considering the numbers of students she had taught. Her approach to teaching and her professionalism have been carried over into her new career and I now count Jillian as one of my dearest friends. She continues to take an interest in me and my career and my ambitions – and has many wise words of encouragement for me on a great many topics. She is also an important reference point to anybody renovating a house! Renovation is a pastime of hers, one of many, and one with which she has had a great deal of success, and an area of expertise she generously shares.

One of my oldest and dearest friendships originates from my youth. Since the age of 12, Roxanne Whitfield has been my friend and an influence in my life. Roxanne and I grew up together, and although we have pursued very different careerpaths, we remain close. We have shared important experiences, and some of the most memorable events of my life so far.

An amazingly creative bunch of people, they bring a unique and professional approach to every task.

Both Roxanne and her family are a constant demonstration of the power of original thought and action. An amazingly creative bunch of people, they bring a unique and professional approach to every task. Roxanne is generous and loyal to her friends, with a wonderfully warm nature. She is a very giving person – to which anybody who knows her would attest. She has a real flair for style and began to display this talent when we were still kids. She and her family were an extended family for me. I was ever welcome, spending a great deal of my time growing up in the Whitfield household.

Undertaking a tertiary course parttime can be a very remote experience. This was particularly so for me. I completed both my undergraduate degree in arts and my postgraduate diploma in business on a parttime basis, and I am completing my master of commerce on a parttime basis. When I began my tertiary studies I was working with a woman named Helen Thomas. Helen gave me the confidence to complete my course, demystifying the academic process for me and, most importantly, she proof read my assignments!

Helen Thomas was my supervisor when I worked at the office of executive personnel in the public service and provided me with my first real promotional opportunity. Not only did her faith in me give me confidence in relation to university work, but also in professional development. Much of what I carry around in my business persona today comes from my relationship with Helen.

The most important lesson Helen Thomas taught me was to have a belief in myself, to trust my own convictions and abilities, and (importantly) always to know where the best spot for lunch, closest to where ever I was working, would be! She was able to demonstrate to me the optimum level of professionalism, taking on the most difficult tasks and dealing with them in an efficient and effective manner. She is one of my models of the true professional.

When I completed my undergraduate studies I made a conscious decision to change institutions if I commenced any postgraduate courses. I'm relieved I remained steadfast in this decision, as my experience as a parttime postgraduate student is vastly different from that at undergraduate level. This change in focus and feeling is achieved by the focus to task held by the staff at Curtin University of Technology. Dr Pam Swain and Associate Professor Alma Whitely, coordinators and teachers of units I have taken, have brought a commitment to their subjects, as well as a requirement and expectation for rigorous research. This is combined with an infectious enthusiasm for their topics. They have made what could have been an ongoing and difficult task a weekly adventure. Importantly they acknowledge and appreciate cultural diversity.

A notable side benefit of completing my postgraduate studies on a parttime basis has been developing friendships with people whom many people might not ordinarily meet. Those to whom I have become closest during the course of my masters studies are two delightful, brave and extremely talented women, my friends Dale Tilbrook and Helen Gryzb, who commenced postgraduate studies, on a parttime basis, simultaneously with me. However, there is one difference – both Dale and Helen are single parents. In committing themselves to study, they have added an extra dimension to their already jam-packed lives. Both are extremely competent and able professional women, who are juggling so many varied aspects of their lives – and so well. They continue in their everyday activities, at a 130 percent level of commitment, while continuing in their roles as mothers.

... they have shown me the value in trusting in your own worth, and believing in yourself.

Amazingly both Helen and Dale have great relationships with their children, despite all the pressures they willingly put on themselves.

Helen Gryzb and Dale Tilbrook have made parttime study a human and enjoyable experience for me. Individually and together they have shown me the value of trusting in your own worth, and believing in yourself. In studying together, we have formed a support group for each other to allow us to let off steam. Both Helen and Dale are generous women, particularly with their valuable time. They have shown me how brave you can be when you have to be. They are ready to listen and to talk to other people about their problems. I know, as they have both listened to problems of mine and have helped me through some difficult decisions. I continue to value these relationships and know that when our courses finish (as they soon will) the links we have will continue.

One of my closest friends is Sheila Anderson, an engineer with one of our public utilities – and by the very nature of her uniqueness in her field is continually called upon to 'wave the flag' for engineering – and women's involvement in the occupation. She attacks this task with a combination of competence, vigour and good humour.

Sheila is not only very talented, clever and an extremely good cook – she is also generous with her time, speaking to groups of women both in highschools and in tertiary institutions about her work as an engineer and women's involvement in the profession. Sheila also contributes to the engineering profession through her involvement in the women's arm of the engineers' professional body.

Whilst eating her 'morning tea' – a biscuit – Sheila Anderson and I have spent many hours drinking coffee and discussing a variety of topics, issues and problems. Between us, we have been able to map out our masters courses, the next few years of our life, the paint schemes for our respective renovation projects, and any other problems. My hope is that I have been as able to contribute to her life as she has to mine.

Lisa White and I have been friends since undergraduate studies – and endures the ongoing slog of postgraduate studies with me also. In particular she has shown me the importance of remaining true to your convictions. She is one of the most talented women I know as well as one of the most 'ideologically sound' of my friends, yet Lisa is always ready to help other people whose values and opinions might not necessarily coincide with her own.

Lisa White tutors Aborigines and students from non-English speaking backgrounds in improving their English skills; participates in church activities; and helps out in the campaigning of local politicians. For a great many years she had a strong link with the Iranian community in Perth – and worked with Iranian women on English skills, their matriculation studies and communication. Strong in her beliefs, Lisa is ever ready to substantiate her ideals with strong and well delivered debates. Her strength and capable nature make her a constant source of inspiration – yet she is not a person to comment adversely or condemn others in their beliefs.

Completing her law studies on a parttime basis – she already has completed an honours degree in politics – Lisa White wanted to do something more to help people. She is studying law as a second degree in an effort to really help people, and to hopefully make a difference. Lisa's studies will take many years to complete – but she remains undaunted and completely committed to the completion of her studies. Currently she is working as an associate to a judge, in an effort to maintain a working link with her studies. Lisa White will, I am sure, achieve all her goals. Her attitude and approach to life and work is a constant and ongoing source of inspiration for me.

I have also been fortunate in experiencing the generosity of men. In working closely with generous people, regardless of sex and gender, I have been able to enjoy my work and feel comfortable in my abilities. Mike Pervan, my partner, and also my father, have been particularly important.

My father – Malcolm Benson – who will never admit it, or at least publicly acknowledge it, is probably the first person with a feminist orientation with whom I ever had contact. My father was the first to show me the folly of underestimating my goals, and of underestimating the full possibilities of life. It was he who dissuaded me from wanting to be a nurse when I was five and encouraged me to think about being a doctor instead. He has always felt that anybody who has the potential should be 'given the Guernsey'.

My father was the first to show me the folly of underestimating my goals, and of underestimating the full possibilities of life.

This attitude is probably what led him into working with the physically and intellectually disabled for a great part of his working life. This was work to which he was dedicated, and into which he invested a great deal of emotional energy – without asking for any reward or acknowledgement. He had the difficult job of teaching crafts and trades to students with intellectual and physical disabilities. The underlying rationale was to help people who had been labelled as not fit for entry into society, to become integrated and functioning well.

My father showed me the benefits and the rewards, and the intense frustrations of working for your principles. He was incredibly strict with me as a child – yet he had a wonderful rapport with the people he taught and worked with and it has been my father who has been most vocal in the encouragement of me to complete my tertiary education – and continues this encouragement in questioning me about studies after finishing my masters degree! It has been my father who taught me the value of competing with myself, particularly in my studies – but it was a lesson I was a long time in learning.

As the numbers of women, compared to men, in our family are significantly smaller, I've often wondered if it was genetic, or if we were taught to be as we are: strong, holding fast to our opinions – or was it a fortunate benefit of my Grandmother's unfortunate life that contributed to this common personality trait within my family?

Many of my attitudes and personal philosophies have been influenced by these people. Through their unfailing generosity and assistance, I am in the comfortable spot I am today. As a consequence, I have come to recognise that it is important to help and assist other people wherever possible. This was one of the reasons for my becoming involved in a professional mentoring scheme in the course of my work at Edith Cowan University. This is a brokerage system that puts recently graduated professionals in touch with their counterparts working in the 'field'. This contact helps the new entrant into the workforce with an entree into networks that might be otherwise difficult to break into. One particularly satisfying aspect of this project was working with graduates who often have a particularly difficult time due to either physical or intellectual disabilities. It was rewarding helping people link into job opportunities in their chosen field, and effectively to show their worth.

At Edith Cowan University, I worked in the area of women's issues and equal employment opportunity for two years or so. Prior to that I worked in the development of human resource policies and strategies for the West Australian government. In working with women, and with people from other countries and backgrounds, I have found that people often have a wealth of ability to give and a huge capacity for sharing themselves and their experiences. Unfortunately, these are often not tapped into.

When I first went into equal employment opportunity, I was asked how I was enjoying the often quite demanding work. I responded that it was like taking a spa! I used that analogy because the ability to work in an area having such a positive benefit on so many people, and that helps to address some of the inevitable inequalities of life along the way, is a wonderful opportunity. It is refreshing for the worker rather than tiring or debilitating. I want to be sure I have made a difference in the organisations in which I've worked, and working in such a rewarding area means it is possible to see results.

I want to be sure I have made a difference in the organisations in which I've worked...

My confidence and faith in what I do have been immeasurably helped by the people whose influences on me have been profound. When I have endured what at the time seemed unendurable situations and experiences, I was lucky to count on the amazing generosity of friends. Friends are the people who have always been there to listen. They are people who have helped me face decisions and undertake actions I might not have had the fortitude to tackle alone. They are people who have always been generous in their time with me – I hope I have been as generous. These friends continue to support me, and (amazingly!) never seem to judge or pass comment about me.

I thank these women for giving me the confidence and inspiration to work in women's issues, equal employment opportunity and, most of all, to care. These are people who have been excellent role models for me in my life and my work.

Descended from a Matriarch

Daphne Milward

Born on 30 March 1940 at Mooroopna, near Shepparton in the north east of Victoria on the Goulburn River, Daphne Milward attended Mooroopna State School and Shepparton High School. Amongst other activities, she worked for many years with the Aborigines Advancement League and remains a member of the organisation.

Daphne Milward has been a member of the Lady (Gladys) Nichols committee, and is a committee member of Koorie Women Mean Business (KWMB), a project established to offer assistance and advice to Koori women developing their own businesses and community enterprises. She is also a director of the Victorian Women's Trust and a member of the Equal Opportunity Commission of Victoria. In 1995 she established her own consultancy firm, Mandala Consulting Services, where she specialises in community development and in particular in cross-cultural awareness.

I belong to a large extended family. Many members of our family have been active in Aboriginal affairs, going back to grandfather William Cooper, whose name is wellknown within the Aboriginal community in Victoria. Grandfather Cooper died in the late 1930s or early 1940s, the year before or the year after I was born. The stories of his activism have come down not only through my family, but through the Aboriginal community generally. He was one of the people who established the Aborigines League, members of which later on established the Aborigines Advancement League. The Aborigines Advancement League is historically one of the major organisations in Victoria to have dealt with Aboriginal issues. Today, the Aborigines Advancement League Incorporated is situated in Thornbury, one of the northern suburbs of Melbourne.

I was raised by an aunt and uncle. It is not unusual in the Aboriginal community for this to happen. Many of us have been raised by various members of our families, particularly grandparents or aunts and uncles. As for activism, it was not so much that I learned about it through *talking* about it. You were in it. It was a way of life, part of your everyday life.

As for activism, it was not so much that I learned about it through talking about it.

In the early 1940s Mum (my aunty) was active in mainstream committees working on behalf of Aboriginal people. My mother was an active member of the Save the Children Fund. As well, education committees were set up at the time, and also committees working to provide housing for our people, on which she was active.

I was born in Mooroopna then, shortly after, we moved across to Cummerangunja, the main mission reserve in the area near Shepparton. (Most of our people, the Yorta Yorta people, come from this reserve.) When I was three or four we moved back to Mooroopna and lived on the flats between Mooroopna and Shepparton. A large number of Aboriginal people lived there, many of whom came across from Barmah, Echuca and other areas for the fruit picking season. After fruit picking came the tomato picking season, and there was also a tobacco factory in the area; my Dad worked there for a time.

Mum's involvement with the Save the Children Fund meant she helped set up a preschool or kindergarten for the kids living on the flats. A band of people from the Save the Children Fund came regularly to bring toys and other items, and everyone sat around under the trees. I sometimes accompanied my mother, because to me it was fun, but I know a great deal of hard work went into running the Save the Children Fund.

Later on, simply because I was there, like everyone else I became involved as a matter of course. There were no demonstrations in the early 1940s, so I was not involved in this way, but there were some bad times which required the community to be activist. People were forced to move out of the flats and into the town or into other fringe camps around the state. My aunt and uncle were one of the first families, along with the Briggs family and uncle Lyn Cooper, who lived in the town. On a gradual basis, through the work being done in Melbourne by those who are now our elders, people gradually moved up into Mooroopna to a little village called Rumbalara. It was established as a transitional village. A lot of the people didn't want to move into Rumbalara, but as soon as they moved out of the places down on the flats, the council came along bulldozing the houses. This meant the people had nowhere to go. Either everyone accepted going into Rumbalara or moved on. From Rumbalara, one by one the families moved into housing commission homes in Mooroopna or Shepparton.

My great-greatgrandmother is the matriarch of many of the families coming from Cummerangunja. I am descended from the Coopers and the Atkinsons: my greatgrandfather was John Atkinson, my greatgrandmother was Bess Murray, and my grandmother was Kitty Atkinson and grandfather Ernie Clements. That is the Aboriginal side of my family. My father was not an Aboriginal person, but I was brought up in an Aboriginal community and didn't really know my father, although I know who he was. My mother, Lilly Charles, married Stan Charles and my mother's cousin, Amy Cooper, was the aunt who brought me up. She married Henry Charles, Stan Charles' brother, so we are all related somewhere. It was from the age of five or six that I was raised by my aunt and uncle, Amy and Henry Charles, whom I call Mum and Dad.

It was mainly through the Save the Children Fund that I received encouragement outside my family. The fund contributed to the cost of my school uniforms and books. If I went away on school camps or other excursions the fund made the necessary payment. Many Koori children from those days would very likely say the same thing: the Save the Children Fund was instrumental in our gaining an education.

Because of the way things were, most of the family didn't go much further in their education than Grade 7 – that was the final year of primary-school. It was an achievement for Koori kids at that time if any of us arrived at highschool, particularly if one did one or two years. If a Koori child went to Form 3 or Form 4, that was a huge achievement. I went to Form 4, 'intermediate' in those days. The choice that was open to girls was to go into the professional course, or into the commercial stream. Being in the professional course meant a student could go on to Year 12, then to university, with the likelihood of becoming a doctor or a lawyer or working in another professional field. The commercial course was for those who wanted to be secretaries or work in administration. I wanted to be a nurse, but the family put a veto on that, because three or four members of the family had been to nursing training and they were not treated well: they suffered racism. Also at the time Mum worked in the hospital in the children's ward as a cleaner. She didn't think it was the best area for me to go into.

My family wanted me to work in a bank, and in those days a child's parents had a great deal of say in what the child's career would be. In the general community, a child went into the father's or parents' business, or worked in grocery stores or banks or whatever other businesses were in town. There were also the orchards and the army.

A young person was lucky if she or he managed to get into a job in the town. It was in the 1950s and early 1960s that the move began of the younger people away from the small country towns where they grew up, into the larger towns or into the cities. This move was

... in those days a child's parents had a great deal of say in what the child's career would be.

necessary in order to gain employment.

I took the commercial stream at school. When I completed Form 4, my Mum dragged me around to almost every bank in town. Thank goodness there weren't any vacancies! Next we went off to the government employment service (it wasn't called the Commonwealth Employment Service – CES – at that time). I put my name on a list and was referred to an engineering firm, W Konigs. They manufactured orchard equipment and machinery for farming. I was the junior typist.

After I had worked at Konigs for some nine months, Pastor Doug Nichols (who later became governor of South Australia) visited the family. He was looking for someone with office skills to work in the office they were setting up in Melbourne, to work toward establishing a hostel for young women. I wasn't really consulted. It was just a matter of course that I was the one who went to work for Uncle Doug and Pastor Stan Davey. Both were pastors of the Church of Christ, and I lived with Stan and his wife, for the office was set up in the manse. There was also an office in Darebin or Ivanhoe, which was run by the manse. I worked there, too. The office was moved several times before the Aboriginal girls' hostel was established in Northcote in a Church of England manse in Cunningham Street.

Twelve to 18 months later, Mum and Dad moved to Melbourne. They became the managers of the hostel, and we lived together as a family again. A garage in the backyard was converted into an office, and it kept expanding as more people came on board. I was the first fulltime employee of the Aborigines Advancement League, as the organisation came to be known.

I was the first fulltime employee of the Aborigines Advancement League...

The hostel provided accommodation mainly for girls going out to paidwork. Before it was established, everyone who came to the city bunked in with relatives. Many stayed with Uncle Doug and Aunty Gladdie, and there was just not enough room! It was difficult for people to get accommodation and there was overcrowding everywhere. Aunty Gladdie in particular worked tirelessly for many years to have a hostel established for young women in Melbourne. It was through her hard work, together with two of her sisters, a brother, Maurice and Doris Blackburn, and Gordon Bryant that the hostel and the Aborigines Advancement League came into being. Those are the names I remember as being closely associated with the early work of the organisation and setting it up. Lions and Apex clubs were helpful, too.

The Aborigines Advancement League was from its inception involved in campaigns, making deputations to government ministers, the premier and the prime minister. It was at the forefront because it was the only organisation existing in Victoria at that time, which was a voice for the

Aboriginal people. Established in 1957, it was instrumental in gaining many, many services for Aboriginal people – better housing and health services in particular. It spawned the organisations that today work for Aboriginal people; most of the people who established the organisations that came later had gone through the league at some time – the Aboriginal childcare agency, the Aboriginal Legal Service, the health service.

Things were done in a quiet way until, in the late 1950s or early 1960s the Aborigines Welfare Board, a government body, tried to close down the Lake Tyers mission. That was when I recall Aboriginal people engaging in marches and public demonstrations. Almost everyone in Victoria came to Melbourne to support the Lake Tyers people, walking through the streets with banners. I was in Tasmania at the time, for it was NAIDOC (National Aboriginal and Islanders Day Organising Committee) day and I went to Hobart to represent the Aborigines Advancement League. I appeared on radio and television and visited universities and colleges.

For that Tasmanian visit, I was the only one available! Everyone else was involved in the march for the Lake Tyers people. When the plane landed in Hobart, the flight attendant asked me to exit at the reardoor, where I was whizzed down the stairs and into a waiting car. Everything was being run to a tight schedule. I had a breadroll shoved into my hand – that was lunch. We arrived at the University of Tasmania and went, almost running, through the grounds to the great hall, then I was led straight onto a platform and placed in front of a lectern. It seemed as if there were a million people in the room. I spoke, and I can't recall if there was even time for questions before I was whisked off to another venue. It was a busy but exciting day, and I arrived home at nine or ten o'clock that night. It was then I saw the news items on television covering the Lake Tyers march. I felt very emotional.

It seemed as if there were a million people in the room.

Anyone who worked with the league was thrown into every activity there was. We had few resources, so whoever wasn't tied up with other work had to step in to do whatever else had to be done. I learnt public speaking through visiting schools, where I talked mainly on the establishment of the hostel. At the time, we were still looking for support and a great deal came from the schools through their social service contributions: classes were asked to take up a social issue, and some of the classes decided to support Aboriginal people. In the early days of the league, as well as Uncle Doug and Stan Davey, Eric Onus and others were involved, Aunty Marg Tucker, Mum and Dad (Amy Cooper and Henry Charles), Uncle Gerry and Aunty Sally Briggs. Most worked on a voluntary basis.

I accompanied Uncle Doug and Stan Davey to many meetings, so I had before me their example of public speaking. I followed what they did, and spoke about the issues in the same way. I was a young woman, so was unable to speak with their breadth and scope, but I was learning all the time and they were great examples. Many other people were activists and public speakers, including the Briggs' girls, Hyllus Maris (who established Worawa College at Healesville) and others. I would like to remember more of the women, but names like Bruce McGuinness and Gary Foley come easily to mind. Lois Briggs (now Lois Peeler) and Margaret Briggs were around my age and are still working in Aboriginal affairs. All the members of Doug's family were active, including his daughters Lillian Nichols and Pam Nichols (now Pam Peterson). Ralph Nichols now runs his own business, doing Aboriginal cross-cultural programs in schools and for major events. Those who married and 'retired' to raise their families came back into the movement, working on projects or in Aboriginal organisations.

I was learning all the time and they were great examples.

Basically, my career simply 'happened'. Initially I worked with the league for four years. Then Uncle Doug suggested I go out into the big, wide world, gaining experience in the wider community. I was employed in the personnel department at G N Raymond's, in Easey Street, Collingwood. They made shoe components – the patterns, heels and innersoles, as well as the boxes in which shoes were packaged, then began manufacturing fancy boxes for items other than shoes. I worked there for four years, then for about 18 months worked with an engineering firm, just down from Festival Hall in West Melbourne. From there I went to the British Government Office. It was situated in the MLC building on the corner of Elizabeth and Collins Streets. I worked as a secretary to the first and second secretaries of the information branch for some two years.

The British Government Office was part of the British diplomatic service, and there was a trade commission as well. We took care of notable visitors from Britain, including the secretary of trade and foreign affairs, and Douglas Home (before he became prime minister). I worked in the area providing information to the general community, and particularly to radio and television stations. We received tapes and videos from England and distributed them. Most were five or 10 minutes duration, but some were long documentaries. They were shown mainly on the ABC, and occasionally on commercial stations, promoting the British Isles.

I had no desire to go overseas, and working at the British Government Office didn't change that. Many members of my extended family, as well as my friends, have gone. Lately, however, I have developed a desire to go. My daughter came back from overseas and has said: 'You *have* to go to see this,' 'You have to go to see that'. Other friends have said: 'Oh, Daph, you'd love this or that place.' Now I think: 'Well, it does sound interesting when you put it like that.' But to me, from what I have seen I can't accept that it would be any better than what we have here in

Australia. The only places that would be significantly different are Europe, the Middle East and Asia, where English isn't the first language. I have never had a desire to go to England or the United States, although over the years I've thought that if I had to go somewhere it would be Canada. The Native Canadians seem to me to be living more closely to their traditional lifestyle, and appear to be in a similar position to our people in Australia. I'd want to visit a reservation, and have no desire for travelling just for the sake of it.

When I left the British Government Office I went to live in Queensland. Some of my friends were there, so I packed 10 suitcases with my clothes and chattels (including saucepans) and off I went. I arrived on the train, together with the suitcases, and stayed in a motel in Brisbane for a week. Then I moved into a hostel or boardinghouse for young businesswomen, and did some temping for an employment agency, 'Manpower'. Jobs came regularly for me. I met up with my friends and was thinking seriously about taking a permanent job, when my Dad passed away. I packed up and returned to Victoria, where I lived with Mum in Shepparton for a time. Then it was back to Melbourne and the league. It was the late 1960s and we were gearing up for the 1967 referendum. The Doug Nichols Hall had been established by that time, and members of the league came in to work, we had photocopiers everywhere, and they were going all the time. We printed thousands and thousands of pamphlets and cards to be handed out at the voting booths. Uncle Doug and Stan Davey, as well as the directors of the Aborigines Advancement League, were being interviewed on radio and television constantly. When the referendum was won, we had a huge celebration at the Doug Nichols Hall.

> ... the whole community was working on issues relating to the referendum.

Bruce McGuinness, Gary Foley, and Bill Onus and Eric Onus were among the activists. They were some of the main spokespeople, but their families were involved and the whole community was working on issues relating to the referendum. There were many, many speaking engagements, and the league continued with its role of providing information to the community on a statewide basis. We weren't working for the community in Melbourne alone; we were working for the communities in the country as well, right across Victoria.

There was need in every Koori community at that time. Koori communities lived along the Murray River, at Dunnstown and Werneth, Mildura, then down to Waubra, Swan Hill, Echuca, Shepparton; throughout Gippsland and at Lake Tyers. There were people at Neerim, Neerim South, Jackson's Tract, Drouin. Then there was the Western District. A lot of miles were covered. During those times, the only way we were able to keep the league going was through volunteer work and support from the Aboriginal community, and through donations from the general community and the trades unions. There was no government funding. Now and again some of the ministers or secretaries of a government department might make a personal contribution, but that was it.

The unions played an important part in Aboriginal affairs. One way was through paying for or organising the provision of goods, including food and clothing, to be delivered to our communities throughout Victoria (probably the trade union movement did this all over Australia). I recall very clearly the people working on the wharves organising through the union for bales and bales of clothing to be sent to Darwin. It was destined for Wave Hill, when the Gurrindgi people were involved in the Wave Hill walk-off, at the end of the 1960s. They were campaigning, with support from the unions, for equal pay. People came from Wave Hill to Melbourne to talk about the campaign, and they went to various union meetings. The unions had great support from the Aboriginal people, and the unions gathered funds to enable the Wave Hill people to continue their fight for equal wages.

The unions had great support from the Aboriginal people ...

When the Whitlam government won the December 1972 election, great change came in Aboriginal affairs. A ministry for Aboriginal affairs was established, then came the department for Aboriginal affairs. Program funds were made available for community organisations to be set up to cover housing, health, education and employment (although there weren't many programs in employment at that time). We had identified positions for Aboriginal people, in government departments, to provide advice. Then, gradually, Aboriginal service units were established within all federal departments. Later the state governments adopted this approach. Activists like Gary Murray, Alf Bamblet and several others began in jobs in the service units, then having seen how the bureaucracy operated they came back into community politics.

The wheels were turning very slowly. Change was not happening sufficiently quickly for our community. We still have the highest infant mortality rate, the lowest life expectancy rate in our community. Our health is not as good as that of the general community. In the 1970s, we had a handful of people going through to the higher school certificate (HSC) and on into university. Over the years, however, programs have increased their assistance and there are many, many Aboriginal people going through university. There are significant numbers of Aboriginal graduates today, compared with the past. However the service units within government departments have been reduced and programs have suffered, just as they have in other areas within both state and federal governments, with the reduction in staff levels in the 1980s and 1990s.

When I came back into the paidworkforce in the early 1980s, after taking a break to raise my family, I took a job with Aboriginal Education

Services in the state ministry of education. The Victorian Aboriginal Consultative Group was established at that time, giving advice to the director of Aboriginal Education Services. I worked as a clerical officer Grade 1. My job was to establish and maintain the filing system. I worked for a long time, just getting files in order. Then I went to the Aboriginal Affairs Unit in the department of premier and cabinet. I went across as a NESA (National Employment Scheme for Aborigines) trainee, employed as a secretary/receptionist/administrative support to the three other people in the unit at the time. Reg Blow was manager of the unit and is now administrator of the Aborigines Advancement League. Errol West, who was at one time at the Aboriginal Education Services, was there too. Joy Murphy was support person for an interim committee that had been set up by the government. (She is now on the Equal Opportunity Board.) Later, Julie Peers (Julie Stevens then) arrived as a trainee. She now runs her own business as a freelance consultant and project worker, and has established a shop at Queen Victoria Market, in Victoria Street, selling Aboriginal art and artifacts.

I took a job with Aboriginal Education Services in the state ministry of education.

When my traineeship ran out, I moved across to the public service board. I worked there with Pam Griffin, who moved on to the Equal Opportunity Commission where she worked as a conciliator and was responsible for establishing police liaison committees within the community across Victoria. She's now working as a coordinator at the Wodonga College of Technical and Further Education (TAFE). When she moved to the Equal Opportunity Commission, I took over her job as Aboriginal liaison officer in the recruitment area. Then I went to the federal public service board, working in the same type of job.

In recruitment, everyone had to sit the same entrance test/selection test. I gave advice about the test to candidates and potential candidates, travelling around the state to promote recruitment to the service. We also held information sessions and took people through practice tests to give them an idea of what the test was about. The only difference between the Aboriginal candidates and non-Aboriginal candidates was that we conducted the tests separately for the Aboriginal candidates, either out in the community or in at the board itself. This was so that Aboriginal people would feel more comfortable. Even today there is a reluctance for our community to have anything much at all to do with bureaucracy. Our community still has difficulties in accessing programs and services, mainly because of stereotyping or the ignorance of other people. Because we are a minority within the general community, in some instances the attitude is: 'Well, we don't really have the time to spend on so few people.' Because there are thousands in the mainstream coming in to access the service, some of those in charge believe they haven't the time to spend on small numbers.

We had some success in supporting Aboriginal people who entered the public service. It was part of my responsibility to provide that support, not just to the supervisors or the employer, but to those who had been recruited, the trainees. It wasn't always possible to give them the support that was really needed. We weren't able to obtain the necessary resources and still do not have the resources, although the department of education, employment and training (DEET) in particular is now developing a mentor program to provide individual support for people coming into the public service or going into private sector jobs under the Aboriginal employment strategies.

> ... *a mentor program to provide individual support for people coming into the public service under the Aboriginal employment strategies.*

From the federal public service board I went across to the department of social security. I was seconded to take over the manager's job in the Aboriginal Services Unit whilst Ron James, who held that position, went on study leave for three years. During the three years I was there, the public service board was abolished. My position (at ASO 4/5 level) was transferred across to the department of social security, so I retained a job there when Ron James returned. It was a liaison position, but I didn't take it up because I went on secondment to the state government for two years. I was with the department of labour, working on the Job-Link program. This was a program established to help the longterm unemployed. It was my job to set up the service for Aboriginal people. I worked out in the northern suburbs, at the regional office in Preston.

Later I applied for the position of manager of the Aboriginal employment strategies, which included the recruitment program also. This meant I returned to the area where I had originally been working. Part of my responsibility was to monitor the employment strategies that had been established, then to negotiate with government departments and private sector employers, to establish more employment strategies. Much of my work was with government business enterprises such as Telecom (now Telstra) and Australia Post, and with higher education – Melbourne, Deakin and Monash universities.

I entered DEET in 1989–90. One of my first jobs was to go to Monash University to talk with the people in personnel about developing an employment strategy for the university. (The University of Melbourne already had one.) It took a long time for Monash to develop its strategy, about four years, and one of the last tasks I did before leaving DEET was to have an agreement signed. That indicates how difficult it was sometimes to work at having a strategy written up, or even getting the initial agreement.

In my time at DEET there were many achievements of significance. A position with the Trades Hall Council was established in 1991 or 1992 – Trades Hall has one Aboriginal/Torres Strait Islander liaison officer. We renegotiated another three-year strategy within the public service, and this has now been completed. Then we had individual strategies with the attorney-general's department, a state position was established in Australia Post and a national position with ACCI. There is an ACTU (Australian Council of Trade Unions) strategy, which includes agreements with state trades and labour councils, and the universities strategy. Now the department is looking to establish strategies at the local level. This is a better idea, because most of the strategies already operating concentrate mainly on the metropolitan area, although Telstra is now employing people who are able to work out in the regions.

I wanted to concentrate on my own spiritual growth ...

I took an early retirement from the public service, had about a week's rest, then established my own consultancy group business, 'Mandala Consulting Services'. Everyone asks me: 'What does *Mandala* mean?' They think it is a Koori word. But the *Mandala* is a spiritual icon, representing the seeking of unity and completeness within the universe.

I had come out of the public service with great ideas of not wanting to become involved in too many activities. I wanted to concentrate on my own spiritual growth, and do something along the lines of helping people with their health through meditation and massage, as I had been working in those areas. But an explosion occurred! I had people ringing to say: 'Can you do this?' 'Can you do that?' In order to do 'this' or 'that' I had to have an income. So I registered my business and have concentrated on delivering cross-cultural awareness training programs. I have worked with federal government departments, local government and in the community. I involve Koori people from the community who have expertise and skills in various areas, and we work together. I have done training programs and team-building, as well as negotiation skills, in the community and am looking to build on that work.

I haven't entirely broken the links with some of the areas in which I previously worked. I keep in touch to offer support to those who are now working in the areas. I telephone them to see how they are going, and they may call me for advice on particular issues. But I have noticed that they have become very confident in the work they do, and the need for advice has lessened.

I am now looking to build bridges and promote a greater understanding between the disparate areas of our community and the general community. We have a multicultural society, and at Mandala Consulting Services we find, in conducting our cross-cultural workshops, that people from other countries have had similar experiences to ours, although they have been through traumas of a different kind. Yet some of the traumas are similar, or have similar consequences – the massacres of Aboriginal people at the time of settlement and the taking away of Aboriginal children from their families are not dissimilar from the experiences of the Holocaust, or massacres of civilians during wartime in other countries.

The Human Rights and Equal Opportunity Commission is currently conducting an inquiry into the removal of Aboriginal children. The reasons and the aftermath are significant. Programs for healing, counselling and dealing with grief are essential. And there is also the question of the descendants of the people who set up the programs and put them into effect – the managers of the reserves and their families, people working in the churches who may have been responsible for the removal of children from their parents or from their communities. They have issues to deal with. The removal of Aboriginal children may have impacted on people across the board.

Aboriginal people have had to suppress their grief and anger, their sorrow and despair.

People three or four generations after the Holocaust still feel the effects of what happened to their grandparents' parents, particularly because their grandparents' parents and other survivors were unable to talk about or deal with what had happened to them. They suppressed their feelings. Drawing comparisons is sometimes useful, and sometimes not so useful. But what is evident is that Aboriginal people have had to suppress their grief and anger, their sorrow and despair at what happened to them, and this has continued on down the generations. It is continuing today.

Some Aboriginal children may have had relatively happy experiences with the families in which they were brought up. But a number have had horrendous experiences. This now impacts on their families, and so the tragedy continues. Resources must be made available to deal with this in a humane, compassionate and caring way.

As a matter of course, in whatever job I have been working, I have set out to help and encourage Koori people, women and men. This has been a part of my job in most positions I have held. I have gathered a family of people around me, with whom I keep in touch. I have been a mentor as a natural outcome of my work and my position in the community. I have two daughters, both of whom now working in Aboriginal affairs. My daughter Karen Milward works as an Aboriginal policy officer with the Municipal Association of Victoria. My daughter Shelly Milward worked as a dental therapist with the school dental service in the department of health and community services for six years. She was looking to expand her experience and now works at Mandala Consulting Services as my office manager. We have a good working relationship: she orders me around a little, which is what I need!

To Do Something *Good*

Joan Kirner

Premier of Victoria from 1990 to 1992, Joan Kirner, AM, previously was deputy premier (1989–90), minister for education (1988–90) and minister for conservation, forests and lands (1985-88); from 1990 to 1992 she was minister responsible for women's affairs. Elected to the Parliament of Victoria in 1982 as a member of the upper house, in 1988 she was elected member for Williamstown.

Joan Kirner retired from parliament in 1994 and is now chairperson of the federal Employment Services Regulatory Authority (ESRA). From 1994 to 1995 she was president of the Victorian branch of the Australian Labor Party (ALP) and was active and influential in the formulation and adoption, in 1994, by the Victorian branch of its affirmative action policy. Amongst many other activities, Joan Kirner is patron of the Living Museum of the West.

University High changed my life. When I was growing up, the careerpath for girls was spelled out by the general community as: go to teachers college, do kindergarten teacher training, or become a nurse. In the western suburbs where I grew up there was no notion that university was even a possibility. University High changed all that. I was there for two years, from 1953 to 1954, and going to university was expected. I clearly recall the first day I attended at university. Dad came with me to pay the fees, we got lost, and dad kept tipping his hat to everyone. It was at the beginning of the age of Germaine Greer.

At University High, a whole new world had opened up to me. It was a selective school as well as taking students from the local community, many of them refugees and Jewish people. Living at Essendon, I had not met children like these before. June Factor was one of them, and became my best friend at school, introducing me to the Eureka Youth League and the Jewish culture of politics, learning and music. She encouraged me to read Russian literature. Gorky's Mother, *which she gave to me, is the best present I have ever received. Reading it meant I went* on to read Dostoevsky and Tolstoy, and on and on.

June Factor's mother, Mary Factor, introduced me to food I had never before seen, much less eaten! There was a chopped liver dish, and bread that was 'different'. Bread in my house was a high-tin white loaf – unsliced in those days. Bread for June and her family was rye, or crusty, or blackbread. And there was a marvellous sticky dessert made of semolina. Food was a culture, not just something you 'had to have'. At home, my father came in from work at five o'clock, expecting tea on the table at 15 minutes past the hour – chops, steak or sausages, mashed potatoes, green peas, then apple pie with cream. Dad and I drew the line at brussels sprouts: we hated them.

My mother introduced June Factor to sewing and knitting. June was unable to knit. When she had her first baby, there weren't Bonds jumpsuits to be bought for children. Everything had to be handmade and handknitted. Mum knitted baby matinee jackets, and June was determined she would learn. June managed to knit two left fronts. Mum fixed the jacket!

My friendship with June meant there was an interesting interaction between our families: a mix of the workingclass Oz family and the intellectual, small business Jewish family with a communist background. This did not cease with my becoming premier. At times June (for many years prominent and active in the Victorian Council for Civil Liberties) became rather angry with me on civil liberties issues, which have always been important to her. This was a continuation of our earlier debates about issues and lifestyles. Fortunately the exigencies of government and our different perspectives did not interrupt our friendship, which has been solid from our school years, through university and up to the present day.

I have always had the confidence of parents, aunts and friends, particularly women friends, and their support. This meant I hit the ground running. I would not have survived two years as Premier of Victoria without the support of women colleagues and women friends. In those two years, they gave me far more than I gave to them – although some of them would argue that this is untrue!

> I would not have survived two years as Premier of Victoria without the support of women colleagues and women friends.

My mother believed girls could do anything. It was my mother who took me to the opera, to musicals, youth concerts, away on holidays. She was a music teacher, so I grew up with Chopin and Rachmaninov. When I could not accept a teaching studentship at an all-girls school, it was she who took me off to University High, insisting the principal enrol me. She was the one who gave me the sense that I could achieve and the drive to keep on going.

My father gave me the sense of what achievement is about. It wasn't a question of achievement 'just for yourself'. It was achievement for other people that was important. 'If you can't do something *good*, then don't do it,' was one of his favourite sayings, and it played a significant part in the development of my view of the world. (He also said: 'Ladies don't wear slacks in the street.' That was part of my culture, too!) A worker in the munitions factory for 40 years until his death as a consequence of a heart attack, my father was in essential services during wartime. He worked together with the women who came into the factory when so many of the men went off to war.

My grandfather was 'Andrew Hood & Son', the cartage people. They held political meetings in the streets of Ascot Vale, standing on horse-led drays. Then they'd disappear when the police or the pro-conscriptionists – Billy's Blue Boys – came around the corner.

My parents didn't only *say* it was important to be involved and 'do things'. They *did* them. Both were community activists in various ways. Dad in particular was active in the community. He supported many boys who were in trouble with the police, bailing them out at ungodly hours of the morning. When my uncle died, my father looked after his family.

My aunt, Mill Cole, was a role model and mentor to me. She worked in the Presbyterian Bookroom. Even when she gave up paidwork on marriage, which is what middleclass women did – she gave me books. There was no public library at Essendon, where I grew up, and mum and dad didn't have much money, let alone know which books to choose. They were keen for me to have a good education but were not too sure how I should get it. *Anne of Green Gables*, *Pollyanna* (whom I couldn't stand), the classics, Dickens and Shakespeare and others, the Christopher Robin books and *Alice in Wonderland* were all presents from my aunt. All her life, until she died early in 1995, Aunt Mill was a supporter and a reminder of my childhood and life as a young woman, and the input she gave to my life through the love of books and reading. When the Special Broadcasting Service (SBS) recorded a program on 'Joan Kirner – This is Your Life' we went out to the village in which Aunt Mill was living. The journalist said to her: 'Has Joan changed much, now she's premier?' Mill replied: 'She wouldn't dare!'

When I began buying books for myself, I read John Steinbeck and Marcel Proust. When I was a child, all the girls were reading *The Scarlet Pimpernel*. Then we read *The Good Earth*, by Pearl Buck, particularly one page that contained sexually explicit material. We went to films, usually the matinees, where I cried buckets of tears over *Black Beauty* and *My Friend Flicka*. I thought Elizabeth Taylor was God's gift to womanhood! I have changed my mind about that, although we have to admire her instinct for survival.

My career in politics has two aspects: the parliamentary political commitment, and my non-parliamentary political career. The former was the shorter part of my political career – from 1982 to 1994 – for I have been active in community politics for 30 years.

In the early days, my activism took place out at Croydon, where I lived with my husband Ron and our children, Kate, Michael and David. When I enroled Michael at primaryschool, we were told that our children would be placed in classes of fifty-four. A bright young mum with a teaching career and high expectations for her children, I replied: 'Not *my* child!'

That was when I learned one of my earliest lessons in politics: if you want to change something for your child, you have to change it for other children and you have to change it together with other parents or other members of the community.

> *I learned one of my earliest lessons in politics . . .*

Much earlier, in my childhood, as a member of the Presbyterian Fellowship I had gone doorknocking against the proposed change of the six o'clock hotel-closing rule. But other than that I had not engaged in organised community politics. So when we as a group of young mums decided we would not tolerate the class-size, we had to sit down to talk about what we would do.

We knew what we wanted. We knew we couldn't get it unless we made a fuss in the media as well as using 'proper' approaches to the authorities. I do not know how we knew that this dual approach was necessary. I had always been a student of politics, so knew that any successful political campaign must have more than one prong, and it maybe that that was the approach mum and dad had to political action, and I had learned it from them. Perhaps it came through talking with June Factor.

I cannot remember the origin of our knowledge of how to run a campaign. But what I do recall is that we learned as we went along.

We began with a petition, sitting down outside the school and encouraging people to sign it. We needed two things – classrooms and teachers. That was what we lobbied for and the demand for them was the substance of the petition.

When the petition received a limited response, we decided to knock on the doors of all households in the area. This meant we met with members of the community and took many subscriptions, joining people up to the parents' club so that they would become involved in further action. I did this with a group of women, some of whom have remained my friends and one of whom, Bunnie Cameron, is living in Williamstown, where I now live. We learned from each other and gave mutual support. We babysat one another's children, so that we could attend meetings. (There was no occasional care for children then – indeed, no real childcare.)

When taking signatures outside the school was not enough, and the doorknocking and a petition arising from it didn't work, I said to my campaign colleagues: 'Well, if we're going to make this happen, we can't knock ourselves out before we get anywhere, through doing all this outdoor activity.' I had three small children and no car, so like the women who had become my colleagues in the struggle, I had to do everything from home. Our political activities had to be fitted in to the time available, had to be juggled around childcare and household tasks, and we had to use the skills we had to best effect.

> *Our political activities had to be juggled around childcare and household tasks...*

We took up telephone lobbying. Every half hour for three weeks we called the public works department. On a Friday I made what proved to be the final call. The man answering the telephone said to another man in the office, in words I overheard: 'It's that bloody woman again! The women from North Croydon. What are we going to tell them?' The reply (again audible) was: 'For God's sake, tell her the minister's decided to give them their classrooms.'

It was 1966. There was no sense at that time of the Australian Labor Party (ALP) picking itself up and moving forward. The 'It's Time' campaign and Gough Whitlam's government were six years in the future. Labor coming to power in Victoria was even further distant. It was just sheer pressure from women that brought this change within the minister's office, and to our children's schooling.

We got the classrooms, but we didn't have the teachers. What to do next? We attempted to make an appointment with the minister. He foolishly said: 'No.' We moved to the next stage: media activism, running a campaign centred around empty classrooms and no teachers. The principal of the school didn't know what to do with us. Nor did the Victorian Minister for Education.

We decided that if the minister wouldn't give us an appointment, we'd sit outside his office until he did. (This is not something I advised when I was a minister!)

We sat there, in the waiting area outside his office. 'What if he doesn't come out?' said the others. 'He has to go to the toilet,' I said. And as they didn't have ensuites in those days, when the inevitable came about, the minister came out. We did sit there for half a day – from morning until after lunchtime – until out he came. It was Lindsay Thompson, a nice bloke with whom I've had a good working relationship ever since.

Lindsay Thompson invited us in, and finally we got our teachers. I became firm friends with the receptionist, a man called Kingsley. After this episode, I was never refused an appointment.

The campaign was run by a group of women who were mutually supportive, and with a mutual interest – our children. Some of us had been nurses and teachers, some were saleswomen, some had other jobs or were involved in home activities. But we were united on one issue. We all knew what we wanted for our children.

Then along came Whitlam and the NEAT scheme. Many of the women with whom I had worked on the class-size campaign took advantage of the Whitlam changes and went to university. The husbands of many of them were businessmen who resented their wives' aspirations. As I had already been to university, I was the one who was at home with the children. I had decided to stay at home for a few years with our children, anyway, and there was no childcare in Croydon. At that time, women looked peculiar if they expressed any desire for state-based childcare. It simply did not exist. My mother lived on the other side of the city and I had no relatives at all in the areas where I lived.

At that time, women looked peculiar if they expressed any desire for state-based childcare.

I was part of a mutually supportive community at North Croydon. Being a teacher, my husband arrived home at a reasonable time – I was fortunate in this respect, and also in that unlike many of the businessmen husbands who were trying to move up the tree, my husband was supportive of me and my activities. With hardly any services, everyone having young children, and most husbands arriving home at a late hour, necessity was a huge, motivating factor in the women getting together. Then the mutual support we gave and received became far more. We began to enjoy it, and to understand the politics of group action.

Many of the women went on to Monash University. My husband couldn't understand what the fuss was about when husbands and wives began falling out over issues such as the women seeking a university education. I did a lot of supporting of the women, who frequently talked through what was happening in their home lives and in their work at university. The conflict was often extraordinary. I had their children after school, because my house was on the way home for many of them.

It came as a real shock to me that some of the women did not see themselves as entitled to make choices. It was a struggle for them to meet the demands made of them as 'business wives', and to dovetail this with their studies and expanding vision of the world.

Since then, many of them have gone their own way, but Bunnie Cameron became a teacher at Williamstown. Her marriage broke down and she moved to Williamstown at the time we did. Together she and I became active politically, we have grown older together, and our friendship remains strong. Williamstown has become a special place to me. I have made many friendships in this historic town. One is with Linelle Gibson, who is considerably younger than I am, and a refugee from the old South Africa. To her, I am a bit like a surrogate mum, and a surrogate grandma to her children. She's been like a younger sister to me in always being there, ready to come over for a chat, or asking us over for a meal. She and her husband have always made it known that their personal support was there, during the difficult years. On week days, for the two years I was premier, day in, day out, she and Bunnie woke me at 6.15 every morning for an early walk and chat. Without them, I wouldn't have made it!

It was when I was in Croydon, taking care of the children and surrounded by women who were only now going to university, that I decided I was happy being 'the community activist'. By this time I was going to Parents' Federation meetings at the assembly hall in Collins Street, next to George's. The meetings were attended by many determined-looking women, sitting there with their hats on and often wearing gloves. But I was annoyed at their agendas: school uniforms, school milk – not more funds for state education, which was starved of resources.

There we were, women in politics but not using our volunteer-power. As younger mums, together we set about making the Parents' Federation and Victoria Council of State Schools Organisation (VCSSO) one of the most effective political lobby groups Victoria had ever seen. We moved from mothers' clubs to parents' clubs and from 'men's committees' to school committees, from committees of advice to school councils with decision-making powers. We insisted that parents (and obviously many parents were women) must have a real say in their kids' education.

I became known as 'the shadow minister for education'. Then I moved into the national level of activism. That meant I had more media exposure. One evening Margaret and Gough Whitlam were sitting watching Bob Moore's *Monday Conference* on the Australian Broadcasting Commission (ABC), when I was a part of the 'great debate' on state aid for schools, which was the focus of the program. Margaret said to Gough: 'You ought to have that young woman on your Schools Commission.' With some help from Race Mathews, who was my local member at the time, and parent activists, Gough Whitlam appointed me to the Schools Commission.

When I moved on to the national stage, I worked in Canberra and from an office in the Commonwealth Bank building in Bourke Street, Melbourne. My work was with a most impressive group of women, all shapes, sizes, intellects, interests – but the one interest we held in common, and which we each wanted so desperately, was for our children's education to be sound, and that there be a decent state school system. All of us believed we (and our children) were entitled to it.

My work was with a most impressive group of women, all shapes, sizes, intellects, interests ...

When we went on delegations to the director general, he served us tea and didn't listen to us. I refused to go. At one conference I moved that we stop raising funds. The motion was defeated, but the debate gained us a new-found respect. Women had moved from a position of asking for and raising money to one of making political demands and never doubting our right to do so.

We began setting the agenda with the director general and the minister. Parent teachers Heather Mung, Jan McKenzie, Pat Reeve, Joan Reidy and I had different skills, different abilities, but we became a high-powered supportive team. I called Joan Reidy 'Sister Hannah' because we carried the banner together and complemented one another's skills. Yet initially the skills the women had were largely unrecognised by others, and often were hardly recognised by themselves. There was so much scope for support and recognition, and our commitment to the cause and to each other meant we gave this to one another.

This support and recognition was important. It worked both ways. Jan McKenzie said I was too policy-oriented: 'You should get out with the people more!' she would admonish. On the other hand, if I had not said to her, a woman, wife and mother who had taken on the role of secretary: 'You can be president of this organisation, which you will do well,' she would not have seen so clearly her capacity to take on the role. Jan McKenzie made the links with the community. I got involved in the political strategies. She was very straight, with a tremendous facility for cutting through the garbage. We built up a strong team.

This became my learning process, a rehearsal for working with the team in Parliament House. It was also central to my ability to achieve positive gains as a cabinet minister. I became minister for conservation in 1985, and my activism in community politics and the work I had put in through those years meant I had a network of women across the breadth of Victoria, regardless of their political party, whom I had supported, or who had supported me. As minister, I attended farmers' meetings. The women would be there – doing the morning or afternoon tea. The farmers, who were wondering what they would do with a socialist, feminist greenie minister, were knocked over when I walked into the tearoom and said: 'Hello!' to the women. 'Joan! It's fantastic to see you,' the women, their wives, would say. The men would be calling me 'Mrs Kirner' or 'Minister' or something else formal. The women knew me, I knew them, they called me Joan and I knew them by name too. One of my advisors was so amazed by my networks, he claimed I had a 'woman in every port'.

> ... a network of women across the breadth of Victoria, regardless of their political party, whom I had supported, or who had supported me.

Back in those days of community work, the network of support and of information was incredible. We lobbied to 'get up' a parent on the Schools Commission. At the time, I was vice president of the National State School Parents' Organisation. Susan Ryan was our lobbyist in Canberra. In 1972 the National State School Parents' Organisation had advertised for an executive officer, interviewing a range of people. Guess who was the best for the job? Susan Ryan! I selected her for her first political job!

Susan Ryan and I began a mutually productive relationship. We were quite a team, with her in Canberra and me in Victoria. The Labor government didn't have control of the senate, so we had to fashion strategies that would secure support from the conservatives. We decided to concentrate on the National Party.

Evelyn Rogers, a mum in Mildura, decided she would organise the Mallee. Did she succeed! As the Schools Commission Bill was being debated in federal parliament and the clause securing a position for a parent was listed – would it be in or out? would we succeed or fail? I met Peter Fisher, National Party member for the Mallee, in Kings Hall. In Canberra lobbying, I was walking through Kings Hall in what is now 'Old Parliament House'. Peter Fisher literally raced through, saying: 'G'day Joan. I can't talk to you. I've got to go to ring my mums!' He telephoned 'the mums' and I called them five minutes later to find out what he had said.

The National Party supported 'the parent-member clause' – because we seemed to have a woman at the end of every country telephone line around the nation.

It has been a mutual arrangement, with support flowing from one to the other and back.

I travel to places in the country now, and people talk about the support I have given them, or that which they have given to me. We talk about what we have achieved together. It has been a mutual arrangement, with support flowing from one to the other and back. I needed the numbers and the cause needed the numbers, but all these women were so much more than numbers. They were advice, they were strategists, they were action, they cared. And when a country woman decides she wants something better for her children, everyone in government or opposition had better get out of the way! They don't give up.

The women were everywhere, remaining supportive right through, regardless of their politics. That's why Heather Mitchell of the Farmers' Federation and I have worked well together: both respect the contribution made by women, no matter what political party they may come from. Providing that the work is on behalf of women and for and with them, and not just 'to them' or 'at them', and providing the issue is one into which we have the same insights: land conservation, children's rights to *good* schooling, public transport.

I met my 'twin' in party politics, Jenny Beacham, in 1973. A teacher, she had become an advisor for parents. She was so good at 'getting things done' in those days. Perhaps people were not game to say: 'No.' Then, there was money around, and we achieved recognition that parent participation was an integral part of decision-making. We were doing this in the education sector simultaneously with Ann Morrow, Lynne Wannan and others doing it in the community childcare movement. Still others were working at it in the community health centres. Community participation had arrived.

The Victorian State School Parents' Organisation employed Jenny Beacham as the service education officer. No doubt the department came to regret this, as from then on we worked solidly together in providing support, information, political strategies and networking for so many parents at the school level, and particularly in the disadvantaged schools program. The disadvantaged schools program was drawn up by my heroine, Dr Jean Blackburn and me, with the support of so many people in the schools sector.

The disadvantaged schools program grew out of mind-boggling experiences I had had. At schools like Fitzroy Primary, English was taught in broom cupboards. I'd go on excursions with the children who lived in the ministry of housing flats and hear them say: 'What's that Miss, over there?' It was wind blowing through long grass, something they had never seen before in their lives, because they'd never ever been to a farm or seen long grass.

At schools like Fitzroy Primary, English was taught in broom cupboards.

I had a view as a workingclass kid that all children must have a good education. So far as I am concerned, it is an entitlement. That seems a reasonable view to me, and it is why I was so angry with the system. Workingclass entitlements were not recognised. The idea was that you could buy education or get it if you had influence, but you're were not entitled to it. The disadvantaged schools program was about putting more dollars into disadvantaged schools – schools in low-income areas. Low-income combined with poor housing and non-English speaking background led to few opportunities. The program aimed at changing this.

I argued and finally gained agreement on the Schools Commission that the way the funds were provided to schools was crucial. It was not only a question of dollars, but one of having committees of teachers and parents determining the programs. The people of Heidelberg (and no doubt many other similar areas) were tired of being researched. They wanted money to *do* something. They knew what they needed as a community: they wanted teachers who'd respect them and work with them, to deliver to their children. It was people like Nancy Spence (a mutually supportive person who once told me she could never do public speaking, ha ha) who made these points to me. The disadvantaged schools program was about all the chances people haven't been game enough to take, and it has brought a huge difference to schools in disadvantaged areas. And 20 years after Nancy told me she couldn't be a spokesperson she was a leader in the fight to save Northland Secondary College from closure by the Kennett government.

As for Jean Blackburn – it was she who taught me that if I wanted to understand decision-making, I had better understand economics. An economic historian, she knew what she was talking about. So, from the time I was together with her on the Schools Commission, over a five year period I began to learn how the broader policies interacted with economics, and the place of social justice. I knew the practical aspect, and she taught me the theory, showing me that economics and social justice are not opposites but work best together. It is not a question of social justice being subjugated to economics. It is an entirely different way of looking at economics. To get the best society and the best economy, it is necessary to ensure that social justice is a firm component of 'economics'.

This is the way I have usually learned: the practice first, the theory later. I learned much of the theory of economics and social justice from Dr Jean Blackburn and Professor Bob Connell. Similarly I learned the theory of feminism after I had done the practice.

Then much later, there was Landcare. The principle we followed was that if you want to get something positive done with land conservation, then it is important to *stop* telling the farmers what to do individually, and to treat the farmers collectively, as the experts, then provide support. We then opened up to the farmers the possibilities of working land on the basis of catchments. Ninety-five percent of farms are, after all, partnerships between women and men, though too often known as 'the farmer' and 'the farmer's wife'. With Landcare, we worked at recognising farming expertise and acknowledging women as farmers and experts too. And this brought me into contact with some powerful agricultural women, such as Heather Mitchell and Pam Robinson. Pam Robinson writes me notes saying: 'Well, you're doing this well, and I don't think much of this . . .' She knows I will take action rather than offence.

With Landcare, we worked at recognising farming expertise and acknowledging women as farmers and experts too.

The relationship I have with Jenny Beacham is one where it is unnecessary for us to discuss where we stand. We work on issues according to the same principles. This means we can always take a shortcut to what we will do about a particular issue, not where we stand on it. This does not mean that we don't stand up to one another when necessary. Our friendship was severely tested when she was state secretary of the Victorian branch of the Australian Labor Party (ALP) and I was Premier of Victoria, and we were running an election campaign in 1992. Jenny had to be very tough. I was far more optimistic than most people. She kept bringing me back to reality. She turned out to be terribly right, of course. We lost the election. But she was always there, and I have tried to be there for her too.

Jenny Beacham and I have been mutually reinforcing about what is important, about how to survive, and even about changes we find are necessary in our lives or to ourselves. There are the endless cups of coffee and phone calls. Like most women, we talk through the issues, whether they be political issues 'out there' or the personal issues which touch us as individuals – and which, in the end, are political in their own way. Jenny is very good at bringing in the experiences of other people to expand debate. In this way, she gains a clear view of what action is necessary and how to strategise.

My staff have been crucial in my party political life, too. This is a slightly different relationship than that which I have with Jenny Beacham and others outside my office, although most of my immediate staffers have been friends and all of them have been ALP members. A lot of them have been from the western suburbs. They are people ranging from my advisors to media staff, to political secretaries – such as Sue Addison, Sue Pickles, Jenny McMillan. All of them are most competent and supportive. People often laugh because in my premier's office I had photographs everywhere of my staff's babies – we were an expanding family. I think of two of my key advisors, Candy Broad and Deb Kiers, as the next generation of first class women politicians.

No woman in politics can survive and be successful without a network of women. Political colleagues are a necessary support, and for a woman member of parliament, women colleagues as supports are essential. For me it has been Caroline Hogg, Kay Setches and Licia Kockocinski, and Margaret Ray and the late Beth Gleeson, in particular. The support is and has always been mutual – and it is difficult to describe it. It is both personal and political, and anything else needed at the time.

No woman in politics can survive and be successful without a network of women.

When I was premier I talked to Caroline Hogg almost every day. It was a lifeline, for it is impossible to work and to 'keep on' without *someone* in the political world a woman can trust absolutely. As well as the political and governmental questions, there are the great personal issues, like the death of a parent, the death of a child. Caroline Hogg and Kay Setches and I went through those events, with them happening to them or to me, and us all just 'being there' for each other when it was important.

Kay Setches is an extraordinary example of how a woman can be: she's always given so much time to so many people, and in so many ways. She has given so much to me and to other colleagues. She gives so much at home. She gave so much as a minister and so much as a member of parliament. Now, she talks of my support for her and particularly how she 'worked out' (from my approach) ways of 'getting things'. She knew I would stand with her on issues, so it wasn't always a matter of agreement, but it was always a matter of mutual respect and mutual support, in working our way through to a decision. This was the way Caroline Hogg and I worked in government, too.

Then there is my family. Through my years in parliament, and particularly those years as premier and leader of the opposition, the family relationship was often strained. Sometimes, at home, under pressure I became the reverse of what feminists say a partner should be – and that is sharing, caring and cooperative. My itinerary began to run the household. My family handled my being in politics in many different ways. Kate, my daughter, went overseas for the last two years of my being in parliament. She couldn't stand it any longer and, besides, she needed to find her own feet. Michael was married and living in Geelong. David was the activist. Ron cannot stand the ins and outs of politics and factions, but he knows what he believes in. He and Caroline Hogg were and are my lifeline to sanity and integrity.

I value, too, people like Joyce Apap and Rachel Storey. When we started the Women of the West, an organisation to bring women in the western suburbs together, Joyce Apap crept along, leaving a meal for her husband and not telling him where she was going. The group and I sought to encourage her as a person. Now she has a degree, she has a paid job, she's on the Victoria Women's Council. She telephones from time to time, either to ask me to do something or to advise her on a matter, or just to say: 'Hello.' Then I have calls from young people who say: 'Can I talk with you. I want a career in politics. I don't know what to do.' Rachel Storey is a young woman, in her early twenties, whom I came to know through the Labor Party. She is on the Victoria Women's Council, too – and now she's working in the office of Bruce Mildenhall, the shadow attorney general for Victoria.

As a local member, from time to time I met with youngsters who just wanted to talk. Than six months later a note would arrive: 'Thanks for that. I've sorted out what I want to do. And now I've done such-and-such.' I will have forgotten about the meeting, and of course it isn't just that meeting that has sorted out what they wanted to do. But it gave them confidence.

> *I was able to make the connection, and to vouch for her in a way that was useful.*

Then there is the young woman who was desperate to be a faction secretary to a minister's office in Canberra. I wrote her a reference. She did an interview. I talked to the minister's offsider. Eventually, the young woman got the job. She thought I got it for her, but I didn't. It was her talent that did that, but I was able to make the connection, and to vouch for her in a way that was useful. She might otherwise not have gained the position, not from lack of talent, but from lack of the right connections.

When I was a minister, I was able to set up various support mechanisms such as the mentoring program in the department of education, and the non-traditional jobs program which places women in non-traditional workplaces, the Rural Women's Network, the childcare for holiday time program. The mentor program was established by Ann Morrow and Pam Sandon. It was for women in senior management as well as for women in the clerical field where pay is low and recognition minimal. We set out both to raise women's expectations and to help them meet those expectations. We moved to have women on selection panels for school principals, and established development programs for women in leadership. It has had a significant effect and there has been a further improvement for women since 1992, when many senior men in education took the Liberal government's redundancy packages, enabling women to have greater access to the top.

The idea was *not* mentoring in the sense of 'pick a winner' and support them. It was mentoring in a sense of ensuring that whoever the woman was, whatever she wanted to do, the possibilities were opened up. The next step was to ensure that women were supported in taking up the new opportunity. The scheme was voluntary, with mentors ranging from Ann Morrow at the top (as chief executive of education) and other senior women, and I assisted when I could.

It is essential to take care with mentoring, for there is little point in the 'pick a winner' scheme, and I have trouble with the idea of 'role models'. Seeing women as 'role models' places too much responsibility on them. I also see the process as an interactive one. I am happy for my experiences to be used as something to be evaluated and examined when others determine the approaches they will take and the paths they will follow. But as premier and in everything I have done, I was and am no more playing a role than trying to be a model. That notion is abhorrent to me.

I have done and continue to do a *lot* of speaking engagements. I try to broaden my support for women by talking about my experiences and saying what I have learned from those experiences. I talk about the issues of image and power and harassment, and the sense that we are moving into a new era, where we are not simply after the tools of power and the rules of power, but we want an equal share of power. That is what we are looking for in a new society.

My focus is broadening, in these days out of the hurly burly of parliament and that direct involvement in party politics at the parliamentary level. I am deliberately making links between my experience so as to strengthen our ability to move forward – particularly young women's ability. I spoke at a Melbourne event where Naomi Wolf talked of the issues in her book, *Fire With Fire*. It was an extraordinary experience and I was fascinated by the response to it. Three-quarters of the audience was 25 to thirty-five. These young women do believe they are equal, but they have found that this is not their experience in the workplace and in relationships with men – they have found that in fact they are not quite so equal. Their belief in equality is not so easy to achieve. Questions keep arising for us and for young women. Can a woman be powerful, can she do a job and still be herself, still have some integrity? I find this reasonably easy to talk about, but everyone has to make her own judgement.

> Can a woman be powerful, can she do a job and still be herself, still have some integrity?

Today I find that I am supporting women by talking about what I *did* – my work in community politics, in parliament and as premier – and I am still *doing*: for example, working to ensure the affirmative action for women rule was achieved in the ALP. Kay Setches was the driving force behind this change, working with me and others, and with the community and women across Australia. It meant a lot of work in the Labor Party, with women from both the right and the left factions. Now we are moving into the next phase. And this is hard work, too.

We are working to establish 'EMILY's List' – a data base and financial and professional support for women in ALP preselections and in elections. It is based on a similar scheme in the United States. 'EMILY's List' stands for 'early money is like yeast' – it will make women RISE.

I have had bad experiences, just as everyone has. In some instances I have given women a great deal of support then felt disappointed by their actions. Everyone has to make her own choices, but is sad when anyone I have worked with closely, and supported against what I thought to be unreasonable attacks, acts wilfully against the interests of women and ignores the principles in which I thought she believed. There have been instances where others have said to me: 'Be careful. Be careful. You'll be used.' Now I see some I supported accepting posts offered to them by a Liberal government with priorities that are not supportive of social justice and the workingclass, of community needs, or even of minimal fairness for all. I think to myself: 'What happened to the sharing and mutual support?' Although the actions of such people do not affect me personally, for they do not touch upon me directly, I am concerned when women take on 'male models of power'. The male model of power is a strange thing for a woman to emulate when she has been a part of feminist and other cooperative activities and relied upon that support. Ultimately, however, it is the woman's choice. That doesn't minimise the disappointment of others seeing this happen, particularly those who have been supportive and who believed in the integrity of those now taking on the male model of power.

I have generally had positive experiences with the media. The women were wonderful. Many years ago, Iola Mathews, when working as a journalist with the *Age*, 'put me on the map', doing one of the very early features on me. I reciprocated, supporting her in her endeavours. I have had a mutually respectful relationship with women in the media, including

Louise Adler and Mary Delahunty, Laura Tingle, Robyn Dixon, Margot Kingston. People may not see it quite in this light: many thought Mary Delahunty was *very* hard on me in interviews on the *7.30 Report*. I don't see it this way. She had a job to do. So did I. Jill Singer once 'chewed me up' in an interview in my early days as minister for conservation. It was a normal professional exercise. My battles have mainly been with men, over power. The male journalists and editors who are anti-feminists threatened by articulate women who stand up for themselves, threatened by women who have power, have been the major problem.

The response of the media can be enlightening, too. I will never forget the time I cried in cabinet – tears of frustration at some nonsense going on. I knew the story would get out, and of course there was a cabinet leak. I was scheduled to do a speech at the Radisson President Hotel. The media were lined up to ask me about my tears and the women – political journalists such as Robyn Dixon of the *Age* – were petrified to write about it. They thought the headlines, over which they have no control, would be: 'Kirner Breaks Down.' 'Kirner Can't Hack the Pace.' The *Sun* kept taking photographs of me by the fast shutter until I looked as if I was crying, but the reaction of the public was very different from what 'the boys' hoped. People thought my tears of frustration were legitimate. They were supportive and, if anything, angry for me.

People thought my tears of frustration were legitimate. They were supportive ...

Then there are the comediennes and television performers. A large number of them 'took me off'. Magda Szubanski, dressed in a black voile tutu and red blazer, was fantastic. Denise Scott and Elle McFeast were marvellous. The Liberal Party constantly asked Magda to do skits for fundraisers for them, for their own political reasons, but she refused every time. She was the prize turn at the World Trade Centre at the *Spot on Joan Concert* which celebrated my first year as premier. We performed together on stage – I don't know who was most like me!

The main reason I am still active, reasonably sane and have some standing today is through the support from people like Kay Setches, Caroline Hogg, Jenny Beacham, Candy Broad, my husband and family. My mother died at the time I entered parliament. Not having her support through those years was a tremendous loss to me. I would have loved to have seen her take on Piers Ackerman (a journalist who was editor of the *Herald Sun*).

In those tough times, women didn't tell me what I wanted to hear. That was *not* the support I wanted – or needed. Rather, it was actually *being there* and remaining activists and friends that was important. In those tough years, they sustained me. I owe them.

PART II
Darkness Into Light

Much More than Tea and Sympathy

Susan Kelly

General manager, Centre for Continuing Education at the Council of Adult Education (CAE) in Melbourne, from 1993 to 1994 Susan Kelly was chief executive officer of Relationships Australia (formerly Marriage Guidance Australia), and from 1989 to 1993 a client account manager primarily with Mentor Human Resource Group, where she consulted on leadership and quality management skills, career development, occupational stress and resources management. From 1975 to 1987 she was a lecturer in psychology and educational psychology at the University of Melbourne and Swinburne University of Technology, prior to which she worked as youth field officer with the Australian Red Cross Society in Canberra, and a migrant and remedial English teacher. In 1992 she became the twenty-eighth president of the Australian Psychological Society, the primary professional and scientific body for psychologists in Australia.

Susan Kelly has written or co-written bestselling books: *A Hard Act to Follow – Step-parenting in Australia Today*, Penguin (1986) with Thomas Whelan; *The Prize and the Price – The Changing World of Women Who Return to Study*, Methuen Haynes (1987); and *Outrageous Fortune – People Coping with Major Life Crises*, Allen & Unwin (1989) with Prasuna Reddy. Since 1979, she has been a regular commentator on national radio and television, and in business and community forums, on relationships, social and psychological issues and the impact of organisational change on workers and their families.

It is not uncommon for children of alcoholics and the mentally ill to seek out substitute parents. When I was young I knew there were significant holes in my development and, at least at some level, I knew that I needed adult support and guidance to get out of them.

As a consequence, during adolescence in particular, I had some very close girlfriends but I also spent a lot of time with my friends' parents.

When I reflect on it, those relationships must have seemed a bit odd to some onlookers. And I have no doubt that at times I must have worn out my welcome. But I think those bonds are what kept me from following an established family tradition of losing the plot and becoming neurotic, even psychotic. I owe much to those adults for caring about me, for listening, offering advice, showing me that other ways of relating were possible, and encouraging me to rise above what surrounded me. Most of all, I thank them for including me in their family activities.

One women in particular stretched her family boundaries to include me. She provided what Christopher Lasch would call 'a haven in a heartless world'.

Elsie Partridge was something of a saviour. A warm, intelligent and generous women, she was utterly dependable. She took me and my younger sister out to places, fed us, provided a bed occasionally, and one day she forcibly intervened to prevent my being injured in one of Mother's frequent violent outbursts.

We didn't talk much about what went on at our home. It was not nice and anyway, when we were away from it we just wanted a rest. Also, we believed in those days that our family was unusual and that few people outside would understand. Sadly we all know now that that isn't true. Our family was worse than many but, tragically, better than some others.

When I did discuss what was happening, Elsie, especially, listened, never judging, never delving and never appearing to derive any vicarious thrill from the drama and peculiar goings-on that were going on across the road. Her support was always compassionate but practical.

Sometimes I took her advice. Sometimes I didn't.

We talked a lot. I asked her questions about her life, her views on marriage and family relationships, her own family history and aspirations as a young woman in England. I also asked for her advice when I had problems, or choices to make. Sometimes I took her advice. Sometimes I didn't.

But one piece of her wisdom did sink in. It echoed around in my head for years, surfacing from time to time. More than once I reflected on her words and they saved me from myself and the fate of many of my peers in Hobart in the late 1960s and early 1970s – that of making an early and probably doomed marriage.

I suppose I was about 14 when Mrs Parb, as I called her, said with such certainty and confidence: 'If all you want to be is married, then anyone can do that.' Simple words but powerful. And I must have been ready to hear them.

Her message was that women can make choices. Women should not be fearful of being 'left on the shelf' – a serious concern for nearly all girls in those days. (I get a bit despondent when I think it hasn't changed much for a lot of young women today.)

She made me see that if you are desperate to have the type of social acceptance that comes with marriage, there will always be some male around to oblige. The difficulty, courage and skill for a woman comes in choosing an appropriate partner, at a time in your life that suits both of you – not just him. Choosing one who is as committed to your personal growth and career as he is to his own, is much harder and takes longer.

It was a liberating insight and probably my first real glimpse of applied feminism.

This is not to say that Mrs Parb was able to satisfy fully her own needs for independence, work satisfaction and so on. As a woman raising three kids in the 1950s and 1960s in Tasmania – almost on her own because her husband was always travelling – choices had to be made. Or was it sacrifices that had to be made? It is not for me to say. But it did seem to me that for all that, she kept a better hold on what it was to be Elsie, as distinct from a mother and a wife, than most women I knew then, and many I've met since.

I found other mother-figures at different times in my life up until I was about 25 years old. One way or another they taught me important lessons. Maybe some of these lessons are learnt as a matter of course in 'normal' families. I'll never really know. But I am aware that I am indebted to those older women like Dorothy, Jenny, my Aunt Joan and my friend's Auntie Kath who talked frankly about life and relationships and helped educate a young woman who was keen to learn. Each of these women also provided true friendship and very practical support in a time of crisis.

I believe that it is because I sought out mother-figures – and to a lesser extent father-figures – and got on well with them, that I was able to come to some acceptance of my parents and an acknowledgment that my family history was just that, history, and not a script for the future. Somewhere along the way, I found I needed surrogate parents less and less. I must have been growing up. Happily for me most of the relationships survived the transition to more equal, less dependent friendships and they continue to this day.

It is not that my mother and father gave me nothing. Paradoxically, they gave me a great deal. And I don't think that, even in my darkest moments, I ever doubted that in their own egocentric way they loved us. In addition to a reasonable genetic endowment and training in the things that make most middleclass kids fit comfortably into new social and employment situations, such as good manners, conversational skill and the like, their greatest gift was to leave me largely alone, to make my own way at school and in friendships.

I heard no strong pro-education values from either parent, but neither did they put up any barriers to my staying on at school and going to university. I can't remember any messages in my childhood that started:

'Girls don't do . . .' There were a few times when what they did greatly assisted the academic path I took and my subsequent success. I was grateful even then because it was the 1960s and I knew that most girls in our workingclass/lower-middleclass highschool didn't get even that amount of support to continue at school.

I can't say whether if there had been any sons in the family, the messages about girls and achievement would have been different. They may well have been, especially in the light of the compelling research that shows that high achieving women are more likely to have been raised in 'brotherless' families than not.

> *We have all become strong, independent and, for the most part, confident and achieving women.*

For almost all the 24 years they were together, my parents were very absorbed in their own conflict, pain and unmet needs. For better or worse, from 1956, when our mother had her major breakdown, we, the Kelly girls, were largely 'self-raising'.

This actually turned out for the best. We have all become strong, independent and, for the most part, confident and achieving women.

My sisters, Robin and Vivienne, and I have been through much together. With only a few hiccups, we have consistently acted as listening posts, absorbent shoulders, and friends for life. For each other we have offered unsolicited but well-meaning, and infuriating but mostly appropriate, advice and support in times of crisis and indecision. And we still do.

I read once about the 'Hansel and Gretel Phenomenon'. We probably fit that bill. Children who support each other and grow strong together as a result of having, what were so indelicately called, 'delinquent parents'. Happily, my parents weren't always delinquent. Father always took a leading role in parents and friends associations at our schools, and even Mother played an important part once or twice.

The time her impact on my future opportunities was most profound and helpful was towards the end of my second year in highschool. I had done very well in every subject; come top in most. This was pretty surprising as only 12 months earlier I had been in a remedial English course and was struggling in many others.

We are not sure what happened to effect the change. Maybe it was the fact that I finally went off the antihistamines that I'd been taking since I was a toddler. I consumed pink drops in water a few times a day from about age two to 12 as treatment for hives, hay fever, asthma, bronchitis, eczema and sundry food allergies. In those days, antihistamines made you very drowsy. I strongly suspect that I slept through primaryschool.

On the other hand it could have been that I finally broke the code of how to succeed at school. Or maybe, and I do think this had a lot to do with it, I was lucky enough to get a great teacher who believed in me. She was one of the first mature-age students, and she taught me in her first year out of training college. Her inspiring teaching had positive spin-offs for all my subjects, and it changed radically the course of my life.

Gwen Filbee was so keen. She saw no barriers to the kids in her class of strugglers developing a love of English literature and doing very well in exams. She had very high expectations of us and, as we now have educational research to support, we rose to those expectations. She made us read and read and read and then talk and write about what we had read. Mrs Filbee was so enthusiastic and encouraging that it was difficult for us not to get swept along by her fervour. She was the Escalante (the teacher of *Stand and Deliver* fame) of Claremont High School in Hobart.

She made us read and read and read and then talk and write about what we had read.

For us, she stuck her neck out. When we all got higher marks for English literature than anyone had thought possible in such a group and the leniency of her marking system was questioned, she invited an external reassessment of the students' exam papers. The case was settled when the second marker recommended an increase in some of the final marks – and no decreases.

But coming top in that class was, temporarily at least, a mixed blessing.

At the end of the year before, I had been streamed into a class that had me doing English, maths, science and so on, but specialising in commerce (basic book-keeping and cheque writing), home arts (delightful euphemism for cooking the inedible and sewing the unwearable) and art.

So in November of that year when I was dux of the class, the horrors of premature academic streaming were becoming all too clear. The principal took the view that as I had done well I could do advanced English with students in a more academic class, but I would have to stay in my regular class and do the lower level of all other subjects. He felt that I would not cope in advanced maths, physics, chemistry and so on. He didn't see it as problematic that with book-keeping, sewing, cooking and art as my major subjects and only basic maths and science, my schooling would almost certainly end at Year 10, and I would have been clearly shut out of every other employment option. The future was unpromising.

With Mrs Filbee's encouragement, I considered other possibilities. I will always be grateful to her, and to my mother who got sober and got her act together to argue with the school that I should be allowed to repeat Year 8 so that I could make different subject choices. Mother challenged the principal's less than flattering appraisal of my ability and agreed to take the responsibility if I found it all too much and buckled under the strain. His conscience clear, I was free to make the most major choice in my career: the choice that made possible all my later achievements and most of the opportunities that have since opened up.

It doesn't bear thinking about what life would have held for me had I not had the support of those two very different women at that critical time. Fewer than seven percent of Australians went on to university in those days; even lower was the percentage of Tasmanian girls who went on. We all know how many bright young women left school at 15 and 16 in those days to be underemployed in a bank or in a department store. And we'll never know what the neglect of that reservoir of talent and energy cost the individuals and the community.

There were three other times in my life when I believe there was a very clear fork in the road I was travelling. To take one route would have been, if not disaster, then certainly a major setback. And to take the other, although initially very painful or demanding, would open doors and unleash possibilities. In each choice, I was helped enormously by other people: one, the aunt of my closest friend, and the other, Bill Mollison, better known for inventing permaculture. He has established sustainable agriculture systems all around the world and won the Alternative Nobel Prize for his achievements. He has made many previously poor and weakened communities self-sufficient. On a much smaller scale, he did something similar for me.

I found myself on the streets – with no place to live and my clothes in cartons.

On 22 April 1970, I found myself on the streets – with no place to live and my clothes in cartons. The violence at home had escalated and Mother issued my dismissal orders. At 7.30 am, and with only an hour's notice, my friend Beth's Auntie Kath took me in as a boarder. She was a widow of limited means and yet she charged only $9.50 per week full board. A pittance, even then. Her spontaneous altruism prevented a child of promise from becoming homeless and a drop-out. It was a very practical intervention and one I will never forget.

I took up parttime housework and continued sewing for money but it couldn't pay all the costs of board, books, bus fares, fees, clothes, and so on. That's when Bill Mollison stepped in. At the time he was my tutor in psychology at the University of Tasmania. He lobbied the local federal MP in the McMahon Coalition government to have the rules changed regarding the payment of living-away-from-home allowance to Commonwealth scholarship holders. He argued, citing the circumstances of me and one other woman as test cases, that if, because of family violence, it was impossible for us to live at home, we should not have to wait the usual two years to qualify for the support (only $22 per week but nearly enough to live on in 1970).

He succeeded. And the two of us, who would almost certainly have had to abandon our studies otherwise, finished our degrees and went on to employment and paying taxes and to returning something of the community's investment in us.

Another critical point was in 1971 and also involved Bill. I had less than three months to go of my BA. I had done pretty well in my courses to that point, considering the incessant background noise of threat, counter threat and Father's imminent bankruptcy. But by the end of second term it all got too much for me. I wanted to quit university.

I don't really know why I wanted to quit then rather than much earlier in the course. As I said, I wasn't failing. Those keen to psychologise might say that I baulked at the prospect of finally being free to leave the family chaos and Tasmania. Fear of flying? Fear of success? Who knows? But, the feeling was strong and I needed help if I was to go the last lap.

Fear of flying? Fear of success? Who knows?

Bill Mollison encouraged me first to take a short rest from study. Then I was ordered to front up at his office every day at around 4.00 pm to review my study program, plan the next steps and, more importantly, cross the date off the calendar. With a combination of encouragement, practical aid and bullying, he dragged me across the line.

I didn't get great marks, but I didn't fail. And I did win a lucrative scholarship to study in Canberra. Bill Mollison never doubted me and my ability and backed that up with action and not a little of his time.

I have said it to him directly, but I'd like to say it publicly too. At a crucial time in my life, I learned to trust again. I handed the reins of my life over to a person who knew that that was what was needed. He cared for me better than I could have cared for myself. And, unlike so many other people who offer help to people in need, he knew just when to stop.

About three months later, I left Tasmania, my life back in my own hands. I had taken a brief break from the burden of making choices and motivating myself, and had been fortunate enough to have a friend who would pick up my burden without any ceremony, fuss or wish for payment or gratitude. But I felt much gratitude then and I still do.

There have been other times since 1971 when I have lost direction and made – or nearly made – odd decisions with potentially huge adverse repercussions.

It was late in 1973, and I was soon to be married. For me, Canberra had been such a depressing and lonely place. I was very vulnerable to getting into a relationship, any relationship, to fill the emotional space that had been occupied by my sisters and close friends who by that time were spreading out, as Tasmanians do, all over the world.

My would-be marriage to Frank was a truly bad match. That was obvious to me only a short time after we broke up. And before that it was obvious to a number of my friends in Canberra and even some of my family. But somehow I lost the plot. I didn't see it. I think that in my effort to show that I was going to really try to make a relationship work and not be like my parents who had abandoned all attempts, I stuck too long at the impossible. Knowing when to leave is a very important skill to develop. I'm getting better at it. And I learnt a lot of what I know in that regard at that time.

> *Knowing when to leave is a very important skill to develop. I'm getting better at it.*

The fact that so many of my friends saw what I didn't, didn't mean that they had the effrontery, honesty, courage (kindness?) to tell me what they saw. Most people wouldn't bother. There's usually not a lot to gain and much to lose by confronting a friend on such basic questions. But there was one who risked it. Kerry Symons turned to me one day about two weeks before I was to be married, and said: 'You've changed. And I don't like it.' Such a bold statement deserved some kind of response. Feebly, I asked: 'How?' And out it all came.

I seemed to have lost my sense of humour. I was sad, depressed, no fun to be with. More than anything, I was cautious and diffident about the simplest decisions.

I couldn't argue with any of that. I had been almost my usual self when I met and attracted Frank – outgoing, confident, funny, pretty good company. But once we were 'an item', my being like that made him feel uncomfortable and jealous. It isn't an original story. Rather, it is one that is played out in couples all the time. It is a natural outcome of a system that values women as property and trophies. I wanted to do what I thought was the right thing to keep the peace. So I had tried to become the kind of person that I thought Frank wanted – meek, accommodating, quiet, uninteresting to any other man.

I am none of these things – humourless, diffident, meek, accommodating, quiet. But I had become, as the saying goes, a shadow of my former self. Although it was a pretty big shadow – I had put on three stone in weight!

Kerry spoke clearly and I knew she meant only to help me. She offered me a mirror and a chance to see what I had become. I took it. With just 10 days to go, I cancelled. The ceremony, the cake, the flowers, the reception. The lot. The guests were uninvited (or is it disinvited?). I stopped making the dress. A friend whipped the icing decoration off the cake and found that it came up quite nicely six weeks later as a Christmas cake. That same friend, Jenny, came with me to remove my possessions from the flat. Through a veil of tears shed not so much for a lost love but for a dead dream, we packed clothes, records, books, canisters, odds and ends and my few sticks of furniture. I went to stay with another friend, and life, of a kind, began again.

Throughout my life, I have been fortunate: blessed with strong and honest friends who have offered support and wisdom at times when I needed both. My friendships have always been central to me, and when deciding how to spend my time, being with friends has always been a high priority. I can't be sure, but I think that most would probably say that I give as much as I get from my friendships.

Some relationships are unequal in the sense that the support always seems to flow one way. Then something happens, the friend calls on you in a crisis and you know that you have been able to return some of the support and insight that she (it is usually *she*) has given you. For me, two such friends are Deb and Beryl. They are the kind who give and give to so many people, always thinking of others, cooking treats, offering assistance, being calm and reassuring: 'Keeping their heads when all about them are losing theirs.'

One occasion, in particular, stands out in my mind. We had three-month-old twins. We had just moved house, the renovations and major house extension had just begun, it was mid-winter, Bill was at work, the day had been very long and I was at rock-bottom. The doorbell rang. Grumping about this additional demand on my depleted resources, I answered the call. There stood Deb, casserole in one hand so I did not have to cook that night and a cake to offer any guests who might drop in. Well, like any self-respecting distraught suburban mother of two babies who has just opened the door to Mother Theresa, I cried, overwhelmed with her kindness.

> *Well, like any self-respecting distraught suburban mother of two babies who has just opened the door to Mother Theresa, I cried...*

Although I've never seen her quite as close to dropping her bundle as I was to dropping mine at that time, Deborah's thoughtfulness and generosity, when she had three young kids of her own, showed me that she knew how I felt and what I needed. These are moments of truth and moments to treasure in a friendship.

Close women friends, in particular, have been there for me through all my high points and low points. And there seem to have been an unusually large number of those in my life.

Beth McLaughlin was my closest friend. Through knowing her, I grew stronger and, if not strode, then certainly clambered out of the quagmire of distorted feelings, mistrust, and perverted loyalties that was my family. I miss her still.

Other friends have been there for me when Beth was killed in 1977, when I had a near-fatal car accident myself, when Father died, when Pat Brotherton, my PhD supervisor and friend was killed, also in a car crash, when I was retrenched in the recession of the 1990s. They shared happy times too: when I married in 1977, when I was coming to terms with having twins at 37, when I finally finished my study ... The list goes on.

Apart from playing a reciprocal role for my friends: being available when their relationships were becoming marriages or becoming history, providing support when they had to make hard choices, offering a place to live, a refuge for months, or just another perspective in a crisis, I have tried to do for other people, what people (usually women, but not always) have done for me.

In my teaching career, I count among my most satisfying times those when I was able to help unconfident students see that they had ability and that they could aspire to more than they had previously thought possible. I have put myself out in a way similar to that which Bill Mollison did for me. Coaxed, cajoled, encouraged and dragged a capable but flagging student or three over the hurdle of lost motivation. They tell me they would have dropped out if I had not been so insistent, even intrusive.

Coaxed, cajoled, encouraged and dragged a capable but flagging student or three over the hurdle of lost motivation.

In one case, a young student who was very intelligent and a gifted artist was struggling with the burdens of a rejecting mother and living in poverty away from her friends and siblings in the country. She was coming to class less and less often and was getting more enmeshed in a drug and binge-drinking culture. Another of my students had committed suicide some months earlier and, irrationally, I believed that I should have seen the signs. But this time I was alert to signs of detachment and self-destructive behaviours.

So over almost a year, I spent many hours with Margaret, listening, talking, supporting. As a 'thank you' she painted me a large portrait of Charlie Chaplin. It is a portrait so large that it takes up most of one wall. On the day she came to install it in our home, we talked some more about her having dropped out of college and what lay ahead. She was still deeply troubled and a real worry to me, because she was getting into increasingly dangerous situations involving violence, alcohol and car accidents, drugs and police.

On that day, she came to the house, hung the picture and stayed for nine months. Bill, my husband, and I found her easy to have around the place, and with both of us she found a kind of peace and acceptance that she had never known. She went for nearly 60 jobs, mainly menial, but was considered over or underqualified. After a long time on the dole, I made her my research assistant, a role she fulfilled effortlessly.

Later, ironically, the department of social security offered her a job. She was soon promoted and, 10 years later, she took longservice leave. It has hardly been the career of a liberated artist. But she is alive, in a happy longterm relationship and her painting and drawing continue to develop.

We did not make a habit of taking in 'at-risk' students and friends, but we did do it a few times and it seemed to be helpful and an important part of a healing process for them.

I have really appreciated the practical support that so many people have offered me. Words of empathy and sympathy are helpful too, but doing something and not being put off by an initial lukewarm response have been the most powerful evidence of their commitment to me as a person. It isn't surprising that I offer the same sort of support to others.

In another context, I am proud of the fact that after having worked with me, almost all my secretaries and support staff say they are more confident. Because I have encouraged their development and created opportunities for them to build new work skills and become more assertive, they now feel able to seek jobs with more challenge, complexity and responsibility – and money.

I am proud of the fact that after having worked with me, almost all my secretaries and support staff say they are more confident.

Jean Russell did the same for me. She opened up a world of opportunities for me when in 1987 she asked me to lead an important committee in the Australian Psychological Society. Jean was a general manager in the Victorian Ministry of Education. In a type of initiative that has in the past been more associated with men because they occupied the positions that made it possible, she used her network to fill the voluntary position. At the same time she increased the skills and the career possibilities for me, the person she chose. I went on to become the national president of the organisation in 1992, and initiated and drove a major organisational refocus and restructure of the society. Since its formation as an independent organisation in 1966, I was the third women and the first female practitioner to head the society. Without Jean's encouragement and practical assistance, it wouldn't have happened. It would all have seemed too hard, a position destined to be taken by someone else – probably a man.

Frequently, I reflect on how much having the support and confidence of others has energised me to try something new. I am sure this is what has led me to encourage others – women in particular – to be players and not just spectators.

White Knuckles and Strong Women

Val Marsden

Val Marsden was born in 1938 in Geelong, Victoria, where she went to school then began her working life as a typist/secretary. Her paid employment was mainly in the private sector, until she joined the public service in Western Australia in 1984, moving into management as first coordinator of the Western Australian Women's Information and Referral Exchange (WIRE). In mid-1987 she was seconded to a policy officer position in the (then) Women's Interests Division of the Western Australian Department of Premier and Cabinet, in January 1988 moving to the post of senior policy officer in the Directorate of Equal Opportunity in Public Employment, then in May 1993 taking up the position of senior policy officer – EEO, in the education department.

In 1988 Val Marsden was the Women's Electoral Lobby (WEL) nominee on the Third National Women's Consultative Council (a federal government advisory body) and in September 1990 she was appointed convenor of the Fourth National Women's Consultative Council as well as being appointed to the National Committee on Violence Against Women for a three-year term. Amongst her many other activities, particularly being active in the Women's Electoral Lobby (WEL) in Queensland and Western Australia since 1972, she has raised two children on her own.

I was born into an anxious world. For the west, 1938 was a time of increasing tensions in Europe. In the Chinese calendar 1938 was the Year of the Tiger. In Europe it was another year of turmoil, of fear and unfounded optimism as Hitler tightened his stranglehold and the rest of the world tried to pretend it wasn't happening. Later that year Victoria had troubles of its own as a long searing hot summer erupted into devastating bushfires at the beginning of 1939 and the term 'Black Friday' was coined.

In the fashion of the times I was born at home, home being a small weatherboard house in what is now an inner suburb of one of Victoria's major provincial cities, Geelong.

While my family was workingclass, my father had a permanent job. Therefore, we always had a roof over our heads, enough to eat and, within the narrow range of consumer goods available in this pre-mass production era, never wanted for anything. By today's standards, there was a general level of poverty which meant that I grew up without being conscious of being poor in a material sense, although that is not to say I wasn't aware of class distinctions.

Geelong was the 'gateway to the Western District' – rich pastoral and grazing areas of Western Victoria. The produce of these areas was shipped through Geelong to interstate and international destinations. Annual wool sales were held in Geelong and the fortunes of the city were intimately linked to the wealth of the farming community.

In this western part of Victoria (first settled in 1834), lived many old families whose wealth was passed down from generation to generation and added to by carefully arranged marriages. The children of these unions attended the private schools in Geelong (of which there were four – two for boys and two for girls). These schools had established international reputations and produced politicians, and civic and business leaders, and their future wives. Yet the incomes of the majority of the breadwinners of Geelong came from work in the factories, and most of the population was workingclass.

This unusual sociological mix meant that we were surrounded on all sides by the evidence of wealth and privilege, and the values of that class prevailed – it meant for many of us never feeling 'good enough'; we could never hope to be part of that society which was so evident all around us. It was no wonder I grew up fully aware that the prevailing view of Australia as a classless society was a myth.

I was the third child in a family of four, and there were about four-and-a-half years between first and last child. My older brother was an asthmatic. At about six months he was hospitalised with pneumonia and the asthma followed. At the age of 24 he died during an asthma attack.

My brother's chronic illness affected the rest of the family in ways I didn't recognise for many years. The need to keep him from getting 'overexcited' and being launched into another bout of asthma with more days off school and possible hospitalisation, meant that excessive displays of emotion – happy or sad – were frowned upon. I vividly recall my sister and myself being asked by my father, when a holiday was being planned, not to let our brother know about the holiday in case he got sick and then none of us could go. For me, that emotional constraint has meant an inability to show excitement or joy or anger, or even to recognise those feelings until well after the event. On the other hand, it has also meant that at times of crisis I'm able to keep a cool head and continue to function.

I grew up in the 1950s, a decade of stifling conformity. Anything 'different' was suspect; any behaviour outside a very narrow definition of 'normal' could become the subject of gossip and character assassination. The pressures on women to conform to a narrow definition of womanhood were strong and the sanctions against those who did not conform especially severe.

The 1950s was the decade when women were actively encouraged back into the home after enjoying a measure of freedom during the war. Then, they had been offered incentives to participate in the paidworkforce, such as childcare, fare concessions, free clothing and medical and dental benefits. In 1950, child endowment was introduced to encourage more childbearing. The same magazines which during the war had carried stories of women courageously doing their bit for the war effort – driving trucks, working in the munitions factories – now carried articles on famous and glamorous women, advertisements for beauty products, and romantic stories where the woman ended in the man's arms and in front of the kitchen sink.

These were my formative years. Those early influences – external anxieties caused by the war, and the internal, family anxieties made me an anxious and reserved child. I became a timid, quiet, sensitive adolescent; not the kind of girl to push the boundaries or even to challenge them. I had to wait another 20 years before I got the courage to do that. However, women, including both my grandmothers, figured prominently in my life in those years. They provided me with a storehouse of memories of role models I was able to draw on later.

Both my grandfathers died long before I was born. My father's father died when my father was about six years old. My mother's father died when my mother was in her early twenties. Neither grandmother ever re-married. My paternal grandmother – whose name of Maude was, early on, affectionately shortened to Ma by everybody – lived in Ballarat. She kept a boardinghouse in Lyons Street at the time I was a child. Having been widowed so early in life (in the days before the widow's pension) she managed a café, cooked for others and kept boardinghouses in order to feed her children. She not only brought them up, she also brought up grandchildren when my Aunt (Ruby – after whom I get my middle name) died of tuberculosis, leaving two small daughters. Ruby's husband went off to the war in Papua New Guinea and never returned; whether it was because he was a casualty or because he chose not to I've never known, but I suspect the latter. Ma later played a large role in the upbringing of the children of the grandchildren she had reared. Their mothers went out to work at a time when commercial childcare centres were practically non-existent and Ma was there to take care of the children. She also spent a lot of time with us as children during our frequent visits to her home in Ballarat.

Ma was a big woman, tall, raw-boned and heavy. An accident as a young girl had left her with one leg shorter than the other and she walked with a limp, using a stick for support. This stick was almost another arm for her. It had a hook at one end which she used to great effect when she wanted to grab one of her grandchildren or, later, greatgrandchildren, as they fought and tumbled and scrambled about her. Her immobility was no handicap. Indeed, for us children it was an asset; because of it she was one adult who was always accessible to us, even if her stories sometimes gave us nightmares and we feared her anger when we misbehaved. She lived well into her eighties and was a much-loved figure of my childhood.

My mother's mother – whose name was Emily but who was to us simply 'Grandma Hancock' – lived in Queenscliff, on Corio Bay not far from Geelong, with my mother's older brother. He was a widower without children and my grandmother lived with him until she became too frail for him to look after, when she came to live with us.

This meant we had seven people living in what was really a two-bedroom house, not a particularly happy arrangement when the occupants spanned three generations but somehow we managed. This was, I suspect, largely due to my mother's ability to be a peacemaker.

I was, like most girls growing up in the 1950s, socialised into believing that a woman's destiny was to be a wife and mother, to be a passenger and never to take the driving seat. I believed that women who remained single and/or childless were to be pitied. Single women were 'old maids'; 'on the shelf', failures because they had been unable to score life's greatest prize – a man. For women, the single state was never seen in a positive light, by men or women.

... socialised into believing that a woman's destiny was to be a wife and mother, to be a passenger and never to take the driving seat.

However, for me the socialisation wasn't entirely complete; I had always believed there had to be more to life than marriage and children. (A Peggy Lee song of the times seemed to say it all: 'Is that all there is?') I knew and secretly admired a number of women who although unmarried seemed to live happy and fulfilled lives: they seemed to me to lead much more interesting lives than any of the married women I knew. But my admiration of them was more wistful than wishful; I couldn't identify with them enough to see how I could emulate them. For someone who needed to conform, to 'fit in', to have as the only alternative role models women who had no status, meant to have no role models at all.

I began my working life at 16 as a secretary, not because I had a burning ambition to type other people's letters, but because there wasn't a lot of choice for girls in those days. Teacher, nurse, secretary, shop-girl or factory hand – those were the limits of choice for us then.

I didn't like the idea of cleaning up after sick people or standing up in front of nasty teenagers (I was one) or working in a noisy, dirty factory all day. My older sister was already a secretary, which meant I at least had some idea of what the job entailed. Clearly I had none whatsoever of what the others involved, so I went to business college and, in the words of Patrick White in *The Tree of Man*, 'became efficient'.

In those days women didn't have a career, we just had a job that would fill in the time between leaving school and getting married and having children: that was our *real* career.

What *I* really wanted to do was go to university. Since my knowledge of university and what one did there was even sketchier than my knowledge of what nurses and teachers did, I didn't know what I would do when I got there or after I finished, but I loved school and loved learning and that was an end in itself.

> I loved school and loved learning and that was an end in itself.

I enjoyed school. Amongst those single women I admired were some of my teachers. I went to an all-girls secondary school and had the privilege of being taught by some wonderful women. At that time the principal of the school was a woman. To us this didn't seem cause for comment, but it must have been quite unusual.

Unfortunately, university was out of the question geographically, economically and socially. In any case I was a timid teenager, finding it easier to retreat into books and live vicariously than to fight to make my own dreams come true. My one form of protest at the limited future laid out for me as a woman was to travel for a few years before finally succumbing to marriage.

Looking back over the early part of my life, it seems that the people I hold dearest in my memory are women – my grandmothers, my mother and my teachers. The only man in my life was my father – a rather stern and remote figure who left home before I got up and got home after dark. I was somewhat in awe of him but envied him his freedom and the broader horizons of men. I think, for that reason, I really would have preferred to be a man. While in retrospect it's women I remember, at the time I thought women's lives were pretty dull and boring on the whole and I couldn't see anything very positive in being one.

In my next phase, I was to become the classic 'disappearing woman'. I married later than most of my contemporaries. If I'd had any way of realising my own dreams I would probably not have married at all. However, in 1965, aged 26, I became a wife. It was the convention in those days to address a married woman as 'Mrs John Smith' or 'Mrs John Brown'. I knew nothing about feminism but I baulked at losing both my family name and my first name. Plain commonsense told me it was absurd.

Having moved from Melbourne to Queensland then to Sydney, we decided, in 1972, to give Queensland another try. By now I was in my mid-thirties with two children and had begun to feel that as a person I had disappeared – I had gone from being somebody's daughter to somebody's wife to somebody's mother without ever being somebody in my own right. Marriage and children were supposed to be all women wanted; they were supposed to fulfil all our dreams. So why wasn't I fulfilled? What was wrong with me? My vague teenage feelings of unease that a future containing only marriage and children lack something – came back to haunt me.

It was about this time that a woman – Elizabeth Dryden – came to the Gold Coast where I was then living and the local newspaper published an interview with her. In the article she talked about how she wanted to start a branch of a women's group, the Women's Electoral Lobby (WEL), which had recently formed in Melbourne. What Elizabeth had to say so stirred me that I was on the phone immediately, finding out details of the first meeting. That was the beginning of a 20-year association with WEL.

Although Elizabeth Dryden left the Gold Coast a short time after launching WEL and I've never seen or heard of her since, I'm forever in her debt because that was a turning point for me.

My involvement in WEL changed my life. For the first time I was able to share my experiences as a woman with other women and begin to find answers to the questions that seemed to have been in the back of my mind all my life – why were women so invisible? Why was it that what we did wasn't important? Why were we paid less than men?

It was through WEL that I became involved in many community issues. For example, early in 1973 a local doctor approached WEL with a request for help in starting a family planning clinic on the Gold Coast. The Family Planning Association (FPA) had been established in Brisbane in 1971 and in March 1972 the first clinic opened. Until WEL agreed to assist, the Southport doctor had met with little enthusiasm for establishing a clinic anywhere on the Gold Coast.

As with many of my other involvements, this was a case of being available at the right time. Another member of WEL, a nurse who had trained as a family planning nurse in England, was interested in working with the doctor to establish a clinic and I was coopted to help. I eventually became the administrator, but first we had to find premises and staff. Shirley, the nurse, located other nurses and doctors for sessional work and I found three small first-floor rooms in one of Southport's main streets which we were able to rent for consulting room, waitingroom and office. We scrubbed floors, painted walls, begged and borrowed furniture, and finally we were, with some misgivings, given the okay by Brisbane. The first clinic was held in September 1973 and initially the service operated for only one day a week. In time, it became a fulltime service and moved to larger premises. In 1991, the year the FPA Queensland celebrated its twentieth birthday, the premises were extended further to include separate education/lecture facilities. Some of the original staff are still involved.

My active involvement in women's issues has brought me great personal satisfaction and helped me develop many new skills. It led me finally to fulfil my childhood dream of not just going to university, but getting a degree – and incidentally proving to myself that I *was* 'good enough'.

My involvement in WEL was directly influential in a major career change and a significant factor in my relocating myself and my two children successfully to Perth in the late 1970s.

There were two reasons for my move to Perth – one was the death of my husband and the other the relocation of my employer.

My husband died in February 1976. The year that followed was a painful one. The support of women friends and the needs of my children were what kept me going. I had to get out of bed each day because my children needed me. I had to go to work too, but the demands of my children were what got my feet over the edge of the bed each day. When I emerged from the first haze of shock and grief I realised I didn't want to bring up two children on my own in south-east Queensland – specifically, the Gold Coast.

I had to get out of bed each day because my children needed me.

Packing up and moving on became crucial. Where to go was the problem. I didn't want to move to a large city, especially not one 'down south', although that was where I had family support. While the humidity of Queensland wasn't for me, the warmth was, and moving to a cold climate didn't appeal. I had also come to some decisions about how I wanted to spend the next few years. I could, I reasoned, spend them looking for another husband, or I could do something for myself. (I obviously saw these options as being mutually exclusive!) At 38, according to the statistics, my chances of finding a husband were fairly slim. I decided I wouldn't waste time on what might be a fruitless search. My marriage had been happy and I wasn't prepared to adopt an attitude of 'he'll do', settling for any man just so I could be accepted back into the world of couples. And, more importantly, I knew women who had managed to bring up children alone without sacrificing themselves in the process.

First, there were my two grandmothers. Both had been strong women living happy and fulfilled lives on their own (or at least without remarrying). Then, closer to home, a woman with whom I worked had been widowed at about the same age as I was. She had raised two children on her own, so I knew it was feasible.

When the firm with which I was working sought expressions of interest from staff who might like to move to Perth, where the company was re-establishing their operations, my hand shot up. I don't think the firm was expecting any of the secretarial staff to come forward – the offer had been to the men. To give them their due, once they recovered from their initial surprise, the firm was supportive and found a job for me in the Perth office. I had never been to Perth, knew no one there and knew only a few people who had even visited the place.

In the 1960s, enroute to England by passenger ship, I had stopped briefly at Fremantle, but had never made it to Perth. It seemed to me to be the chance of a lifetime, the chance to make a new start. But if the move was to succeed, I needed to know about the after-school care situation in Perth so that I could settle my children in. If they weren't happy, I wouldn't be able to settle.

My involvement in establishing an after-school centre at my children's primaryschool in Queensland meant I was aware that such services existed. Whether there were any in Perth was another matter. I used my contacts in WEL to find out and was delighted to discover that Perth had a co-ordinated program which had been in place for a number of years. It was run by an organisation called 'OSCCA' – the Out of School Child Care Association (incidentally begun by a woman – Marion Brockway). I discovered that there was also an after-school centre (not part of the OSCCA program) operating from a church across the road from Subiaco Primary School. As it happened, the centre was also open before school, a bonus I hadn't expected.

Armed with this knowledge I soon made up my mind – yes, we would move to Perth and so we did – in August 1977. Being able to get this information, so crucial to my being able to move across the country with two small children whilst keeping the disruption to their lives to a minimum, made me realise how important it was to have good information when making decisions.

I became active in WEL almost immediately after my arrival in Perth. My experiences and those of others made us very aware of the importance of getting policies in place that gave formal recognition to the needs of women. The first step in doing that was to get a women's adviser to the premier: someone who could provide a women's perspective to decision-making at the highest level. As well, we wanted consultation with women in the community so that the advice given could reflect the variety of women's experience. And, finally, we wanted somewhere for women to go to receive the kind of information needed to enable women to take control of their lives.

This didn't seem too much to ask, but it wasn't until the election of the Labor government in 1983 that we had any success. Very shortly after the election, the appointment of a women's adviser was proposed, as well as the establishment of the Women's Advisory Council (WAC).

Once WAC got underway, one of its first projects was establishing a women's information service. Many attempts had been made in Perth over the years to establish such a service. One had been run for some years by Women's Liberation from a small room in the old Padbury buildings in Forrest Place. Lack of money and burn-out on the part of the women who tried to keep the service going finally forced it to close. WEL itself had provided a telephone information service for some years. Both services simply scraped the surface of the need that was there, a need that had been recognised elsewhere through the establishment of a service called the 'Women's Information Switchboard' (or 'Switchboard' for short) in Adelaide, South Australia, some years before. The Women's Advisory Council, together with a consultant brought from Adelaide (Deborah McCulloch) and supportive women MPs, did the lobbying and groundwork to gain approval for the establishment of a Perth service, and early in 1984 it began to take shape.

The opportunity came for a change of direction. To work in such a service, with and for women, appealed to me enormously and when advertisements appeared for the staff – one coordinator and a number of information officers – I was interested. However, should I be successful in gaining a position, it would mean a career change. It was scary. I had been a secretary since the age of 16 and although I had felt for some years that I had grown out of the role, it was still a leap into the dark. But I didn't want to be an information officer. I wanted to be the coordinator, the person who made things happen. This meant an even greater leap. I had often talked and written about the unacknowledged and unappreciated skills of secretaries. Now I would have to prove it, and frankly at that stage I didn't believe a word of my own rhetoric. What I said about others was different from what I applied to myself.

I had often talked and written about the unacknowledged and unappreciated skills of secretaries. Now I would have to prove it ...

Like most women, I looked at the job description and focused on the things I couldn't do, rather than focusing on the things I could do, knowing that the gaps would be filled through experience. The insistence of a woman friend finally propelled me into applying. She nagged and prodded and finally said that if I didn't apply she would never speak to me again. In the face of that threat I applied for the position of coordinator and, to my delight (and terror), won the position.

Being involved in the Women's Information and Referral Exchange (WIRE) gave me the opportunity to bring together the knowledge I'd gained through my own experiences and to use that knowledge to help others. That was the basis on which WIRE was established – that women were able to take control of their lives if given access to the information they needed. The people who could best provide that information were other women.

The Women's Information and Referral Exchange (WIRE) was an overnight success. Women found the philosophy of women helping women, within a formal structure, supportive and empowering, and they poured in the doors. Staff dealt with over 3000 enquiries in the first six months of operation and for the next four years averaged around 18 000 enquiries each year.

What WIRE provided obviously tapped into a deep need. It was too good to last. The service was eventually brought down through the activities of a woman associated with WIRE (not a WIRE worker), who was charged and found guilty of misappropriation of investors' funds. The outrage and betrayal felt by all women became overshadowed by the politicisation of the issue, resulting in the closure of the service, which left Western Australian women without an essential resource.

The loss of WIRE meant the loss of a central focus for women's services. Housed in the same building as WIRE were a number of other coordinating bodies for women's services, including refuges and learning centres. With the closure of WIRE, those services were forced to find other premises. Fortunately, they did, but the interaction between them, which enhanced the ability of each to meet women's needs, was lost. The service replacing WIRE, staffed by only one officer, is a travesty of the original service.

Time for moving on arrived. When I first became involved in the Women's Movement, we had no idea of what we were taking on. Naively we believed that if we pointed out where discrimination and injustice to women occurred, those in power would feel compelled to set things right. One of the problems with being shut out of power and excluded from decision-making is that there is no opportunity to learn about power and how decisions are made. What we did not appreciate, back in the early 1970s, was the power of male culture.

In 1988 I came to the conclusion that just goodwill wasn't enough to make things happen for women. By then we had equal opportunity and anti-discrimination legislation at state and federal levels and it seemed to me that, with this to support us, some real changes could be made.

It was for this reason I decided to make another career change. I applied for, and won, a policy position in the Office of the Director of Equal Opportunity in Public Employment (ODEOPE), the body established to assist the public sector in implementing equal opportunity for its workforce.

The director at that time was Liz Bredemeyer, a former president of the Women's Advisory Council. We quickly found we had similar views on many issues and Liz became a personal friend and also my mentor. She gave generously of herself and her experience to assist me in making the transition from an operational to a policy role. On many occasions since, she has used her knowledge and skills to help me and other women. For example, she set up mock interviews to help us in applying for other jobs. Knowing how this has assisted me, I've tried to pass on what I've learned to other women in the same way.

A chance remark by another women friend finally thrust me into university. Through WIRE I came to know the (then) librarian in charge of the Western Australian State Library's information service, Infolink – Kate Haslam. Through Kate I discovered there was an alternative adult university admission process and that, if I were accepted, I could study externally. I sat the test, which required me to answer some multiple choice questions and/or write an essay. Being the anxious person I am, I decided to do both to maximise my chances. Within several months I received an offer of a place and a few weeks after that my letterbox began to fill with lecture notes, study guides and assignments.

Looking back over some of my essays and the journal writings I was required to keep in some of the subjects, I'm struck by the excitement with which I tackled study in those early years. I went through a spurt in intellectual growth that was the most exciting and rewarding I had ever experienced. As an external student I had no access to the interaction between student and lecturer or other students that is such a vital part of the university experience, but at the time this was an added challenge for me: any discoveries I made were *mine*.

It took me 11 years to get my BA, but I didn't feel that was such a disadvantage. It meant that in the later years I was reading papers, books and journal articles which were discussing contemporary issues and involved up-to-the-minute debates. Later in my study I was able to tackle topics which didn't exist, or were not the subject of academic writing, when I began.

Whilst I was slowly working my way through my studies, my children completed their own schooling.

Whilst I was slowly working my way through my studies, my children completed their own schooling. Both began university; my daughter graduated as a secondary school teacher. Friends, too, began (and finished) studying fulltime, while I plodded on. In 1990 I was lucky enough to be able to become an internal student at last. Then, in 1991, on leave from my job, I could take on a halftime study load as an internal student. That was a satisfying year. In 1992, I completed my final unit and nothing would have stopped me from turning up at the graduation ceremony in 1993 to be handed that all-important piece of paper – my graduation certificate.

Then came a real chance to give something back. In 1988 WEL nominated me for membership of the Third National Women's Consultative Council (NWCC). I was thrilled and excited when the nomination was accepted and I was appointed: here was an opportunity to do something for other women at the national level.

I found my two years on the Third NWCC a rewarding experience. We tackled many issues, among them ratification of ILO (International Labour Organisation) Convention 156, dealing with workers with family responsibilities. This was an issue of particular significance to me. From my own experience I knew how difficult it is to balance work and family responsibilities.

For some time considerable pressure had been placed by women's groups on the federal government to ratify ILO 156. With increasing numbers of women in the paidworkforce, it was becoming obvious that they were suffering under the double burden of their paidwork and unpaidwork. The NWCC was influential in having the government focus on this issue. In March 1990 a one-day conference was held in Melbourne to promote public awareness of the ILO Convention. The conference coincided with an announcement by the federal government that ratification would go ahead.

As a consequence, the NWCC produced two valuable publications about the convention. One was designed to help women to understand what ILO 156 was all about, and the other (published by the Fourth NWCC) pulled together the papers delivered at the conference.

At the end of the third council's term I was asked to convene the fourth council. I was thrilled but terrified: all my old self-doubt and insecurities came rushing to the surface. I recall a dream, just after I had accepted the offer, in which I was sitting atop a tram which was careering down a hill. Clinging on for dear life, I was trying to keep it under control. Here was my subconscious, expressing terror at my leading such an important body.

> *I was thrilled but terrified: all my old self-doubt and insecurities came rushing to the surface.*

As it turned out, convening the Fourth NWCC for the first 18 months of its term (work commitments prevented me from staying on for the full three years) was a rewarding and exhilarating, if exhausting, experience. In many ways it was not unlike my dream! I owe a debt of gratitude to the women on the council who gave so generously of their time and expertise. I am particularly indebted to my deputy, Lydia Philippou, who was unstinting in her support and encouragement and whose formidable skills contributed significantly to the success of the council.

One of the issues I was keen to pursue during my term as convenor was that of the implications for women of enterprise bargaining. Work on a conference to draw out these implications began under my leadership and came to fruition under the leadership of my successor, Kaye Loder. That women could have a raw deal under a de-centralised industrial relations system, unless certain safeguards were put in place, was of concern to me. Whilst unions had identified many of the potential problems, the subject needed a specific women's focus.

Other issues we examined during my time as convenor were employer-sponsored childcare; women and the environment; women and housing; and the measurement of the value of the unpaidwork of women through time-use surveys conducted by the Australian Bureau of Statistics (ABS).

Through my membership of the NWCC I became a community member of the National Committee on Violence Against Women (NCVAW). One of the rewards of being involved in the Women's Movement over many years has been the acceptance into the mainstream of issues once considered private and the responsibility of individuals: childcare, violence against women, and sexual harassment.

The establishment of the NCVAW was therefore a major breakthrough. Its work culminated in the development of a national strategy on violence against women, contained in a document launched by the prime minister, Paul Keating. The policy is at government level and at assisting service providers around Australia to work collaboratively in the elimination of all violence against women.

When the NCVAW wound up in June 1993 I was appointed to a taskforce established by the Western Australian chief justice, David Malcolm, to examine 'gender bias' in the law. Work in Canada on helping the judiciary to deal in a less biased way with women and Indigenous people in the courts was influential. I had come across much material on the subject during my final year at university and been excited by what was happening. The chief justice was impressed with the Canadian initiatives, and this was significant in his establishing the taskforce. My appointment to the taskforce gave me an opportunity to use the knowledge and experience I had gained through my studies, and my involvement in the NCVAW and the NWCC, to assist women at the state level.

... my life so far seems to have been teetering between confidence and a longing for the limelight, and agonising self-doubt.

Reflecting on what's gone before, I see that my life so far seems to have been teetering between confidence and a longing for the limelight, and agonising self-doubt. Whenever success seemed within my reach I would be racked by feelings of inadequacy. It is as if there is another person inside always dragging me down, keeping me from enjoying my triumphs.

Once, in a workshop, I described my attitude to life as being similar to that of people who are afraid of flying: the so-called 'white knuckle brigade' – those people whose fear makes them grip the arms of the seat until their knuckles show white. They're afraid that if they relax their vigilance for a second, the plane might fall out of the sky. Well, I said to the group, that's how I live my life: in a constant state of anxiety, feeling that only by worrying about everything will I keep disaster at bay.

Fortunately for me, at crucial times in my life, when my knuckles have been at their whitest and when that negative person inside has been doing her best to hold me back, I've had the support and encouragement of some remarkable women. They have given generously of themselves, their knowledge and their skills. At all the important turning points in my life, it has been women who have helped me to overcome my fears and the demons of self-doubt threatening to drag me under. I'm very grateful to them. If I have been able in the past to return some of that generosity I'm glad; I hope to be able to continue to do so.

Neither Singularly Saints Nor Sinners

Kay Saunders

Kay Saunders was born in Brisbane in 1947. Educated at the University of Queensland where she was awarded an honours degree in anthropology and sociology and a doctorate in history and anthropology, she is now reader in history and has authored seven books, most notably *Race Relations in Colonial Queensland* (1975, 1988, 1992); *Gender Relations in Australia* (1992), co-edited with Raymond Evans; *War on the Homefront* (1993); and *Aboriginal Workers* (1995) co-edited with Ann McGrath and Jackie Huggins.

Like many of her generation active in the anti-Viet Nam war and anti-conscription movements as well as the Women's Liberation movement, Kay Saunders later became an official prison visitor to the Women's Prison in Brisbane. She is currently director of the National Australia Day Council, and council member of the Australian War Memorial and Australian National Maritime Museum.

Kay Saunders has one daughter, Erin Evans, born in 1970, and was one of the first women to be awarded a Commonwealth Industry Scholarship.

In 1993 Jackie Huggins asked me to read the manuscript of her mother's biography, Aunty Rita. *We discussed how, despite the vast differences in our lives emanating from our class and racial origins, we who shared the same birthday had so much in common – our early lives were dominated by the effects of our fathers' injuries sustained in the second world war and by our mothers' pathological reactions to loss and grief. I told Jackie how I felt extraordinary shame about my earlier life and admired her courage and forthrightness in confronting deeply disturbing past events. I wondered if I possessed that honesty and bravery. As we concluded this discussion we began talking about how important it is to be a good mother – caring, wise and forgiving – and how we both hope we lived up to that ideal. We left the manuscript behind and joined our children. My adult daughter, Erin, was reading a magazine and Jackie's son, John Henry aged seven, was playing with his toys. Together we affirmed our beliefs about our responsibilities as mothers and the joy that role had given us. But for Jackie's generosity and encouragement on that day – and on so many others in the past – I might have described my life through a conventional narrative, beginning when a degree of my professional success was first identified, then simply charting its subsequent linear route.*

My father, Eric Saunders, gave me a lot of encouragement accompanied by intense pressure to achieve well academically. His father, Frank, had read English at Cambridge University in England; his uncle Ernest was a lecturer there and his uncle Cecil had been a senior engineer for the Anglo-Persian Oil Company (later BP). His cousin, Mollie, had studied chemical engineering in the 1930s although she suffered an enormous professional handicap by virtue of her sex. My father often talked about his grandmothers, Louise Bass Saunders and Harriet Watts Sizer, who had been active members of the Women's Christian Temperance Union (WCTU) in Cambridge, suffragettes and fervent supporters of Emmeline Pankhurst. His mother Florence Sizer Saunders was in the WCTU in Queensland and an active supporter of her brother, Hubert Sizer, a leading conservative politician from 1917 to 1940. Uncle Hubert led the pro-conscription campaign in Queensland in 1917.

His cousin, Mollie, had studied chemical engineering in the 1930s although she suffered an enormous professional handicap by virtue of her sex.

Like my father, these ancestors subscribed uncritically to notions of British racial and cultural superiority. Not surprisingly, given their conservative politics, they were extraordinarily antagonistic to the labour movement and the workingclass. In retrospect I see that these people whom, apart from Uncle Hubert, I never met, were crucial in my development, although I rejected their ideological world view. My strong puritanism and belief in the work ethic emanates from them and perhaps, as my story will show, were my salvation.

My mother, Elizabeth Walsh Saunders, came from an entirely different background. Her father, Peter Walsh, was an Irish navvy on the North Queensland railways, her Scots Catholic mother, Elizabeth Duff Walsh, had been a barmaid in Charters Towers. My mother was born in a tent on the rough mining settlement in the remote Duchess field. At seven she had been sent to Brisbane for her education and went to live with her Aunt Catherine who had married a wealthy German businessman, Oswald Englander. She went from extreme poverty to a house with several servants and a cultivated European atmosphere. As a child my favourite person was my Uncle Oswald who was, in effect, my putative grandfather. He encouraged my interest in primitive cultures and spoke at great length about his impressive collection of Chinese, Japanese and Indian antiques. His suicide, after a bankruptcy in 1956, effectively shattered my life. My mother had a severe breakdown and withdrew totally into a solitary world of tears, and his wife, Catherine, left in the house denuded of its magnificent furniture, antiques and paintings, went spectacularly insane.

With my father's constant trips to Greenslopes Repatriation Hospital on top of all this, I felt extremely isolated and unable to communicate my grief. I spent as much time as I could with our neighbours, the Sue-Tins, who had come from Hong Kong. Their house bustled with life – Chinese operas playing loudly on the hi-fi, voices shouting and laughing. Mrs Sue-Tin was totally unlike any woman I'd ever met. To the disgust of our middleclass suburb, she once showed a group of workmen how to push a wheelbarrow full of bricks. In her estimation, Australian work practices no doubt left much to be desired. But unlike an anglo-Australian household, she supervised extensions to their house and negotiated with the workmen as well as running the household with five children, whereas, as was quite clear to me from observations about my family, middleclass anglo-women were financially and socially dependent upon men. Lady-like adornments of music, playing bridge and making tapestries were their chief occupations. I strove to be independent and not simply decorative, well-dressed and well-married.

> ... she supervised extensions to their house and negotiated with the workmen as well as running the household with five children.

The tragic implications of women's dependency were forced upon me in a traumatic manner. Catherine became increasingly disturbed and her main conversation was about God's instructions to her. I hated having to visit Catherine, especially when I had to do it alone. At the Anglican organisation to which I belonged, the Girls' Friendly Society, visiting the sick and needy was highly stressed. My father regularly reinforced my duty to visit my kin. This was an intolerable burden to a child of only nine and ten. In 1958, when I was almost 11 years old, Catherine attempted to kill me as she believed God wished to preserve my purity and this could be accomplished only by my death. When I ran terrified to a neighbour's house and the police were called, I was not to know that this act would be crucial in my later development. Catherine was taken to the state psychiatric hospital. My mother, rather than being relieved that I was still alive, reacted with destructive vengeance. I had ruined the family's good name and reputation. She implied for years to come that I had even caused the pivotal bankruptcy of two years before. So two years of almost catatonic withdrawal were replaced by years of aggressively violent denunciations, accusations and reprisals. I was given no counselling and was told I must never speak of these shameful events.

My mother insisted we leave the district, which meant selling the beautiful colonial house where my father had been born. As I was very withdrawn at school, often in unironed uniforms, teachers did not warm to me, nor did other pupils, until the final years of highschool. When I entered secondary school in 1961 it was not compulsory, as 14 was the leaving age. The overall standard of education in Queensland was low. Few girls entered the mathematics/ science stream I undertook. Any encouragement I received in the senior forms was from my friends, Miles Finamore and Geoff Newman, both of whom later studied engineering.

Few girls entered the mathematics/ science stream I undertook.

Apart from my Dalmatian dog, Nita, my sole friend in the crucial years between 11 and 15 was an elderly spinster in our parish. I was allowed to visit Mollie Gayford because she had come from Cambridge. We often gardened together and visited other old ladies to collect flowers for the church. She was wonderfully supportive and kind though she never directly asked me anything about my life. She understood implicitly and without her I do not know what might have happened to me. Miss Gayford was a very independent woman who rejected conventional domestic life of husband and children. I now read Barbara Pym novels and remember another eccentric Anglican spinster with much affection.

My professional success today must be seen against this terrible background of neglect and trauma. Had we been workingclass I would have been sent into care but, by virtue of Uncle Hubert's standing in the community, I was effectively left to fend for myself. I always maintained a burning ambition to go to university so I could be financially independent. Even when I arrived at the University of Queensland in 1966 there were few female role models to follow. Most of the women were tutors whose role was defined as an extension of the secondary school teacher. That was still the case when in 1975 I became a tutor in history. Often women colleagues reinforced these low expectations and did not encourage my ambitions to become a senior academic. The few women on the senior staff in my undergraduate studies were older spinsters who presented an image I so unkindly wanted to avoid at all costs. Being attractive to men was at a premium in those heady days. My one role model was Margaret Cribb who taught political science. She was intelligent and elegant (rejecting the still dominant notion that only frivolous women are interested in their appearance). Margaret was an excellent teacher and a scholar, showing how a successful career and family life could be negotiated. As a mature scholar today, I often use Margaret's pioneering studies on the intersection of industrial relations and the state. Young women today should never forget that 30 years ago there were few role models, few successful women and minimal chances for professional advancement.

I found life at university totally liberating, especially in the atmosphere of the upheavals wrought by Australia's involvement in the Viet Nam war. My father paid for me to attend classes in my first year as my record at school was too mediocre to win a Commonwealth scholarship. Considering the fees were the equivalent of a worker's annual wage, I was still dependent. When, at the end of my first year, my father was diagnosed as having multiple sclerosis, my mother accused me of 'causing it' through my disrespect and disobedience. In the middle of examinations I came home to find all my belongings in the street and the house covered in black curtains. Her destructive abuse when I entered the house still, to this day, rings in my ears. Strangely my mother was an exemplary grandparent and Erin has many treasured memories of her.

Fortunately my boyfriend's parents took me in and gave me a temporary home. Meeting Raymond Evans and his wonderfully warm and generous Welsh family helped change my life. In Raymond I had an intellectual companion who encouraged my development in the academic, emotional and political arenas. We married in late 1968 and had a daughter, Erin Evans, two years later. At this time I was undertaking a doctoral candidature in anthropology and had to fight hard to keep my Commonwealth postgraduate award. The practice and policy was that a woman had to forgo the scholarship if she gave birth. I believe I was the first mother to retain her scholarship. Regardless of this battle, I had a difficult time as I had to have a caesarean and had little money. I could afford only three months off my scholarship as 'maternity leave'. Because of a violent alcoholic supervisor, I was forced to change disciplines, departments and supervisors. Having coped with all this I learned how to monitor my time and be ruthlessly efficient. Alongside came the terrible realisation that this was not an even playingfield. Ambitious women could not compete equally with men, especially if the women had children.

Having a child actually assisted my studies: rather than being totally obsessive about my PhD, I could enter into a delightful world of play and joy.

At 25 I looked a careworn woman of 55 but nothing deterred my determination never to be dependent. Having a child actually assisted my studies: rather than being totally obsessive about my PhD, I could enter into a delightful world of play and joy. Erin was fortunate to have a wonderful daycarer. Mary Smith had four older children; she looked after her husband's elderly Aunt and also did dressmaking. I admired her strength and she was a source of guidance to both Erin and me. Through her Erin learned to appreciate the importance of the domestic life I had rejected as my main priority.

I also chaired the first Women's Liberation meeting at my house in Brisbane in mid-1971. Unfortunately I found these women were not supportive because they saw children as women's primary oppressor. So my role as a mother denied me their support and my role as an intellectual prevented me from relating well to domestic women. Two younger friends, Lindy Raine and Bruce Hawker, often minded Erin for me and this gave me invaluable respite from work and domestic duties. We remain friends and I look back on their kindness and generosity with enormous gratitude. Lindy is now a senior producer at the Australian Broadcasting Corporation (ABC) in Brisbane whilst Bruce is a political adviser to Bob Carr, the New South Wales Labor premier.

My sister-in-law Gaynor Evans, who was also undertaking a degree in anthropology and sociology, was a mainstay of these years. My friend Suzanne Gould gave me much emotional support but, having married an old friend, John Wachner, she unfortunately (for me) left to live in London and Israel. I remain close to John and Sue and still treasure their friendship. Sue's mother, Peg Gould, was later the mother I always wanted – kind, understanding, loving. Her constant words: 'Darling, you're so clever!' and her acts of unconditional love have been precious to me. Peggy and Sue had suffered enormous tragedy in their lives and this bound us all together.

Apart from Gaynor my first female intellectual friend was Kathryn Cronin whom I met at the State Archives in 1970. Pregnant with Erin, I was looking through bundles of documents on the plantation system whilst Kathryn was studying the Chinese in Queensland for her honours thesis. We struck up a conversation in the reading room of the State Archives. When I was offered a publishing contract in 1972 by the Australian and New Zealand Book Company, I expanded the project to include Raymond and Kathryn. Both were stimulating and generous collaborators. From this collaboration we wrote *Exclusion, Exploitation and Extermination: Race Relations in Colonial Queensland* which was published in August 1975 to extraordinary public furore. In the early 1990s it was released for a third time with a new introduction.

I was looking through bundles of documents on the plantation system whilst Kathryn was studying the Chinese in Queensland for her honours thesis.

My other crucial female friend who taught me so much was Carmel Shute, whom I met in 1973. She was one of Raymond's honours students. Unlike other women in the Women's Liberation movement, Carmel was not anti-child. She was warm, affectionate, with a wonderful laugh and a sense of humour. She guided my reading into more left-wing feminist texts, such as Emma Goldman's *Living My Life*. Carmel and I wrote several review articles for the journal *Hecate*. I admired her immense skill and precision with words and ideas. I was sorry when she left Brisbane (she is now in Melbourne with the Public Sector Union (PSU) and, in her spare time, a leading light of Sisters in Crime) for her friendship could not be replaced.

In my career as an academic there were no female mentors in my new field. I was fortunate in having been sponsored by Denis Murphy to whom I served what was effectively a long apprenticeship: all too often women are not sponsored and, lacking a patron, cannot extend themselves out of lowly ranked positions. I was also fortunate to work later with Ross Johnston who, likewise, was generous with his guidance and advice. As well as working with Raymond, I learnt my craft directly from Denis and Ross. Denis Murphy's death in 1984 was a terrible loss.

Later, when I was more well-established, Geoffrey Bolton extended his considerable expertise in negotiating within the academic hierarchy to offer me career guidance and advice. We worked successfully on a chapter in *Gender Relations in Australia*. His wit, urbane charm and intelligence has been a source of much merriment. In my own office I have experienced enormous support from the administrative staff, especially Serena Bagley, Angela Hall, Suzanne Lewis and Mavis Little. I rely upon their advice, admire their good sense and enjoy many moments of mirth with them.

Now, as a senior academic I hope I can emulate the good example I was shown. Unfortunately, with the restructuring of the tertiary system, there are no fulltime tutors and senior tutors. Postgraduate students merely get a few hours tutoring and no sustained 'on the job' training as academics. I have gone out of my way to give an abridged period of instruction to parttime tutors who have worked under my direction. Most have been women. I fear that, despite their talent, persistence and determination, their futures are bleak. But I have attempted to further their careers. As an example, one tutorial assistant, Maree Ann Reid, came in from the American field but proved herself a diligent and enthusiastic teacher of Australian history. When Lyn Finch and I were awarded a large Australian Research Council (ARC) grant in 1993 we employed Maree Ann as a senior research assistant.

> ... she has now established herself as an academic and political activist in Toowoomba.

I have been fortunate to be able to guide the early careers of several gifted women. I co-supervised Ann McGrath's honours thesis in 1976. She has gone on to become a notable scholar in her field. Ann and Jackie Huggins were co-editors with me on a book, *Aboriginal Workers*. We worked harmoniously as a team and I found it an energising and rewarding experience. Katie Spearritt, now (amongst other roles) active in the young women's group of WEL in Melbourne, Victoria, is one of the most talented students I have supervised and taught. She and I collaborated on an innovative study on childbirth practices in colonial Queensland. Raymond and I chose her to contribute a chapter in our edited volume *Gender Relations in Australia: Domination and Negotiation*, published in

1992. Libby Connors was the first doctoral candidate I supervised and she has now established herself as an academic and political activist in Toowoomba. I have guided Joanne Scott in the path (hopefully) towards success by assisting her in locating opportunities to speak at conferences, going over the rough drafts of papers and publications. Jackie Huggins and I collaborated on a conference paper and publication on the difficult subject of feminists' ethnocentrism. That was particularly rewarding for it made us both examine our most basic premises about feminism and whether white women can ever truly shake off their racism. We concluded it was virtually impossible.

My most enduring and successful collaboration and friendship (apart from that with Raymond Evans) has been with Lyn Finch, whom I initially taught as an undergraduate in 1983. I was subsequently her temporary doctoral supervisor and we have given a number of conference papers together, the most significant in May 1992 at the international conference on a reappraisal of the Battle of the Coral Sea sponsored at the Australian National Maritime Museum. I was one of the two academic advisers for the program. We also included in the program Yuriko Nagata, who has undertaken splendid work on Japanese internment in Australia during the second world war. We were the only women presenting papers – hardly surprising given the nature of the topic.

Earlier, Lyn Finch and I worked harmoniously together on an otherwise disastrous research team. We spent several weeks in the field travelling thousands of kilometres, a true test of whether you are compatible colleagues. Tensions in the team initially, in my opinion, emanated from crossed perceptions about its structure. As the only widely published author both here and internationally, with a good track record in getting major projects finished on time, I saw myself as managing director of a less experienced team. Some others involved saw it as a democracy where we could all have equal say. This reflects a wider problem where, I believe, women all too often unwittingly subscribe to the 'tall poppy' syndrome in an attempt to refute male hierarchies. Democratic notions of a collective are seen as the ideal, whereas university policy is to have experienced senior chief investigators responsible and accountable for the final product. Junior team members are supervised and directed by the team leader. Perhaps this model works better in the sciences than in the humanities.

The other side of this false democracy is the emotional pressure that can be exerted on senior female professionals to give far too much assistance to less experienced women, especially those who have not followed the masculinist model of a careerpath. A misguided sense of generosity can lead one to pretending publicly that a colleague has

> ... *the emotional pressure that can be exerted on senior female professionals to give far too much assistance to less experienced women.*

equally pulled her weight, whereas, like men, women have to learn by trial and error to be able to stand independently on their own two feet. If they fail, they fail. In the end it does the beneficiary no good by propping up poor performance or, in extreme cases, no performance.

Generally I have enjoyed far more pleasant and cordial relations. When Lyndall Ryan held meetings in her home of the Koala Klub, a loosely based group of historians, she sponsored a unique intellectual soirée in Brisbane. Lyndall has been extraordinarily generous with her time and energy – constantly – and I have often benefited from her good advice. I have always admired Ann Curthoys and often talk over professional issues with her and follow her advice. She has that rare combination of academic brilliance, professional integrity and personal warmth. Joy Dimousi, with her wicked wit, is a valuable new academic friend and adviser.

My experience has not only been in the narrow defined academic sphere. In 1983, I, along with two religious sisters from All Hallows' Convent, undertook voluntary teaching duties in the Women's Prison. Sister Beatrice, all of 83, consistently told 'the girls' (as the prisoners liked to be called) that everyone could break the law – it all depended on one's chances in life. We laughed and teased her about her misdemeanours. I often thought, when I listened to stories from my students' lives, how easily I could have joined their ranks as our childhoods had all been riven with emotional trauma and intense instability. Only the money and class position was different.

In 1985 Tess Livingstone and I wrote a film script together and it proved immense fun. Tess had been a student of mine and is now one of Queensland's most prominent journalists. It was a wonderful collaboration and we deeply regret that the producer could not raise the capital to see it reach the screen. I was also fortunate to meet Dee Dee Glass, a highly respected director and producer with her own London-based company. She was interested in producing, for Channel 4 in London, a documentary on Joh Bjelke Petersen, former Premier of Queensland. Tess was also to work on the project. She was a vital member of the team as she had all the political contacts. Unfortunately, again, raising capital prevented completion of the project. But I learned a lot from these two talented women in fields quite different from my own. Both have also been supportive to me personally at a time of crisis.

In 1992 I was appointed as a director to the National Australia Day Council and have been fortunate to work with Lois O'Donoghue, Shirley de la Hunty and Matina Mottee. They are all extraordinary women with impressive achievements and a determined sense of integrity and cooperation that one does not encounter regularly in the back-biting world of academia. Our male colleagues are charming and listen to our opinions without brushing them off as unimportant or claiming our good ideas as their own. In 1994 I was appointed to that Bastion of Masculinism, the Australian War Memorial. Beryl Beaurepaire, as chairperson, has shown the degree of leadership that should inspire us all.

The last 30 years have witnessed great advances for many Australian women. But we should never be complacent nor should young women underestimate how hard it was to struggle in a professional world without female mentors who encouraged success and advancement. My mentors were necessarily sympathetic men and this is not uncommon. But I see changes. My daughter has undertaken doctoral studies in bio-technology under the excellent supervision of Susan Hamilton and John de Jersey. Erin has, moreover, consistently talked over any project I am working on, and offered assistance in proof-reading texts and preparing indexes. Her loyalty, her warmth and emotional generosity have given me strength and deep contentment. Although we were divorced in 1982, Raymond Evans has continued to provide sustaining intellectual partnership. We, along with Clive Moore, are currently undertaking a massive project to document the Australian federation movement. Clive and I are currently engaged on a book on Australian masculinities. Working directly with women like Kathryn Cronin, Lyn Finch, Dee Dee Glass, Jackie Huggins, Tess Livingstone, Joanne Scott, Carmel Shute and Katie Spearritt has been rewarding both personally and professionally.

Her loyalty, her warmth and emotional generosity have given me strength and deep contentment.

My story therefore contains mixed messages about women's generosity. Women can be enormously destructive and where it is mother and putative grandmother doubly so. Women do not always instinctively reach out to provide emotional support. They can be a professional hindrance by inferring that women should stick together – at the ***bottom*** of the rung. The successful 'tall poppy' then suffers constant criticism and undermining, mostly from her female colleagues. But women can also offer intellectual companionship, emotional support and a strong sense of camaraderie. They are diverse and not easily categorised. Women are neither singularly saints nor sinners, but complex humanbeings driven by a myriad of diverse and often contradictory forces that impel their own actions and thoughts.

A Strong Commitment

Edith Morgan

Born on 1 February 1919 in the Melbourne suburb of Essendon, Victoria, Edith Morgan attended Essendon State School then Essendon High School, leaving school before her fourteenth birthday. Some 40 years later, in the 1970s, she graduated in socialwork from the University of Melbourne. For a number of years she was a member of the Social Security Appeals Tribunal (SSAT), hearing appeals from decisions of the department of social security in relation to pensions and benefits.

Edith Morgan has been a member of the Communist Party and the Australian Labor Party (ALP). She is a member of the Union of Australian Women (UAW) and Older People's Action.

I had to make my own way for a long time. I was the third child in a family of eight children, with two boys above me and one below me. I held a very menial status.

The boys were the focus of my mother's attention; they were the 'stars', every one of them. As for us girls, I and the two who were closest to me in age married as soon as we could. We removed ourselves from the family circle because there was no support at all for us. I was extremely angry about that and still am. I carry great anger about the way women were treated in our family.

As growing children, we girls were denied any education. It was the Depression, certainly, but each of my sisters is intelligent and creative – and none of them has achieved anything *great* in her own right. This is tragic. Women are obliged to fight constantly for a bit of space. I have always had a strong response to women and to the place of women in our society, particularly those who are denied space of their own. This has led me to work with women and become involved in women's organisations.

I have taken a political stand on the issue of social justice, equality and the downgrading of women. If I have had any impact over time, it has been because of the organisations in which I've been involved and my role in those organisations.

For many years I was very unsure of myself. It took a long time for me to develop sufficient confidence in my own integrity to 'take off' and do something about myself: something outside my role as the mother, and outside my role as supporter of a husband. I was into my forties before I embarked on my path as a political activist in the Women's Movement.

I was into my forties before I embarked on my path as a political activist in the Women's Movement.

Early on, I was involved in general political movements. I was a member of the Communist Party for many years, then in the 1950s I was strongly involved in issues related to education and general public services. In whatever organisation I joined, I took on the role of president or secretary. I didn't seek out either position, but somehow that was where I ended up.

I left school at the end of my thirteenth year. I turned 14 in February and had I continued on at school my family would have had to pay for me: that was how it was at the time. My two elder brothers (both of whom were bright, with high intellectual capacities) won junior scholarships. One of them, Ken Caldercott, won a Commonwealth scholarship, which was a grand achievement. There was a great deal of concentration on the boys and encouragement for them, not so much from dad but certainly from my mother. She was extremely socially mobile, but her attitude was: 'Well, the girls will be alright. They'll marry someone.' Growing up with this means a young girl learns that her destiny is tied to the life she will have as a married women.

I cried when I left school and remain bitter about being denied the right to go on. With no support, it was impossible to fight the dictat that I should leave. As it was, I remained fulltime at home until I reached the age of nineteen. Mum had twins at 42 and suffered a stroke, so I spent the intervening years supporting her. That was how long it took me to break out of the hold my family had on me. This cannot have helped but have an immense impact on me and my future life.

My mother was a creative, intelligent person. She was not a feminist. She was a Methodist and saw that anything she was to achieve in her life would be achieved through her sons. There was no question at all about that. She did have achievements of her own – she was a wonderful cook, she could sing, play the piano, and was a marvellous dressmaker. But gradually all her talents left her, because she had too many children. Some women can cope with eight children; some can cope with four. Some people can't cope with one child, or any children. As the family grew, my mother withdrew, became depressed, suffered from high blood pressure, developed varicose ulcers, then had a stroke and from there onwards it was a matter of 'all down the hill'.

These were the years before anti-depressant drugs came on the market. So from the age of 50 my mother's health was very poor; from 53 she was more or less a vegetable. All this was due to the impact of bearing children she never should have had in the first place, together with living with a man who was insensitive to her needs, and who shared with her the inability to talk about sex. I assume that it was all this that led to her despair. She lived until she reached the age of sixty-three.

At 19, I was untrained, so took up shopwork. I went out to get a job because I had become so miserable at home. I worked at a delicatessen in Footscray for two or three years. Then I was married. Now I see myself as something of a 'blob' in those teenage years. That is my vision of myself: not a lot of fight in me, but seething anger; not knowing how to break through the burdens of a sick mother and tiny twins with whom I didn't know how to cope. Once I went out to work, however, the world looked different. I developed my own personality. I began to see myself as an integrated person rather than as someone spread into the family group, with a shadowy and ill-defined existence, whose sole role was as chief cook and bottle washer.

I began to see myself as an integrated person rather than as someone spread into the family group, with a shadowy and ill-defined existence ...

I married in 1941, at the age of 21. I had a boyfriend who was rather persistent, and there was Bill. I met Bill at a dance, held at the Masonic Lodge in Collins Street, Melbourne. He was an intelligent and earnest young man who had been brought up in the Catholic Church and had made a stand against it. He was a reader and had a socialist ideology. The persistent boyfriend had none. The situation grew more dramatic every day. Finally, Bill and I ran away to South Australia, to marry in Adelaide, then we went to New South Wales and lived in Sydney. If it had been like it is today, we wouldn't have bothered to marry, but marry was what people did in those days. It was good for me that I went, as it pushed me away from family. Bill joined the Royal Australian Airforce (RAAF) and I joined the Communist Party.

I come from a committed political family. My father was an extremely political man, a trade unionist and leader amongst men. He worked at the Spotswood workshops as a fitter and turner. All the men came to him, Jack Caldercott, to talk about their problems. My father was a most humanitarian man. Yet ironically he had no real sensitivity to mum or to her position. He loved his daughters, but had no great vision for us. To be fair, he had no great vision for his boys, either. Yet he was a great, loving man, a singer and player of the cornet. He belonged to a band and he is the one in the memories of us girls, far more than mum. It is sad that none of us can recall ever having been cuddled by mum. We always knew there was something very solid about dad – that he would support us if it were necessary. But with mum, this solidity was not there. She found it very, very difficult to have any close physical contact with her daughters.

My father was a strong advocate of the workingclass. He was a strong anti-racist and none of us was allowed to make a single racist statement, ever. His background was central to his position on these issues, as he came from New Zealand and had a great love for the Maori population, some of whom were his close friends in Auckland. My father had great integrity and was very, very strong. He took us to Festival Hall to hear the Red Dean of Canterbury when he visited Australia. (The Red Dean was the one who had been to Russia and had praised socialism as a viable alternative.) We were introduced to political ideas from a young age, and there was no doubt that the political ideas holding sway in our household were not only left wing, but left wing radical.

My husband had very little education. He was an intelligent fellow: he was a navigator in the airforce, and navigators certainly were not stupid. When he returned from the airforce I wanted Bill to go on to university to develop his capacities. With the study he had done in the airforce, he could have begun at university at the level of second year science. But Bill refused. He had dreams of making millions by working as a salesman in insurance. He did this all his life, but he didn't make any of those millions! It was his dream, and he didn't want anyone to be his boss.

My branch of the Communist Party centred around the Sydney suburb of Mosman. Penny Ward (married to Russel Ward) and Marie Child were members, and the women members formed an interesting and lively group. They wanted me to become even more involved by joining the education program and learning methods of promoting communist ideas. Unfortunately I didn't have sufficient energy. My husband was supportive only so far, and it was difficult to find someone to look after the children. I would say to Bill: 'Will you be able to look after the children on Saturday afternoon?' 'Oh, I don't know,' he would reply. 'I might have important things I want to do.' At the same time he'd tell me how lucky I was. His view was that men lost out by being denied the privilege of having children. Yet on the other hand it was seen as a most unimportant job. I lived with these conundrums, and in the 1950s I and other women in the Mosman cell of the Communist Party organised to form a childcare cooperative in the Mosman Junction area. It was one of the first movements to establish a cooperative childcare scheme to enable women to go out to work. It was completely unfunded

> *His view was that men lost out by being denied the privilege of having children. Yet on the other hand it was seen as a most unimportant job.*

and was our contribution at that time to the need for childcare.

It was 1942 when I joined the Communist Party. Questions of housing, public health and education became prominent after the second world war. I became very involved in all of them and took a leading part in campaigns in our local area. It was fashionable, then, to be in the Party. I left at the time of the Hungarian Revolution, when there was a great deal of turmoil, questioning and debate, in the Communist Party. This coincided with the enquiry held by the United States House of Representatives into 'Un-American Activities'. Central Intelligence Agency (CIA) agents were spying on members of the United States Communist Party. There were factions in the Communist Party all over the world. Some members adhered to Trotsky's teachings. Others were opposed to the Trotskyites. I had a great admiration for people on both sides.

After I left the Communist Party I retired from party politics for almost 10 years, until 1967. Partly this was because my son was very ill. At that time he was constantly being raced to hospital, which meant it was not easy to be involved in political activities. It was the Viet Nam war and Jim Cairns' activism that brought me back to party politics. I joined the Australian Labor Party (ALP).

Nonetheless, in the 1950s in Melbourne I became active in the community, in local politics. I worked grading eggs, and it was at this time I simultaneously had a leading role in school organisations. Much later I began work with the local council as its first socialworker. Many women become involved in community and local issues when their children are at school. It is inevitable that this should happen, because a woman's links are often generated through the children going to school.

> *I worked grading eggs, and it was at this time I simultaneously had a leading role in school organisations.*

But it was a repressive period for women. In about 1951, when I was still living in Sydney, I joined the Union of Australia Women (UAW). In the early 1960s the UAW produced a regular magazine which is astonishing to look at now, for the UAW was regarded as 'radical' yet the articles relate to traditional womanly activities, including recipes. It was a terrible time and it wasn't easy to live through it. In Melbourne, women in the UAW included Betty Olle, Alma Morton, Yvonne Smith, Marj Oke and Betty Irvine (whose husband was in the Builders' Labourers Federation (BLF) who were (and are) remarkable women. And brave. They conducted weekly peace walks through Melbourne at a time when to talk peace was to be a traitor. The UAW fought against the oppressive nature of the political system, and when we were not permitted to take placards up to Parliament House, members used their ingenuity to take their message right up to the doors of parliament: we wrote or embroidered political messages on our aprons, and wore them as we walked around the city and up the steps of Parliament House.

Up to my time of working with the women in the Mosman cell of the Communist Party, then with the women in the UAW, I had had no active support from other women. On the contrary, I had had negative learning. When I was about nine years of age my mother, struggling with her own health problems, said to me: 'You'll never make old bones either.' That chilled me to the soul: fancy an adult saying that to a young child! So whenever I felt depressed, particularly during those repressive days of the 1950s, I would immediately think of mum. This spurred me on! Negative learning can be very, very positive if the impact is so real that it lives within you. I am not a depressed person, but at times anyone can be 'down'. Then I think of mum. She didn't live to be old – although at the time 63 years of age wasn't too bad. But from the age of 40 onwards, there was no 'quality of life' for her. This made me vow I would never live my life as she had.

I joined the Labor Party when I lived at Warriewood, in the Casey electorate. I stood against Race Mathews for preselection. A number of us were extremely critical of the way we thought the Labor Party was being made to take a backseat in the electioneering in the federal seat of Casey. No one else was standing, so I nominated. 'He shouldn't get this seat without a fight,' I thought. The vote was close. I believe there was a rigging of the figures: some people were allowed to vote although they had only just joined the Party, rather than having the required year's membership. I could have challenged the vote, but didn't. I had never thought of winning the preselection. I missed out by three votes. He was preselected and went into federal parliament in 1972, at the time the Whitlam government came to power. The vote was taken at Trades Hall, in Victoria Street. I received an incredible ovation. Race Mathews held Casey for three years, lost the seat, and later went into state parliament, in the Victorian Legislative Council.

I was in the Socialist Left faction of the ALP. The faction was very alive in those years. Our family and others were strong in the branch and the federal electorate assembly (FEA) and the Party itself. Our branch was active and held an important place in the ALP. Casey kept the issues alive, particularly around the Viet Nam war. It was only towards the end of that war that Whitlam was prepared to come out publicly on the issue. There was a strong feeling in sections of the ALP that the Viet Nam war shouldn't be discussed because (they thought) it would be 'electorally bad'.

My involvement in the Casey electorate was important politically for me and for other women, as well as for the men, for it showed that women *were* entitled to be outspoken, *were* entitled to stand for preselection, and *could* do well in preselection battles. At the time, however, it was not really an issue that I was a woman and Race Mathews a man. It was the political issues of the era that were decisive. If a woman with the same views as Race had been standing, I am sure I would have stood against her.

> In my political work at that time I did not feel I had a supportive network of women around me.

In my political work at that time I did not feel I had a supportive network of women around me. My sense of politics came from within me, and from my family's involvement in the trade union movement and political causes. My eldest brother, for example, was very involved in the Communist Party until he left the Party, like I did. He was also strongly committed to the 'underdog' in the Spanish civil war. He travelled all over Australia showing films and raising support for the side of liberation, until they lost at the end of the war.

I had a strong sense of myself as a woman in an oppressive male dominated world. I retain this sense of self, and see that the world has not changed much: a person only need watch television to see the dominance of men, blabbing away and making a mess of the world as they blab on and on. Their grey and black suits dominate, taking over the world. It is difficult for women to endure that sight, particularly when women viewers want to see changes in social justice and women's equality.

Still, changes did come about in 1975, International Women's Year (IWY). Bon Hull, who later co-wrote a book on women's health, *In Our Own Hands*, was involved in the development of the Women's Health Cooperative in Collingwood. As the Collingwood council socialworker, I argued the issues through the council, and arranged for Bon to attend a meeting to speak to the council. This was an important period in my life. I came into a vacuum and moved the council to support many constructive proposals for improving the position of people in the Collingwood area. Not only did they agree to the establishment of a health centre in Johnston Street, but the council gave money for the development of the Women's Cooperative.

My position as socialworker with the Collingwood council came about as a consequence of my 'going back to school'. Almost 10 years after I returned to Melbourne in 1958, and by the time I was 47, I heard of the Council of Adult Education (CAE). I learned it was possible for people to return to an interrupted education, to complete courses they had not finished, and to qualify for entry to higher studies. For almost 35 years I had borne the anger of having to leave school at thirteen. Now was my chance! I made application and completed my matriculation in two years, at Box Hill High School. I could have done everything in a year, but I was terrified of going to university and knew that that was my destination after I gained matriculation. When the time came, I applied to the socialwork faculty in the University of Melbourne.

There was no 'scheme' at that time, no mature-age entry. A person was entitled to sit for the matriculation examination at any age, but there was no leeway for entry to university. After I went off to university, a large number of women in the Casey electorate took up adult education. I was anxious all the time! At least four women from the electorate followed me to university. One of them, Jane Tibbie, studied Australian history. Others took up teaching. Throughout my years at university, I knew these other women were watching and waiting to see how I fared. All the way through university, I was carrying the torch not only for myself, but for many, many women. I felt I was bearing a beacon, lighting the way forward.

After graduating, I began work with Royal Melbourne Hospital as socialworker. I stayed only two years, because I couldn't abide the hierarchal, separatist nature of public hospitals. On one occasion the workers in the maintenance section went on strike. We were asked to act as cooks and other support staff in the kitchen. I argued strongly in our section (the socialwork section) that I had never been a strike breaker and I certainly wasn't about to start! The director of the socialworker section and one other went to help out. The rest stayed with me. I felt a great sense of achievement!

It was whilst I was working at Royal Melbourne Hospital that the huge moratorium march against the Viet Nam war took place. We were asked not to participate: a directive came down from up on high; we were not to go. I argued the issue through our section, saying: 'I *am* going!' The only ones who remained in the section were the director of socialwork and a woman originally from Hungary, who was a good socialworker but may have been politically opposed to our attitude to the Viet Nam war. Every other socialworker came out with me. I had a strong sense of my persuasive powers.

It was an amazing day. The trams had been stopped for the rally. There was magic in the air. People left their offices, left the hospitals, surged into the roads marching toward the city centre. Crowds of people walked along the footpaths to the assembly point, spilling into the roadway. There was no background noise of trams or trains. There was no disruption of cars or taxis in the streets. It was magic. Magic.

The trams had been stopped for the rally. There was magic in the air.

We marched from Treasury Gardens and took over the city square. The streets were blocked all around, right up Collins Street, right up Swanston to Bourke Street. It had an amazing impact, and the names of the people who spoke were not important. I cannot recall them, now. It was the feeling of solidarity as people came together to express their anger at what was happening in Viet Nam. That was the breaking point of our involvement in the Viet Nam war. People were having an impact, and we knew it. We had come from difficult times – from the deadheart of the 1950s, into the 1960s where we'd been breaking through barriers, then into the 1970s, when people came together around an issue about which we all felt so strongly, and were so angry, and we were determined to end war.

Political activism was still difficult, however, particularly where women's issues were concerned. On one occasion I went to Canberra to the ALP national conference, during the period Gough Whitlam was in power. I attempted to make my voice heard on the question of women who are an underclass, the women who are forever in poverty, always subjected to poor housing, who have no status. Even the Women's Movement has not handled this issue very well. Today, the Women's Movement is extremely middleclass, and although there is lipservice to widening the parameters to ensure representation of Aboriginal women, poor women and so on, there seems to be an unwillingness to look at class in perspective: why are the women in poverty there? What is it in our society that ensures we have an underclass? The Women's Movement lacks this perspective.

At the Canberra ALP conference, no attention was paid to the issue. The lack of response was, I believe, because changing the situation can happen only through strong political direction and a complete redressing of the balance of power and resources. This is not on the agenda – wasn't then, isn't now. We are not good at enabling women who are in this position – in the poverty traps – to take the floor to talk about their situation and circumstances. We need to empower people, particularly the poorer people, to be articulate, and to provide real opportunities for them to speak. This is the only way we can bring about the massive social change that is necessary to improve the lot of the underclass, to lift *everyone* out of it.

We need to ensure that women can talk about their real feelings. Women often speak in a guilty way about the way they have 'looked after' their husbands, and generally they believe that their efforts have been inadequate, that they have failed in some way. Yet we need to get under the surface comments women make, to see the reality of their lives. Women live with husbands who drink, who have sexual demands the women feel obliged to 'go along with'. These women care for their husbands over and above what any humanbeing should be obliged to do, and way beyond what any humanbeing is entitled to. It is difficult for women to raise these issues in public, to speak out against the 'right' of men to dominate them sexually, to see them as sexual objects, to see them as rightly confined to minor decision-making in marriage. Yet it is women who are the *strong* ones. It is women who hold marriages and families together, against tremendous odds. Women manage to scrounge a bit of money from a parttime job, or a

> *Women often speak in a guilty way about the way they have 'looked after' their husbands . . .*

casual job in a factory or on the shopfloor. Then they spread it across, feeding families, going without, teaching themselves to cook mince in 56 different ways. The world doesn't recognise this and women, unfortunately, often fail to see the truth themselves.

Well I remember not having sufficient underclothes, for years and years. How difficult it was, with four children. I kept saying: 'I'm going to leave. I'm going to leave.' But I had no money. There was no support system for women. My mother or father wouldn't allow me to land on their doorstep with four kids, having left my husband. It just wasn't on. This was the world I lived in in the 1940s, 1950s and 1960s. Many women live in this world today.

In the 1970s I read *The Female Eunuch*. *The Female Eunuch* gave me a framework through which I could analyse the anger and boredom I felt about marriage and the feelings of lack of integration of myself. It, and Germaine Greer, made far more sense to me than did Betty Friedan's *The Feminine Mystique*. *Everyone* was talking about *The Female Eunuch*. And I read Simone de Beauvior's book, *The Second Sex* at about this time, too. It was more of a struggle: her books are not easy to read. But once I put my head down, I found her words energising.

It was when I was the socialworker with the Collingwood council that I gained the first concrete support from women in achieving a goal for myself. It was 1972, and the 'old guard' Labor men on the council didn't even *want* a socialworker. Mine was a political appointment – and I certainly got there with the support of the women on the council. I knew they were supporting me, because they were vocal about it, and there was no doubt that they were behind me. The women continued to be supportive of me, both in my role as a socialworker and of me as a women. They were strongly involved in all the committees – housing, agedcare and so on. Sadly, toward the end of my time with the council, one or two women councillors did not wholly support my recommendations, particularly in relation to the highrise flats. Back in 1972, these were not seen as 'part' of Collingwood. It was as if aliens had come into the middle of the municipality and the council had no responsibility for them, or for the buildings where they lived. The council were providing no garbage services or cleaning of streets. It took a considerable time to get the council to acknowledge that the people living there were ratepayers, paying rates through the housing ministry certainly, but nonetheless paying for each flat. There was also a question of whether other services should be provided to the estate. We did a quick breakdown of who received services. The services were going to the private households – the older residents around Clifton Hill, Abbotsford and so forth. But the

> *It was as if aliens had come into the middle of the municipality and the council had no responsibility for them, or for the buildings where they lived.*

council was putting forward as a serious proposition the notion that we oughtn't to provide these services to the flats!

I took the town clerk to the highrises for a visit, simply to walk around the estate. He had never been to the estate or walked through it, despite having been with the Collingwood council for many years before I came to the council. It just wasn't seen by him as part of his domain! I emphasised that it was vital to focus on that section of the residents as equally important as any other section. This took a considerable time and lots of energy.

When Hoddle Street became a six-lane highway (previously it was one street), I suggested the council do an impact study of lead levels. I gained no support on that, not even from the women, despite its being such an important issue for everyone and particularly for children's health. There may have been a suggestion that I was presumptuous to move into areas like this, but I saw them as directly relevant to the municipality, to the health and wellbeing of residents, and to my work as socialworker for the council.

My position became permanent, despite the difficulties that had arisen in having the council accept the initial appointment. Eventually the position moved into the corporate structure and it is now far removed from my policy of the open door. True it is that this policy developed its own problems after two or three years, because it was impossible to see and talk with everyone who came in the door. Nonetheless, it is necessary for councils to provide a person or staff in a role such as this, to ensure that the concerns of residents are properly taken into account in council policies and activities.

It was the time of the radical lesbians in green dungaree overalls and truncheon boots. Strong words were said about men, particularly as rapists.

Just as there are problems in municipalities in ensuring that the voices of the people are heard, difficulties arise within the Women's Movement in terms of ensuring that everyone has an opportunity not only to speak, *but to understand the issues*. Many conferences, seminars, meetings and celebrations were held all over Australia during International Women's Year. One meeting was held in the Lower Town Hall in Melbourne, the intention being to have a series of meetings, over a period of months. I worked desperately to ensure that women from the Collingwood estate would attend. A good number of women said: 'Yes, we'd love to come.' They did. But it was a disaster, for the debate went into areas that were not yet on the agenda of these women. It was the time of the radical lesbians in green dungaree overalls and truncheon boots. Strong words were said about men, particularly as rapists. Certainly this was an issue of direct relevance to the women from the estate, just as it is to all women. But the passion and intensity with which the radical women spoke, and the language they used, was not inclusionary. At the next meeting, no one from the estate attended. I remember Bon Hull getting up to ask: 'Where are the women from the estate?' I pointed out why they weren't there. After that, the action fizzled. There were no more meetings! This illustrates why it is important in the Women's Movement to ensure that we recognise varying levels of consciousness. It is important not to act to alienate women who want to be included, have pressing issues they need to have addressed, and who will connect with the issues being raised if only we can frame them in a way that includes all women.

In more recent years I have been involved in issues relating to older people. Alma Morton, Marj Oke, myself and several others wrote a submission for funding of a group of old people to run a lobby advocacy group. The idea was to take the issue of older people away from the welfare basket. We are a group of older people managing our own affairs, with project officers whenever we have had funding for a project. We take up issues such as health, nursing homes, age discrimination. We have taken these issues and our perspective on them to both state and federal governments. Since the change of government in Victoria in October 1992 we have no longer been able to discuss the issues with the state government. However, many of us are or have been working on federal government committees. The Australian Older Women's Network (OWN), too, plays a leading role in advancing the status of older people, and there are many strong and vital members, such as Betty Johnstone and Maureen Hewitt, who work hard to lift the profile of older women.

We take up issues such as health, nursing homes, age discrimination.

I believe we have advanced the cause of older people. Older people have gained status such as we've never had before. Older People's Action provides a focus and a voice and has been particularly effective in issues relating to user rights in the context of nursing homes and hostels. Now there is a Charter of Rights for people in nursing homes or hostels. The charter establishes security of tenancy, the right to have a room of your own, the right to be heard, and a right to have residence committees established. The idea is to ensure that the voice of older people within the institutions can be heard, ending the total lack of power older people have had in hostels and nursing homes. A Charter of Rights cannot right all the wrongs. Nonetheless, without any charter, in the absence of very articulate older people or relatives or friends who come behind them and push the issues, the industry is willing to overlook the rights of older people who are residents.

A problem which continues to confront us all, however, is that of *power*. To improve the position of people who are disadvantaged and oppressed, it is necessary to *want* change and look carefully and without quibbling at where the changes should be. What *are* the most important elements in changing society in favour of or at least toward equality for women? That is a big question. It means throwing out so many traditional models. It's frightening to the people in power, because they are doing very nicely, thank you. It can also be frightening to people who are in groups that are organised to represent the interests of particular sections of the community. *Some* sections of the community *are* relatively well organised. *Some* sections of the community, although they undoubtedly have problems – who doesn't? nonetheless are relatively advantaged. *Some* sections of the community can be greedy and arrogant, demanding more, more, more. *Some* sections forget about, or don't even recognise, the disadvantage of others. They set their own concerns way above the needs of persons who are less well-off. It is those divisions that create the difficulties confronting any movement for positive change and doing away with inequality.

It is those divisions that make it difficult, sometimes, to work together toward a common goal.

My work has mainly been with women. It is my strong sense of independence that has carried me through, for despite experiencing feelings of inadequacy, I developed a strong commitment to doing a task myself if I could possibly do it. I learned not to rely on anyone.

> *It's frightening to the people in power, because they are doing very nicely, thank you.*

A Smile Speaks Any Language

Joyce Apap

Born in Malta on 5 October 1949, Joyce Apap arrived in Australia on Australia Day 1966, at the age of sixteen. She left Malta on 6 January 1966, just two weeks after she married.

Joyce Apap holds a BA in social sciences (community development) from Victoria University of Technology, and a graduate diploma in education and training, gained in 1993. In September 1993 she was appointed to the Victoria Women's Council. Her pastimes include reading and learning, and she enjoys weekends away, meeting with women, and talking and relaxing in coffee shops. In October 1995 she became a grandmother.

My mother and father were married for 10 years before children were born into our family. Then in 1943 my elder sister, Carmen, was born. I was the fourth child, born in 1949. My grandmother died not long before my birth, so I was given her name – Josephine.

Back in those days, women didn't go to a doctor to find out why they were not pregnant. But there was a view that a woman without children was impaired, deficient, a failure, or just plain sick. My mother had to endure the sniping remarks until children suddenly began to come naturally. Four children appeared, one after the other. All were born at home and looked after by a female midwife, family, and neighbours. In Malta, people did not have homebirths through choice; rather it was through poverty. Childbirth was women's business.

When I was two years old, my father died suddenly, at the age of forty-six. My sisters and brother and I went to orphanages. The girls were in one orphanage, while my brother went to an all-boys orphanage. Neighbours had offered to take us in, but my mother said: 'No.' She wanted to keep us together. At the orphanage we were looked after by nuns, while my brother was cared for by priests. My sisters left the orphanage before I did. I left at 11 years of age.

My younger sister, Marcia, was born after my father's death. Mother was pregnant when father died. Dad died in March 1951 and my sister was born in October of that year. Marcia had to go to a babies orphanage. She was not kept together with us.

In Malta, after church the people congregate on the church steps, laughing and talking.

I often heard my mother talk about my father, describing how, because I was the youngest child, he took me on his shoulders to church, for Sunday's Mass. In Malta, after church the people congregate on the church steps, laughing and talking. Food is an important part of our culture, and in our family it became a tradition to go off to the cakeshop: my father would walk across to the road to the best cakeshop in the village, taking me on his shoulders. He would then buy cakes for us all, for afternoon tea. That is why, I think, I have a liking for cakes!

Although I cannot remember my father, my mother repeated this story to me many times and I will never forget it. It makes me sad to remember that I did not grow up with a family – father, mother, brother and sisters.

I enjoyed school and often said I wanted to be a nun. I love and admire strong women, who are like the nuns in the orphanage. They were good role models. Whenever we children played games, I took on the role of the mother; I was always the caring person. This made me feel close to my mother, although we were separated. My mother visited us once a week or once a fortnight: she came whenever she could. But her life was hard, as she was obliged to work in paid employment to earn money to keep herself and to put towards our upkeep. (Ordinarily women in Malta did not do paidwork: they remained at home, looking after their families.) It seems I have taken my mother's example to heart, because I work hard in all I do, putting 100 percent into everything. This, I believe, is what my mother taught me.

My mother was the caretaker and cleaner at the local primaryschool. Everyone knew my mother. She was the one who gave out the codliver oil and served up the milk. I was 11 years old by this time, and left the orphanage to go home to live with my mother, brother and two older sisters. Our younger sister, Marcia, stayed in the orphanage. As students, my two elder sisters and I attended the school where my mother was caretaker. After school, we helped mum to clean up. She would let us children help her to hand out the milk and ring the bell for school. If there was milk left over, we were allowed to take it home to drink or use it to make cheese.

In Malta, school is 'in' for half a day, then the children go home, returning to school at two o'clock, staying until four, then going home again. I attended school until I completed Grade 6; I was 14 years old. Then it was time to sit for an examination for entry into highschool. I didn't pass the exam, so I left school and went to work as a maid in the house of a rich woman and her son. I also worked in factories, making T-shirts, until I emigrated to Australia some two years later.

The rich woman with the son was a bad employer. I was afraid of her and terrified she would sack me. I received £1 and 50 pence for the week's wages, of which I gave £1 to my mother and kept the rest. The woman's son often created mess about the house, but in his mother's eyes he could do no wrong. I was there to clean up after him. This increased the stress of the job, as I was the maid and was therefore required to clean his mess. He deliberately created chaos, and there was no excuse for not ensuring that everything was spick and span – at once.

In the early 1960s my elder sister Carmen emigrated to Australia. She sailed in a group, and the priest looked after them. Some time later, in 1966, I married and followed her. All I knew about Australia was that my sister thought life was good. Yet she was lonely, and wanted someone from the family to join her.

I arrived at Port Melbourne, travelling by the *Roma*: it was the ship's last trip, and the journey from Malta took a month. There were many different nationalities sailing to Australia for a new life. On board, we were separated, women on one side of the ship and the men on the other. I did not like this. I made many friends on the ship, and some of the Maltese families settled in one area of Melbourne – St Albans. I continue to see them and we often talk of our experiences on board the *Roma*, coming to Australia.

English is taught in school in Malta, for the Maltese were British subjects; Malta became a republic, and independent, in 1964. However I had a basic education only, so although I often said I understood when people spoke English to me in Australia in those first years, I had difficulty in understanding what was being said, particularly if people spoke quickly. Even now, as I grow older, I find that Maltese comes more easily to me than English. My children and husband and I speak Maltese to one another: fortunately when my children were at primaryschool, Maltese was one of the major languages of ethnic minorities and it was taught at their school.

Originally, my husband was in the Maltese Army, which was part of the British Army. He was stationed in Germany for three years. Initially I went out with his friend, but we broke up because he made a mark on my neck. When this happened, my mother was shocked and most upset with me. I did not know what the mark meant, or the significance of it. My mother wanted me to stop seeing the man, who was much older than I was. I said to him: 'Why did you do that to me?' He replied: 'Well, you let me.' I told him I had no idea what it was and did not understand why he had done it to me. We broke off the relationship. It was then that I approached his friend, Joe (who is now my husband), who was on holidays from the army. I asked him to help me make up with my boyfriend. That was how I met the man whom I married.

At this time I was planning to go to Australia. My sister Carmen was homesick and wrote asking for someone from the family to travel to be with her. I was next in line: my older sister Antonia had a boyfriend and they were already engaged; my brother Paul was the father-figure and had to care for my mother – so it was left to me. I told my mother I would go to Australia.

When Joe and I began dating I told him of my plan. Joe's holidays were coming to an end and he was to return to Germany to continue in his posting. My mother was very fond of him. Joe made her laugh so much that my mother crawled on the floor with laughter when he joked with her. Hearing of my intentions, Joe decided to resign from the army to go to Australia with me. My mother was not happy, for I was only 16 years of age. She did not want me travelling to Australia as a single woman – with Joe! *Travelling with a man . . . !* So, six months after Joe and I met, we were married. Two weeks later, we travelled to Australia as a married couple.

I didn't know my husband very well, but he showed me a great deal of love and gave me many material things. He sent me gifts and beautiful clothes, purchased for me in Germany, and wrote letters to me every day. It was Joe who bought me my first watch. I was so happy – I felt *very* lucky and *very* RICH. My mother often laughed about the letters, for they ran to 10 or 12 pages, all of them written with many hugs and kisses scrawled everywhere.

The Maltese who were already in Australia went to meet the ships coming in . . .

At St Albans, where my sister was living and where we settled in Australia – and continue to live after 30 years – was a large Maltese community. Maltese families from the *Roma* and other boats settled in North Melbourne, Carlton and Fitzroy because these suburbs were close to Port Melbourne, where the ships docked. The Maltese who were already in Australia went to meet the ships coming in and, as people came down the gangplank, went up to ask the new arrivals if they needed somewhere to live. This meant the newcomers were not stranded, and those who were settled and had houses were able to take in lots of boarders to contribute to expenses.

My sister first lived in Fitzroy, then moved to St Albans, which was a new suburb at the time, with no roads or footpaths and poorly lit streets. Land was cheap in St Albans. There were many factories close by, in Sunshine and Footscray, where migrants could get work. The west was an industrial area in those days. Housing and rental accommodation were far less expensive than in other areas. Maltese and other migrants settled in the west as that was where the work was available.

In St Albans, I lived across the road from a Maltese family who happened to be from the Maltese village from which I had come. I did not have to speak English with her, and didn't want for anything. She was not in paidwork, staying at home to look after her family. She had five children: her oldest child was older than I was.

At this time, women were expected to stay at home caring for children and the household, rather than go out to work. It was similar to the situation in Malta. Both Malta and Australia have changed: now in Malta (just as in Australia), married women are going out to do paidwork, and now many more girls and women are remaining at school longer and getting an education.

For two years I played the 'homebody' role: but not only did I not do paidwork, I didn't have babies. I began to grow concerned. I was sexually naive when I married: I thought that as soon as a woman did IT, a baby was delivered up to her! My mother had to put me right, laughing and with tears in her eyes. But two years without a baby? It didn't seem right.

I regularly visited the doctor, asking why I wasn't pregnant. He would say to me: 'But you're just a child.' Nonetheless he drew many diagrams for me to illustrate how I might get pregnant. I was thoroughly bored. Each day I waited for my husband to return home from work. Around four o'clock I'd sit outside on the porch, talking across the fence with my Maltese neighbour. I spent two years doing a lot of reading. I learnt how to cook. I went back and forth to the shops for an outing, because this meant I met lots of Maltese people – the workers at Coles were Maltese, as were those at the milkbar, and the butcher was Maltese and selling Maltese food.

I went back and forth to the shops for an outing, because this meant I met lots of Maltese people . . .

It was the 1960s, and the *Women's Weekly* was *my* magazine. At the time Ita Buttrose was editor, and the first item I read in each issue was her editorial. At that time, she and Maggie Tabberer were my role models, as well as Denise Drysdale and The Go Go Girls, who regularly performed on television. I had great admiration for those three women – Ita, Maggie and Denise.

Ita Buttrose was a mother figure. In her columns she wrote of her concerns for her children and it gave me the family I didn't have. I make friends easily, and find that when I do I want to adopt them and include them in my family. Ita became one of the family. Maggie Tabberer was as big as I am – and I thought she was really classy! Denise Drysdale was a little chubby like me, too, and she was doing all the things I would have liked to do but didn't. I went from school to work, then married. My sisters went dancing. They went out with boys. Apart from that brief time when I met my husband, I had none of that. Because I married so young, I missed out on my teenage years. I was able to live part of the excitement through watching and listening to Denise. Denise Drysdale also had a great deal of spunk. She didn't allow herself to be 'put down': if her mate on the program, Ernie Sigley, said anything that bordered on the derogatory, or attempted to discount her, she snapped back with a quick and clever remark. I admired her ability and her determination to stand up for herself.

> ... *a great deal of spunk. She didn't allow herself to be 'put down'.*

Role models were important to me, too, in coming to terms with aspects of my life and giving me hope. My childhood had been fraught. Apart from the years in the orphanage, when we were living with my mother we knew she had difficulties with money. She was paid £30 a month, and as soon as she received her pay-packet she would send me to the shop to pay the grocery bill. At that time in Malta, the tradition was to purchase goods every day, with the shopkeeper writing it all down in a book. Sometimes the monthly bill added up to more than £30, so we couldn't cover it. I knew we were often behind, and I grew accustomed to seeing my mother constantly worried about money.

Gold in Malta is used like money, and mother would ask me to: 'Take the box and go to the pawnshop.' I would pawn the gold in the box, use the money to pay the extra we owed at the grocery shop, then later in the month I'd be off to the pawnshop again to retrieve the gold.

From the age of 11, to 16 when I left for Australia, I played a responsible role in our community. The neighbours and people down the street often asked me to write letters for them, to send to their relatives in Australia, Canada or England. They had young children who were unable to write, or who did not know how to read and write. The neighbours trusted me with their family secrets. One woman would tell me what to write for her, admonishing me not to repeat any of it to anyone else. Then another would approach me to write her letters, and say similarly: 'Write so and so, but *don't tell anyone what is in the letters.*' This meant there was a great deal of responsibility resting on my shoulders. It also meant that I was brought up knowing about Australia and America. I had also grown up with ideas about Canada. When I was growing up, my mother would say to us that before I was born the family had intended to emigrate to Canada. My mother would say to me: 'You would have been born a Canadian citizen.' Yet my family didn't make it to Canada: my mother did not pass her medical examination. She had cataracts in one of her eyes. This prevented the family from migrating to Canada.

After almost two years of staying at home, waiting for my husband to return from work and chatting with the neighbours, I went out to work, taking a job at the Liberty factory in West Melbourne, sewing swimming-suits and brassieres. Many Maltese women from St Albans and Sunshine worked in the Liberty factory. Maltese men worked across the road at the Southdown Press factory, printing *TV Week*. We travelled by train from St Albans, talking and laughing all the way to work. I did not last long in this job, as I had fallen pregnant – at last.

It was not until the 1980s, however, that I became involved in the Women's Movement.

I always enjoyed reading. I was hungry for knowledge and longing to practise my English. I read the local paper regularly, soaking up the community doings and the news of the neighbourhood. It was there that I read about a new group starting up – Women of the West.

The article came to my attention at a very low period in my life. My children were having problems at school. Teachers telephoned me to talk about it. This upset me. I began to think there was something wrong with me. I would ring the infant health centre sister when I was not feeling well. She would come to visit me at home, have a cup of tea, and talk. She was concerned for my welfare.

All at once, a great deal of sorrow related to my childhood began to surface. I was angry at my mother for placing me in an orphanage, I was angry at our being poor, and I was angry for not having had the opportunity to really know her.

At the time, the Olympic Games were on. Every time the Australian national anthem played, I burst into sobs, so that I frequently found myself choking with tears. Now, as I think back, I realise I may have been searching for my identity. Even now, I am Maltese in Australia and called an Australian when I visit Malta. This is how it is for people who leave their country and culture of birth behind, taking a new life in a new country and a new culture. It doesn't mean that I or any others from different countries do not feel strongly for our new country, Australia. We do. But we carry with us memories and a life from the country of our birth, and where we grew up.

At this time, my husband was aware of my unhappiness. He took to leaving me notes saying: 'I love you. What is wrong?' I didn't know *what* was wrong with me. Then I read the 'Women of the West' item in the local paper. There was a telephone number at the end of the article. I took courage and rang, then spent an hour talking to the woman, Fran, at the end of the line. I kept repeating: 'I'm from an ethnic background, I'd like to join the women's group, can I come? I can't speak English.' Of course, I was speaking English all the time – this was the language she and I were using to communicate, for it was the only language she had and it was the one I was using at the time!

Fran encouraged me to attend, so I decided to go to see what the group was about. The first meeting was at Footscray TAFE and the speaker was to talk about domestic violence, based on her book *Even in the Best of Homes – Violence in the Family*. Fran told me the name of the speaker as if I should automatically know who it was! I didn't have a clue! But I decided I would go. The meeting was set for an evening during the week, and at that time I had four young children. How could I tell my husband I was going to a meeting? In our culture, only prostitutes go out at night – at least, that was what my husband constantly told me, and that was what we were brought up to believe.

I spent days sitting on the toilet. I was really, really scared.

I decided I would tell my husband I was to attend the meeting, and then just – go. I spent days sitting on the toilet. I was really, really scared. Yet I went. I walked out and went by myself. I made sure the children were alright, that tea was cooked, and everything necessary to be done, was done.

I didn't even know where Footscray TAFE was. I didn't know what domestic violence was, either, in those days. Perhaps I knew that wives were beaten, but I didn't know about economic and psychological violence, and didn't think about any of it in the terms I do now. But once I was at the meeting, I even got up and asked a question!

That was the beginning of meeting with women. For a long time I felt threatened in the group, because I thought I was isolated amongst a bunch of classy, knowledgeable women. But I *loved* going to the Women of the West.

My mother often said – following an old Maltese proverb: 'Be with people who are better than you.' I followed her advice, and although I felt scared and stupid amongst the group, simultaneously I was extremely interested in the group. These women were teachers, teaching adults in technical and further education (TAFE), and there were politicians, too, and in particular Joan Kirner. Most important of all, the women were discussing women's issues in the west. Fran, Renata, and Ann Hilda were there, together with many other women, discussing the issues with them and with Joan Kirner.

These women became the women I could relate to. They encouraged me to develop my ideas. Everyone at Women of the West made me feel welcome. I was the only woman from a non-English speaking background (NESB) in the group. The women in the group could (and did) ask me questions! I'd think to myself: 'My goodness! They're asking *me!*' I quickly learnt how to contribute, because after they asked a question, they automatically expected me to answer. What amazed me was that they listened to what I had to say. They were asking ME my opinion. These women were classy! I would look at the clothes they wore and worry that I didn't have the same sort of clothing. Thinking about it now, I realise it was quite silly of me to be concerned, but it was important then that I fit in.

The Women of the West were concerned about women's issues. I thought to myself: 'I've always been fighting for my rights!' For many years I had worked as a cleaner, and I earned the label 'troublemaker' because I stuck up for myself and the others, and the other cleaners encouraged me. The Women of the West said to me: 'You speak with passion and feel very strongly about issues. Why don't you go back to school?' 'But,' I said, 'I can't.' I didn't know it was *possible* to return to school. I said I didn't have an education. Initially I was embarrassed to say that I went to Grade 6 and no further. I concealed it because I was ashamed. Then one of the women got the papers for me. She helped me to fill out the application for the ethnic diploma at Victoria College.

I didn't know it was possible *to return to school.*

I was called for an interview. When I arrived and sat down, the interviewing panel asked me what I read. I replied: 'The *Women's Weekly*, of course.' They showed me a copy of *Australian Society*. 'Where did you get that book from?' I asked. I had never seen it before. They asked me if I did voluntary work. 'No,' I said, although I went regularly to kindergarten with my children and did fundraising, and helped at the local school. But – 'No,' I said. 'I don't do voluntary work.' I simply thought I was doing what all mothers do, and didn't think it was important or could be relevant. Voluntary work? I didn't *know* it was 'voluntary work'.

Needless to say, I didn't do very well. They didn't accept me. In a way that was just as well, because it made me talk with my friends about the experience. Renata listened to what I had to say, and was furious. 'But you *do* do voluntary work,' she said. 'You know that you come home from your cleaning job at 10 o'clock, then you make cakes for the stall.' 'Is that voluntary work?' I asked. 'Yes! What do you reckon it is!?'

Renata gave me a pamphlet about the Women's Information and Referral Exchange (WIRE). I telephoned them and asked if I could do some voluntary work. The woman on the other end of the telephone was so excited. 'We have an offer of voluntary work from someone!' she cried out. When I went in, I said: 'I've come here to learn.' They said to me: 'It's what you're going to give us that's important.' I had never seen it like that before. *I'm going to give them?!* I had always thought it was *others* giving to me, what *I* would learn from *them*, not what *they* would receive from *me*. As it was, I did learn a great deal. I sometimes say to people that I am like a flower – I need to be watered and nurtured. If I am nurtured, I become more and more responsive and learn more and more. If not, I shrink. I am like a sponge. When I stop learning, that is when I stop growing.

I did the training course and worked with WIRE in a voluntary capacity for two years. I did the five to nine shift. In those days I was still doing my cleaning job with Australia Post, at which I had worked for 16 years, together with other Maltese, Greeks and Italians. We met each day on the railwaystation at five in the morning and formed a real community, working hard, full of life and dreams, talking and joking.

After finishing cleaning I collected the children, went home to do housework and prepare the evening meal, then it was back to work at WIRE for the evening shift.

I then went on to the Western Institute (now Victoria University of Technology). It happened that Ann Hilda, one of the women in the Women of the West group, was teaching at Footscray TAFE. She told us a university was scheduled to be built in the western suburbs. I wrote a note and passed it up to her: 'Please let me know when the university is to open.' Even before it opened its doors, I put in my application to study for the ethnic diploma. Ann Hilda had called me to attend an interview about enroling for the course. We were three women at the interview. She informed us that the course had not been funded. She then asked me if I would like to study something else. 'Oh yes,' I said. 'What can I do?' She suggested I do bridging courses. 'What's that?' 'Reading and writing and return to study.'

In 1987 I joined the Western Institute and did these subjects in my first year. Dr Barbara Brook was my teacher, and the class was myself and one other student. Some people were sceptical about the idea of a workingclass university. There were snide remarks about its not being as 'good' as the University of Melbourne. Well, I was so happy about the Western Institute. *I had an opportunity*, someone had told me I could go – I hadn't known until I was told – and I realised there could be so many women out there, like me, who didn't know their rights and the opportunities available to them. They needed direction or encouragement, like I did, and which I was fortunate to receive.

I completed the first year and didn't look back. I give true acknowledgement to the women who supported and encouraged me, for if I hadn't met them, I don't know that I would have done all I have. But if I say anything of this sort to these women, they instantly reply: 'But you had it in you!' They would remind me that I fought at union meetings, when I was a cleaner. That I had always had a fierce, determined, even desperate look in my eye! Yet – the possibility is always in my mind that maybe I wouldn't have gone back to school without the Women of the West behind me. I feel extremely lucky that I had the opportunity. The Women of the West set me going, and women have supported me all the way.

> The Women of the West set me going, and women have supported me all the way.

The woman who shared the classes with me at the Western Institute studied with me at nights. During the day we studied in the library or in the women's room. There were women from non-English speaking backgrounds, like me, coming to the university to study. It was so good to see non-English speaking background women studying and getting an education. We cried on so many occasions when the going was tough. But we kept at it, coming from knowing nothing at all, to where we are today. Sometimes other women said to me and other non-English speaking background women: 'Oh, you got a pass.' They acted surprised, as if they could not believe that we had passed. Yet we had worked very hard. And we had overcome many barriers, including those in our own heads. I didn't have the confidence that I could study or write or put an essay together. *What's an essay?* Yet when someone said to me I could do it, I did it.

Another teacher, Katy (Kate) Hughes, who taught me in the subject 'reading and writing', would say to me: 'This is a Year 12 subject.' I would reply: 'Then I can't do it.' She'd say: 'Yes, but if I don't tell you it's a Year 12 subject, you will do it. But as soon as I tell you it's a Year 12 subject, you say you can't do it!'

I studied when the children were asleep, and on weekends. On Saturday afternoons I would drop the children at the pool, then go to the library to study. It worked well for me.

It was around 1988, a year after the Western Institute was established, that Women's Studies was introduced as a subject in the bachelor of arts degree. Not everyone at the Western Institute wanted Women's Studies. (Perhaps they were worried about a 'backlash' from the community.) I became involved and thought that many women like me (of non-English speaking background) would benefit from such a course – learning about women's history, women's rights, that women can do anything if we want to. I entered the course. It was new knowledge for me. I had never heard or known about women's history before. After 12 months of doing bridging courses, I was ready to start on a degree. In 1988 I applied to do two subjects in the BA. I took Women's Studies and communication. I enjoyed Women's Studies, but the communication unit was *horrible*. Once the teacher made a remark about my clothes: I saw no reason for dressing up for school, so wore tracksuit pants. This clothing was the target of the remark.

Barbara, a Polish woman, and I sat together in the communication class. She would say to me: 'We're doing communication but we are not communicating with the teacher.' We would crack up with laughter.

After the first assignment was handed in to the teacher, we discovered that most of the class had failed. There was a student who cried so much, she was so upset by the experience, that she never returned to class. I almost did the same. I thought of giving studying away. Yet I went to the teacher and told her: 'I will do the essay again, and I'll be back.' I wanted to show her that I was there for a purpose, that I wanted to learn. It was part of the learning process, that episode. I went back, but the other woman dropped out completely. The teacher was sarcastic. In my opinion she was a poor communicator. But I survived it.

I enjoyed Women's Studies. I hadn't known anything about women (apart from being one!) and everything was new to me. I was blurry-eyed and starry-eyed, listening, comprehending and taking time to read some materials three or four times to understand the ideas. But I enjoyed it. I was hungry for knowledge.

Barbara Brook and Katy Hughes taught Women's Studies and we had some wonderful times. Many of the issues were those that are not talked about in 'polite company'. Everyone was so *forward*. I tried not to be shocked. Now I don't get shocked any more, but in those days I was astounded at some of the discussions. I wouldn't dare tell my husband what we talked about!

> *Many of the issues were those that are not talked about in 'polite company'. Everyone was so forward.*

In 1989 the Western Institute offered a community development program. I switched courses. I had a desire to work in the community. I wanted to inform the people of the resources available, and how to access those resources. I wanted to make sure they could discover how to go about doing whatever it was they wanted to do. I completed the BA in community development, then went on to do a postgraduate diploma in education and training. In 1995, with one year to go to complete the masters degree, I deferred as I was tired and needed a break.

There was also an incident on Mother's Day that made me think. My older children did not come to see me on that day! *My children didn't come.* Now, I had always let my children know I have a dislike of Mother's Day. My line is that mothers work hard all year, and one day means nothing. It is an artificial 'celebration', with women smiling whilst receiving further symbols of their oppression, as gifts! – irons, washingmachines, ironing-boards! But the children had always come, anyway – it is a day everyone celebrates and they did, even though they knew I didn't like it. (It made me sad, too, for I was drawn on the day to thinking about my mother.)

The day after Mother's Day I telephoned my eldest son to find out what had happened. Joe and I had been interstate, in Sydney for the weekend, to see *The Phantom of the Opera*. Although we had seen it before, Joe had bought tickets for he knew I loved the show. But we were to be back in Melbourne by 2.00 pm and I had told the children of this plan before we left. 'What's wrong with you – why didn't you come?' I asked. 'Why should I come?' he replied. 'You're always in front of the computer, studying.' It was true: I regularly spent Saturday and Sunday studying, because when a person works outside the home and also has a family, she doesn't have time to study, and besides – she is tired. There isn't time to concentrate on studies during the week. Weekends provide the only free blocks of time.

I said to my son: 'You know I've been doing this for eight years. It's not the first time!' But it made me realise that children grow up and may miss out on some of the contact children like to have. It was then that I said to myself: 'Well, I've achieved what I want to achieve.' I used to say I would go all the way and do a PhD. But for now, I'm satisfied. What I wanted to do, I've done.

Before I completed the degree, I had a picture of going up to receive the certificate and giving a speech. I believed that a piece of paper would give me confidence. As it was, I received the piece of paper – and *nothing happened!* My confidence didn't improve.

When I worked as a cleaner, I talked about politics, what was happening in the world, articles that appeared in the newspapers – people ignored me. But when I mentioned I was studying – *then* they would listen! Really listen! So education is very important: both education learned at school, and education about people's life experiences.

Like a lot of people, I believed that no one would listen to me or class me as knowing anything if I didn't have a piece of paper. It is as if having a degree legitimises anything a person has to say. It places 'what you learned at school' above life experience. Yet some people can be 'good' academics but not have experienced *life*. I feel I have something of both, now.

> *I believed that no one would listen to me or class me as knowing anything if I didn't have a piece of paper.*

I have no idea where my tenacity came from: the will to be in the forefront of demands made by the cleaners, then going back to school and sticking it out through university, even when the going got tough. (I usually refer to university as school, perhaps because this takes me back to the childhood schooling I never had.) Even as a young girl I worked so hard, helping my mother clean the school. So it is as if I've always worked hard. Even coming to Australia, particularly at such a young age, was difficult, and I have done well. I was never afraid of hard work. I knew we were poor and I knew there were rich people in our street and how they lived.

I always wanted a family, a mother and a father. At the orphanage I had before me a fantasy, a picture of the sort of family I would like to have. The picture consisted of a man who would be the breadwinner, who would work and provide for me, protect me and look after me for ever.

The notion was very strong in Malta that boys are 'better' than girls. Education for girls was seen as a waste. Girls get married. To have girls in the family is a drawback, because girls are a greater responsibility than boys. Whatever boys do, there can be no wrong, according to accepted wisdom in Malta, but whatever girls do . . . ! Well, they can get pregnant for a start! My brother was the only one in our family who gained an education. He was the father figure in our household, and this would have had an effect on me as well, in the way I grew up and the ideas I developed. My life has been full of struggle and instead of going under, I have just kept on struggling.

In Australia I took on many roles without realising I was becoming a leader. When my children were at kindergarten I attended the parents' meetings. The committee needed a president, secretary and treasurer. I was drafted. I recall asking: 'Okay. What do I have to do?' They replied: 'Oh, nothing, just open the meeting.' I thought I could manage that, so I took on the job as president of the kindergarten.

I took on many roles without realising I was becoming a leader.

I visited my sons' school to talk with their teachers. I was reluctant to become involved because I believed my English wasn't good. One of the teachers, Carmelina de Brinkis, taught my children Maltese, so I spoke with her in Maltese. As we sat and talked she said to me: 'Why don't you get involved with the school?' I replied: 'Oh, I don't know and . . .' I thought I couldn't do it. I wasn't on their level (meaning 'educated'). I didn't want anyone to laugh at me. I was afraid. But she asked me what she could do to encourage mothers from non-English speaking backgrounds to become involved in the school. 'Why don't you do a multicultural luncheon?' I asked. 'This is how people will come. Invite them, they will see that it is really important. Send a note telling them about it. Don't do it through the newsletter.' It worked. Then I became a member of the school council.

It was then that I realised: *These people are like me.* I could communicate. Perhaps my English was not 100 percent, but we understood each other. From there, I became involved in other groups. In our local community centre, I facilitated the multicultural women's group. But at the time, if anyone had asked me if I was working in the Women's Movement, I wouldn't have thought about it in those terms. We were women having coffee together, chatting about women's issues. Was I running a group?! Later, for the first time ever, I organised a celebration of International Women's Day for Maltese women. We held it at the Maltese Community Council Centre in Parkville. It was the first time the Maltese centre had held a function for women.

Over the years I have come to recognise the effort I put in to relating to people. I have English and Maltese, but I make sure I can use one word that has a significance for women of other cultures. I have worked frequently with women of varying ethnic backgrounds. When you smile and say: 'Good morning' to a Greek woman in her language, you know you put a big smile on her face. It's *her* language. When I walk down the street and hear a Maltese voice, I feel *good*. If a woman is Italian, I'd say: 'Come sta.' If she's Greek, I'd say: 'Ti kanis.' If she's Spanish, a smile, and it's: 'Ola.' I made sure I had a word in the language that made people feel comfortable. One of the difficulties for women of minority ethnic background is that we are all isolated, despite living amongst our people. The most important aspect of working with women and gaining support for women's issues is breaking down this sense of isolation. The coordinator of the Neighbourhood House where I worked often said that the way I related to women from different backgrounds and cultures was my best feature. For a smile is universal, it speaks any language.

My work in family violence has also involved supporting women attending court to obtain intervention orders. When I was employed as domestic violence outreach worker for the Maltese community I thought at first that the women wouldn't come to me, because I was too wellknown. But it didn't work out that way. People came to see me. It was very difficult for me working with my own community. Sometimes I knew the women and their husbands. Working for the Maltese community was like working with your family. I worried for my own family.

When I had to go to courts, the men would come to talk to me. I told them that what I was doing was my work. The men would write down my car number. Sometimes they rang me at home. My telephone number is not in the telephone book, but they would find it out. The work made me sad and very angry.

I had to be strong to enforce my policy of not taking my work home with me, to my family. This is an issue for all minority ethnic background women who are involved in their community and who become involved in the Women's Movement, for we cannot remove ourselves from our community and do not want to do so. But it means that I might give professional help to a woman, then meet her in the street the following day, or meet her at a social function. This is the difficulty I experienced in working with the community in which I live.

I have encouraged other women to do what I have done. I would have been one of the first women from my area (the west), of my age, a mother with little formal education, to go to university. I was 38 when I began school. I am seen as a role model for other women from minority ethnic backgrounds. I have been asked to talk with other women about my study and my experience. In my job as outreach worker, then at the Neighbourhood Houses where I worked, women would come to me, saying: 'I know what you have done, that's why I'm here.' 'You really encouraged me to come, and to go on.' Many women came to me, talking to me and telling me I was the reason they were there. I felt proud that other women could relate to what I had done. It is like sharing the load and the struggles of studies and of being at school. And I didn't tell the women that it was easy . . . studying.

I felt proud that other women could relate to what I had done. It is like sharing the load and the struggles of studies . . .

Whilst working as further education coordinator at one of the Neighbourhood Houses, I enjoyed interviewing the women who came saying: 'I want to do something but I really do not know what I want to do.' I would ask them: 'Tell me, when you were really little, what did you dream of doing, but have never done?' They would say, perhaps: 'I wanted to be a nurse but I couldn't, because I married, had kids.' I would reply: 'You can do it now. This is how you go about it.' I would ask: 'How far did you go in school?' They'd reply: 'Oh, Form 4.' I would say: 'Gee! That's even better than me. I went only to Grade 6.' Then the women would look at me and say: *'No!'* They were astounded. *'And you're doing this job!'* I would tell them how it was that I went back to school, learning to read and write in English, then went from there on to another step. I explained it to them as steps. *Take one step at a time, then it doesn't seem so daunting.* I explained that once the first steps have been taken, a person can consider what she will do next. She can then determine whether she does want to go on to complete a degree, or whether she wants to do something else. I remember when I used to say: 'Oh! a degree! *Three years fulltime.*' I would think to myself: 'I'll be 60 by the time I've finished.' Well, I've done two degrees, and I'm not 60 yet! I'm not even fifty! Aim at achievable goals. You can do it. Anyone can do it – with a bit of support!

But together with acknowledging the support I have received, it is important to note that undermining can take place too. In one of my positions, I received conflicting messages. I was used as the example of the 'successful' 'ethnic woman'. I was portrayed as the role model: 'Look at what Joyce is doing.' The fact that I had gone to school and gained a degree from university was, on the one hand, regarded highly. Yet on the other hand it was used to undermine me: as if there always had to be an announcement about 'what Joyce has done', as if it were not simply a natural outcome of my own hard work and determination. It was as if I was the 'poor cousin' who had 'succeeded'. As I went further and further in my education, I found that there was an attitude on the part of some women that I was not passing examinations and assignments through my own efforts, but that 'special rules' were being made for me and other 'ethnic people'. I began to say: 'Look! They're not passing me for my good looks! I'm working really, really hard!' Then the messages began to go out: 'Joyce is stressed out. She's too busy studying to do her job.' I love studying, and at one time put it ahead of my family, but I was certainly performing my job in the appropriate way – competently and professionally.

It was as if I was the 'poor cousin' who had 'succeeded'.

This was a bad experience, but I do not allow it to colour my views about *all* women. There was a great deal of emphasis at my workplace on 'conflict resolution', but I felt that even if attending the courses and learning the techniques might be useful in some settings, it certainly didn't work in relation to my job. I began asking questions about the structure of the workplace and this led to continuing conflict, and eventually the matter was resolved at the door of industrial arbitration.

But at the same time this negative experience was happening, something good was occurring for me too. I was appointed to the Victoria Women's Council. The convenor was chosen, then over 100 applications for membership of the council were received. Three Aboriginal women were selected, then 50 women were interviewed, of whom 12 were chosen. I had seen the advertisement in the *Age* and was interested. I cut it out. Then I had a telephone call from Joan Kirner, who was our local politician, who said to me: 'Joyce, you just have to get involved. Get your application *in* at once!' I said: 'I'm thinking about it.' That wasn't enough. 'Get your application IN!' That was the extra encouragement I needed. How could I *not* apply after that? I wrote the letter the day applications closed – and faxed it in. I still have a copy of it.

Now when I look back on the situations I've been in – the positive and the negative, the instances where I have been supported and that where I was not, the strongest message that comes through to me so powerfully is that *I've survived*. I have had great encouragement from many great women. 'Keep going, Joyce. You're right', they would say. 'Don't give up!' This means a great deal.

> . . . *the strongest message that comes through to me so powerfully is that I've survived.*

I think back on those early role models, such as Ita Buttrose, and continue to be grateful for her example. I saw her several months ago on television talking about menopause. I still relate to her, because I am coming to this stage in my life too. And I think she has been and continues to be a role model for many women: a woman with a career, she shows that women *can* succeed in many fields, and that it is not necessary to 'have a man'. Many women believe that without a man they cannot do anything. It is important that prominent women project the truth.

As for Maggie Tabberer – she still has class, and I still admire her. Then I went to see *Hello Dolly* when it was playing in Melbourne and suddenly, there was Denise Drysdale on stage! I hadn't known she was in the show. She had a small part, but a great impact. At the interval I was leafing through the program and talking about Denise's part, and a woman standing alongside me overheard. 'Oh, you like Denise too,' she said. 'Yes, I think I've sort of grown up with her and her go-go dancing on *Kommotion*.' 'You must be my age,' said the woman. So, there I was, at the theatre, with a woman striking up a conversation with me because, although we had never met and probably will never meet again, we had been similarly affected by Denise Drysdale and her television performances. Perhaps

Denise stood for the childhood and teenage years I never had, and that is very important to me.

I believe that everyone has something to contribute. The academics who taught me at university had a powerful impact on me, and I have moved on from those days when I sat watching television, but no one can take away what Denise Drysdale, Maggie Tabberer and Ita Buttrose gave to me by being women who stood up for themselves, refused to be put down, and kept *on*. And they're *still* keeping on – just as I am. We need to recognise and acknowledge each other.

PART III
Contradictions

Women Must Keep Talking

Joyce Nicholson

All her life, Joyce Nicholson has been surrounded by books. Born in 1919 in Melbourne, Victoria, from the age of 12 she began helping her father in his publishing business, after school, in school holidays and then fulltime. After the second world war she gave up paidwork for marriage and had four children. She then started writing and reviewing children's books, radio scripts, articles and so on. In all she has written what she calls 'a mixed bag' of 32 books, which she feels reflect what she was doing at the time of writing – children's books, how-to books and, in 1972, when she became a committed feminist, books and articles on feminism and the fate of women.

In 1968, after occupying many roles and holes in her father's business, generally 'filling in', as is so often the fate of women, Joyce Nicholson was finally elevated to what, she maintains, had she been a son, would have been her role many years earlier. She was appointed managing director. It was great fun and she was a great success.

Try as I can, search my memory as much as possible, I do not remember one single woman who, in my early years, helped or advised me to aim or work for the future that, although I did not realise it at the time, was the one I most wanted to achieve. I was surrounded with love. There were my mother and several loving aunts, and this love provided me with great security and the basis for strength, but all of them preached that a woman's role was to be passive, supportive, non-achieving, and the greatest happiness for a woman was to be found in marriage and motherhood.

The one person who influenced me in a different direction was a man. My father. He too believed in marriage for women, but also taught me to be capable, confident, independent, strong. I do not think I am strong. I think I am as weak as water, but people keep describing me as a 'strong woman'. If that is so, it is because of my father. There was nothing in my father's eyes that I could not do. We were great mates. He took me to the football and cricket. We went on long hikes in the country together. Above all, from the age of 12, I went in to his small publishing business, during holidays and after school, to help him. I learnt about printing, editing, design, and management. In my teens he left me to run the business, while he went interstate. He was a great man for initiative and new ideas, but he was not good at detail. He left much of the detail to me, and that was very educative.

But a formal education was not considered for me. My mother sat by my brother night after night to make sure he studied and qualified for the university. The family even found enough money for him to attend Queen's College. But education was not considered important for girls and, although I had also planned to go to the university, at age 15 it somehow happened that I left school and went into Dad's business fulltime. I do not remember any conversation about it, but it must have been somehow discussed. I know I was beginning to be interested in boys and that my mother bought me some very smart ready-made clothes from Cann's. Until then I had always worn clothes made by my mother – very well made too – but the store clothes seemed glamorous. Perhaps for one brief period I believed I wanted to leave school and start earning some money.

Something must have happened at home to influence me. All I needed was one word of encouragement and I would have stayed at school. I always loved school.

All I needed was one word of encouragement and I would have stayed at school.

Although I was often top of the class at the Methodist Ladies College (MLC) not one woman there tried to keep me at school. What a bleak story it sounds for a committed feminist. I was a perfect example of sex role conditioning. But maybe it was these early experiences that later led to my feminism. Worse was to follow. Predictably, being blonde and slim and compliant, I married a man considered very eligible, tall, handsome, dark, good at sport, educated at one of the best schools, Scotch College. I met him at the university. For I did get there. I soon discovered what a terrible mistake I had made by leaving school so young, so Dad suggested I do a parttime university course, which I did, ending with that most useless qualification, a pass arts degree, but very suitable for women – nothing too difficult or clever. I was married during the second world war and worked for Dad during the war years, managing the business for several months when he went overseas.

My father's business, which he founded himself, was D W Thorpe Pty Ltd, and it published the journal and reference books for the book and stationery trades. I worked in it, including Saturday mornings, for about 12 years after leaving school, so I knew thoroughly every aspect of it.

There was only Dad and me and a junior typist through all those years, and had I been a son, it would have been accepted that one day I would take it over. Predictably again, however, when peace came and my husband, whom I loved passionately, was returned to me, I gave up paidwork and proceeded to have four children. It was a custom in the 1940s for women to be sacked when they were married, but I left of my own free will, longing for the happiness of being a wife and a mother.

It was a custom in the 1940s for women to be sacked when they were married, but I left of my own free will ...

For a while I was indeed very happy. I had a son and a daughter and we lived in a rented house that was small and convenient. But then we had two more children, and moved to a big two-story house in the fashionable part of Hawthorn. We also owned a seaside house, and gradually the terrible truth began to dawn on me. It was hard work and, although we lived at a high standard, there was never any money for me. It all went on the two big houses and school fees, once again for the best schools. Worse still, I began to find I HATED being a wife and mother, much as I loved my children. I wanted to be doing something else, similar to what I had done before marriage.

But fate was not kind to me. During those ghastly years I did not find one of my close or casual friends who shared my despair. The Scotch College mothers not only worked harder and entertained better than I did, but they seemed to enjoy it. My old university friends seemed happy with their lot. Not one woman I knew well worked outside the home. Two were doctors and worked parttime, but all stayed home, giving the impression of domestic bliss.

Although there was no suggestion I should return to Dad's business ultimately to manage it, my Dad did give me a lifeline during those difficult years. He suggested I review children's books at home for his main publication, the trade journal for the book trade. Also, he began to employ young men to 'take over' the business (never a thought by any of us that I would make a good 'young man'), and as Dad never took the trouble to train those men properly, they always got into a muddle when he was away, so I was regularly called in to tidy up the mess – another suitable female occupation. My children were all at school by this time, so I would dash in to the office for a few hours, and then home again to cook dinner.

Reviewing children's books led to writing children's books, also suitable for women and something I could do at home. Again it was a man I remember who helped most there, Lloyd O'Neil, who was starting his own Australian publishing company, Lansdowne Press, and suggested I write some Australian animal stories while he would provide photographers. These were a great success. Practically every year then I wrote either a picture or full-length children's book. Even here I did not receive much support from women I knew well. There were often suggestions that my writing showed I was not satisfied with my married life. If I had known then what I know now I would have answered: 'Too right, I jolly well am not satisfied.' All I did was feel guilty.

If I had known then what I know now I would have answered: 'Too right, I jolly well am not satisfied.'

Two notable exceptions were Barbara Graham and Joan Harris, old university friends, who were always supportive, and would tell me how they had bought my books as gifts, often even sending them overseas. It made me feel good. And there were often women I met casually who seemed impressed with my efforts and made me feel proud. Also my writing brought me in touch with women from a different world. Because I wrote books and had four children, I was considered newsworthy, so every new book brought women journalists to the house to interview me and arrange for my photograph to be in the paper. My confidence grew. Then Ada Norris, who founded the Children's Book Council in Victoria, asked me to organise the first children's book week. It too was a great success and although she was difficult to work with, Ada Norris was supportive and appreciative of my efforts. I did this for four years, and met some wonderful women who not only helped me, but made me feel I was doing something worthwhile outside the home, women such as Ena Sambell, Ethel St John, Geva Macmillan, Nance Donkin and Vi Pritchard.

Although still feeling guilty, I slowly rebelled against my accepted role. I went to a Writers' Week school in Adelaide and had the great good fortune to spend several days with two outstanding women, Florence James and Mary Durack. For the first time I met role models, who were not only achievers but felt that women usually had a rough deal in life. Florence told me what was wrong with a novel I had written, which when I re-wrote was published as *The Convict's Daughter*. I returned home with my head full of new ideas. My children slowly grew older, as did my Dad, and he decided to retire and appointed yet another young man as managing director of the business. It should have been my job, but I never thought of it. If only there had been some aware women in my circle to point out what was truly my heritage.

But fate again took a hand. The young man proved more and more inefficient, and Dad asked me would I work in the business for several days a week to 'keep an eye on things'. Anyone with experience in such a situation knows how impossible it is to 'keep an eye on things' if one has no authority or access to important papers. So I found myself the satisfying job of editing the book trade journal, for which I was paid less than the young man's typist. But I thought I was content, as I used the money I earned to pay someone to cook dinner each night. To me it seemed marvellous. Then an amazing thing happened. After about a year, a very small occurrence in the office made me suddenly positive that the young man was not only inefficient, but dishonest. One day after passing the secretary's office, I noticed she was altering one of the account books. What gave me the strength to act as I did then, I will not ever know. I had never been good at standing up for myself, something people who know me now will not believe. Perhaps it was frustration born from years of being passive and supportive and over the previous year putting up with what were actually impossible conditions in the business.

'I want to take all the account books home,' I suddenly found myself saying.

'You can't do that,' said the secretary. 'It's not possible,' said the managing director, appearing at the door, having overheard the conversation.

'Well I'm going to,' I said. I quickly found a box and started filling it with as many account books, cheque butts etc as I could find. I knew them all, for they were similar to the ones on which I had worked years earlier. Thankfully, no computers then. As some of the documents had been hidden by now, I had the humiliating task of crawling round on my hands and knees and looking behind and under books and furniture with two pairs of hostile eyes watching me. I finally left the office, carrying my load, went straight to the home of my sister, Lois Woodward, dumped the box on her table, saying: 'There's something terribly wrong here,' and went home to be sick for days.

My sister then, and later, was wonderfully supportive. She sorted out the papers, and the final result was holding consultations with the accountant which concluded with the dismissal of the young man. At the next directors' meeting, my Dad finally said to me: 'Well, Joyce, I guess you had better take over the company.' 'I don't think I know enough,' I said. Can you believe it? Such was my socialisation. You see, I knew a lot about editing, but not much about the politics of the book trade. Then I thought that I couldn't make more of a mess of it than the young man had. So I took the offered job.

I knew a lot about editing, but not much about the politics of the book trade.

It was 1968 and I was 49 years old. The strange thing was that I found once you sit in a seat of power, you receive all the information you need. Minutes, pressreleases and reports land on your desk, and I quickly learnt all about the book trade. For six months I sat at my desk, writing, editing, trying to get the journals somewhere near coming out on time. They had been appearing as much as two months late. And while I did that my sister sorted out the cupboards and drawers which my predecessor had left in complete and utter chaos. It appeared the business had become so muddled that he could not cope. Every month he started a new file, putting away in a cupboard what was waiting to be attended to, to be forgotten. Lois sorted it all out, and gradually order was restored. After six months

I could leave my desk occasionally and began attending trade meetings. I was starting an absolutely marvellous life.

I then gradually built up a great staff of women, Penny Somma, Vivienne Brophy and Pat White, to mention only a few, who helped me to create a successful business from one nearly bankrupt. I loved the work, I had all the authority one could desire, and I earned an ever-increasing income. The work involved often travelling interstate, which seemed very glamorous to me. Everything was better than I could ever possibly have imagined. Still, believe it or not, I was not completely happy. Still I felt guilty. I felt there was something wrong with me. I should be home enjoying being wife and mother.

Women are not all the same, any more than men are all the same, all wanting to be plumbers or doctors.

Then, late in 1971, another amazing thing happened. I read *The Female Eunuch* by Germaine Greer, and suddenly my entire world changed. It was as if a burden had rolled from my back. I understood my sex role conditioning. I need no longer feel guilty. There was no good reason why every woman should like being a wife and mother. Women are not all the same, any more than men are all the same, all wanting to be plumbers or doctors.

Even better things were to follow. I started going to meetings of the Women's Electoral Lobby (WEL), and met hundreds of women who felt exactly the same as I did, who had experienced the same doubts, worries and guilt as I had. The happiness that the Women's Movement brought to me cannot be described. No longer need I feel peculiar, different, a freak. I could stand tall and hold my head high. The confidence I gained cannot be assessed. After all those years of feeling I was swimming against the stream, I found the strength of sisterhood, of women swimming beside me towards the goal of achieving more equality for women. Just a tiny few of those women were Beatrice Faust, Jan Harper, Katy Richmond, Noelene Chappell, Di Gribble, Hilary McPhee, Eve Mahlab, Josephine Capp, Helen Glezer and so many, many others. I was a different person, and through the years since then it has been the same – there are so many more women one meets all the time to share one's problems, to encourage, to praise. One amongst others is Eva Cox in Sydney, who is regularly interviewed on radio about women's issues and speaks articulately and strongly for women – like others who do so, a joy to hear.

When I took over Thorpe's it must be said that the men in the two trades were wonderfully helpful. They had known my father for years, many of them had known me also, mostly when I had been younger, and they were aware of the problems in the business, some of them more aware than my father and I were, and they came to sit down opposite me at my desk, asking: 'How can I help you?' I thought people may believe I had pushed the young man out, but as far as I know, and fortunately it was not until years later that I was told about it, there was only one man, a publishers' salesman, who went around accusing me of this.

There is probably no industry where men are more understanding and sympathetic to women than publishing and bookselling. Spending one's life producing or selling books has a civilising effect on people, and I doubt if women are treated better in any other trade. They are not well-paid but no one in the book world is particularly well rewarded, and bookmen do appreciate and award women, as well as being aware of such matters as discrimination and sexual harassment. Alas and alack, however, no group of men is perfect, and as I became more established and the company more successful, I did become aware of how even in the book industry the work women did could be trivialised. Although I held the same position as my father, and ran the business much better, in my almost 20 years of being described as 'one of the most important women in the trade', I was only once asked to address an important meeting. Everyone thought and said I was wonderful, but no one offered me a position of importance, outside what I was already doing. Who knows? Perhaps I did not deserve it.

... in my almost 20 years of being described as 'one of the most important women in the trade', I was only once asked to address an important meeting.

But this was where other women in publishing and bookselling were such a strength to me, as I guess I was to them, women such as Sally Milner, Hilary McPhee, Di Gribble, Liz McDonald, Anne O'Donovan, Pat Healy, Eve Abbey and many more. Sometimes, different ones at different times, we would get together and laugh about the thoughtless things men did to us. One simple experience we all suffered was our invisibility. I would tell the others about the time I was on the export development committee of the Australian Book Publishers Association (ABPA) – I went to the Frankfurt Book Fair every year, then. At a general meeting back in Australia, Geoffrey King, the president, was hearing the reports from the various committees. He looked around. 'Oh, there's no one here from the Export Committee,' he said. I put up my hand. 'What about me?' I asked diffidently.

Hilary McPhee's story is about the first publishers' conference she attended. It was in Canberra, and at the opening cocktail party someone said to her: 'Who are you working for now?' 'Heinemann's,' replied Hilary. 'Oh. Who is their representative here?'

The very next day at the opening meeting of the conference, Hilary McPhee and Sally Milner were sitting together, with several men on either side of them. When the rollcall came, and everyone was asked to stand up in turn and say which company they represented, these two were not given the chance. They were passed over from the men on their left to the men on their right. Hilary is now one of Australia's leading publishers and

Sally Milner, with her own company for many years, was the president in 1991 of the same Australian Book Publishers' Association (ABPA). This 'invisibility syndrome' is like the 'don't take any notice syndrome'. You make a perfectly sensible suggestion at a meeting, and no one takes any notice. A few minutes later a man makes the same suggestion, and all the other men present think how excellent it is. How we women would get together and tell these tales and roll about laughing. It was laughter that kept us sane. Just like the Blacks in Doris Lessing's wonderful book, *African Laughter*, about Zimbabwe.

How unkind this is to the many close male friends who showed me so much kindness, and still do, during my years in the book trade. I could name dozens of them, but then this book is about women, not about men.

When I was asked to write this piece, the request was that I write about how women had helped me and how I helped other women, and I must admit I felt just as blank about the second part as I did at the beginning about the first. But when one starts to remember, it is amazing what comes into one's mind. At first I honestly found it hard to remember any women I had helped. Yet I know I have. When I was given an Order of Australia for services to literature and the book publishing industry, I received a host of congratulatory letters, many from women who said how much I had helped them. Some of these women I could not even remember, and with those I could remember I had no idea what I had done. When I wrote *The Heartache of Motherhood*, again there were so many letters from women saying how much I had helped them, for they felt just as I did, and it relieved their guilt to know they were not alone in finding it hard always to enjoy motherhood. Yet all I was doing was writing what I felt. I was not thinking: 'How can I help other women?' When I gave a speech at the Mary Owen Dinner in 1991, which I thought would be an awful failure (for all I did was tell the story of my life, particularly my socialisation), I was amazed at the reception the speech received and the number of women who came up afterwards to tell me how much I had helped them.

> ... *we all must keep talking and persistently agitating.*

I had two simple aims in that particular speech. One was to be a little bit amusing, if possible, and I could not believe how much shared laughter resulted. The other was to tell women that we all must keep talking and persistently agitating if we are to achieve any sort of real equality. Women have to change the world, slowly and gradually, for themselves. No one else will do it.

Perhaps that sums up where I have helped other women. I have possibly been a role model and my willingness to talk of my miseries and my problems has helped others. Secondly, I know I have always, since 1972, done all I can to encourage women, to stand up for them, stop men putting them down, stop women putting themselves down, tell women they can achieve things if they really try, tell them they should apply for promotions, apply for increases in pay, realise their worth, know they can do things as well as men, if not better. The only actual example I can remember is a young bridge friend of mine, Juliet Pettitt, who was telling me how unhappy she was in her librarian position, so typically I asked her why she did not apply for more money or another job. So she did, and received a promotion.

I asked her why she did not apply for more money or another job. So she did, and received a promotion.

Probably the three years I spent actively working for WEL helped other women considerably, although I never saw it that way. There was so much joy and euphoria in working with other women of similar views, there was so much laughter at our meetings and conferences, there was so much comradeship in everything we did, that as far as I was concerned, I was the one who benefited, not other women. Yet now I think more about it, most of the women I worked with were middleclass, already with good jobs, so the conditions we wanted to change were not really about to alter our own lifestyles much, although the process certainly altered our attitudes to ourselves.

The first WEL meeting I attended I started to edit the WEL *Broadsheet*, first with Jocelyn Mitchell and then by myself. I was able to offer a big empty room in our Hawthorn house to be used as the WEL office, and how I loved the women who staffed it, typed out the *Broadsheet*, and then printed it out on the old cranking Gestetner we acquired cheaply. I was part of the hoard of women who interviewed politicians before the 1972 election and recorded the views of each one on matters of concern to women. Then I went with Helen Glezer to interview Creighton Burns of the *Age*, and he not only agreed to publish the results in a four-page supplement just before the election, but was willing to print 30 000 copies on green paper for us to use as publicity.

We also attended every political meeting possible, in some electorates calling our own meetings, and asking awkward questions, particularly about sex education, family planning, contraceptives and abortion, subjects that were taboo until then. This was probably one of the most successful things we did. Much of the equal opportunity legislation that came in over the following years has not brought the good results we believed it would. The basic fact that women not only bear but rear the country's children makes it hard for many to make use of legislation, no matter how good it is. But the knowledge women gained through the free discussion of contraceptives can never be lost. Believe it or not, back in the early 1970s, these matters were mostly not mentioned in public, and girls and women were amazingly ignorant. Once these private matters were made public women have never been able to be forced back into ignorance.

In regard to the WEL survey, the Liberal Party members were shown to be much less sympathetic than those of the Labor Party (ALP) and when Gough Whitlam was swept into power we felt it was all due to our work. It wasn't, of course, but we did add our bit.

When the next state elections came round, in May 1973, WEL organised a large forum in the Dallas Brookes Hall in East Melbourne, and the four party leaders agreed to attend to be crossexamined. I was given the task of summing up what the leaders said in reply to family planning questions. I also went with Eve Mahlab before the forum to see Ron Casey of Channel 7, to suggest he televise the program. He agreed, and when Eve asked for a payment of $3000 I nearly dropped through the floor. But I did not bat an eyelid, and Ron agreed. Eve always believed that women underprice themselves and constantly urges them to ask for more. How right she is.

Channel 7 telecast the program twice, once live, and again the following day. It was a great success, and many women, as well as men, were made aware for the first time of feminist ideas and of unreasonable male attitudes. There were many other actions in which WEL took part which helped women learn more about their rights. I remember now how amazed I was at the number of times younger women would come up to say to me: 'When I heard you get up and talk I thought I would never be able to do anything like that. And now I do it all the time.'

> ... *many women, as well as men, were made aware for the first time of feminist ideas and of unreasonable male attitudes.*

Now I join every women's association I hear of and subscribe to every feminist magazine. I have a large library of books written by women, thousands of them, and every picture hanging on my walls is painted by women, except two by my sons. I once felt a bit of a nut about this, especially when men seemed to think it was a bit odd. But don't most men collect men's paintings and men's books? Look at the antiquarian book lists. They are nearly all books by men, and the male books are always more expensive than those by women. Then in May 1987 Judith Woodfall wrote an article 'My Home and I', for the *Age*, and she described my house as 'a home dominated by women and their work'. That made me feel good and not a nut any more. Women can be wonderfully supportive.

One of the most influential things I did for women was in 1988, when I launched a 'Million Dollar Appeal' for the Victorian Women's Trust. I sold my business in 1987 and because the Women's Movement had done so much for me I wanted to do something for it. I had all sorts of ideas like scholarships and trusts, and then I went to a meeting addressed by a young Jewish male lawyer with considerable experience, Jon Faine, who is known for his work on law reform and, at the time, had a program on 3LO, the ABC station in Melbourne. He explained how he had been employed in large law firms where legacies had been left for trusts to be set up for particular aims, and that large sums of the money donated were wasted on administration. He said, if one wanted to leave a legacy, one should choose some organisation that supported the sort of causes that most equalled one's own ideas, and then trust them and leave the money to them.

After much thought I decided for me this was the Victorian Women's Trust (VWT), for it helps under-privileged women to start businesses, form cooperatives, set up forums, conventions and carry out projects that the more established sources of support are not interested in helping. So I suggested to Jenny Florence, then the VWT's administrative officer, that I launch this special appeal. I started it with, for me, a substantial donation, and I paid the expenses of the appeal. I have also willed the VWT what is also, for me, a large amount of money. The appeal still has not reached a million dollars but it is slowly growing, and it brought much publicity, and once again we all enjoyed the euphoric experience of women working together for women. I did not enjoy the publicity at the time about the money I was donating, but I wanted to set some sort of example. It may be just coincidence, but I felt many women heard about the VWT for the first time, still support it, and that since then it has gone from strength to strength.

I did not enjoy the publicity at the time about the money I was donating, but I wanted to set some sort of example.

Once again, however, I felt I gained more from this gesture of mine than others did. There were all the wonderful women who came to the house to help address envelopes and stick on stamps. There were the women who donated large sums of money and those who worked on the appeal council with me, Val Byth, Marion Webster, Eve Mahlab, Janet Bruce, Ann Morrow, and once again my sister, Lois Woodward. Above all, there was a young woman, Fran Kelly, who was assigned by the VWT to liaise with me. What a fine young feminist she was, caring, helpful, with a great sense of humour. She was working for Quit then, and was disappointed she was not appointed to a feminist program with the ABC in Sydney, 'The Coming Out (Ready or Not) Show' (and which is now called 'Out Loud') in which she was interested. Instead, Fran Kelly went on to be employed on AM and PM on 3LO, programs heard nationally every day of the paid working week, and now I hear her regularly, cross-examining politicians and other leading people, mostly from Canberra. Every time I hear her it gives me a warm glow. *There's my young Fran*, I think.

What is so important about all this and what I have done is that women should keep talking to women. Although it is disappointing that many men find feminism strident and threatening, it is even sadder that so many women do not support it or even understand it. It is our job therefore to keep working for it, keep talking about it, informing women, until they all become our sisters and join us in our quest for equality. We need every forum there is for women to talk and women to listen.

Gorgeous Girls, Great Women

Natasha Stott Despoja

Natasha Stott Despoja is an Australian Democrats' senator for South Australia. At 26 she is the youngest-ever female member of the Australian Parliament. She has grown up in the Women's Movement and represented young women on the South Australian Women's Suffrage Centenary Committee. Amongst many other offices and activities, she has worked as a freelance journalist, community radio producer and political consultant, was women's officer at the University of Adelaide in 1989 and in 1991 was state women's officer with the National Union of Students (NUS).

A former president of the Students' Association of the University of Adelaide, Natasha Stott Despoja is committed to improving education quality and is a staunch opponent of fees for education. For recreation, she is happiest when 'hanging out' with friends in Adelaide's Rundle Street cafés and keeps a steady supply of chocolate on hand for those occasions when a politician's life is not a happy one.

'The Gorgeous Girls.' Hardly the name for a feminist collective, it was, however, the first women's group to which I belonged. The group gave an assortment of pre-pubescent girls, who didn't quite fit in with the other students because of appearance, ethnicity or divorced parents, a chance to talk about boys, make-up, homework and pop music. Through this network, whose entry card was a patterned ruler, I found out what a condom was, even if I didn't quite understand its purpose. Like most things in primaryschool this group was short-lived but it was the beginning of something that would be ongoing in my life – being a part of women's networks. 'The Gorgeous Girls' was my first glimpse of how women can provide support for each other, just as the group's disbandment, when two members had a fall-out, taught me how fractious these groups could be.

I am from a small family. Although my mother, Shirley, is the fifth child born to Jessica Stott (née Swinfield), she is the youngest of a youngest and experienced an isolation from her brothers and sisters because of age and education: she was the first in her family to attend university. This isolation was compounded by geography and her decision to marry Mario Despoja, a Croatian immigrant, whom she met when he performed well on a television games show in the early 1960s.

As the storybooks would have it, this tall and handsome man, with thick accent, managed to win the topic of 'Australian history' and the heart of the female reporter sent to interview him. Of course the fairytale ends there.

I was born in Adelaide on 9 September 1969, my length the same as the column space in the newspaper, the *Advertiser*, where my mother worked. We moved to Canberra in the early 1970s where my brother, Luke, was born and my father was a public servant in the department of Aboriginal affairs, under Gough Whitlam.

My parents were Labor (ALP) voters and staunch unionists. One of their attempts to imbue a sense of unionism and collectivism in my bones was when they placed me on Dad's shoulders at a country town Labor rally so I could see the great prime minister himself. Similarly, my memory of Whitlam's dismissal on 11 November 1975 is forged because I recall my parents' shock and disbelief as they watched it on television in the livingroom in our house in Queanbeyan.

Schoolgirl camaraderie was not necessarily a feature of my early school years. Enrolment at an all-girls school in Canberra ended when I refused to wear the regulation hat, and to nap at the required times. This rejection of single-sex education led to my involvement in a coeducation experiment at an all-boys school along with a handful of girls. Parents of the boys wanted Canberra Boys Grammar to be the Eton of Australia so the girls were eventually kicked out again.

I remember this period – when I was a member of a small band of primaryschoolers – as creative. I was encouraged to paint, sing, learn piano, read and act. I have fond memories of the friendships formed with the other girls.

I also remember leaving this environment; being bundled with my brother into a car in the middle of the day and driving to my aunt's house in Melbourne, Victoria. It was my mother's brave escape.

The importance of support groups is made clear when you lack them, and my mother's experiences have taught me the importance of support for women.

The importance of support groups is made clear when you lack them, and my mother's experiences have taught me the importance of support for women. It has made me seek supportive networks as well as create them. It has also toughened me so that I consider self-reliance and independence paramount. This means I often fail to utilise or create the networks I should, denying myself and others shared experiences and strategies.

These days we can talk more openly about the reality of families and how good families can be heaven on earth and bad families can be hell. I have benefited from this long battle by the Women's Movement which has shown that not all families are supportive and that women and children *often* suffer.

I saw how my mother lacked support: in her work at the *Advertiser* she watched as male colleagues were promoted above her; at home, while she worked nightshifts to support us, some babysitters were only too happy to tell us this behaviour made her an 'unfit' mother. This perception was connected with her severe hearing loss, a disability that has worsened over time so that she, like 11 percent of the population, experiences an isolation we cannot imagine. My mother was granted custody and worked to support two, usually warring, kids.

Shirley Stott Despoja is my strongest role model, someone who survived the roughest times without the assistance she desperately needed. It is often hard for children to compete with that kind of strength. The only way I was able to help her was to be her ears and happily escort her to opening nights which she attended in her capacity as South Australia's first arts editor. She is a living symbol of what feminism is all about and her influence in my life was obvious from early in my schooldays.

She is a living symbol of what feminism is all about and her influence was obvious from early in my schooldays.

'Girls can do anything boys can do – except boys can't have babies.' For this politicisation of my Grade 3 class I was given the role of the bride at the end-of-year school play. Outspoken girls learn their lessons early. I did not, however, reject outright the traditional female roles. Back in a coeducational environment I decided I would be a nurse or a ballet dancer, maybe both. Despite 10 years of ballet, knee problems put a stop to that but I have an enduring love of the arts and a wardrobe full of crab and canary costumes. The desire to help people through a profession like nursing soon gave way to an interest in social justice and the legal system.

Social justice meant equality, especially for women. My outspoken feminism was reluctantly tolerated by some teachers and the few who encouraged my beliefs, such as history teachers John Davies and Bernice Robbins, won my admiration. More debilitating were those teachers who baited me or labelled my views a 'phase' and even marked my work down because of them. I can see how writing an essay in my Year 11 maths exam entitled 'Mathematical Supremacy is a Patriarchal Myth' could be seen as provocative but it was wonderful revenge on a teacher who was surprised I had any maths ability considering my sex.

I did not always understand why it was the girls in my classes (more often than the boys) who made fun of feminism or who joined in the teachers' taunts about men being superior to women. But I am reminded of a quotation I read, written by Rosemary O'Grady, lawyer and journalist, along the lines of: 'The powerless often side with the powerful in order to survive.'

Highschool saw the creation of more sophisticated support networks, revolving around debating, politics and music. My closest friends and allies (male and female) shared my interest in social justice issues, public speaking and episodes of the D-Generation. These networks existed within the schoolgrounds and soon extended to the creation of a formal network of secondary school representatives which, in the International Year of Youth, created the first statewide secondary school representative body in South Australia. It was a role encouraged by an open-minded school principal, Diana Medlin, and provided opportunities to develop skills few young people learn, such as public speaking, media work, submission writing and liaison with government bodies.

It was invigorating being part of a union that empowered young people, a group whose views are often trivialised, patronised or ignored.

This marked my entry into politics. I had been a member of student councils throughout school but the creation of the State Council of Students coincided with debate over the reintroduction of tertiary fees, an issue that cut to the core of my beliefs: the need for equal access to education for all groups in society. My opposition to charging fees for higher education stopped me from joining the Labor Party (ALP), where I had thought my pro-union ties would lead me, and propelled me into a period of re-emerging student activism and the burgeoning National Union of Students (NUS).

> ... *an issue that cut to the core of my beliefs: the need for equal access to education for all groups in society.*

Women On Campus was a significant part of this activism. We knew fees would hit women hardest. Tertiary fees, in whatever form, would be a psychological and economic disincentive for traditionally disadvantaged groups to participate in higher education.

I have marched in women's rallies and protests all my life, all part of growing up a feminist. It was a natural response, upon arriving on campus, to join the campus women's group which had experienced a revival in the mid-1980s due to the efforts of hard-working feminists like Susan Coles, Kathy Edwards and Arna Eyers-White. Women On Campus no longer maypole-danced around the cloisters (as they had in their early days!) but it was a powerful and supportive network involving feminists from a variety of political perspectives and backgrounds. Through this network we provided support for women with speakers, self-defence classes, counselling and entertainment and, in turn, it was an invaluable support group for me when I ran for the Students' Association women's officer. It has since become a strong tradition to run women's tickets during election time to promote female candidates, regardless of political association but mindful of their feminist beliefs.

Adelaide University was forward-thinking enough to have been one of the first higher education institutions to create the position of a women's officer within the Students' Association. My first job in the position was as part of a team fighting a challenge to the position by a male engineering student. The case, in the state's Equal Opportunity Commission, was eventually dismissed and the position allowed under positive discrimination. This symbol of the backlash against feminism on campus is typical of the way structures and support for women have been manipulated and undermined by anti-feminists. It was also typical of how our energy is used fighting battles we believed won and, in this case, diverted our attention away from the day-to-day needs of women on campus.

> ... *a strong tradition to run women's tickets during election time to promote female candidates, regardless of political association but mindful of their feminist beliefs.*

'Sisterhood is powerful' and it was at this time at Adelaide University. We reclaimed old slogans as well as the night, invented and re-created campaigns and took on the administration, our sexist peers and the doubting Thomases and Thomasinas. We successfully fought for additional security and lighting for the campus, instituted annual lighting and security checks, and revived the Blue Stocking Weeks which have since come to prominence all over Australia.

While involving difficult issues like rape, sexual harassment and sexist curricula, my job was also to promote positive events for women such as 'theme weeks' on women's health, sport and education. At the risk of 'mainstreaming' women's issues, this was all part of providing events that would cater for as many women as possible while enticing those women who had not thought about the position of women in society to get involved. Campaigns ranged from providing free sanitary products, female speakers and bands on the lawns, to a national campaign which targeted a dubious product, touted as a contraceptive and sanitary device. These campaigns brought women together and were exciting and empowering.

During this time I realised the value and power of the media. It was an effective tool for attracting attention to women's issues on campus whether inadequate security or promoting events including Blue Stocking Weeks and an AUSTUDY wedding. Imagine the surprise of Adelaide residents on discovering the city's statues had been covered in blue stockings? Or lecturers arriving to find their overcrowded lecture theatres full of sardine cans?

Kicking up my heels in blue stockings with my sisters on campus was followed by jumping the 'hurdle' from being a women's officer to a so-called 'leadership' position when I became president of the Students' Association. In elections on and off campus, I have always run as a member of a team of like-minded men and women so that emotions and workload are as evenly shared as the beer and pizzas.

Kicking up my heels in blue stockings with my sisters on campus . . .

These support networks could not always translate to the academic boardrooms or university councils. Despite a show of bravado by insisting on dressing like a student (always wear jeans) I found the endless stream of academic and other meetings intimidating and often unproductive. I was often the only student and only woman in many meetings and unable to create alliances. My aim was to gain the respect of the establishment not necessarily their affection. Some student representatives try to enjoy a social relationship with the university administration, to counter their isolation, a position I found untenable. Brokering deals with the establishment or the government implies students have similar power when, in fact, student power comes from sheer numbers. It is unfortunate that these numbers are rarely tested or paraded in front of arrogant and complacent decision-makers.

In my first year on campus, students were flexing their numbers in the streets around Australia. They burnt effigies of then education minister, John Dawkins, lobbied Labor politicians and shouted slogans of protest. To no avail. In 1988 the Higher Education Contribution Scheme (HECS) succeeded the Higher Education Administration Charge and signified a new period of user-pays education in Australia, condemning many talented graduates to large debt levels.

While I suffered the tokenism afforded to student leaders by the administration, I was also conscious of the splintered nature of student activism. Our common goal: the fight for a publicly funded and accessible education system, was often compromised by student representatives mindful of Party loyalty and unwilling to jeopardise their political careers. During my time in campus politics I valued party-political independence and loyalty to a group of like-minded progressive, pro-education and pro-feminist students, above all else. I did not crave the often superficial camaraderie of the political parties on campus and my decision, years later, to join a political party, was a result of my beliefs, not in spite of them.

I joined a political party that did not have the same historical and political baggage of the old parties when it comes to women. The Australian Democrats have had three female leaders and, at one stage, had more female members of parliament than male members. When Senator Janine Haines, then leader of the Party, addressed my Australian politics lecture, she was the first politician I heard use the word 'patriarchy' and describe women's oppression. She did not shy away from issues like maintenance defaulters, and the treatment of women in politics and the media. Her appeal was instantaneous and her decision to leave politics after her unsuccessful bid for the lower house seat of Kingston in 1990 was devastating for me and many supporters.

While much inspiration comes from women, one of my strongest supporters in politics has been a man. Senator John Coulter became leader of the Australian Democrats in 1991 and was willing to overcome the usual reservations about young people to employ me, aged 22, as an adviser/researcher on issues including education and youth. I have never seen John Coulter impatient with or threatened by young people. He is one of the few politicians I have met who is fearless: fearless of multinational companies, of being radical, of new ideas or people. That kind of support in politics is rare and to be treasured.

Through my role as a staff member for John Coulter and the next leader, Senator Cheryl Kernot, I was able to see into the belly of the monster that is politics: writing speeches, amending laws, meeting people through my work in portfolios that ranged from education and youth to Aboriginal and Islander affairs. I have seen how women are treated in parliament: the sexist and snide remarks and even a building that is not 'woman-friendly'. Despite a hairdresser, a gym and a meditation room, there is still no childcare in Parliament House in Canberra, something I recall Janine Haines mentioning in her university lecture years before. In this atmosphere it is more common to find alliances based on factions than sex or gender.

... how women are treated in parliament: the sexist and snide remarks and even a building that is not 'woman-friendly'.

Politics is about gaining and maintaining power. Once you attain that power you can wield it for positive change but how that power is attained is also significant. I do not like seeing women abuse power or play the boys' games. It is distressing when successful women in politics or any profession say they have made it on 'merit' and fail to provide support for their sisters who are coming behind.

I see the importance of groups like EMILY's List (Early Money is Like Yeast) which have formed in the United Kingdom, United States of America and Australia and are about providing financial and emotional support to women to succeed in politics. However, the development of cross-party links is essential.

I am discovering common interests and problems with other young women in politics and we are trying to develop cross-party support groups, no matter how informal. I have role models among my peers. Young female politicians like Cassandra Gelade and Leeza Chesser (rising stars in the South Australian Labor Party), and Fenella Barry (Wilderness Society) come from different perspectives but face similar obstacles. It is also true that some of the most prejudiced views against me and other women come from women who espouse feminist ideals yet may never have met or spoken to me.

I speak to many schools and conferences as a way of educating girls about politics and overcoming their reluctance to get involved in a profession with a popularity rating lower than journalism and used-car sales. Girls still consider politics a male-dominated and male-oriented profession and the importance of young female mentors can not be overlooked.

> ... *men who were patronising and glib, especially when I was able to run rings around them on policy.*

I ran as a candidate for the senate at the age of 23 (albeit in an unwinnable position) and quickly found myself debating seasoned politicians: women who made fun of my youth and men who were patronising and glib, especially when I was able to run rings around them on policy. The comfort of having a political party 'backup' does not always make up for the sense of isolation you experience when standing alone at the podium or facing a barrage of questions from an unhappy crowd. Usually the toughest political battles are fought out within your own ranks.

While one man asked me if I went into politics to find a husband and a preselector said he wouldn't vote for me if I 'was going to get married and pregnant', my most disturbing experience was when a woman challenged my preselection on grounds that were eventually ruled out of order as 'vexatious'. It is not that I do not expect women to challenge each other, it is a good sign to see more women competing for positions of authority. But I do not like seeing women played off against each other, especially by men eager to consolidate their power-base.

Women in politics cannot be expected to share the same views but I do expect that they will not perpetuate the patriarchal dominance of the parliament.

I grew up with the notion of 'sisterhood'. Like the term 'feminism', it was never a dirty word. Despite evidence of emerging networks among young women, recently 'second wave' feminists like Anne Summers and Helen Garner have lamented a lack of 'third wave' feminists. We are there. There is a group of third wavers and our brand of feminist continues to evolve. I do not think that there are fewer women willing to call themselves feminists but I believe the definition of a feminist is as diverse and wide-ranging as it ever was.

Nevertheless, women of my generation are taking that risk, they are willing to define themselves in this way and overcome some battles that the second wavers did not have to face. We are learning how to support each other and build networks among women despite the emerging backlash against feminism and conditioning which teaches us not to be competitive or assertive and to hide our success.

The feminist movement, like any political movement, experiences its own set of factions, rivalries and even hierarchies. When I met Naomi Wolf, I was surprised by how conciliatory she could be. In *Fire with Fire* she argues that women should accept the diversity within our movement, something I agree with, but I am angered by a sinister trend which sees women using the language and rhetoric of feminism against us. Writers like Camille Paglia and Katie Roiphe, with their hard-hitting brand of 'anti-victim feminism', receive media acclaim and chastise other feminists for going 'too far'.

> *I am angered by a sinister trend which sees women using the language and rhetoric of feminism against us.*

My association with journalists (family and friends) has given me insight into the male-dominated media world and has taught me that manipulation of the media by women is necessary if we are to get our voices heard. My mother suffered for writing about 'women's issues' like domestic violence and sexual abuse. Today I see my peers fighting the same battles, wanting to appease newspaper proprietors by not being too radical, too feminist, too honest.

I see a new kind of journalism emerging, tuned in to the views of young people and a fairer society. The national broadcaster, the Australian Broadcasting Corporation's Triple J encompasses this new no-fear journalism and promotes assertive and progressive women like Angela Catterns, Helen Razer and a female current affairs reporter, Sarah MacDonald, all supportive of other women and unashamed promoters of young talent. The Canberra Press Gallery is increasingly characterised by leading political journalists who are younger women, like Laura Tingle, Fran Kelly, Lenore Taylor and Christine Wallace. Women like these and journalists like Fiona Carruthers from the *Australian* – to whom I am personally indebted for her pursuit of stories promoting women and for tackling the vexed question of the 'third wave' – make the path a little easier for the rest of their sisters to tread.

I have chosen a profession that, at times, can offer wonderful camaraderie and support but which also pits people, especially women, against each other in a ruthless manner. Women's survival and eventual equal representation in male dominated arenas like politics will happen only if supportive links are established across professions. And while these formal networks characterise my professional and political life, I could not do without the regular lunches, chocolate and TV nights, magazine swaps and coffee gossip sessions with girly friends and comrades, Melissa McEwen, Kirsty McKenzie, Misha Schubert, Amanda Forbes, Jane Sloane and Robyn Pedler, and many more who provide fundamental emotional support along with my marvellous male friends Craig Chung, Bernard Cohen and Andrew Knox. It may seem a far cry from the 'Gorgeous Girls' at Stradbroke Primary but this kind of grassroots support, encouragement and promotion of each other is what my idea of feminism is all about.

An Empowering Journey

Melinda McPherson

Melinda McPherson grew up in Melbourne's northern suburbs and has actively pursued study and work in the field of education. Following completion of her year 12 at a Northcote secondary all-girls school, she gained degrees in music and drama education from the University of Melbourne's Institute of Education, then taught in secondary schools for four years.

Having consistently maintained a keen interest in justice issues, the politics of ethnic and cultural difference, and feminism, Melinda McPherson currently works as an education officer in the higher education sector and is undertaking a masters degree in Women's Studies and education at LaTrobe University, Melbourne. Her interests include reading, the criticism of popular culture, travel, music and people, and during 1994 she backpacked through Europe and the United States of America.

As a child, my religious education focused strongly upon the Christian message of helping others and giving of oneself. The story of 'The Good Samaritan' remains firmly fixed in my mind, as do a number of other stories which represent Jesus as a caring, loving, and giving mentor. Unfortunately I was not old enough at the time to realise that *Bible* stories are supposed to elicit differing responses from men and women (that is, men serve the 'lord' by leading on his behalf, while women serve the lord through doing what men say the lord wants – serving men). But the message of obtaining joy through mutual support and cooperation – that idea of community remains strongly with me as I contemplate the effects of such values as 'aggressive, healthy, competition'. It is through the generous living of those around me that I have come to learn and grow in my relationships and understanding of the world and it is from my own generous living that I hope others will draw inspiration and hope. I believe strongly in the value of creative cooperation, and it is for those with whom I have participated in cooperative emotional, working, and recreational relationships that I write.

My mother went out to work when I was in early primaryschool. She was able to go into paidwork because my grandmother offered to mind my youngest brother, who was two at the time. While my mother's income assisted our family in acquiring things we were told we 'otherwise wouldn't have', I was also acutely aware that my mother worked in order to achieve a sense of purpose. From an early age this appeared natural to me, and I wasn't aware until I reached highschool, where mothers were supposed to volunteer for canteen duty, that ours was an unusual situation.

While my mother is still the primary source of domestic labour in our household, my father contributed significantly at home and encouraged my mother to follow any avenue of work or cultural activity she desired. Mum hates doing the housework. Despite efforts to learn to sew and cook, both she and I have remained dysfunctional in the area of housewifery. I cannot cook, sew, clean, tidy, iron, dust, vacuum, wash, or sweep with any degree of precision or enthusiasm. I am envious of those who are able to prepare meals boasting just the right flavours, or construct garments with an eye for perfection.

> *I cannot cook, sew, clean, tidy, iron, dust, vacuum, wash, or sweep with any degree of precision or enthusiasm.*

I didn't think twice about completing secondary school and going to university. A highly motivated student, I valued education greatly. Dad worked as a labourer in the wool industry while mum was a secretary. Both parents encouraged me towards success at school. However their encouragement was more than 'career' orientated. I will always remember my mother's view: 'Education is never wasted – it doesn't matter in what area it is, it is never wasted.' From this I am quite sure I derived my strong desire to 'acquire knowledge'.

Mum is hardworking and intelligent, however a combination of religious upbringing, socialisation, and personality directed her during her late teenage years into the pursuit of a career which entailed little responsibility or status. In a sense, I am sure some of my mother's own desire to pursue further education was lived out through me. Mum is sometimes afraid of herself and unsure of herself, which renders her unable to follow through with or believe in her own thoughts and ideas. Instead she prefers to follow the advice of an 'authority'. This has been a great source of conflict and pain in our relationship, and has made it difficult for me to make some of my own choices free of reservation and grief.

My parents' encouragement of me towards educational achievement has been phenomenal. While many of the other girls at school looked to fashion models, television stars, and other such 'visually enticing' women as examples around which to mould themselves, I can remember aspiring most of the way through primary and highschool to emulate professionals such as teachers and lawyers. To me, their knowledge, intelligence and highly developed ability to articulate philosophical ideas was exhilarating and, in some senses, sexual. In other words, I believed that if an individual were to attain some of those qualities, then in many ways she or he would be revered, desired, and respected by others. I don't know whether or not I worshipped any 'famous' female role models – but I do know that I had no aspirations to emulate 'Brooke Shields' as my friends did.

My earliest mentors were kindergarten and primaryschool teachers. As far as I could tell they possessed personal strength and intelligence – two qualities I aspired to myself. To this day mum reminds me of my first day at kindergarten – a day she believes anyone could tell just how I was going to 'turn out' . . . 'I took you to the frontdoor,' mum sadly reminisces, 'and you took off without even turning around to wave goodbye like the other children did.' Poor mum.

I remember the names of all my primaryschool teachers. Only two of these teachers were male. Both exercised an authoritarian, aggressive approach to punishment in the classroom (as did most of the women teachers), however one of my Grade 6 teachers had an excellent sense of humour. We gave him a really hard time! My perception is that male teachers did not automatically command the admiration of students as female teachers did. More influential as role models were some of my secondary school teachers. My parents had offered me a choice of single sex Catholic schools to attend. I chose the one that appeared the more academic. Most children my age seemed to want to be at school for the social interaction and, while I made many lasting friends, I felt I was there to learn.

My perception is that male teachers did not automatically command the admiration of students as female teachers did.

Our Year 7 music coordinator was an excellent communicator, manager and musician. Whilst managing a difficult music department on her own, she oozed enthusiasm and is probably one of the greatest reasons for my becoming a music teacher. She ran choirs, wrote the music curriculum, trained musicians for the musical, performed herself – and loved her art. She now has two beautiful children and continues to share with other students her knowledge and love for music.

My Year 8 English teacher was one of the most powerful women I have ever encountered. She ran her classes like an army camp – and had the greatest knowledge and understanding of the world I had ever seen. I was scared to death of her – so was everyone else – but I learned so much from her that I remember to this day. I understand she returned to university to become a lawyer. I pity her legal opponents – she had nerves of steel and a tongue of acid.

There are so many teachers to whom I owe thanks – but my Year 11 maths teacher must surely be acknowledged. She worked tirelessly in her first year out of university to assist me and my classmates in our pursuit of mathematical excellence. This 'first year out' teacher was asked to take over the Year 11 maths B class from another teacher who had been injured in a car accident. Her classes were clear and concise, and she spent endless afternoons with us, helping us over problems in her own time. The result of her effort was A's for both my mathematics subjects that semester – and an admiration on my behalf that lasts until today. 'The Lenz', as we nicknamed her, left teaching for the computer industry.

On both academic and extra curricular levels, I loved school. I worked with one of the music teachers in Year 9 to present a series of guitar classes. I had learnt guitar for a number of years, and loved teaching. I also tutored a number of fellow Year 11 students and others from different levels in mathematics, legal studies, and music. I loved communicating and could not decide whether to become a lawyer or a teacher. What now appears to be a choice between two extremely different careerpaths did not, at the time, seem so far apart.

I loved communicating and could not decide whether to become a lawyer or a teacher.

Having very little idea of the monetary facts of life, I chose to become a music teacher, and took up the cello so I could enter college. My mother did not really want me to become a music teacher – she didn't think I was making a wise career choice. When I look back, she was probably right in some respects. However I am a very stubborn person (a characteristic I derive most definitely from my father), and eventually chose Year 12 subjects which would assist me in becoming a teacher. Throughout my schooling, I was heavily interested in social justice issues. Racism made my blood boil, as indeed friendships were made and broken in my school based on one's ethnicity. My interest in the class struggle did not fully develop until university.

The woman who taught me cello from Year 12 through to the end of my college course was talented and understanding. I admired her greatly. She had played for many important people in many important places – and was revered in her industry. When I first visited her, I could barely scratch out a simple tune, however her patience and skill saw me through to the completion of my tertiary course. With so little previous experience it was a miracle I passed cello in my Year 12, let alone achieved a grade in the eighties for some of my practical college exams.

My cello teacher had a small but beautiful house, with a lovely studio for lessons. During the years I studied with her, she married a computer specialist. They moved to a bigger house, with even larger rooms set aside for her music making. I greatly admired the way she had organised her life. It is true to say that I was as much fascinated by her skill as a musician as I was by her personal self. She was working in a field she loved, was extremely skilled, had wonderful friends, and had the energy to juggle everything in her life at once. She believed I could achieve and, partly in response to my own ambitions and her faith in me, I did.

My years at secondary school and university were replete with support and influence offered to me by some very special women. Three close friends in particular, Ombretta Fanetti, Genny Kinnaird and Amanda, completed tertiary degrees whilst sharing with me many of life's harrowing and joyful experiences. Ombretta pursued a bachelor of arts at LaTrobe University. Amanda (a woman determined to succeed), had transferred from town planning to commerce at Melbourne University, and Genny was at Rusden, although still very much in the wilderness so far as determining upon the career she wanted to follow. My friends came from extremely diverse backgrounds, but in those years all shared the same sense of purpose and freedom I did. All were achievers, each motivating herself over and above the various obstacles life provided.

During my first year of college, I left home. I had begun a relationship with a boy in the army who came from Adelaide, South Australia. Unfortunately my very religious parents didn't approve of the nature of the relationship, and so after 18 years of having the television stations changed at home whenever a 'breast' or 'bum' was revealed, I decided to leave. In many ways my parents still supported my education, but for the first two or three years away from them I was financially 'on my own'.

My relationship with the boy was a complete disaster. He slept around behind my back, often drank heavily, and was both verbally and physically violent toward me at times. During these three years I leaned heavily on my close friends and in particular confided in one who was in the midst of a longterm relationship breakup herself. I suppose one always has to look on the bright side of things – and it is indeed true that my interest in gender construction and psychoanalytic feminist theory comes from this sad experience – but it was one of the darkest times of my life.

I sought counselling because I couldn't deal with the relationship breakup. I was an extremely naive 18-year-old, and the overwhelming lessons of Catholic teaching – which were still embedded in my brain – made my understanding of the situation more confusing. Despite all the pain I developed an uncompromising resolve NOT to fail my university course because of this revolting boy. A counsellor helped me realise I hadn't done anything wrong (although it took a long time to reach this understanding) – and that I was justified in my dislike of the attitudes and behaviour of this male being. However the question of 'why' gnawed at me. 'Why' did he do this to me? 'Why' was he like that? 'Why' did I react the way I did? 'Why' did other people see my situation as unfortunate but not devastating?

For a long time I thought there was no point in continuing with life. If boys were allowed to do what they liked and girls just had to put up with it – and if this so called 'religion' of my mother's ex-communicated women for not wanting to remain permanently spiritually bonded with virtual animals – what was the point of going on? Was I supposed to be an intellectual, sexual and emotional slave for the sake of following these 'tried and true' values? Why was I the one seeking counselling – the one to be labelled 'not quite right' – when this guy could go on living his life as a 'pretty nice, ordinary bloke'?

Well – this was my rude awakening to women's rights (or our lack of them). Whilst working at a hospital during my years at college, I made great friends with a number of the older women, one in particular who kept being drawn into relationships with violent men. However, she was a remarkable example of the human spirit. She had endured the horrific marriage to a man who did such things as forced her into sexual relations if she wanted housekeeping money, and so on. She worked for women's refuges and had very open ideas about sexuality. This woman at the hospital was also a great sense of support during my own longterm relationship and had the finest sense of humour about life.

> *I made great friends with a number of the older women, one in particular who kept being drawn into relationships with violent men.*

I am sure this was the beginning of my feminist awakenings. While I always had a strong sense of my rights as a woman, I had never really considered what was lacking in the world for women. Being in a violent relationship that I had difficulty leaving, I truly believe I learned an empathy for women in relationships that most other 18-year-old girls would not have had. I know that my friends were on unfamiliar ground, which made me feel even more isolated.

Despite this difficult set of circumstances, the female role models just kept presenting themselves during college. Our head of department in music was approachable, encouraging, and professional. My music method lecturer also remains, for me, an image of vibrancy and success. She seemed to have an unending supply of brilliant musical/teaching ideas to share with our classes, and never hesitated to connect politics with her vision for teaching. What fascinated me about her was her brilliant networking capacity – something I had not really encountered before.

I have come to see that 'networking' can play an important part for women wanting to gain opportunities in their chosen fields. I have also observed in my own places of work that equality of treatment and opportunity dissolves into a mirage in the face of male networking power – the most obvious examples of which are the 'old boys' clubs'. I dislike the 'bloodsucking' nature of this supposed networking, where I have observed employers treat certain employees like 'scum of the earth', and then go on to overtly emotionally caress someone from whom they hope to 'gain a favour'. However I do believe there is a place for developing friendships, sharing skills, supporting new ideas, and generating enthusiasm within the workplace amongst individuals.

One male lecturer in education also remains in my mind. I had a furious fight with him over the reasons for my having become a teacher. Still thinking in the liberal mould – that the individual can overcome any negative circumstances in order to achieve OR that the individual is not stupid enough to do what society 'says' she should do – I was emphatic that I had entered teaching of my own choice and not as a result of some 'gendered segregation of labour'. My Year 12 score had been sufficient to enable me to do a number of other more 'economically viable' courses and I 'thus hadn't been socialised into teaching. It had been an informed choice!' 'Aaah!' said this lecturer, 'but I am not disputing your personal reasons for teaching – within the context of what I am describing, they make no difference. You and three quarters of the rest of the teaching profession are women, and all of them I am sure have just as good reasons for becoming teachers as you did. The fact is you have chosen a female dominated profession, and there are social politics behind your decision.' Was I boiling! I had envisaged myself as being somehow 'better' than those girls who had become secretaries and nurses (how arrogant does that sound!). I must say that this lecturer was extremely clear thinking, and always interrupted my stubborn, fixed thoughts with radical, social, political ideas. Before I entered his classes, I had very little idea about the effect of economics on education, and grew to have a firm understanding of the socially constructed barriers to achievement of the underprivileged. My final education submission for college examined the state government's implementation of a social justice strategy within the schools.

I had envisaged myself as being somehow 'better' than those girls who had become secretaries and nurses (how arrogant does that sound!).

At this stage I had still not gelled my personal experiences of life (and men) with feminist theory. I had my own theory that men had a *pact*. They could do whatever they wanted (for example sleeping around, being violent) as long as they weren't caught out. And if they were caught out everyone else had to pretend they were disgusted, even if they were doing the same thing themselves. This was as far as my idea of 'feminist theory' went.

Well – when college finished so did my vision for my future. I had met an interesting man who was involved in politics, but I shared no interest in politics myself. To me, the politics of university boiled down to how many people you could manage to sleep with before you reached the ripe old age of twenty-three. Having had a number of relationships before this, I had virtually condemned myself to the hell of believing I had no sexual value at all. This had impacted greatly on my vision of my own intellectual ability as well. While I never failed a subject at college, I didn't have the educational direction I had lived with my whole school life. My belief that the only men able to be faithful were conservative moral prudes had left me believing that I could never really find a partner who would understand or support me (let alone love me).

I received an outstanding grade for my ministry of education teaching interview and, consequently, a number of working offers. I became employed as a teacher in a Catholic all-boys school (probably wanting to work within the system with which I was most familiar – and because I couldn't get away from the nagging encouragement and pride of my mother). I revelled in the joy, peace, and happiness of having a relationship with a partner that was affectionate, caring, and supportive. My partner was understanding and alert to my needs. He encouraged my academic pursuits and supported my desire to travel abroad. He did not, however, dispel any of my belief in the theoretical 'pact' I believed existed amongst men in general.

My initial years of teaching were both interesting and miserable. While my relationship with the man I had met at university was moving in a positive direction, my reasons for teaching appeared slowly to be vanishing. I was working in classrooms with boys from Italian, Lebanese, and Greek backgrounds. These young students had so many social obstacles to overcome – and once again I suppose my old fears that they would grow into monsters, no matter what I did, came back. What a shock to the system to see my first class of Year 10 drama students jumping over desks and virtually hanging from the rafters! So much for my commitment to the social good! Some of the boys were friendly, helpful, intelligent, mature, and hard-working. I probably related best to those who had a real yearning to learn – as this was the way I had felt at school.

I gained a level of control over my students within that all-boys school, but left the job prematurely. This was more due to my lack of direction than the students' circus antics. Slowly, it seemed to me that my 'knight in shining armour' resolve to teach was disappearing. The money was the pits, the hours were long. My dedication was absolute – but I had lost the zest. There seemed to be lots of hard work, but very little reward. There also appeared to be no careerpath – and I didn't want to remain stagnant. In summary however, teaching demands as much of YOU as it does your teaching skills. The work does not finish at 3.30 pm, and the holidays are merely opportunities to continue work in the home environment. It is an exhausting vocation.

Slowly, it seemed to me that my 'knight in shining armour' resolve to teach was disappearing.

With my partner's support I left my job (despite the fact that the recession had hit) and took on a job at LaTrobe University. The secretarial back-biting and generally primitive attitude of possessiveness and power in that office forced me to reconsider teaching. I had virtually completed a graduate diploma in drama in education, and so (with my bachelor of education in music), was qualified to teach at least two disciplines. I was extremely lucky to be offered an interview at the secondary school I attended as a student, and so took the offer immediately. This was partly due to the fact that my work at LaTrobe had finished, and the lack of work in Melbourne University at the time. Also, it was to be a challenging coordinator-role.

In the graduate studies department at LaTrobe I had come across a thesis on male violent behaviour. This was my first experience of structured feminist analysis. 'Finally!' I thought. 'My own experience has been so carefully and accurately articulated in a psychology book by someone else,' and I began to realise that others thought as I did. The thesis partly dissipated my sense of isolation. However it wasn't until I found a book entitled *Eunuchs for the Kingdom of Heaven* by a German author called Ute Ranke Heinemann that my interest in feminist theory blossomed. How can I describe my exhilaration at Ute's uncompromising and damning theological analysis of the Catholic Church and many of its inhumane rules! (Unfortunately Ute was sacked from her position in a Catholic university in Germany.)

> In honestly challenging the structures that are, in courageously and emotionally articulating and sharing their ideas...

I know that these women did not write down their thoughts specifically for me. I know that they have experienced life and perhaps suffered in ways I have not. I also know that their commitment to their ideals and their articulation of those ideals is the contribution they want to make to feminist – to human – discourse. However, it is through these women's personal struggles, and their articulation of those struggles that I have come to a greater understanding of myself, my sisters, and the world. In honestly challenging the structures that are, in courageously and emotionally articulating and sharing their ideas and in cooperating with other women through this sharing of thoughts, I have insurmountably benefited from their generous living.

I have since enroled in a master of education course at LaTrobe University, in Women's Studies. I am acutely aware of the fact that many of the women in my course have come to their understandings of feminist discourse from the personal assistance they have provided to other women in shelters, health organisations, political forums and so on. I am also aware that I find it difficult to thrash out ideas in my own mind, and that I often need to say the wrong thing in order to understand the right thing. I have learnt more about psychology, philosophy, politics, education, and bureaucracy in this course than in all of my years of schooling. My experience of living, learning, and teaching in areas with high numbers of non-English speaking background people has caused me to focus particularly on the social effects of the intersections of race, sex and gender on specific communities of people.

I believe that the struggle towards obliterating oppression in all of its many and varied forms lies not simply with the white western feminist struggle, but with the ability of all social movements to expand their agendas to include issues of racism, classism, sexism and so forth. Viewing the absolute hysteria taking place within some sectors over the High Court's 1992 Mabo decision on the Land Rights of Indigenous people causes me great sadness. It reminds me of the staunch resistance nineteenth century women met in fighting for the vote or for an education, and the frenzied resistance mounted against Afro-Americans wanting to enter United States universities many decades ago. To me, each of these events do not go a millionth of the way to creating fairness and freedom, yet they are met with responses that indicate their implementation will bring a fate worse than death to those currently in power.

While it was a negative personal experience that eventually led me to the course in Women's Studies, and personal experience of positive role models which has led me to reflect upon the nature of women as a powerful source of learning and growth, I have yet to determine in what direction these new understandings will lead me.

While I now work as an education officer in the higher education sector, I hope I was able to share something of my skills and attitudes with the students I taught at the secondary level. I truly wanted to empower the girls I taught during my second appointment. I particularly enjoyed working towards this goal in my public speaking classes where I felt I could help many of the young women come to 'voice'. Due to a combination of socialisation and varying cultural backgrounds, the students at this school were very easy to discipline. While that was great for my stress level, it posed a whole variety of other problems with respect to their learning. Our school environment was very supportive. Our girls participated in a wide variety of academic, spiritual, social, and sporting activities, although cultural politics still held a firm grip on social interactions outside the classroom, as they had when I was a student.

What issues do I see as important if change and progress are to take place in our world?

The encouragement of cooperation, empathy, creativity are all important elements of an environment in which change can be fostered. The white, western, middleclass Women's Movement has finally begun to acknowledge that issues affecting women other than themselves are also women's issues – poverty, racism, famine, war. The time has come where some kind of positive space can be created for men who want change.

Not many women want to exclude men from their own and the world's processes of change. In order for change to occur, not only should I be teaching little girls and young women to value themselves and their power, but also little boys and young men to value all aspects of themselves (for example, the ability to demonstrate emotions) and the importance and difficulty of struggle for those who live different realities (women, those from language backgrounds other than English, racial and ethnic minorities, and more). What good will it be for our enlightened, empowered, creative daughters if the other half of the sex/gender equation continue to live in their own world of antiquated values and power politics based around fear. The time has come to educate boys as well as girls for change. Not that we should take sole responsibility for it – but that we should share responsibility with those who share our commitment.

> *Not many women want to exclude men from their own and the world's processes of change.*

Challenging ourselves and our ideas is also important to change. For some the challenge may involve simply getting through the day – for others it is conquering fear, whether that fear be of women's power, gay pride, or fear of making decisions on one's own. In 1994 I spent four months overseas travelling alone. Sometimes I was really afraid, however the experience was irreplaceable and I believe I have grown a great deal because of it.

On a more social level, we need to be living our lives in such a way as to confront crippling ideologies (such as racism, sexism), thrusting our views, ideas, and needs into empowering discourse, and allowing an arena for the development of each individual's creative, intellectual, spiritual and physical potential in such a way that, as far as we are capable of giving, each person's life becomes an act of living generously.

Life and Belonging

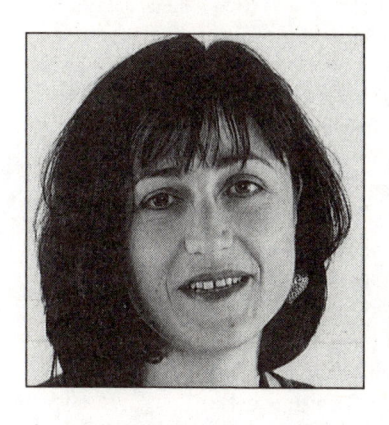

Carmel Guerra

Carmel Guerra was born on 20 October 1961, in Melbourne, Victoria. She holds a bachelor of arts and diploma of youth affairs from Royal Melbourne Institute of Technology (RMIT) and is coordinator of the Ethnic Youth Issues Network at the Youth Affairs Council of Victoria. As a director of the Victorian Women's Trust (VWT), she is a member of the fundraising and membership sub-committee and is keen to ensure that more women (including young women) of non-English speaking background are encouraged to participate in the Victorian Women's Trust and its activities.

In 1995 Carmel Guerra edited a book on young people and multiculturalism, titled *Ethnic Minority Youth in Australia*.

Benevento, the small town in Italy where my parents were born, is famous for its liqueur, 'Stregga'. Stregga is similar to Galliano, and most people who visit Benevento quickly learn about it, if they have not known of it previously. In Italian, it means 'witch' – perhaps a peasant version of a bag lady, but one with mystic powers. Many women from that part of Italy, in the south, near Naples, are renowned for having mystic powers.

My parents came to Australia in 1956–57. They married in Benevento. Six months later, Dad arrived in Australia. Mum came out a year later. I was born four or five years later and was raised in the northern suburbs of Melbourne, in Victoria. I lived there all my life and now, as an adult, have bought a house in the northern suburbs. I attended Thomastown Primary School, then went to Lalor High School.

At the time, my parents wanted to send me to a Catholic school. They were generally strict about aspects of our growing up but somehow, I don't quite know how, we children won the debate and my sister and I went through the state school system. All my friends were off to the state school, so we kicked up a big stink, saying: 'Why *should* we go to the Catholic school?'

On reflection, I don't know whether I did better by going into the state system, or whether I would have done better had I gone to the Catholic school. Thomastown was a very workingclass suburb and both the primary-school and the highschool were fairly conservative. But by the time I arrived at Lalor High School in the early 1970s, it had begun to change. It was multicultural.

I did the higher school certificate (HSC) as it was then called, passing all subjects except English. That was devastating, for I had always been a B student in both English and English literature. I passed English literature, but froze during the English examination for it was the first HSC exam I sat. Either I performed badly or didn't answer the questions at all, I don't know which – yet I don't recall walking out feeling any more upset or worried than I did for the other four examinations. When I saw the results, I went crying to the English teacher, sobbing: 'What am I going to do now?' She was just as devastated as I, because I was one of her students who was hoping to go to university. She persuaded me to go back to study English, but I wasn't sure it was what I should do, so took a year off. Had I been a struggling student, I might have thought that my failure in English was connected with my minority ethnic background, although I am a second-generation migrant and my English is better than my Italian. But I had never thought such a thing would happen to me, and I had failed *so badly*. I received a high C for English literature, yet in English my result was something like forty!

I had applied to do the youthwork course at Phillip Institute in Coburg. Phillip Institute had a fairly lengthy application process, including a written application and interview. I got in! This meant that my English result was doubly devastating. 'Oh, my God,' I thought. 'Now I can't even accept the offer because Phillip would not accept me without my HSC.'

My English teacher was a lovely old woman, an 'old school' teacher who'd been in the field for a long time. She was probably in her late fifties, and was an HSC examiner herself, and because my score was so low, a total fail, knew it was impossible to find out why. 'Carmel,' she said to me. 'You can't give up.' It was a real pep-talk, and eventually she persuaded me to return to school, taking English at night at University High. I mixed with lots of other mature-age students, which I enjoyed.

> *'Carmel,' she said to me. 'You can't give up.'*

During the year off, I did some voluntary work at CYSS (Commonwealth Youth Support Scheme) centres locally, working as a volunteer with unemployed young people. It made me ask: 'Do I really want to do this?' I met some extremely tough kids. They were only two or three years younger than I. Almost immediately, I confronted complicated and difficult situations.

In Year 10, like most other students, I visited my careers teacher. I set out wanting to be a journalist: I had no interest in becoming a lawyer, teacher or doctor, although that was what my parents wanted. 'I'll be a journalist!' I thought, although I don't know exactly why. It may have had something to do with my inquisitive nature. I liked the idea of investigating issues and analysing ideas and situations. Yet at that time, there weren't so many people of minority ethnic background in journalism. My careers teacher, an incredibly conservative, middleclass man, was not impressed. 'Why don't you go into nursing or teaching?' 'No,' I persisted. 'It's journalism I want.'

> 'Why don't you go into nursing or teaching?' 'No,' I persisted. 'It's journalism I want.'

Then, by Year 12, I had talked myself out of it. In Year 11 I inclined toward socialwork. For some reason, I have no idea why, the idea of youthwork became predominant in my thoughts. At the time it was not a career in the way it is now, and was particularly unusual for someone with my background to go into or even think about. But I had always been interested in 'people issues', particularly those affecting young people. Perhaps I identified through my own childhood and upbringing.

So it was back to the careers teacher. 'There's no way you'll get into a youthwork course,' he said.

I had great pride in returning to see him when I was accepted into the youthwork course. 'Up your nose!' I said (figuratively speaking). He had given no reason why I wouldn't be accepted. I believe he had 'boxed' me into a certain career option, according to what is a typical (and 'acceptable') career for a woman, particularly a woman of migrant background. He could not see beyond the realm of his own perspective.

But some teachers at the school were different. The physical education (PE) teacher, Sue Watson, was my softball coach. This episode in my life began when I and some other girls, both of anglo and non-English speaking background (NESB) hung around together. Through the PE teacher we began playing sport. Sue was married to an Olympic basketball player, so they were 'Mr and Mrs Fitness'. But she was not the kind of PE teacher who fitted the traditional mould of just getting out there on the field, and playing. She had a social conscience. Purposely she went out looking for us girls, wanting to get us involved because she could see that we were not participating. We discovered we were pretty good ball players. We became the northern suburbs champions, then won through to the state school grandfinal, coming runners-up in the state school competition. We lost by one run, because someone tripped over, injuring herself, which meant she couldn't finish. Otherwise it would have been our game.

This was a profound experience for us all. It gave us the sense of succeeding in something. We followed softball through from Year 9 to HSC, and all of us completed Year 12. Sue Watson was the one who was a constant, there the whole time, ensuring we kept playing. She was the type who took us home, inviting us over for dinner, taking us out to various activities outside the school. She created a strong sense amongst us of its being important to *do* things. She travelled the world with her husband's Olympic team, and after Year 12 she kept in contact with us, wanting to know what we were doing, and what we had done with our lives. She urged us to complete our education and go to university. Most of us did.

> *We were so concerned about our body image, because there were so many skinny girls in the class (all anglo-Australian) ...*

I had had no real interest in sport before then. At primary-school I had played some sports games, but none of us had ever formally wanted to attach ourselves to any sport at school. For non-English speaking background girls, there was a real disincentive to joining in, particularly swimming. We were so concerned about our body image, because there were so many skinny girls in the class (all anglo-Australian) – then came the Mediterranean girls (us), who were rarely as skinny as the others. We suffered from paranoia about being exposed to the boys. Softball was a sport where we could feel that we were not being harassed by them. Sue Watson was the motivator and role model who brought about a major change in all of us.

However, when we did take up sport, there was a contest with the boys. 'Ownership' of the school ovals was the issue: we had to mount a huge campaign to gain access to a proper oval on which to play softball. It was only when they began to realise that we were good that the school authorities allowed us to use the oval – it was 'the boys' soccer field'. The soccer oval and the space we used as a softball oval overlapped. Soccer balls ended up on our field and softballs went onto theirs, precipitating enormous battles between us. Finally we gained primary use of the field – only because we were winners of the regional sports competitions!

Besides Sue Watson and my English teacher, one other teacher at Lalor High was an important influence, giving me real encouragement and support. George Sorgi was my Year 10 Asian history teacher. It was his first year of teaching and he had our class, where there were many students of minority ethnic background. He was one of the few migrant teachers who was employed in the school, and was an outspoken gregarious character. He was chubby – like a teddybear, with curly hair, and was a fantastic teacher. To that time, we had learnt only Australian history. He introduced us to Confucius, eastern philosophy and the entire history of China. He related his own experience of success, and in everything he did the message came through: you can be a migrant and succeed. 'My parents came here, and this is what happened to me . . .' He was from the northern suburbs, too, and had chosen to return to work in the Thomastown area.

Whilst a volunteer at CYSS, I was impressed by several women and the way they went about their work affected the way I developed my approach. One of the youthworkers at the CYSS centre was the first person who had ever talked to me about 'women's issues' as feminist issues, on an intellectual level, and why it is important to consider them. At school I had observed how teachers *always* paid more attention to the boys, and that those who gain the most attention are those who yell the loudest. I quickly learned that a girl is picked on if she is seen to be the one answering all the questions, and that it was necessary to be quiet because the boys had to answer. But women's position in the world was not something that came through to me on a conscious level until the youthworker at CYSS began talking with me about what it was like for young women in the program who were unemployed. She also talked with me about the importance of women workers moving into youthwork: at the time it was a male-dominated industry. The youthworkers were men who hung around the streets playing at being 'peers' with the boys. She presented the alternative view: 'Look,' she said firmly. 'There need to be more women in the field, and it is a great thing that more are coming into it.'

As for family influences, my grandparents were in Italy, so we children didn't have an opportunity to visit and be with them, although as a child I returned to Italy several times and met them. Knowing more about them now, I find there are many qualities I have probably inherited from them, particularly independence. I am very much like my grandmother on my father's side: they say I have her personality as well as her looks. I met her only once, when I was ten.

My mother is an incredibly forthright woman. She did not go to school, so didn't ever learn (formally) to read or write. Her parents sent her to school but she hated it, finding it was irrelevant. From a young age, she went out to work. But she taught herself to read signs and do the shopping without any problems. 'Look, Mum,' I'd say. 'Buy Omo instead of Cold Power.' Then I'd think: 'How would she know which is which?' But she does.

For my mother it was important from the beginning that her children continue their education. She was never one who said: 'I want you to leave school early because I want you to get a job and get married.' There is and always has been within our family a strong sense of wanting to succeed. As children, some of my cousins received a strong message: 'Go be a secretary. That's good enough.' With my mother it was always: 'Go to university. Do it. It's good for you, you need a career, you need money to look after yourself. Make sure you make yourself secure.'

She was never one who said: 'I want you to leave school early because I want you to get a job and get married.'

My mother knew about higher studies because there were people in our circle who had gone to university. She knew that in order to be a teacher or enter some other profession, it was necessary to attend university. For her, to be a teacher was to have a good career. In Italy, teachers are held in high regard. Their status is akin to that of doctors. (Teachers from Italy are horrified to discover the low esteem in which teachers are held in Australia.)

When I went into youthwork, she did not understand the job. Now I am a policy officer, she does not understand what I do but as I fly interstate for meetings, and meet politicians, knows it is important work.

At University High I met pupils who, like myself, had failed only English. Many students were returning to school after time spent out, in paid employment. Nightschool gave me an opportunity to meet with mature-age students in an extremely positive teaching environment. Because the students were, mostly, older, there was far more simulating debate than had ever occurred at Lalor High. I was only 19, and was able to listen to a whole range of people from varied backgrounds talking about books and life. They had a passion for what they were doing. That was very different from when I was at school previously. It made me regain faith in education. I had returned to school thinking it was a huge chore: 'What am I doing, going *back*? What will I *do*?'

I took a job at a shoe store, working parttime during the year, so that I could earn income.

In hindsight, it is easier to see that going straight to university from highschool may have deprived me of experiences that are now vital to my work and to my development. Now I recognise I was also fortunate in having the year off, for in being 'unemployed' I had many opportunities. I took a job at a shoe store, working parttime during the year, so that I could earn income.

At University High I read John Fowles' *The French Lieutenant's Woman*. This was my first introduction to his work and even now it is one of the books I reflect upon, for it made me think concretely about the role of women. Yet it was through my own experience that I had begun to question women's position in society, and to understand what I was seeing in the world around me. I did things, and things happened, that I knew were 'not right', but had no theoretical context in which to place it. It was not until I arrived at university that I was exposed to what might be called traditional mainstream feminist theory.

At university I read *The Female Eunuch* – fairly late in life, in 1979 or thereabouts. The book had been out for many years and people kept talking about it, but I was only 10 or 11 when it was originally published and had no idea of its contents. Then lecturers in sociology began referring to it. 'What's the book about?' the students kept asking. I read it and thought: 'Oh, my God! Now I understand what is happening to me.' It was a real revelation. Marilyn French's book, *The Women's Room*, was probably the other most significant book. In the early 1980s a friend gave it to me, saying I should read it.

Yet everything I read lacked an ethnic dimension. At the time I was living and breathing my ethnic identity, so I felt as if I understood it. Reading *The Women's Room* and *The Female Eunuch*, as well as *The French Lieutenant's Woman*, brought into my awareness the fact that I was a woman and what that meant, both in real and theoretical terms. It was not until then that I began to see that being a woman and being of minority ethnic background were not two separate parts of me, but were interrelated. Before, I had seen them as separate.

In my course at university, only four or five of us came from a non-English speaking background (NESB). We quickly saw that no one else talked about what it's *really* like in our part of the world. Everyone else drove from the eastern suburbs, across the freeway, to attend university. The four or five of us who were of non-English speaking background all lived in the northern suburbs. We were experiencing 'migrant issues'. No one knew what we were talking about. We were breaking new ground. In about 1982 we began to say: 'Hey! There is something not right here.' We had begun to question, and to realise that it was *not ourselves* who were 'out of place'. It was the way people saw the world that was the problem. Or what they failed to see. 'Why aren't there issues in the course and under discussion to do with who we are and what we're about?' we asked.

> *We had begun to question, and to realise that it was not ourselves who were 'out of place'.*

In my second year, I did a placement with Bruce Wilson from Melbourne University, based at a school. Bruce was an educational researcher, and I and a fellow socialwork student did research on NESB students' participation in school. It gave me an opportunity to do *real* research around understanding the experiences of children in schools and learning about educational attainment and the effect of background and ethnicity. I learned a great deal from Bruce Wilson.

It was at this time that questions of dealing with ethnicity in a feminist context began to arise for me. Many lecturers at university were feminist and lesbian, and this was confronting to many students, particularly to those of us from a minority ethnic background where such issues are so often 'under the carpet'. I also learned about group-work for women, and learned to understand how women operate differently from men, and why.

It was only much later that work like that of Rosie Braidotte and others came into the curriculum. Women in their thirties and forties who are moving into academia are beginning to change what is taught and how it is taught. One is Georgina Tsolidis who, over many years, has researched non-English speaking background girls and education. Currently she is at Monash University and her report, *Educating Voula*, was published in 1986 by the Ministerial Advisory Committee on Multicultural and Migrant Education.

I graduated from university in 1983. It wasn't until the mid-1980s, when I became more active as a professional, that I began looking out for material on women and ethnicity. I had assumed, before then, that it was not there. But when people of non-English speaking background began to move into the profession in greater numbers, the material began to be published. The experiences of migrants and non-English speaking background girls and women in school and at work began to emerge in the literature.

> The experiences of migrants and non-English speaking background girls and women in school and at work began to emerge in the literature.

It was then – in the 1980s – that I discovered that educational ideas and methods were still very much as they had been when I was at school: no attention paid to non-English speaking background issues or students. This became the basis of my work in the mid- to late 1980s when we were developing girls-only programs and looking at why CYSS unemployment schemes had to incorporate programs specifically targeted at girls. Girls had to be given space. Yet we weren't winning the battle. The response was: 'If girls want to come, they should be allowed to come.' 'What's wrong with boys? They're not going to hurt the girls.' 'Why should girls have more resources than boys? It's *their* problem if they don't want to come.' There was so little material available to support policies we knew, from our own experiences and from direct experience working with anglo-Australians and non-English speaking background boys and girls, were essential.

My own experiences were central to my thinking. For some children of migrants it is essential to return to 'the home country' at some time in their lives. I first went to Italy as a child of 10 years of age. I have fond memories, but they are vague and I was too young to understand. My second trip was a very personal journey, and a major psychological and emotional experience. The urge to return to Italy had begun when I did the second year placement and discovered there was very little in the youthwork literature about *my* experience. In the third year placement I and a colleague, Fran Linardi, were placed at the same agency. We went to university together and became, and remain, good friends. We realised it was ridiculous that there was nothing in the curriculum relating to multicultural issues. When the university didn't respond to our concerns, we agitated more strongly. We organised a major forum for all third year youthwork students and teachers. It was 1983. We invited Al Grassby to speak. He'd been around for a while, and for us it was a coup to have him visit and talk to the students and teachers. I had read *The Whitlam Years* and had studied the reforms that had occurred in immigration, and the White Australia Policy which had been abandoned not so long before. It was revolutionary that Al Grassby came to speak about immigration policy, multiculturalism and what he had done as minister for immigration and ethnic affairs in the Whitlam government.

By the time I graduated from university and moved into the paidworkforce I knew what I had to do. My university experience taught me that my work *had* to incorporate activism. I knew I could not possibly contribute to the full simply by going out into the field, doing casework with families. I knew also that it was imperative for me to return to Italy. I didn't feel 'Australian'.

My university experience taught me that my work had to incorporate activism.

This feeling of not being Australian came in so many ways. One aspect which seems so simple, but to a child growing up and then to that child as an adult is so fundamental, relates to children's stories. Today, when I am together with anglo-Australian friends, particularly those who have had a far more middleclass upbringing than I, I have no conception of what they are talking about when they refer to tales that are so familiar to them. I wasn't reading until I was in primaryschool, and if someone were to ask me about books we read at that time, I could answer nothing about them. As a child I didn't read *Alice in Wonderland,* or *Winnie the Pooh,* or *The Wind in the Willows*! I didn't read the Billabong books. I read them as an adult because I felt I had to. Everyone else was talking about them, and I didn't know what they were talking about.

My friends, who were mostly migrants or second generation migrants, and I didn't go home to read. Our parents didn't read to us. It was school that encouraged us to read. Teachers asked us to report back on books, or we did projects which forced us to read. Our parents might have bought us encyclopedia, but we didn't know how to use them. Parents did this, thinking it was the right thing to do, but not understanding the books themselves. Mum and Dad told us stories that had been passed down through the generations. We knew the story of Red Ridinghood and Cinderella. Red Ridinghood is 'Il Capucco Rosso' in Italian, and is a universal story – at least for Europeans. Around our dinnertable or when friends came to visit, it was folk stories we heard, ones their grandparents had told them, or they spoke of their family or friends and events that had involved them.

There were other differences between us and the children at school who were anglo-Australian. I was not allowed to go away with the school to camp until Grade 6, because my parents wouldn't let me: 'Good girls don't go on camps.' By Grade 6, Mum had changed her mind. This change of heart came through my friendship with a girl who lived down the road. We were good friends (and remain so), and often visited one another. For anglo-Australians, her family was incredibly open for the 1960s and 1970s. Vicki often came to visit and eat spaghetti. I went to her house and ate lamingtons and scones. I didn't know what a lamington was until I went to her home! She'd have Vegemite sandwiches, and bread and butter with hundreds and thousands sprinkled on top. I'd throw my lunch in the bin, and want to share hers. She asked her mother to make an extra sandwich for me.

It was a major coup. But she bore the flack from my aunties who said: 'Oh, Maria's sending her daughter to camp!'

It was this friendship, and Vicki's mother talking with my mother and visiting occasionally, that led to my mother allowing me to go to camp. It was a major coup. But she bore the flack from my aunties who said: 'Oh, Maria's sending her daughter to camp!' 'Oh, no, she'll turn out like all the Australian girls now!'

My cousin and I are the two in our family who entered a non-traditional field. Socialwork was 'non-traditional' in the 1980s. 'What are you two doing? Socialwork? Youthwork?' our relatives asked. They were bemused, for there were our other cousins going into law or administration, or working as teachers. We were soul buddies during our teenage years and paved the way. We said we would do something, then we did it, and occasionally we were told to go to our rooms, where we would cry, then be yelled at. Sometimes, we'd just go, saying: 'We're going!' We fought the battles that made it easier for my sister to go out when she became older. Because I was going to discos at 16 and 17, she was able to go to discos and parties, and go out on her own. But again the aunties complained, saying we were being radicals and: 'What kind of mothers are you?' Because we stuck together, we won the battles in the longrun. Now the generations following us have not had a difficult time at all. Everything has to be negotiated, but there is a great level of understanding. But we were the 'black sheep' of the family, entering an unknown field then heading off to Italy for a year of travel and study.

Our parents were full of anxiety. Their children were never coming back! They would never see their daughters again!

In 1983 I graduated from university; I was in my early twenties. 'I don't feel Australian,' I thought. 'I don't look Australian – whatever "Australians" look like. I don't feel that people treat me as an Australian. The kids with whom I work don't feel they get a fair deal. *I* don't feel I get a fair deal. I need to go to Italy, because that is where I belong.'

The Italian I spoke was a dialect. I wanted to learn to speak Italian.

I travelled with my cousin. We went to Italy, wanting to find ourselves. My cousin, Pina, and I lived in Siena for six months, studying the Italian language at university. Yet in Italy I *knew* I was not Italian. There was I, at 24, arriving 'back' in Italy, thinking: 'Oh, my God. I don't belong here either!'

It was emotionally devastating, thinking I had no identity. 'Where do I belong,' I asked myself. 'I don't belong anywhere.' There was a real sense of loss.

Then, at the university in Siena, we met up with other lost souls: the children of first generation migrants who had 'returned' to Italy for the same reason. There were 10 of us: two from Canada, two from Argentina, some from Switzerland and the United States. The entire class was ordered to speak only Italian, not in their native language, to ensure that we would *learn*. One day, the topic was the migration experience. Several of us said we *had* to speak in English, for we had to express what we felt. We couldn't express it in Italian.

We began speaking in English. Suddenly an incredible euphoria spread over the room. Ten of us looked around saying with wonder: 'We all feel the same!' 'We are the only 10 people in the room who understand what we're talking about.' No one else had any idea! 'What are they talking about?' 'Feeling as if you don't belong?' 'What do you mean, you don't belong? You were born in Australia . . .' They were not migrants. They were not the children of migrants. They had no sense of our feelings, our experience, our lives. For them, there was no sense of understanding.

'What do you mean, you don't belong? You were born in Australia . . .'

The 10 of us, together, came to a realisation that we were the consequence of a process. It didn't matter what we did, we had to learn to live. Our children would feel far more settled than we ever would. We were the consequence of our parents' migrating. We were born in a country we had not chosen to move to. We were born in a country that had chosen not to accept us. The group of us decided that the only response was to move to a desert island, to make up our own country for all the people around the world who are the children of migrants!

Ever since that moment, I have felt at ease with myself.

It took that trip, and that personal connection with others who said: 'This is what's happened to me, and this is why . . .' I returned to Australia a somewhat more content person.

At the Italian language school in Siena, the teachers said it was a common phenomenon to have English-speaking Americans or Greek-speaking Greeks or French-speaking French who were 'lost' in the country of their birth, and 'foreign' in the country of their parents' birth. That year, there were more of us than usual. It was a symbolic message to us: we were there, all at the one time, needing to be there. Most of us were women, and we maintained a connection with each other, writing for several years. Then the letters simply faded away, and stopped. Perhaps we finally felt we had gained what we needed.

After living in Italy for six months, I travelled around Europe and Eastern

Europe. In 1987, I returned to Australia. I felt as if I was coming home, but there was trauma also in this, for I recognised that if I had never left Australia I may have felt more secure in 'knowing' that I belonged in Italy, whatever the truth. There is nothing worse than fulfilling your dream – then discovering that it is just that. A dream. I had believed: 'I'm *really* Italian.' Reality was thrown back at me as soon as I landed in Italy. Australia was my 'home'. Yet I had not felt as if I 'belonged'.

> *I recognised that if I had never left Australia I may have felt more secure in 'knowing' that I belonged in Italy, whatever the truth.*

I was forced to come to terms with my need to make life in Australia. The adjustment was difficult, for I knew that returning to Australia meant I had to rebuild my life.

When I returned I thought I would not be able to work. Returning was a painful process. I began applying for jobs *everywhere*. At first I thought I should work in Sydney. I went to an interview and was offered to a job with the Parramatta council, in the western suburbs of Sydney. Then I realised that I was running away. The time had to come when I said: 'No, Carmel, you need to deal with who you are and what you are and what you want to do in Australia.'

I made a conscious decision to remain in Melbourne to create something positive. I wanted to work with others on the issues I had lived through, so for a while I worked at creating a young women's program in the Northcote area. I did some consultancy work for another organisation, around young people's issues. I worked in North Richmond highrise estates with young people. Then I gained employment with the Youth Affairs Council of Victoria.

I had travelled full circle: from CYSS, where I had worked before going to university, then to working with CYSS on work experience, then a 'real' job, for four or five months, helping to set up the migrant women's program: devising a scheme to encourage young women to participate in labour market activities.

I came to the Youth Council of Victoria through Lesley Podesta, who was at that time the director. Fran Linardi, Kominos Zervos, myself and several others had been working for a number of years as a network of youthworkers, trying to place migrant youth issues on the agenda. Lesley Podesta knew me and of my work, and invited me to apply for a job to set up a network bringing together organisations and individuals to advocate on behalf of migrant or NESB young people. I set up the infrastructure.

That network is still operating. Now I am employed as the coordinator. A key aspect of our work is to train human service professionals in developing appropriate work practices in ethnic communities. We provide cross-cultural training as well as anti-racism training, and provide an information resource base for young people, workers and agencies, and maintain contact with ethnic youth organisations.

During that time, I met Mary Crooks. I was appointed to the Youth Policy Development Council, and she was chairperson. I found her to be incredibly intelligent, stimulating and forward-thinking, with a strong sense of social justice and equity. She assisted me enormously and guided me on how to put together a booklet titled *Young People, Social Justice and Multiculturalism*. It documented the issues of young people and placed them in a societal context. This experience provided the framework for my further work on these issues at the broader socio-political level.

In 1994 I was awarded a Churchill Fellowship to travel to Europe and the United States to study issues of refuges, youth and ethnic minorities. I had known nothing at all about the Churchill Trust, but in discussion with a friend, Stefany Durack, I mentioned that I had reached a stalemate. 'Where do I go from here?' I asked. 'Apply for the Churchill Fellowship,' she said. 'Churchill? I know about Winston Churchill, but what's that got to do with anything?' She worked in the public sector in Perth, and one of her friends had received a fellowship. 'Oh, yeah,' said I. 'I don't think *I'll* get one.' She rang up the Churchill Trust, asked for an application form, then sent it to me. 'Carmel. Investigate this,' she instructed. 'You've got to be joking,' I said. 'How could someone like me ever get one of these?' But I began reading the form. Next, I applied. Then they called me for an interview.

That was an amazing experience. Here I was, sitting at a table surrounded by a panel consisting of representatives of important societies and associations. 'Do these people have any idea of what I'm taking about?' I thought. 'Absolutely no idea.' But there was no point in dropping my bundle. 'How will I sell this concept to them?' Obviously, I did a good job, for I was awarded a fellowship. When I looked through the list of 40 or 50 people around Australia who had been granted a fellowship, I saw that there was only one other person on the list who appeared to be from a non-English speaking background. Yet there was such a crying need for projects to be focused on this area. There had been little or no work done on the issue of refugee and migrant young people at the time. To their credit, a convincing argument won the committee over. This gave me some hope – perhaps there is an ability in people and organisations to change when given the opportunity. But the problem is that people need to know that the opportunity is there. I found myself being given a unique opportunity. And if Stefany Durack hadn't mentioned the Churchill Fellowships to me, done her bit then *made* me follow through, I wouldn't have known about it!

All my working history, I have consciously worked with migrants, have sought to work with migrant young people and migrant women. The battles I had to wage in order to get where I have been and where I am were vital. They were about getting young people, ethnicity and migration on the public and government agenda. The 1990s are so different from the 1980s. In the 1980s it was about wanting to be heard and demanding that something should be done. In the 1990s it is far more about articulating the nature of the problem or situation. There are good stories to tell, but the recording of the migrant experience has been largely tokenistic. In the past, when we were fighting so hard for our voices and ideas to be heard, at least we had a sense of power and ownership over the information and issue of migration and ethnicity. Now people say: 'Oh, yes. It's a good story. Can you write about it?' Yet power and structure have not shifted (if they have moved at all!) to accommodate us. It is extremely condescending to be on the receiving end of such intellectual gibberish.

I am grateful in some ways that I had to struggle and fight battles. As a youthworker in the early 1980s, I saw the need to create an organisation for non-English speaking background youth. We had to fight battles for funding and even for the acknowledgement that our demand was legitimate. Now at least we can look back and say: 'This is how far we have come; in the 1980s there wasn't *anything*.'

> *I had to challenge those men who at school told me I couldn't do what I wanted to do.*

I wonder about the influences that made me into who I am and that directed me into the areas in which I have worked. I had to challenge those men who at school told me I couldn't do what I wanted to do. It was the male careers teacher and the male maths teacher at Lalor High School who provided me with those negative experiences that motivated me to take risks. There were the positive experiences, too, from people such as the English teacher and Sue Watson, the PE teacher, and the teacher of Asian history working with kids in his 'old' area because he understood them. There were the youthworkers I met, and others during my early work history.

My desire to change practices I saw as unfair and unjust stems from my own experiences as a child and adult. I wanted to change the system of which I was part, and that I found discriminatory. I believe I have to give back something to the community and work toward making changes for the young people and migrants living in Australia today.

As One Door Shuts, Another Opens

Christine Ramsay

Christine Ramsay is an exhibiting photographer who mainly exhibits her work from her studio and occasionally with other galleries. She does private commissions and contributes to publications and, in conjunction with her work as a photographer, is an independent manager/publicist/consultant to other artists who require her expertise.

As a photographer, Christine Ramsay combines harmoniously her love of travel, art, architecture, interior and graphic design. She enjoys dining out (but gets cross when she feels bloated!), music – especially the classical guitar – and shocking films. She is a member of the National Gallery Women's Association in Victoria.

I was born to Chinese parents in Singapore on 2 August 1940. I arrived in Australia in 1957, as a student, to attend highschool in Adelaide so that I could enter university. After one year in highschool, I went on to the University of Adelaide, in South Australia, where I did a bachelor of science degree. As far as Singaporeans are concerned, it is quite the 'done thing', for families who can afford it, to send children to England, America or Australia for tertiary education. My family selected Adelaide because I had a cousin there who could keep an eye on me.

I was interested in the humanities, especially literature, but took science because I wanted to study medicine. As it turned out, I continued studying science and subsequently went on to do a doctor of philosophy in organic chemistry. Thus I commenced on a careerpath I had never planned – and ended up running an art gallery for 18 years.

I gained the bachelor of science with honours, then married a colleague, also an organic chemist, and we worked for two years in London, England, and Boston in the United States of America. When my husband was appointed to a job in Melbourne, we returned to Australia. I wondered what I should do with myself, so enroled at the University of Melbourne and commenced my PhD. I was most efficient during this period of my life: I had two daughters while I was completing my PhD, so had it all done in one fell swoop!

As my older daughter was about to start school, the only option for me, so that I could have coinciding holidays, was teaching. I had to consider that for the next 15 years there would be holidays for the children three times a year, including a two-month break at Christmas time. Apart from teaching, no job can give a parent so many holidays. I did a diploma of education and taught school for a year. By the middle of my first teaching year, I realised that being in a classroom was not for me. The opportunity to establish an art gallery arose. I was extremely excited. So Raya Gallery, the first gallery in Australia to specialise in contemporary South-East Asian art, was born. I set it up in my own home, the house where we still live. I ran the gallery at home for six years, then moved it down the street to Cotham Road, Kew, a Melbourne suburb, for another 12 years.

By the middle of my first teaching year, I realised that being in a classroom was not for me.

Life has many twists and turns – all unexpected until events actually occur. That is the beauty of it – as one door shuts, another opens.

My inaugural exhibition of paintings by Singapore artists took place in the spring of 1972, after a Singapore friend who trained as an accountant gave up her career to set up a gallery in Singapore. My interest in the visual arts was sparked during my stay in England and America. Through Marjorie Chu, I mounted an inaugural exhibition of sufficiently high quality. To start me off in the gallery business, she acted as my guarantor. Walking into an artist's studio and announcing: 'Hey, I'm starting a gallery in Australia. I would like to show your work,' is not the best way to ensure top artists will agree. 'Who are you? Will I ever see you again?' would no doubt be the response.

I knew little about art, nothing about how to keep records, nothing about accountancy and had no business training. After all, I had been in science for 12 years: I had done cancer research in London and Boston and on returning to Australia I had studied for my doctorate. With this as my background, everything I achieved in the gallery world was by way of a learning process – on the job. That was the most exciting part. I taught myself and asked for a lot of advice. I may not have used all the advice I received, but people were certainly generous with it. I met wonderful people who were open and giving.

My childhood was unusual. I have a brother and a sister, but there is an age gap of eight years between my sister and me. I was brought up like an only child, by my grandparents rather than my parents. This meant that the people I interacted with and who were closest to me were much older. There was a two generation gap. My grandmother was my mentor and mother-figure. My grandfather was the one who paid the bills, but Chinese men don't have time to play with little girls!

Between me and my grandmother and my 'amah' (a Chinese domestic servant) there was a 50-year age difference. While they spoiled me shamelessly, through their love and approval they also gave me a strong reference point. There was no pressure from either of them. I was not required to live up to some standard or vision they had. They didn't stand over me, or sit next to me, making me spend two or three hours after school doing my homework. But they instilled in me the desire to achieve, to be educated well, to excel in school. The most contradictory but remarkable thing about their influence was that both women were illiterate: they couldn't even write their own names. My 'amah' had to thumbprint everything. My grandmother could sign her name, mainly for legal documents, but that was it! So these two completely illiterate women instilled in me a strong sense of myself. Still, to be *so* high-achieving – it's a mystery even to me!

I was not required to live up to some standard or vision they had.

My primary and secondary schooling was completed in Penang, an island off the north-west coast of Malaysia. I had an idyllic childhood growing up on that small island with fine white sand on endless stretches of beach, gentle hills which appear to turn purple in the late afternoons, sudden tropical rain followed by the seductive scent of the frangipannis – it was like a country town, very, very safe and untouched by tourism. It was then a British colony and I revelled in the British system. It is true that some people had a bad time with the Brits. But there was a large number who were unaffected by the colonial system on a day to day basis and who thrived on what was good about it.

I attended an English-speaking school and the teachers were some of the best anyone could have, anywhere in the world. These teachers who were prepared to travel to the 'Far East', almost half a century ago, to live and work, were special. They were not 'drafted'. They *chose* to come. They were adventurous and enquiring. Misfits and maniacs must have applied too, but the selection board was thorough: to my knowledge, there was not one nasty incident reported. Generally, the teachers who came under the colonial system were dedicated and compassionate. I had the very best of the British educational system. Our final examination was known as the 'Senior Cambridge Exams'. My only regret was that, as a child, I did not study Chinese and missed out on Chinese history and literature. I was only western (British) educated, but I did thrive on the system, and loved it. That in itself is a contradiction. Life – how a person ends up, how a person 'is' – is a contradiction.

None of our British teachers imparted the attitude that they were 'here to teach the little heathens'. We were fortunate in that sense. One of the teachers, an Irish woman, opened up a whole new world of literature, poetry and theatre to us. She came from the source as it were: rather than a Chinese teacher trying to teach English literature to Chinese children, we had someone from the very source of the novels, plays and poetry. She was inspirational and many students, especially myself, kept up our friendship with her for years and years, until she died. I remember her with great affection and admiration.

The year I spent at school in Adelaide is a trifle hazy. I was mainly trying to come to terms with living without my comforts and my family, because until I was 16 years old I had a personal 'amah' to clean up after me. To be left on my own for the first time was a shock. I boarded with a migrant British landlady and expected her to cook all my meals. Once she left a pot of meat on the stove. I ate it all up. When she came in, she asked: 'Where's the meat? Where's the meat?' 'I ate it,' I said. 'Oh, God! You ate my cats' meat.' The meat was for her six cats!

So I was coming to terms with what life was like away from home, and was studying hard. At that time it was necessary to do the leaving examination, then leaving honours to get into university, and ordinarily it took two years. I did it in one year, then went straight into the science faculty.

I can recall no one inspirational during my university days, neither at the University of Adelaide nor when I was doing my doctorate at the University of Melbourne. What hit me, rather, was the reverse: how women subjugate themselves in order to secure a husband. One extremely bright girl took exhibition prizes year after year. She enroled to do her masters degree rather than a doctorate, the reason (as she said) being that the man she was courting was enroled to do a doctorate, and she couldn't possibly be better qualified than he! Yet year after year she had taken the exhibition. This was puzzling for me and quite contrary to my upbringing.

... how women subjugate themselves in order to secure a husband.

Yet again, I encountered another contradiction. Here was I, brought up by two completely illiterate old women, yet they did not raise me to spend my days devising the best way to catch a man. On the contrary, they instilled in me a desire for outstanding achievement.

From the time I was in secondary school, without any prompting whatsoever, I rose at four every morning to study for examinations. Where did this motivation come from? I believe it was from the two women who cared for me. As a child, I wanted them to be proud of me and my achievements and this motivation has continued as I became an adult.

My 'amah's' favourite story was the one of a poor scholar sitting for the Imperial Examinations in ancient China. He was so poor that he could not afford to buy candles to study at night. Instead he caught fire flies, placed them in a bottle and studied by their light. He eventually gained the highest grade possible and went on to be a great scholar. His story remained fixed in my head. The woman who told it to that small child is today 85, in good health, and has gone back to live in China.

My grandmother and 'amah' were *always* there, encouraging.

Over 18 years, as director of Raya Gallery I travelled a great deal. In the early days, my art came from South-East Asia, mainly Singapore, Malaysia and Hong Kong. I recorded as much as I could as to what went on because the art was new to Australia and I had to show Australians the process by which it was made. This was particularly necessary if the artist did not accompany the exhibition. If the artist was present, she or he talked to the viewers and buyers. So from the earliest time of the gallery, I was taking informal portraits of the artists and recording the tools and materials they used. I used photography, my own photographs, for the recording. Photography was by no means an unfamiliar medium as I was printing black and white photographs during my secondary school days. So what was initially an interest and hobby developed over the years into what is now my professional pursuit.

I designed many of the invitations to the exhibitions and used colour photographs as illustrations. I taught myself to look at things artistically. I would look at someone's painting and say: 'Hey, this is good but if he had left out this part, this part, this part, it would be great!' So when I came to do photography as an art form, I knew immediately what I wanted. It was a game I taught myself, through doing my own work.

This is how it has been with so many aspects of my work – learning on the job. Another spin-off is that I have become one of the most meticulous accountants on earth today, simply because I had to keep all my books. With photography, I try to capture the essence of my subject rather than the whole, be it landscape, architecture, nature, still-life or people. When I was at school and also as a young mother, I spent countless hours in the darkroom printing my photographs. Nowadays, I have become lazy or, rather, have lost interest in darkroom techniques. I send all my unexposed films to a laboratory.

I spent countless hours in the darkroom printing my photographs.

The Chinese love photographs. Like the Japanese, they are constantly photographing themselves with everything! I rarely see a Japanese tourist without a camera – snap, snap, snap. The Chinese love to be photographed, too. Of course I cannot speak for 1200 million Chinese, and generalised statements are what they are – generalised – but in my experience 'camera-shy' has never been a Chinese problem. A large number of family photographs I have from the past are formal portraits taken in studios. The subjects bothered to dress up, go to the studio, and have their photographs taken. I ransacked my grandmother's cupboards after she died, looking for photographs. I have albums of photographs dating back to the turn of the century. Some of them are from the nineteenth century, particularly the 1890s.

Why this love for the camera, recording pictorial reminders of family members, times, celebrations and places? There are many Chinese like me, third or fourth generation born outside mainland China. Our forefathers – in my case, my greatgrandfather left China in 1870, as a boy, and did not return. We are South-East Asians who have been brought into a lifestyle much influenced by the British, as Singapore and Penang were British Straits Settlements. This multiplicity of influences leads to an eclectic society. Although I am Chinese by birth, I think in English and many of my family think in English too. We are a mixture of many things. I think that this love of being photographed is yet another contradiction. By and large the Chinese are shy people – low key. Perhaps it is the western influence? Every year, on the birthday of my grandfather or grandmother, a photographer would be called in and the whole family clan would pose for hours for one photograph after another. My grandmother, who loved to be photographed, would have a solo session after the group ones were finished.

In 1986, together with Morag Loh, noted historian and writer, I mounted a seminar cum photographic exhibition entitled *Survival and Celebration*, which centred on the Chinese women in Australia and their affiliations over 130 years. There were hundreds of photographs on display, collected by Chinese women spanning the early settlers to the present. My family has far more photographs than I do, despite my being the professional photographer in the family. They have albums and albums of wonderful historic works – every family gathering, every party, every holiday. They have photographs of whatever they did of any significance. My family is not unique; many others have done the same. It may signify a search for identity, wanting to preserve something of the past and pass it on to future generations.

In 1986 I organised a group of friends to Central Australia. I had travelled extensively – Europe, America, China, South-East Asia, but never to Central Australia. The red centre's landscape was overwhelming. It was mind-shattering, and I was inspired. I even came to understand a little about the concept of 'dreaming'.

I looked at the magnificent landscape artistically: how could I capture it? How would I capture it artistically? That was the starting point of my career as a serious photographer. When the photographs came back from the laboratory I was extremely happy. I had taken 30 rolls of film. Now I am very economical. I shoot just enough for an exhibition: I know precisely how much is needed, after so many years at it.

That was the starting point of my career as a serious photographer.

In August 1988, one of my artists dropped out. He had a family crisis, which meant his exhibition could not be put together in sufficient time to take up the date that had been set aside. This meant that in three months time, there was 'free' space at the gallery. I slotted myself in.

I knew it would be a conflict of interest. A gallery director should never compete for sales and publicity with his or her artists. When the time comes, it's time to give up the gallery! This is why people who are artists trying to run a gallery simultaneously with exhibiting their own art have such problems. The golden rule is: do not compete with your own stable. Yet in this case I thought: 'Why not? If I don't launch myself, who's going to launch me?!'

The space was available. I couldn't fill it in three months. So for my first solo exhibition I gathered together everything I thought was exhibitable. There were landscapes, and to make the exhibition more interesting I photographed 20 people who played a significant part in my artistic life. Fortunately those whose portraits were on display did the decent thing and bought their own portraits: they couldn't *not* buy their own portraits. This paid the bills!

So I held my debut exhibition in 1988, another exhibition in 1989, and by 1990 I knew I wanted to move on. My farewell exhibition in that year consisted of images of Singapore. It was a most fitting end to my career as a gallery director.

To date, I have held 17 solo exhibitions, mostly at my own studio but also at the Westpac Gallery, Victorian Arts Centre, the Council of Adult Education (CAE) gallery, two commercial galleries and an overseas gallery. I show about three times a year at my studio: any more would be overloading the buyers. My photographs are small in format as I want them to be intimate. I like people to come close up when they look at one of my photographs, rather than gazing from afar at blown-up images.

As director of Raya Gallery from 1972 to 1990 I nurtured many artists over time. I believe in a long and fruitful interaction with an artist – guiding, talking, exchanging ideas, challenging and being challenged. I was not interested in one-offs – 'come in, sell, go away' exhibitions. If one wants to run a gallery as a purely commercial venture, it is possible to turn around 20 to 25 exhibitions a year: in – out, in – out. I had between eight to 10 – at a leisurely pace. I also used the gallery as a base for holding lectures, painting demonstrations, poetry and musical evenings. This meant I was not simply exhibiting art. Raya Gallery was a meeting point. I liked using the phrase 'the artistic meeting point of eastern and western traditions'. Over the years I learned a great deal about ethnic and Asian architecture and on one occasion did a wonderful celebration, a community-based show

I liked using the phrase 'the artistic meeting point of eastern and western traditions'.

with lectures and an exhibition. I did a great deal of work with the Australian Natives Association (ANA) of which Frederick Dunlop was president for many, many years. I arranged all their anniversary exhibitions.

I have worked on a number of voluntary committees and mounted a community awareness exhibition for the pleasure I derive from it and in the hope that I will give back something of what I have received in support and encouragement.

I was active in the Australian Asian Association of Victoria when its president, Edward 'Weary' Dunlop was alive. I met Weary at a picnic in the late 1960s and he became a great inspiration in my life. I hosted many Australian-Asian functions at Raya Gallery. I enjoyed working with the original core members; their interest was genuine. In later years, and after Weary died, I lost interest. The association seemed to have taken on a different persona. It was time for me to close that door.

The other committee to which I belong is the National Gallery Women's Association, an official fundraising group for the National Gallery of Victoria. I have been on this committee for 17 years. We hold functions throughout the year and assume a public relations role for the National Gallery. In 1979 I was invited by the then president, Elizabeth Summons, to join. Liz is a remarkable woman – a patron of the arts, witty, intelligent and a great organiser. She could get anyone working around the clock for her on a voluntary basis. This last talent is probably the greatest asset for anyone leading a voluntary committee. Liz opened many doors for me. Through her I met important collectors and people of influence in the art world and gained access to private collections, for viewing. It is essential for a gallery director to have these kinds of contacts. The art world is elitist, however much we may like to think otherwise, however much we may like to subscribe to egalitarian ideals. Knowing the 'right' people also gives one the confidence to operate in this world.

An even earlier mentor was the wellknown fabric designer, Frances Burke, who died in 1994. Articulate and strong-willed, Frances was a talented artist in her own right. When we became friends, she had given up her fabric-printing business. She was generous with her time and advice and helped me to understand what makes the art world tick.

My philosophy, as director of Raya Gallery, was to welcome everyone. I am a 'people person', thrive on people. That I am Chinese gave me an edge in the art world, especially as I specialised in contemporary South-East Asian art. I was different, could not be categorised, and hence was more memorable to people.

Morag Loh, in collaborating with me on *Survival and Celebration*, showed me how two professionals with diverse expertise and strengths can combine them to produce a highly successful project and at the same time a warm and lasting friendship.

I have also found satisfaction in pushing along someone else's career. Once I saw an artist's work at a show, and liked it so much that I sought out her name and address; then I contacted her, visited her studio and offered her an exhibition at my gallery. She was a mature artist but had never had a solo exhibition because she could not afford the framing. Framing of paintings requires a large capital investment. For some artists, $3000 or $4000 is a great deal of money. I had the facility at Raya Gallery to exhibit paintings matted but unframed for I had a highly sophisticated panel system to which artworks could be pinned in such a way that their presentation matched that of framed works. A large proportion of overseas work exhibited at my gallery was done on paper, for example Chinese brush paintings, exquisitely scrolled but unframed. To display them effectively, I had made a pin on/panel system somewhat similar in approach to that I had seen at the Hong Kong museum. Returning to the artist: all she had to outlay was $50 for extra matts. I loaned her the bulk of matts from my stockroom. I even cut them for her. She has gone from strength to strength.

I have observed marked differences in the way men and women go about trying to get an exhibition. If the artist is unknown, it is difficult to find a good gallery. From my experience, men manage to secure exhibitions more successfully than do women. Male artists are more able to cope with rejection and this gives them an advantage. Women are often overly sensitive to a negative response. An artist can ask: 'Would you like to exhibit my paintings?' Or the question can be framed: 'You wouldn't like to exhibit my paintings, would you?'

The number of times women have used the second approach in asking me for an exhibition was unbelievable! Immediately it sets up the negative, and I can think of a good reason for it. If I had replied: 'No,' then she would not feel so bad. Framing the question in the negative way is a means of self-protection. I can understand this self-protection as I tend to do it and I have to constantly remind myself not to do so. Another tactic is to make a joke of things, so that you won't feel so terrible or embarrassed if you are knocked back.

Male confidence, on the other hand, can be unpleasant. I recall the time a Chinese artist from Shanghai came in to the gallery. He was the type who placed himself in the category of the gods. He brought along a bag of his paintings, demanded I look at them, and wanted an exhibition. 'No!' I said. I thought he would kill me there and then. I feared for my life. You see, in Shanghai no woman would ever say that to a man under the same circumstances. He left in a huff but for a time whenever I saw a Chinese man coming into the gallery I would hide in the toilet. I preferred to lock myself in to having an altercation that might end dramatically – for me.

AS ONE DOOR SHUTS, ANOTHER OPENS

In my childhood, I had unconditional support from my grandmother and my 'amah'. In my adult life, I am fortunate to have a tolerant husband, and that's a great help. He supports me in most of what I do – well, 95 percent. We have differences of opinion, fights, arguments, but in the end, there is 95 percent support! This means I have no problems in 'giving back' to other people. I am not begrudging in any way. If people ask for my help and I am able to give it, I do. That I give another person something does not mean I lose it. It is like a game: the more you give, the more you receive. That is the more farsighted way to regard the support any person gives out to others. Perhaps that is the notion that underlies Christianity in its best sense. Incidentally, I am not religious.

That I give another person something does not mean I lose it.

Of course, this philosophy can backfire: a person can give support then, instead of reciprocation, be 'kicked in the face'. But these instances can be put to one side: they are few and far between. The way I see it, once a person feels she has received support and encouragement from another person, then she has no qualms about giving to others. Life would be terribly boring without contradictions and unforeseen events. I look forward to shut doors and open, new ones.

The Women in My Life

Mary Owen

Born on 8 February 1921 in Melbourne, Victoria, Mary Roberta Owen was educated at Korowa CEGGS (Church of England Girls School) and Lauriston Girls School (from which she matriculated in 1936). She graduated BA from the University of Melbourne in 1986 and is a past deputy chancellor of LaTrobe University.

Since 1972 Mary Owen has been a member of the Women's Electoral Lobby (WEL), and was founding coordinator of Melbourne Working Women's Centre. She has written numerous submissions to government, articles for books, and articles and 'letters to the editor' on various matters concerning women. Now retired, Mary Owen is concentrating on the pursuit of an unmeanstested age pension – to be funded by a compulsory levy on income and the abolition of current tax concessions for superannuation, which favour the wealthy to the detriment of low-income earners.

I've had a fortunate life, although I certainly didn't think I was fortunate when I was a child. One of my favourite sayings was: 'It's not fair!' This incensed my father because it usually implied – or was explicitly – criticism of my stepmother. To his credit my father was ever conscious of the debt he owed his second wife for taking him on with three children under the age of five. We three did not appreciate this at the time. We could see only that there was a difference between the way we were treated and the way in which our younger sister and brother were treated. With the wisdom of years and the experience of motherhood, I can now understand that a parent can make allowances for the behaviour of her own children which she does not extend to other people's children.

I don't think my stepmother was aware that she treated us three differently. Probably she unconsciously rationalised her attitude by the thought that, by the time her first child was born, we were old enough to understand and to obey. This could not be expected of 'the littlies'.

Of course, we never did make up the gap. Her daughter was always three years younger than my sisters, who are twins. There was the same gap of three years between that daughter and our one and only brother, but he and she – the two younger ones – were always linked together as 'the littlies'.

I have no childhood memories of being petted, helped and encouraged; quite the reverse. We children were expected to help with household tasks, to wash our own socks, iron our blouses, do our own school homework; to devise our own entertainment; and to compete in school sports. What I learnt more than anything was to compete. For me, the prize most worthy of competition was my father's approval. I wanted to be the best at everything.

Being the eldest, being the best was not difficult at home – at least in the sphere of physical achievements. How proud I was that I could slice French beans more finely than any of the others! Yet ultimately this was not very smart because I was left to slice up three pounds of beans while the others had only to shell peas – accomplished far more quickly.

The **Book of Ecclesiastes** *says:*

Cast thy bread upon the waters: for thou shalt find it after many days. Thus spake the prophet.

If you throw a pebble into a pool of water, it will make ripples. If it is a small pond the ripples will extend to the limits of the pond; in a large lake they will eventually flatten and vanish. To 'cast your bread upon the waters' conjures up visions of an ocean where a bottle cast into the sea eventually arrives on a beach thousands of miles away.

Something of this philosophy has permeated my life, although it is difficult to say where I got it from. Was it a sense of noblesse oblige: *that those who have received more blessings should share them with those less favoured? My parents instilled some such notion into me although, as a child slicing beans, I did not count myself 'blessed'.*

I was, I think, a very self-centred child and, although I helped my siblings in various ways, I think it was rather to show my superior proficiency than to give them comfort. And until recently I have scarcely acknowledged the debt I owe to several women who, now I consider it, have helped mould me into the person I am.

> It was many years before I had some understanding of the difficult job my stepmother must have had.

I suspect I have mostly tried to do what I wanted to do because I wanted to do it. That has, on occasion, included helping others – particularly women – but that has probably done as much for me as it has for anyone I may have helped.

My mother died when my twin sisters were born. I was only 16 months old. Not surprisingly, my father married again and in due course I had another sister and a brother. It was many years before I had some understanding of the difficult job my stepmother must have had. I was probably a spoilt brat when she took me on. She and my father thought children needed discipline. Praise and sympathy were therefore in short supply.

I am sure my parents aimed to teach us to stand on our own two feet and to be independent. I suspect that, unappreciated though it was when I was a child, this attitude has stood me in good stead throughout my life. Yet, seeing other children petted and indulged, I thought myself to be very hardly done by. I was lucky in having one sure refuge where I felt loved and special – my Auntie Marge.

Auntie Marge has, I think, been the greatest influence on my life. A painter and my godmother, she took her godmotherly duties seriously. When my mother died she (I think) felt herself called upon to discharge those duties rather more than the average godmother.

It was bliss for me to stay with Auntie Marge and be treated as an only child. She didn't criticise my parents or encourage me to feel sorry for myself, but I knew she loved me. She allowed me to read all her books and she encouraged me to write. After she died I found she had a collection of my early efforts stowed away.

My childhood was dominated by women.

My childhood was dominated by women. Our household consisted of parents, four girls and one boy – the youngest – plus a live-in maid. When we were very young a nursemaid came every afternoon and we had a laundress who came once a week. Apart from my father, the only men with whom I can recall having regular contact were Sykes, the Scottish gardener, who always made us shortbread for New Year, and John, the Chinese fishmonger, who came once a week and cleaned the fish my mother selected (usually garfish, which I hated because they seemed to be full of fine bones) under running water from the gully trap.

On Christmas Day two or three great-uncles came for midday dinner, giving us exciting presents. They all seemed to have wet, drooping moustaches which tickled when they kissed us. They were fine uncles.

Each of the all-girls schools I attended was run entirely by women. Apart from the first year at the second of these, I loved school and had crushes on various teachers. School was the most important thing in my life. I went as early as I could each morning to play tennis before lessons began and most afternoons after school I played baseball, hockey or tennis, although I wasn't very good at any sport. I made the hockey team only because we were such a small school that there were not many to choose from! And that reminds me of the only man I can remember being associated with school: Mr Robb, who came to watched us play hockey, keeping time with a large stopwatch. Once he took me to afternoon tea at the Robur Tearooms in the city. This was an event indeed but I suspect I did not tell my parents about it, for I am sure they would not have let me go had they known. How innocent I was and how lucky in this case that there was no need to be otherwise. Mr Robb and I talked about sport and the dear old chap behaved impeccably.

My greatest joy was swimming and I *was* good at that. Every afternoon in the summertime – unless it was really chilly – I was down at the Malvern Baths, swimming up and down, up and down – 32 lengths was a mile and I would do at least sixteen. In my last year at school I became self-appointed coach for the younger girls in our house and taught several of them to swim. Although this was the only place available for meeting boys of my own age, I really was not interested in them. They seemed so juvenile and I could never understand why other girls got so excited about them. I was there to swim.

Years later, when my daughter asked me to coach her in diving I was appalled when, after about half an hour of telling her what to do, she said: 'I don't know what you mean. *Show* me!' I had to get up on the divingboard to demonstrate. She came equal first in the diving event for the combined Church of England Girls Schools sports! And, so far as I know, she never dived again. A bit like her mum. I couldn't resist the challenge of trying something new but, once I had accomplished it, I could seldom be bothered doing it again. Am I a dilettante? There are so many interesting activities and ideas to explore that I can seldom bear to concentrate on any one thing long enough to become an expert.

As a child, I received mixed messages. On one hand, I was supposed to be the brains of the family and was expected to do well at school. On the other, I cannot recall being praised for anything; I was more often chided. Perhaps with time I have forgotten the praise, but if I came home with the news that I had come top of the class in English or second in the egg-and-spoon race, I was told not to 'skite'. The general feeling appeared to be that parents should be careful not to let a child develop a 'swollen head'. Later I learned that my father often skited to other people about his children's achievements. In childhood I felt I did not come up to expectations. The most common remark in my school report book was: 'Molly could do better if she worked harder.'

> *I was supposed to be the brains of the family and was expected to do well at school.*

I worked hard – in spasms – but there were so many distractions: tennis, hockey, swimming and friends. Whatever I did, I did with great enthusiasm. One of the maxims we were taught was: 'Whatsoever thy hand findeth to do, do it with thy might.' I sure did! And it has taken me many years to learn not to find so many things to do. Yet the rest of this biblical quotation (from *Ecclesiastes* 10.9) is: 'For there is no work, nor device, nor knowledge, nor wisdom, in the grave, whither thou goest.' A sobering thought, I suspect it has been driving me, unconsciously, most of my life.

We were a conventional middleclass family, nominally Church of England (C of E) although my parents went to church on formal occasions only. My two sisters and I were sent to a Presbyterian Sunday School, mainly to keep us occupied for an hour or two and because a young woman, who taught in the Sunday School, lived nearby and was willing to take us and bring us home.

I also went to extra classes to study for an exam offering a scholarship to Presbyterian Ladies College (PLC). I came top of our group but did not win a scholarship.

When we were old enough to go by ourselves we went to a C of E Sunday School and I was duly confirmed as a member of the Church of England. My parents believed this was 'the right thing to do' but, later on, when I became involved with an evangelical group, they thought that was going a bit far. They were right. There I met a man who said he loved me and, because at the age of 18 I thought every girl must be married but that I was so unattractive that no man would want me, I promised to marry him. Later, when I had doubts, my early training that one must always keep one's word prevented me from breaking that promise. The marriage was a disaster for reasons which, I suspect, are responsible for many broken marriages: we came from very different backgrounds and at no time ever seriously discussed our expectations of marriage.

I was duly confirmed as a member of the Church of England.

I am not quite sure what my expectations were but I think I just took it for granted that our partnership would operate as did that of my parents: my husband would go to work and earn the money, leaving me to run the household as I saw fit. My husband, I think, had an idealised vision of a family. His father was an important figure in his life: he had been first mate with the Bristol Steamship Company and had married his cousin, Mary Ann Morgan, daughter of a Welsh miner. Mary Ann's mother died when she was quite young and her father remarried. She and her brother and sister were brought up by their maternal grandmother. Seventeen when she married, Mary Ann was 19 when her first son was born. Six years later the second son – my husband – was born. Her husband was seldom home and it must have been hard for that young woman, brought up by her grandmother in a small Welsh village, coping with two boys on her own. My husband's memories of his father were of the revered head of the household, captain of a ship, taking them out for treats and waited on by an adoring wife. I expect that is the way he pictured himself. Poor man. I saw things differently.

For as long as I can remember I have always loved reading and meant to be a writer myself – an author. I was forever starting stories and frequently not finishing them. The only one I have now is one I found among Auntie Marge's papers. It was all about naughty girls being punished.

English was my best subject at school and I took it for granted that I should top the class. Alas, the only year there was a prize for English was in Form 6, matriculation year, and I was beaten by two-thirds of a mark by a girl who had never figured as being 'good' at English. We had a different teacher for English that year – an older woman who had taught at the school for years. I am not sure whether she was more impressed by persistent hard work than by creativity, or whether she just thought I needed cutting down to size. It took me a long time to get over that disappointment. The only prizes I ever won at school were one for general excellence (whatever that meant) when I was about 10 and another for scripture when I was twelve.

I thought the only way to a career in writing was to be a journalist. My father did not think it a suitable career for a girl but knew me well enough not to say so. He told me that, if that was what I wanted to do, I should have to learn typing and shorthand; so I took these two subjects as extras during my last year at school. I did well, winning a half scholarship to Dacomb Business College. I would have liked to go to university but it would have been a big expense and, in any case, I was only 15 when I matriculated. In those days a student had to be 17 or 18 before being admitted to the University of Melbourne. The scholarship could not be wasted. So, to business college I went. It was all very boring and, being unused to the lack of discipline, I frequently crossed the road to Coles ladies' lounge, knitting a jumper while I read a novel propped on my knees. My wardrobe consisted of a couple of cotton frocks and two skirts: one made from my old school tunic, the other from a pleated skirt – originally attached to a bodice. Mother had bought a huge piece of the material cheaply and had had skirts made for all four of us girls by an old woman (she seemed old to us) who came to sew for us. After I began at the business college mother made a special effort for me and had the old skirt and the tunic remade in a more stylish fashion by a French dressmaker recommended to her by one of her friends. My 'Coles ladies' lounge jumper' was an addition to my wardrobe.

I had achieved a speed of 60 words a minute in typing and 120 in shorthand...

After two terms at the business college I had achieved a speed of 60 words a minute in typing and 120 in shorthand, and was considered ready for a job. Dad sent me to see someone he knew at the Commonwealth Bank. While waiting to be interviewed I was appalled at the school-like atmosphere of the huge office in Collins Street and was relieved when the man said they could not take me on because I did Dacomb shorthand and all 'their' 'girls' did Pitman's, which meant they could read each other's notes if necessary. He referred me to someone else and in no time at all there I was in the typical female role of typist/stenographer.

After a few months of typing boring form letters I was moved to the editorial section where I enjoyed helping prepare a regular newsletter. Then came the second world war. I went to work for Broken Hill Associated Smelters and in 1942, at the age of 21, I married a second lieutenant in the Royal Australian Naval Reserve, the man I had met at the evangelical group, and went to live in Adelaide. He was attached to HMAS Torrens, the naval depot, but was allowed to live out when not on nightduty and we had two rooms in a house in Larg's Bay near the depot.

After the war we settled in Melbourne and produced three beautiful children – two girls and a boy. I strove to maintain standards set by my mother but without the household help she had had. We seemed never to have sufficient money. My husband thought me extravagant and, by his standards, I probably was. After his father died in 1929, at the beginning of the Depression, he was the sole support of his mother until she qualified for the age pension in 1942, his brother having married quite young and being unemployed for some time. No wonder my husband was always very tight with money. He maintained he must save for our children's education and for our old age – worthy sentiments but, once we had separated, he refused to pay the children's education expenses and I received none of the superannuation benefits accumulated for the benefit of us both.

I received none of the superannuation benefits accumulated for the benefit of us both.

In the early days my husband was loath to pay bills from doctor or dentist. This embarrassed me, so I took in typing. Although I did well out of this work, done at home between housework and childcare, I was unable to save any of the money I earned. I did not want to admit to my parents that I was not being adequately provided for and I attempted to keep up appearances, probably indulging the children more than was good for them. I made most of their clothes and my own.

When our youngest child, David, began kindergarten my mother-in-law came to live with us and agreed to mind him in the mornings, which meant I could take a parttime job. The arrangement was that she paid no board and had all her pension for herself. My job was close to home – still typing and stenography. It was advertised as a fulltime job but I managed to persuade the boss that I could do all they needed between 10.00 am and 4.00 pm and would accept a wage of £12 a week instead of the 13 guineas they were offering. No one had heard of enterprise bargaining in those days but, with full employment and good stenographers hard to get, I did not find it difficult to make such arrangements to suit my needs. It did not occur to me that I was being unfair to the other poor women who had to work the full shift. One can work harder if one works a shorter day.

I had somehow managed to persuade my husband to buy a secondhand car from a neighbour and, as my poor mate was too nervous to learn to drive and I had had a few lessons some years earlier, it was decided that I would get a licence first; he would learn later. He never did, so I had full use of the car. I dashed home at lunchtime to drive David and a neighbour's child to kindergarten. The neighbour brought the children home.

I was full of guilt about these arrangements and was determined not to exploit my mother-in-law. I employed a woman to clean once a week and her sister to do the ironing. The cooking, shopping, sewing and other chores I did myself. One of the 'other chores' was cleaning the lavatory as my cleaning woman informed me that job was beneath her. Cleaning the lavatory was certainly beneath my husband, who was conscious of being a 'white-collar' worker. He did help with the washing up but informed me, when I proposed taking on a paid job outside the home, that he did not mind my 'having a little job' so long as I did not neglect my children. I tried not to, and am now sure I erred in the other direction. I taught them nothing about running a household. I did try, at one time, to have them share the ironing, but Grandma disapproved of David being expected to iron the handkerchiefs and I found she was doing them herself.

After two or three years the firm for which I had been working moved to the other side of the city and I found another job – selling food mixers door-to-door. This was the beginning of liberation for me. We were paid on commission and, for the first time, I was paid the same rate as the men. My total wage was better than most of the men earned because I was better at the job than they were.

We were paid on commission and, for the first time, I was paid the same rate as the men.

I worked at that job for about six years but my husband hated my doing it, partly because he was embarrassed that a wife of his should do such 'demeaning' work; partly because he was ashamed to admit that his wife did any paidwork at all; but mostly, I think, because it gave me such confidence in my ability to compete with men.

There were endless rows. Eventually I agreed to give up selling and take a desk-job as the proprietor's private secretary. Even that did not satisfy my spouse. I moved to another job close to home where I was constantly underemployed and bored to tears. After several more jobs I went to work for a union where, among other duties, I produced the union journal. There I remained for 12 years until 1975, International Women's Year, when with Sylvie Shaw I became one of the first two coordinators of the Melbourne Working Women's Centre. At the age of 54, I gave up a secure job and my real commitment to the cause of women began.

There was a one-off grant of $40 000 from the Whitlam government – that was all. My conscious reasoning ran something like this. My children are now more or less off my hands (financially). It is time (that famous Whitlam slogan) to do something for all women. Another six years until I reach pension age. If I stay in my current job, I have no hope of saving enough to make me independent of the age pension. I am probably in a better position than most women to run the risk of having one year's employment only and probably would not have much trouble in finding another job or two to last until retirement. On the other hand, we might set something going that will change attitudes to women in the paidworkplace – and the world could be a better place.

But my activism had begun when I was in my forties. For many women, 'change of life' is an ominous phrase and a threatening one. I looked forward to the day when I should not be bothered with 'the curse' and constant fears of pregnancy, before the days of the Pill. For me, menopause was a non-event. The real change in my life came when my second daughter, Wendy, persuaded me to go to a meeting addressed by Dr Bertram Wainer. I was 47 and my second life began.

I looked forward to the day when I should not be bothered with 'the curse' and constant fears of pregnancy...

I wasn't really unhappy in my first life although I complained about lots of things. This may have been because I was naturally argumentative and contrary. Essentially, that first life revolved around family and I took little part in outside activities apart from hockey and tennis, the fundamentalist religious group of my late teens and, later, the school mothers club, the Scouts mothers club, the local church (where I taught in the Sunday School) and a weekly game of tennis with mums from the church.

In my second life, I became involved in the world of politics. Long before Don Chipp set up the Australian Democrats 'to keep the bastards honest', Bert Wainer founded the Progressive Reform Party (PRP) with much the same idea. Until then it had never occurred to me to join a political party. A swinging voter, I had voted for men (they were all men, then) who sounded the most convincing when elections came around. I forgot all about politics in between times. Bert persuaded me I could help change what was. It began with my old habit of sticking up for the underdog.

I particularly remember three issues: the campaign to have seatbelts made compulsory in all cars; the enquiry Bert Wainer started into the Victoria Police Force; and the campaign to remove the laws penalising abortion.

In my sheltered life I had had little to do with the police and I was appalled at the stories of police brutality which poured in in response to an advertisement in the daily papers inviting people to tell us of injustice which they felt they had suffered at the hands of police. I and my elder daughter, Rosemary, volunteered to interview several of those who responded. No doubt we were very green (nothing to do with the environment) but the consistency of the stories we heard was convincing. The names of the same police officers kept coming up from different sources.

In the end, the Kaye Enquiry (headed by a queen's counsel) found three senior police officers guilty of corruption and they were sent to gaol.

The abortion issue was inextricably woven with the corrupt police. The story was told by Peggy Berman and Kevin Childs in their book, *Why Isn't She Dead!* – dedicated by them 'to the Liberal Party Government of Victoria, without whose studied neglect of the problem of unwanted pregnancy this book would not have been necessary'. What I learned through my association with Bert Wainer and the Progressive Reform Party heightened my growing awareness of discrimination against women and, even before the PRP dissolved, I became absorbed in and into the Women's Movement.

> *I became absorbed in, and into, the Women's Movement.*

Wendy was also responsible for my awakening to feminism. She lent me a book (recommended to her by the English teacher at Canterbury Girls High School): *The Feminine Mystique* by Betty Friedan. This book made a great impact on Wendy at the time and on me too. I had already separated from my husband, so neither Friedan nor the Women's Movement can be blamed for that. They simply helped me to understand what had happened.

I had a fulltime job which I needed, as I had two children still at school and one at university and was getting no financial assistance from my husband. Such spare time as I had was spent mostly on the Progressive Reform Party. Many members were women. Most were far more politically experienced that I and I listened with fascination to their accounts of membership of political parties. The only skills I felt competent to offer were typing and shorthand; so I became minute secretary and spent hours typing lengthy minutes of meetings and wonderful policy proposals.

I also had some skill with words and editing, which I used after an abortive attempt, with two other members of the PRP, to view the Victorian parliament in action without first submitting our names and addresses at the door. The custom was to alert members if there were visitors from their electorate – so that they could be on their best behaviour. We wanted to see how they performed when they did not know they were being observed. We had put out a media release in advance, stating what we proposed to do. I think one radio station bothered to send someone along but next day the evening paper carried a sensational report of the 'assault on Parliament House' in a column entitled 'On the Spot'. I responded with a letter to the editor of that paper and writing letters to editors has become more or less a habit since then.

Inspired by the PRP, I became interested in a number of public institutions and their effects on citizens. Among other things, we sought a better deal for contributors to the Hospital Benefits Association (HBA – health insurance). I found that, although I had joined the HBA during the war while my husband was away in the navy and had paid a family subscription for all the years since, only one of us could vote at the annual meeting and that one was my husband as family head! We succeeded in having that regulation amended but it heightened my awareness of sex discrimination and the need to get government to do something about it. Eventually the PRP disbanded and I joined the Australian Labor Party (ALP).

It was at about this time that a PRP woman suggested I join a new women's organisation called the Women's Electoral Lobby (WEL). Primly I replied that I did not believe in separate male-female groups. My friend replied that WEL had a few male members who believed in the feminist cause. This set me thinking, for the first time, about the meaning of feminism. Now when I hear a woman say: 'I believe in equal opportunities for women but I'm not a feminist,' I laugh to myself as I recall my own earlier ignorance.

One day I read a paragraph in a daily paper which said that WEL planned to interview all candidates for the forthcoming federal election, quizzing them on six matters of vital concern to women. 'Here at last are some women who are not just complaining about their lot but are doing something practical to change it,' I thought. In September 1972 I joined WEL.

I had not quite comprehended the value of collective knowledge and experience ...

These were exciting times. When one Sunday morning I turned up at the advertised venue for the first meeting, no one had a key. We adjourned to someone's flat in Carlton where, miraculously, a photographer from the *Age* found us. (It was, of course, no miracle: some competent woman had managed to let him know where we were.) In those early days I was often amazed at the way in which WEL women seemed to be able to organise (apart from the mislaid key to the first meeting place!) and the vast amount of knowledge they possessed. Despite my own involvement with the Progressive Reform Party, I had not quite comprehended the value of collective knowledge and experience and had not realised that women could initiate action.

The Women's Electoral Lobby opened up a new vista for me, of women working together for other women. That was the whole reason for our existence: sharing our experiences, DOING things to make life fairer for women.

It is not modesty which causes me to say I cannot think of any particular woman to whom I have given support which has enabled her to change her life. Through WEL and the Working Women's Centre, I have been involved in so many collective efforts of support for women that it has become a way of life. Individual cases do not readily come to mind – except one. A woman sent me a donation for the Melbourne Working

Women's Centre (WWC) with an accompanying note: 'I attribute being employed at this moment to your good advice. And it has certainly made a difference to my life.' She had been on the way to a nervous breakdown through pressure of family commitments and discriminatory treatment from her employer. The strain of combining the two roles was great, yet she said she needed the job 'not for the livelihood but for my personal survival'. She went on to be very active in the conservation movement.

More recently I have been touched by hearing – from out of the blue – from two women, each of whom says I influenced her life. Beth Wilson is now the President of the Mental Health Review Board. In 1992 I was amazed to read her story, 'Beyond the Legal Mystique' in *Breaking Through*, where she says I inspired her and that topics I raised in the media influenced how she looked at the world. *Beth had inspired me!*

Beth Wilson and I were classmates in higher school certificate (HSC) English literature at Prahran High School night classes. Both having left school at 15 and working in fulltime jobs, we had something in common. Yet mine was a fairly undemanding office job and I was doing only two subjects at night. Beth worked all day on the floor of a frozen food factory and was doing four subjects in one year. She was always so bright and cheerful and very funny, and I thought: 'She deserves to succeed if ever anyone did.' When she received top marks in all subjects and qualified for entry to law school, I wept for joy. To think I may have influenced the direction Beth took later is a reward higher than I could have imagined.

Heather O'Connor, another old friend, surprised me too. At a function in 1994 she said: 'I'll never forget how you helped me when I first became involved in the Women's Movement. I was just terrified of all those bright women and you took me under your wing.' I recall nothing of this but was immensely grateful to Heather for those comments.

I should like to think, too, that I had some influence on the career of my dear friend Kerry Lovering. In 1974 the department of labour and immigration advertised for two executive officers in the Women's Bureau. One was to advise on policy formation on issues relevant to work in the paidworkforce, the other to develop and maintain public relations for the bureau. I applied for the second position, suggesting to Kerry that she apply for the other. Some time later I met Kerry at an International Women's Day march. Had she put in an application? 'No.' I persuaded her that she should. She did, and got the job for which *I* had applied! Since then Kerry Lovering has held several highlevel positions and is now in South Australia as head of the Workers' Compensation Board. She would have arrived at the top anyway, but it is nice to think I may have had a small hand in pushing her over the starting line.

Individual cases may be difficult to recall. It is even more difficult to understand what motivated me. I am sure most help for women has come from collective efforts and the enveloping aura of sisterhood to which I was first exposed in the early 1970s is a very real part of this. What I have learnt is that, if you want to change things, you have to change public opinion; and to do that you have to have the numbers. You must work as part of a group.

> Most help for women has come from collective efforts and the enveloping aura of sisterhood...

There have been many important women in my life. Many of them are now dead and, to my shame, I doubt if I ever acknowledged to them that I thought I owed them anything. I am taking this opportunity to record the names of some whose influence I now remember and appreciate. There will be other women whom I shall remember from time to time and wish I had included in this tribute and I am sure there will be others, later on, who will enrich my life in various ways.

Aunt Olive, who gave up her job to look after me and my two sisters when my mother died.

My stepmother, who took on three children under the age of five and taught me to be independent.

Auntie Marge and Auntie Dall, who loved me and made me feel special.

Fanny Withers, my grandmother, who showed an independent spirit and took on the art establishment and the Victorian government,

Nurse Nelson, who provided loving care and suggested I should become a doctor because I had the brains.

The Misses Irving, Margaret and Lillian, who established Lauriston Girls School and set an example of strong, upright women.

Kay Irving, their niece, who regularly led a horse from Jordanville to Ashburton, arriving at 7.00 am to meet me, so as to give me riding lessons before school.

June Borgeest, a neighbour and my closest friend, who provided a refuge, humour and support when my husband was unbearable.

Beth Wilson, who had not had my advantages but rose triumphant.

My daughter Wendy, who introduced me to Betty Friedan and was responsible for my meeting Bertram Wainer and my subsequent involvement in politics.

Liz Carrell, who suggested I should join WEL.

Edna Ryan, who taught me about sisterhood and has been my model and inspiration for more than 20 years.

Three young women at the University of Melbourne who invited me to join with them on a Psychology II project. One of them (Annie Cantrell) later said I had helped her, and invited me to address a class she taught.

Nancy Kudis, who sold supermixers with me and taught me how migrant women survive.

My sisters – Shirley, Joyce and Marian who, with their husbands, provided wonderful support when I badly needed it. I must add a special 'thank you' to

Joyce, with whom I was staying in 1995 when I suffered a minor stroke. I believe it is largely due to her prompt and loving care and that of her daughter, Dr Judy Craig, that I have suffered no permanent effects from the stroke.

What I have learned is that , if you want to change things, you have to change public opinion; and, to do that, you must have the numbers – you have to work as part of a group. The Women's Electoral Lobby has been my group and the ripples from the Women's Movement are being felt around the world.

> *Cast thy bread upon the waters: for thou shalt find it after many days:*
> **Ecclesiastes** *11.1*

PART IV
Good Fortune, My Company

A Traveller, Not a Tourist

Jill Lennon

Born in 1939, Jill Lennon moved nomadically around New South Wales country towns with her parents, both teachers, until incarceration at a Dominican Convent in Sydney to learn the art of being a lady (an impossible task!). She studied at the University of New England, Armidale, from 1957 to 1959, graduating with a bachelor of arts degree, then completed the diploma of education at the University of Sydney in 1960, followed by 10 interrupted years of teaching interspersed with serial resignations and wild spending of accumulated superannuation money on overseas travel. She finally saw the light and joined the Australian Broadcasting Commission (ABC) and from 1974 to 1985 worked as a radio producer – an incredibly creative and exciting time.

In 1985 Jill Lennon leapt over the wall with voluntary redundancy when the rot began to set in, and flogged her body and skills in various capacities – including equal employment opportunity (EEO) officer at the then Northern Rivers College of Advanced Education (CAE) – now Southern Cross University – and communications consultant with the Bicentennial Older Australians Project and the health department's 'Homereach' project for non-English speaking background (NESB) carers. Together with her partner and friend of 22 years, Gwen Bloomfield, she currently operates a coffee shop in the Byron Shire on the New South Wales far North Coast, and is supporting her aged mother who is still very puzzled about the way her daughter turned out.

There's nothing quite as flattering as being asked to ruminate on one's past and, at this turning point in my life, I relish the chance to reflect on the inter-connectedness of women and our mentors.

Over the last 22 years the most constant source of support and encouragement has been my partner Gwen Bloomfield. We've often speculated that had we not met and braided our lives in the way we have, I would probably have settled down predictably as a 'career woman' in teaching, respectable and safe and conservative, squirreling away my superannuation and being a centrepiece at school reunions. Instead, with her as my companion and guide, as I have wavered at the crossroads when I could see other possibilities for change in my life, it's been Gwen's urging me to: 'Go on, do it!' that invariably provided me with the shove to leap into the void and run the risks – to embrace feminism, to change jobs, to be a traveller rather than a tourist, to drop out altogether, to move to the country, always in search of the new experience.

This has created a life of constant upheaval with all the anxieties that go with change – a feeling of moving through a landscape rather than being part of it, of not being around in women's lives long enough to build on friendships and establish continuity or intimacy, of watching contemporaries move vertically up the career ladder with all the 'goodies' that go with that, while I stumble in a horizontal fashion into the unknown. 'When are you two ever going to grow up?' once hissed a 'successful' career woman recuperating from a multiple bypass! However being a boundary rider, an observer, an adventurer, has also been incredibly exciting. It's enabled me to work as a secondary teacher, an ESL (English as a second language) teacher, a broadcaster, an EEO (equal employment opportunity) officer, a researcher, a restaurateur, a community healthworker. It's brought me into the lives of non-English speaking carers of frail elderly people, female inmates of prisons, academics, musicians, writers, actors, judges, socialworkers, poets, politicians, ferals and 'alternatives', radical women, femocrats and bureaucrats – and having a taperecorder and a microphone for so many years as my tools of trade has provided the opportunity to meet incredible people of vision, talent, commitment and sensitivity. It's a technicolour world that would never have appeared without Gwen Bloomfield's support and encouragement.

And while my conditioning in the 1950s was thorough, and the 'shoulds' and 'oughts' still recur from time to time in the stilly watches during the rough passages, when I feel life would have been so much easier had I run along the predictable patterns laid out for a girl so clearly then, it's Gwen who conjures up the exciting moments of life past and the exciting possibilities yet to come.

Being committed to each other in this way has presented a lot of frustration in attempting to build close and separate friendships with other women, with some refusing to see us as anything other than an excluding symbiotic couple – often, I suspect, because of their own oppressive negative experiences within the institution of marriage. Being labelled and dismissed in this way has often been painful and alienating and impeded my attempts to connect with others; consequently the few friendships along the way remain very precious and are carefully tended.

My earliest experience of being nurtured and valued as a unique individual rather than as the youngest member of the Lennon family in a small country town – 'the Headmaster's daughter' – began on the day when, at the age of eight, I met my piano teacher. Sister Margaret Rose, a Catholic nun, a 'Brown Joey', was immensely talented, handsome, and awe-inspiring and all I wanted to do was be near her as often as possible! By introducing me to the wonders of classical music and insisting on excellence, she tapped into something profound, creative and deeply satisfying I believe resides in every humanbeing but few of us realise. I still have a clear memory of sitting alone at the piano in her Music Room, playing scales and awaiting her arrival for my lesson (Mary McKillop and the Sacred Heart gazing down solemnly from the mantelpiece, smell of highly-polished floors), feeling a mixture of fear and excitement as I heard the familiar swish of her habit and the rattle of her large Rosary beads as she glided down the corridor. Had I practised enough? Would she be pleased?

I also accompanied the girls' choir on the church organ, and we would often go over together to the empty church loft while she introduced me to the intricacies of 'silent fingering' and the magic of organ stops and swells. Playing a Mozart Mass on Sundays, encircled by angelic voices, while Sister Margaret conducted and the priest intoned Latin from the altar, was the closest I ever came to a mystical experience.

Playing a Mozart Mass on Sundays, encircled by angelic voices, was the closest I ever came to a mystical experience.

Sister Margaret Rose was not all sweetness and light – my brother hated her and called her 'The Sphinx'. As he soon found out, her anger was dreadful to behold and she quickly dispensed with those not serious about their music. A rap over the knuckles on a cold winter's day in Glen Innes stung almost as much as your pride. I still remember so clearly the occasion when a motley collection of us – Protos and Tykes – was in big trouble for smashing beer bottles outside the convent gates late one afternoon after our theory lesson. I was the only bad girl in the group and refused to own up when the Inquisition was conducted into this scandalous incident. Sister Margaret then singled me out, accused me, and instead of ranting and raging as she had already done to the downcast male culprits, drove arrows through my heart with the words: 'All I can say is I'm bitterly disappointed in you.' Boiling in hot oil would have been a far sweeter punishment than this threatened withdrawal of love and approval!

Even after I was bundled off to boardingschool to salvage what was left of my formal education – a miserable and alien three years – she remained my friend and confidante at holiday time. She always appeared interested in my tortured tales of adolescence, and often we would share our time simply by making music together, playing duets and duos. With her as a role model I quickly became a 'marriage resister', exploring other possibilities despite the constraints of the 1950s on a young girl's dreams. Joining the convent had a certain appeal for quite a while, till I realised my intentions weren't entirely honourable!

> *I quickly became a 'marriage resister', exploring other possibilities despite the constraints of the 1950s on a young girl's dreams.*

There is a postscript to this story. Several years ago, I impulsively sent a letter to my old music teacher at the Head House at North Sydney, not knowing whether she was alive or dead, because I wanted to thank her for the way she had enriched my life. A couple of weeks later two elderly nuns knocked on our door (clearly wondering why they hadn't seen me in church!) to say Sister Margaret was indeed alive, had received my card and asked them to track me down. They warned me that she wasn't very well, without specifying the exact nature of her illness.

So it was an awkward and sad final encounter that day when we met over the polished tea service in the parlour of the convent and I realised that she was suffering some form of dementia, with large gaps in her memory and our conversation. (Maybe it was just as well, in light of my politics, sexuality and godlessness!) I fled from the scene, pursued as much by thoughts of my own mortality as by the shocking change I had witnessed. But I'm still pleased I made the pilgrimage – it was vital to acknowledge her importance in my life, even if we couldn't communicate now as we had then.

Over the last 22 years of my nomadic life, I've been dragging a grand piano with me all over the countryside, long after I stopped playing it, and I realise now it's because it still symbolised something of the innocence and devotion and support I experienced as a child with this nun. I've just handed it on to an intense and solitary 16-year-old, in whom I can see the same dedication to her teacher and the same passion for excellence.

Fresh out of university and teaching at the age of 21, I knew at some gut level it was vital to get myself overseas as soon as possible if I was serious about breaking the marriage circuit and learning to stand on my own two feet. That two years of work and travel with my old friend Peg was the transforming experience I hoped it would be, and while the terms of the teacher's bond enslaved me to the department of education back in Australia for the next four years, it became my personal mission to identify any secondary school girl who was labelled as unacceptable or unconventional and hold before her through literature and music and history the possibility of other choices, other lives.

I particularly valued the time when a student would ambush me outside the classroom to talk further about a particular poem or novel, as I knew she had been touched in some significant way, and I always tried to listen seriously in the way I had been taken seriously as a child. As a means of getting students off the treadmill and away from school humdrum I often organised visits to professional theatre companies. I felt enormously privileged when I had this chance to expose curious minds to the power of the imagination, and we'd return to heated discussion and argument over themes and character and interpretation.

Years later, when I was spending the day in gaol along with 120 other women who had caused 'serious alarm and affront' on Anzac Day in a demonstration against women raped in war, one of my former students emerged from the throng (also under arrest!) to tell me how significant I had been as her teacher when she was a 15-year-old. Now a qualified doctor, and clearly on the verge of feminism and lesbianism, she had left the safety of her marriage in pursuit of ideals she was still grappling to identify – another risk-taker, another soul who had escaped some of the bonds of patriarchy!

> ... *another risk-taker, another soul who had escaped some of the bonds of patriarchy!*

The dawning of the United Nations Decade for Women in 1975 marked the start of a whole new experience in living generously with others. It was exactly the right time for me to be working within the Australian Broadcasting Commission (ABC) as a radio producer, as a group of uppity feminists seized the moment and took on the establishment, persuading them to 'give the girls a go' with a weekly radio program on women's issues – the now legendary 'Coming Out Show'. (In 1995 Liz Fell and Carolin Wenzel edited a great 20 year retrospective on the program, published by ABC Books.)

A small nucleus of us supported each other through highly stressful and exciting times, and I learned so much from competent and confident ABC women including Liz Fell, Ros Cheney, Janet Bell, Kate Millar, Julie Rigg and Robyn Ravlich. In order to maintain creative control we operated from the outset as a collective – the Australian Women's Broadcasting Cooperative – within the creaking hierachical structure already in existence – such impudence! For the first time I could see just how powerful and productive and stimulating collectives could be, pooling our ideas and energy, always trying to listen to differing opinions with attention and respect. This is not to say there wasn't a lot of shouting and anger too at times, but we knew it was important to stay there until there was a resolution we could all accept, be it our collective response to criticism on high about program content and balance, or cooking up a submission to open up career opportunities for women in radio.

At regular intervals we would descend *en masse* to Broadcast House to present our petitions and argue our case with 'Management' (so feudal!)

– very disconcerting for them and great fun for us! (After a while 'His Secretary' took to asking ahead of time about our numbers so there'd be enough chairs – often only the board room was big enough!) There was a real sense that we were the forerunners of change – and an amazing camaraderie and sisterhood emerged that cut across program departments (walled cities) and job classifications. And out of the radio each Saturday came the raw experiences in very un-BBC (British Broadcasting Corporation) voices of real women in all their array and disarray, invariably gathered by other women within the ABC who had escaped from behind the typewriter or filing cabinet for the first time.

> ... women within the ABC who had escaped from behind the typewriter or filing cabinet for the first time.

There was such talent among so many of these 'handmaidens' – many with degrees and amazing creative lives of their own 'outside' as writers, poets, musicians, photographers and more – and now there was a chance at last for them to learn basic broadcasting skills from us experienced women and go to air with lots of support. When I took over as coordinator of the Women's Unit in 1979 and 1980 I took particular pleasure in working on a one-to-one basis with such women who tentatively came in with a good idea but didn't know how to turn it into a radio program. Teaching a woman how to work a portable taperecorder or conduct a basic interview seemed such a simple exercise to me, but to see the delight and terror and boost to self-esteem that invariably followed the first legitimate interview was a stark reminder of how easily we as women are kept in line by the withholding of information or skills.

Some of the non-production women on staff were to discover from their time working on 'The Coming Out Show' that they didn't have the temperament or aptitude for radio production; others who had been waiting in the wings for years for a chance like this just took off! Often their politicisation as feminists came later as they joined the lobbying for breaking down the old careerpath structures that effectively locked them into their roles as producers' assistants or clerical typing staff. Today I see that many of these women who got their first big break back then through their association with 'The Coming Out Show' and the Australian Women's Broadcasting Cooperative (AWBC) – both from within and without the ABC – are now in key positions as producers and executive producers. With any luck they too have learned the lessons of living generously.

The other exciting part for me about being involved as an experienced producer with a feminist program was the chance I could provide for politically active feminists in the real world – clever women such as Sue Bellamy, Joyce Stevens, Eva Cox, Carole Deagan, Sabina Erika – to explore and expand on their revolutionary or provocative ideas, using the resources of the medium to full advantage, and getting national exposure. Sue's programs on Virginia Woolf, and Eva's tribute to her stepmother Hepzibah Menuhin, are still remembered by some listeners to this day. The beautiful songs and voice of Judy Small were first heard around the countryside through a 'Coming Out Show' we made together long before she made her first record album. In turn it was Judy who generously approached me to compere a live concert in Sydney when she actually did launch her first album. (This was a vote of appreciation from Judy which turned out to be a terrifying public ordeal!)

Unfortunately, as is well-documented in feminist literature, one of the occupational hazards of collectives is their propensity to become closed and excluding, and our AWBC collective was no exception. The managerial appointment of the first equal employment opportunity officer to the organisation was a controversial one as months of research and report writing and hundreds of hours of women's own personal time had gone into the submission for such a position to be created (this was well in advance of the mandatory state and federal legislation). We recommended this position to be advertised internally in the first instance, providing a career opportunity for one of the many competent undervalued women on staff already immersed in the ABC 'culture' and well aware of its subtle and not so subtle discriminatory practices. So when an 'outsider' was appointed who resided in Broadcast House close to management, she was put into the 'them' rather than 'us' category by disappointed members of the cooperative who viewed her as a managerial puppet. Consequently life was very difficult and isolating from the outset for Elsa Atkin. I was to experience a similar isolation myself when some years later I worked as the EEO officer in a tertiary institution, and discovered to my shock and horror that the greatest support came from the principal of the college and the greatest suspicion and hostility from key women in the unions! That I too, despite my impeccable feminist credentials, was perceived as a 'them' and not an 'us'!

Conscious of the alienation and the buffeting Elsa Atkin was experiencing from both above and below, I tried to be sympathetic and supportive to her in those early days whenever we met in the corridors, as she recounted a minor triumph or a particularly rude run-in she'd had that week with a man in a grey suit. Years later, when she was well in her stride, Elsa was to tell me how important even that minimal support had been to her at the time, and she repaid me with enormous generosity when she successfully tendered for a large Commonwealth grant to train long-term unemployed rural women in the ABC regional centres right

The beautiful songs and voice of Judy Small were first heard around the countryside through a 'Coming Out Show' we made together ...

around Australia and invited me to oversee the scheme for the year. I revelled in the entire experience. Gwen and I felt like Ratty and Mole from *Wind in the Willows* setting off in search of adventure – travelling and living in a motor-home with me biking into a different regional office each week, from Geraldton to Launceston to Cairns, working alongside the trainees, sharpening their skills, firing their imaginations, encouraging and supporting them and fighting their battles if they were being exploited or ignored. While there was never any guarantee of ABC jobs at the end of the scheme, many of these talented women went on to become producers and presenters on both radio and TV, and a survey I conducted later indicated that even without the jobs, the experience had been an amazing boost to their self-esteem.

For me the best experiences have always been the shared ones – being involved in the 'Sapphoteria' restaurant for women in Sydney during its brief but glorious life; being part of the collective (an interesting blend of heterosexual left theatre women and radical lesbian feminists) writing and staging 'The Awful Truth Show'; joining forces with Viv Binns, community artist, and others, to create a Mother's Day event in an art gallery; working with Benedicte Cruysmans, a human dynamo in the health department, to produce truly useful and accessible information for Italian carers, respecting each other's expertise and learning from each other along the way.

> *It constantly amazes me when I meet men and women intent on clutching their talents or knowledge fiercely to themselves to serve their own personal ends...*

It constantly amazes me when I meet men and women intent on clutching their talents or knowledge fiercely to themselves to serve their own personal ends – as if by sharing, living generously, something will be permanently taken away from them or they will somehow be diminished, as if exposing ideas to dissent and debate by others is dangerous. Eva Cox in her recent Boyer Lectures on the ABC entitled 'A Truly Civil Society' talks about Robert Putnam's and Francis Fukuyama's notion of 'social capital', the reservoir of trust and mutuality that holds people together. Putting this into practice is currently absorbing my time, as Gwen and I support my aging disabled mother who is struggling to maintain her independence at home in this final stage of her life and as we prepare to launch ourselves into the next adventure – a business enterprise involving the skills and energy of local women living on the poverty line, while at the same time being available to encourage, listen to and act with the women whose lives intersect with ours.

Unseen Energy

Ruth E Lechte

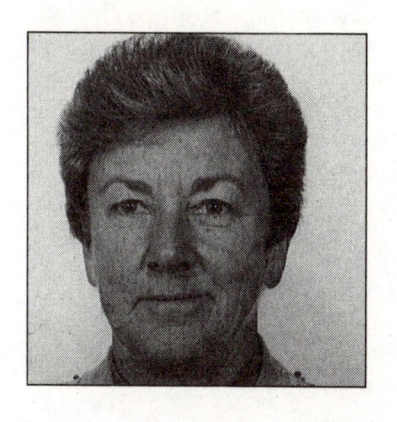

Ruth E Lechte was born in Victoria, Australia and attended school in Melbourne. In the 1950s she taught science in Melbourne and London, England. In addition, in the United Kingdom she worked at youth centres in Birmingham and London. Then returning to the southern hemisphere she founded the YWCA (Young Women's Christian Association) of Fiji and from 1961 to 1973 was its national executive director.

During 1973 and 1974 Ruth Lechte worked, travelled and studied in Asia, Africa and the Middle East spending some months based at the YWCA headquarters in Geneva. From 1974 to 1984 she was Pacific Area director of the World YWCA and from 1985 to 1994 director of Energy and Environment/Appropriate Technology with the World YWCA, working in 90 countries (and physically present in 52!). Amongst many other activities she has carried out organisational work at United Nations' women's conferences in Mexico (1975), Nairobi (1985) and Beijing (1995). She is currently consulting for the Asia Development Bank, preparing the environmental education strategy for the department of the environment, Fiji government.

Looking back on life lived so far, it is a source of pleasure to recall, applied to oneself: '. . .what is so very good about the support and help human beings give to one another, which need not be reciprocal this one to that one and that one back to this one, but can be like a chain, link to link, passing the support and encouragement along, down the generations.'

We were born and raised in a rural community. Our antecedents came from agricultural families, efficient and dedicated farmers of pioneer stock, accustomed to battling adversity. They had an unquestioning religious faith, which among other things had supported our father through the horrors of Gallipoli and France in 1914–18.

The focus of childhood was on the activities of a small community with a large social input from the church. While my parents would not understand how my beliefs now reach beyond traditional Christianity, there is no doubt that the moral values and caring for others which was the ground of an extended family involved in overseas mission work and local service to the disadvantaged, set the scene for later life.

A small community gives more than usual opportunities for leadership; one is now swamped by numbers. Parents and teachers were able to channel a personality with an apparent natural facility for leadership ('bossiness'?), which was generally considered to be verging on the 'ratbag', into productive – or at least controlled – occupations.

> ... *an apparent natural facility for leadership ('bossiness'?), which was generally considered to be verging on the 'ratbag'.*

Great sacrifices were made by our parents to send their daughters to church schools. There was no whiff of feminism at the Methodist Ladies College (MLC) Melbourne in the 1940s, believe me. (There is little even now: the principal has always been male!) The emphasis was on academic excellence, service to God, the community, and to the nuclear family. Our parents' main concern was that we be brought up 'in the faith' while being given the best education possible (they had left country schools at ages 12 and 14). Mother was a music teacher, and at MLC we had wonderful participatory musical experiences which have been a valued part of our lives since.

Music and sport, in my case, were of some detriment to the activities of the classroom. Teachers were thus generally not role models: yet I fell into teaching as a career – for want of a better idea. It gave an opportunity to gain skills which could be used universally, and led to overseas travel and further study.

It transpired that science teaching was a good choice. A farm background, scientific knowledge, and teaching, have come together with later community development training into three decades of grassroots work in appropriate technology and advocacy for the environment.

There followed episodes of shortterm employment and backpack travel in Britain and Europe. One job was in a community centre with a strong Quaker influence, in London's East End. Earlier, at the Selly Oak Colleges in Birmingham, I had attended Quaker meetings and peace conferences and been part of anti-nuclear activist groups. This laid the basis for an ongoing and pro-active peace stance, especially in the Nuclear Free and Independent Pacific Movement. The inspiration of the groups in Birmingham and London was surely 'generous' and, I hope, 'repaid' – I certainly acknowledge their influence, and have since tried hard to similarly influence young women in peace work and advocacy skills and activism.

There were real role models at Kingsley Hall. Much has been written about Doris and Muriel Lester, raised in comparative wealth, with strong religious faith. They moved to the slums of London in the Depression, worked politically with socialist friends, and spent time in gaol for living on the allowances government gave the unemployed, to prove the amount was inadequate. As pacifists they opposed the second world war while living through the bombing in the heart of the target area. They founded two Kingsley Halls in London's East End, named for their dead brother. Their stories were challenging, their pacifism and links with the Friends and with socialist principles irresistible, and while my own activism is expressed more in feminism and rural development, much of its genesis lies in London and Birmingham and the influence of two remarkable women.

> As pacifists they opposed the second world war while living through the bombing in the heart of the target area.

Undoubtedly my upbringing had sown the seeds of commitment and service; it was always assumed that such would be our behavioural pattern. It took a concrete example of opposition to the 'principalities and powers' by two rather unlikely 'ladies' to begin what has become a lifelong urge to identify and oppose political and patriarchal manipulation. They were focused on putting the skills into people's hands which would enable them to control their own lives. This has translated into the same focus for work with women in my own case: assuring control by women of their lives without pressures from patriarchy, culture, religion or political leaders inhibiting their personal growth and economic wellbeing.

Both Doris and Muriel Lester were elderly when we worked at Kingsley Hall, but they were firm in their activism. The work we had to do was difficult and often frustrating, in the days of 'teddy boy' gangs, but the Lesters never doubted our ability to carry it through.

Younger women will not have been influenced by me in the same way as I was by the Lesters. Pragmatism, rather than their single mindedness, has been necessary for my activities. But in the 30-plus years which have passed since then I have consciously taken every opportunity to assist young women, rural women and communities, to analyse violence, and to be politically active in combating violence against the poor, weak and disadvantaged, against women, and violence which is detrimental to the environment/creation.

The Lesters' political activism took another form. In the 1920s and 1930s they spent periods in India, in ashrams and centres, with Gandhi. Gandhi stayed at Kingsley Hall in Bow when he came to London on several occasions to confront the British colonial government, campaigning for India's independence and for peace. My 'cell' on the roof of Kingsley Hall was where he had lived. The Lesters toiled for the end of colonialism in all its forms and in all places – a strong influence in my later opposition to Pacific colonial administrations and practices.

Now there is neo-colonialism to confront. The tradition of earlier non-violent peace activists must be continued and strengthened, and their ability to recognise oppression, whatever form it takes.

The early period of my life in Fiji was influenced by an Anglican with strong Quaker connections, Marjorie Stewart, who founded the Pacific regional community education women's training centre of the South Pacific Commission. She had spent many years in Africa and the Carribbean and had a strong commitment to community development principles. She believed implicitly that rural people and the urban poor could manage the development of their own communities and the uplift of the individuals therein, and their destiny, perfectly well, given the skills and knowledge.

> *She believed implicitly that rural people and the urban poor could manage the development of their own communities*

Marjorie chaired the board of directors in the formative years of the Fiji Young Women's Christian Association (YWCA) and gave it a program orientation it has never lost. She founded a monthly meeting in the YWCA on public affairs, not always regarded kindly by the authorities. She travelled extensively for the Fiji government bringing education and training to communities before the introduction of universal suffrage, and classes for women who were to vote for the first time.

Marjorie is remembered by her ex-students around the Pacific with affection and I join them in the awareness that if she were here she would assure us we are not doing well enough, for peace. She lived to be 90 years of age and was a peace activist all her life, engaging in retreats for reconciliation and teaching in peace studies. She was especially active in her own troubled country.

I trace her influence ever since in peace activities, and in my own professional life with women internationally. Her impatience with anything short of excellence was formidable. We need to replicate it.

The international general secretary of the World YWCA, Elizabeth Palmer, was the next strong influence who moved me onwards and upwards. Elizabeth never asked if you wanted to hold down a certain position in the organisation, she just appointed you and expected you to do it properly! She facilitated growing and learning experiences, in my case an International Training Institute, a study tour of the most difficult countries and situations, and then a Pacific regional appointment as a World YWCA staff member. I later moved from the Pacific to the world as a fieldworker undertaking international environment program work and appropriate technology activities from an international desk in the World YWCA while remaining based in Fiji.

The 12 years as a Pacific regional worker were probably my most formative, they coincided with or created my consciousness of feminism as a force and moral imperative. My Pacific sisters in Melanesia, Micronesia and Polynesia are so much part of my 'be-ing' that they form a personality environment which defies description. I am humbly aware that this has not been reciprocal. While there are certain activities I have been able to put in place, their generosity and skill in building on that has been a revelation.

In provincial elections in the Western Solomon Islands in the early 1990s women campaigned for the first time. They did not win any seats but stirred up enormous interest and scared the traditional leadership nearly silly! We were able to support this effort by providing resources to hire canoes, travel to remote communities, provide food and accommodation and print manifesto material. What a very satisfying way to pass on the torch! Watch out for next time!

They did not win any seats but stirred up enormous interest and scared the traditional leadership nearly silly!

There is some sense of inadequacy in the next step – how to hand on from these and many other women role models, with their support and encouragement, a similar motivation to the thousands of young women I have had the great good fortune to contact. Who knows? Some of this is being written in a village in Transkei, surrounded by rural women training in tree planting skills. Marjorie would love it! It's another way of support and encouragement.

There have certainly been opportunities to ease the process along for women faced with difficult struggles, as in the lead-up to independence in New Caledonia and Vanuatu. In many cases women are now facing their own politically independent but oppressive and misogynist national governments. It becomes important to facilitate women's activities and actions, not to coopt their work.

Peers and contemporaries, colleagues and sister activists, have left indelible influences too numerous to enumerate on my life. So have organisations, for example various Intermediate Technology groups, Greenpeace, and many women's associations such as that in the East Sepik in Papua New Guinea and others on whose boards and committees it has been enriching to serve.

Rushing about the planet in heavier-than-air machines allows time to read, adding to the general backdrop and foundation of what one is and knows. More recent knowledge builds on what went before, which undergirds it. Vanessa Redgrave makes sense of Lillian Hellman. She also teaches us so well to develop an inner metering system for spotting crap! Vandana Shiva (author of, amongst other works, *Staying Alive*) makes sense like a blinding light when you've lived trying to overcome the disasters created by 'development experts'. And reading technical journals keeps reality alive – almost without exception they lack a gender analysis.

It is not necessary to know women personally to be the recipient of their wisdom and guidance.

There are others met fleetingly but, read and absorbed, they are generous in their sharing: Mary Daly and Rosemary Reuther – for example. Of those never met, one recalls the singer Holly Near, who, while living in a one-room flat and driving a 1982 car, has made over $10 million for peace work and international understanding!

Such women 'live generously' because their activism and convictions are shared.

Such women 'live generously' because their activism and convictions are shared.

Many women have enriched what could otherwise be a tedious 'committee attending' life, Wangari Mathai of the green belt movement in Africa for example. And I treasure my working colleagues, the staff of the World YWCA and the International Women's Tribune Centre. There is a real sense in which it can be said that the teamwork of years shapes one's thoughts, ideas and convictions, distilled from generous colleagues. As retirement approaches I see that international field work, while stressful in many ways, has given me an unparalleled opportunity to meet and work with thousands of women. The next period must be constructive, and translated into continuing opportunities for action. One to one co-operation may decrease with the movement away from a professional appointment, so one must apply energies for fewer 'bandaid' solutions and more retooling of structures. Advocacy and networking puts in place conditions conducive to women's advancement and reduces influences which militate against their wellbeing and attainment of 'fullness of life'. Necessary skill training includes the 'how-to' of:

- political involvement/decision-making;
- education for girls, especially overcoming discrimination in science and technology training;
- wage equality;
- equal opportunity for professional advancement;
- childcare;
- shelter and housing;
- awareness raising on issues, and work and training for advocacy;
- environmental rights;
- total attitudinal change to women's and men's roles as they are currently understood and expressed.

What drove/drives these women from whom I have learned, and with whom I have lived, played and worked? From where does the strength and power come?

I am fascinated by the concept of Unseen Energy – a technological question which if pursued and extended touches the issue of the Source. From what/where does Energy flow? And is this Source what is called God? I am not religious, there is no feeling of need to 'worship' the Source – while possibly being in awe of it. If I go to a church, synagogue, Quaker meeting or temple, it is for community and for meditation. Of course, a church can speak to my upbringing – the music in a cathedral overcomes the excrescences! Not feeling religious has nothing to do with anything, but it feels right to be aware than an intelligent and harmonious unseen energy seems to be governing all activity in life whether it can be identified or not. And it has become 'seen' in the people whose input has been so generous all my life. 'God is a verb, not a noun.'

The most generous has been my partner, who has given love and support unstintingly, with an understanding of how to rein in the wild streaks of my personality while not repressing innovative notions, no matter how unusual.

From all these influences age causes life to distil down to essentials. One is taught what is 'right' and 'wrong' from the earliest years. Now much of this appears trivial. Bawdiness or blasphemy as traditionally understood no longer seem serious to me when compared with environmental destruction – which in itself is a form of blasphemy. Puritanism bores me and I'm sure distracts people from deeper issues. Really, I find few things offensive any more: three maybe. Violence in all its forms – certainly. Stupidity – indeed. And mendacity, untruthfulness, bending the facts, a form of communication heard more often from leaders and despoilers than is the truth.

A point in life has been reached stemming from all the love, help, encouragement and trust which has gone before, received from so many people living generously – and willing to give in such a way that the result is often a stance very far from their own. We don't discover who we are alone, or simply alone. We become who we are in relation to the people in our lives, to the natural world, and the resulting ambience those people, the world and ourselves create.

> ... *with an understanding of how to rein in the wild streaks of my personality while not repressing innovative notions, no matter how unusual.*

Raised 'Living Generously'

Audrey McDonald

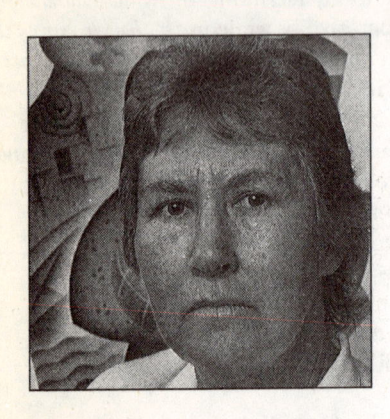

Audrey McDonald, OAM, has been a lifetime activist for the Women's Movement and progressive causes. Born in country New South Wales, at 19 years of age she was elected a trade union official, also representing women in the hospitality industry. In 1967 she was elected national secretary of the Union of Australian Women (UAW) and worked in a voluntary capacity for 30 years. She has been a prominent activist in the peace and South African solidarity movements.

As a member of the Women's Advisory Council to the Premier of New South Wales, Neville Wran, she helped secure official marking of International Women's Day for the first time in Australia. She was awarded the Order of Australia Medal (OAM) in 1989 for her 'service to the Trade Union Movement and to Women's Affairs'.

Voluntary community organisations consist of people who give of themselves, their time, energy and finance to the causes in which they believe. They are people with a social conscience, dedicated to the concerns and wellbeing of others.

The Union of Australian Woman (UAW) is comprised of such women, and there I have devoted a great deal of my life with women who 'live generously'. Much of what has happened in my life is their story too.

The UAW was founded in 1950 to improve the life and status of women as citizens, workers and mothers in a peaceful world. It was founded by workingclass women, women who were not well-off but who gave of themselves. Most had no opportunity for higher education, no opportunity for positions of power or status. But they worked hard all their lives and were dedicated to improving their lot and that of others. They have supported the struggles to attain humanrights, dignity and an improved quality of life at the local, national and international levels.

I was brought up around such people in the Women's Movement and trade union movement.

Commencing in 1965 as the national publicity officer and then national secretary from 1967 until 1993, for almost 30 years I have worked on a fulltime voluntary basis for the UAW. Previously I worked as an official of the Hotel, Club and Restaurant Union (HCRU) and then the Liquor Trades Union (LTU) after their amalgamation. I worked, too, in leading capacities in many arms of the peace and solidarity movements, especially the Australian ANC (African National Congress) Support Committee.

Like many bush kids I came to the city so I could attend highschool. I stayed in Sydney for the rest of my life.

My father's parents were from the Rhine Valley and immigrated due to hard times in Germany. My mother's family were of English/Irish stock and worked on building the railway line through to Tenterfield in far northern New South Wales. In the 1880s both families took up small selections at Sandy Flat, 13 miles south of Tenterfield, and raised 10 children.

My father's mother washed on a flat rock in the creek. But she had the first iron roof in the district. When the youngest was born, the oldest daughter went for the local midwife on a draught horse.

... did her mending and fancy work whilst minding the sheep.

My mother's mother lived across the valley and did her mending and fancy work whilst minding the sheep. My mother, the youngest, went with her. Mum was acclaimed throughout her life for her beautiful needlework.

This then is what women did in my grandparents' days. Both died before they were 55 and we never knew them.

I was born in Tenterfield in 1937 and grew up on our small farm with two brothers. As a young person, there were a number of people who shaped my life: my parents, teacher, close relatives and my trade union.

For my younger brother and me, our days consisted of up before daylight to get the cows, help do the milking, feed the poddies and the pigs, home for breakfast and then walk to school a mile away. After school it was home, catch the horses again to get the cows, do the milking and home for supper. The day finished with doing homework under the kerosene lamp or playing hide and seek out in the paddock in the dark.

School was intermittent. Sometimes we had a teacher, sometimes we didn't. Ours was a small, one-teacher school with about 20 kids. At various intervals I was away from home at other schools, locally and in Maitland. On reaching sixth class my teacher, Mr Braid, urged I should go to Sydney to attend highschool. My parents, who had little education, were anxious I have this possibility. My father was a forward thinking person who saw the need for girls to have a good education.

Pa and my brothers stayed on the farm whilst Mum and I came to Sydney to live at the People's Palace (the Salvation Army's private hotel which accommodated many country visitors). Mum stayed in the city with me for the next three years apart from when we went home in the school holidays. She got a job at the Palace as a housemaid and joined the Hotel, Club and Restaurant Union. Before long I began working in the milkbar after school and at weekends in the diningroom as waitress, then cashier.

> *She got a job at the Palace as a housemaid and joined the Hotel, Club and Restaurant Union.*

I attended Crown Street Girls High. School was difficult. I was not accustomed to a city environment and my lifestyle (in the city centre) was unlike that of other students in suburban houses. But we made the most of it, making many friends amongst the hotel staff. They were women who had come to the city for work or for medical attention or to care for sick relatives.

Apart from a few close relatives whom we saw regularly, it was the union that became our family.

I entered the paidworkforce whilst still at school. Towards the end of this period I was called upon to give evidence in a union case on the issue of underpayment of wages. I had been paid half wages as a junior when there was no junior classification. The union won the case and I received £700 in 'back money'. I continued to work there as the receptionist and switchboard operator after leaving school. At 17 I used the backpay to go overseas as the union representative to the 1955 World Youth Festival in Warsaw and to a Food and Tobacco Workers conference in Sofia. On return I worked in a metal factory and became a member of the Sheet Metal Workers Union. Tom Wright was secretary of the union and I met other 'sheetie' officials who also influenced my view of the world.

I renewed my acquaintance with the Hotel, Club and Restaurant Workers Union (HCRU), working in the office for a period, then in a club and a coffee lounge. I was elected as an organiser of the union and worked as such until the end of 1961. I organised among women in restaurants, boardinghouses, retail shops, the railway catering workers and the train buffet staff. I greatly admired people in the union such as Flo Davis and Vic Workman.

Through the HCRU I met my husband Tom who was an official of the Building Workers Industrial Union (BWIU). I came to know other BWIU officials like Pat Clancy, Frank Purse and their families. And on the annual May Day preparations I worked with officials of a number of unions such as the Wharfies and Metal Unions.

These then were my mentors: people I looked up to. Mostly they were men, except for Flo Davis. But then there weren't many women at union leadership level in those days. I recall attending the ACTU (Australian

Council of Trade Union) Congress in 1957 in Melbourne and was one of just a few women delegates.

Flo introduced me to the UAW which I joined in the mid-1950s. There I met women such as Enid Hampson, New South Wales secretary, and a most creative and capable woman who gave encouragement and showed great interest in members' work. Phyl Keesing was New South Wales president. Afterwards she and I worked nationally for many years. She was a gracious, charming woman always objective and devoted to the women's cause. She helped me tremendously throughout the 1970s and the 1980s in running the organisation nationally, in particular in policy making and in preparing publications and submissions.

Throughout my time as national secretary there have been many activists in the organisation at local branch and higher levels who have been my mentors. They are too many to name. But they have always been there: helpful, dependable, willing, thoughtful and dedicated.

For several years after leaving the HCRU to have Daren, our son, in 1962 I was active in the BWIU women's committee and the local branch of the UAW at Maroubra where we lived in a housing commission flat. The women's committee was an important part of the life of the BWIU. It was affiliated to the UAW and supported its campaigns. The women's committee participated in the BWIU campaigns and sought to activise women who mostly were not in the workforce. This experience broadened their outlook. But being active centrally wasn't easy so I mainly directed my energies to local activity. The UAW Maroubra Branch which was in the Randwick Municipality took up childcare as its main campaign.

'Childcare' in those days was a dirty word. But the UAW was accustomed to doing things that weren't popular – campaigning for equal pay and the right of women to paidwork, maternity leave, price and profit control, peace and opposition to the Viet Nam war. We collected lots of signatures on a petition to establish a childcare centre and had a deputation to the Randwick council. We were told our place was at home in the kitchen. So we campaigned even harder.

In the UAW we supported one another. Mainly we were young mothers. We would meet at one another's homes and Bonnie Jago, the only one with a car, would take us to and from meetings and to the various activities within the area as well as to meetings with other branches and to their functions.

. . . indoor living, lack of space, needing not to irritate the neighbours with noise, no play area or backyard.

Flat living had its difficulties – indoor living, lack of space, needing not to irritate the neighbours with noise, no play area or backyard. For both the mother and child social contact is essential. I needed my own interests and Daren, our only child, needed social contact. Also Tom had a demanding union job with numerous night meetings. So when Daren was a few months old we booked him in to the local kindergarten where he began when he was 20 months. At that point I began going in to the UAW office and subsequently became national publicity officer.

Those of us who were activists in the organisation, and held leadership responsibilities, were able to do so because of the generous support given for one another. This is what sisterhood is all about. To care and help each other. To care for the organisation which cares for all women. Family support also has been a large factor in enabling us to be active.

With the political and social turmoil of the late 1960s and early 1970s many women who had never been active became involved in the Women's Movement. This was the period of modern feminism. Women's role in society had changed. The Pill meant more and more women were able to plan their life and their careers.

This was also the period of the Viet Nam war, conscription and the massive peace demonstrations. The UAW participated in all the peace rallies. Members were involved in the creation and actions of the Save Our Sons (SOS) movement.

It was a complex period. On the one hand, our members shared many common objectives with the women's liberationists. But we were ill at ease with their tactics. On the other hand, we agreed around many women's issues with the conservative women but differed with their broader politics. Yet it was a period in which there was a broad unity of women's organisations, except for the extreme right.

> *Structured leadership was challenged by those who favoured 'collectives'.*

Although our political goals may have been similar, the UAW found it difficult to have a common working relationship with radical feminists. Our women felt intimidated. Structured leadership was challenged by those who favoured 'collectives'. But we felt organisations could function in a businesslike way and still operate democratically and flexibly.

Despite political differences on the left which affected the UAW to some degree, we continued to campaign around prices and living standards issues, child endowment and maternity allowances, childcare and needs of working women, preparations for International Women's Year (IWY) 1975, peace, and international solidarity issues such as Chile and South Africa.

One of the main contentious issues within the UAW was the question of international work. Some felt we should concentrate on local issues and that international matters were not so important.

Freda Brown was president of UAW and a vice president of the Women's International Democratic Federation (WIDF) to which the UAW was affiliated. Freda made an outstanding contribution both nationally and internationally. The UAW benefited greatly from her participation in the international movement. I personally learnt much about the international work in this period and it became dear to my heart. It meant that the UAW was well-informed about the developments in the Women's Movement overseas. The WIDF's status at the United Nations (UN) also meant we were able to keep abreast of UN plans for International Women's Year in 1975, the Mexico Women's Conference held that year, the UN Decade for Women and subsequent events.

Most of our members had a warm regard for international solidarity and sisterhood and strongly supported the WIDF. We were closely in touch with women in many countries. Members contributed in a practical way towards aid to women and children in other countries, both in money and in kind. At the same time we built close links with migrant women and their groups in Australia.

The UAW's activism around international questions was matched by work around many national issues. In particular we campaigned with the support of the trade unions. Militant left unions such as the BWIU, Seamen, Wharfies and Metal Workers gave the UAW moral and financial support and we cooperated on deputations, conferences and other projects in the interests of women and their families.

The UAW participated in education and training programs with the Trade Union Education and Research Centre (TUERC). Classes on public speaking, meeting procedure, how to organise functions and other such practical activities were organised. Our members blossomed and gained confidence.

Classes on public speaking, meeting procedure, how to organise functions and other such practical activities...

We cooperated with the TUERC to organise seminars on issues of vital importance to women but which were also important to other sections of the community – rising prices and consumerism; women in politics; women, unions and the workforce; farmer-worker relations.

One such seminar on women in the workforce, held in 1974, produced an Australian Charter of Women Workers' Rights. The basis for this arose from my attendance at the Third World Working Women's conference in 1972 in Prague. Organised by the World Federation of Trade Unions (WFTU), the conference decided upon a world wide Charter of Working Women's Rights. The Australian Charter, which was the basis of the UAW's *Hand Book for Women Unionists* printed in 1975, was put to the ACTU by the Metal Workers Union (AMWU) and became ACTU policy.

At that time I worked on a parttime paid basis for the Trade Union Education and Research Centre. Bill Brown was administrator and I was assistant administrator. As well as education programs, we produced a quarterly magazine the *Modern Unionist*. I gained much knowledge about journalism and magazine production, running classes and organising conferences from Bill Brown who was a creative journalist, writer, educator and political activist. Over the years we worked together on many committees and, like others, I benefited greatly from working with him.

The election of the Whitlam Labor government after a long period of conservatism that had done little for women and had committed their sons to Viet Nam, gave impetus to the Women's Movement. This, combined with the rise of modern feminism (Women's Liberation) in the early 1970s, the persistent work of women's groups like the UAW, and the United Nations plans for an International Year of Women, saw the government begin to involve women's organisations in policy formulation on women's rights. For the first time the UAW received government recognition and its views were sought.

With Freda Brown now WIDF President, the UAW was well placed to propose initiatives in support of major international events like IWY 1975, the Mexico World Conference of Women, the United Nations Decade for Women, the International Year of the Child in 1979, the Copenhagen Mid-Term Review of the Decade in 1980, and the Third World Women's Conference, Nairobi in 1985.

By 1976 New South Wales too had a Labor government. The UAW for the first time was represented on a government body through my appointment to the newly established New South Wales Women's Advisory Council (WAC) to the Premier, Neville Wran. This was a very rewarding experience personally and for the organisation. I was able to put forward a number of proposals from our organisation which included celebrating International Women's Day. This led to the New South Wales government being the first in Australia to officially mark IWD on 8 March each year.

Being on the advisory council was also a learning experience – seeing first hand the functioning of government. The most satisfying experiences were being able to organise and participate in broad consultations with women in the community – getting to know all their problems and bringing those issues before government.

Non-government women's organisations throughout the 1980s and into the 1990s continued to exert their influence on government individually, collectively and through the Office of the Status of Women and the National Women's Consultative Council (NWCC). Many important changes have taken place for women, though still more needs to be done. Women must continue to strive to improve their status.

The Australian New National Agenda for Women (1993–2000) and the preparation for the Fourth United Nations World Women's Conference and the Non-Government Organisations (NGO) Forum in Beijing, China in 1995 was a further landmark in the struggle for equal rights and a better life for women. The UAW was actively involved in the 1995 preparations. Women were urged to participate in the NGO Forum. Such events which bring together thousands of women from many countries are truly inspiring and demonstrate a great feeling of sisterhood. Preparations give women a voice in national and international decision-making.

The UAW has paid much attention to women's development. Its style of work, training policies and planning strategies have all been important factors in encouraging our members to come forward and play a role in the Women's Movement. A collective style of work is critical to making one feel a valued and integral part of any organisation. The UAW believes in both strong leadership and strong membership participation. We have done much to create opportunities for members' participation and leadership within the organisation. But an effective, vibrant organisation must also be businesslike or no decisions are reached and no plans put in place.

The UAW organisation discourages 'tall poppies'. We have an unwritten understanding, which I encouraged, that each member should be able and prepared to turn to anything, whether speaking at meetings, writing placards, washing up or cleaning. Living generously is about developing good 'all rounders'.

> ... *each member should be able and prepared to turn to anything, whether speaking at meetings, writing placards, washing up or cleaning.*

We organised classes around different topics – meeting procedure, rules of debate, speaking at meetings, writing articles. Members would prepare five minute contributions on a topic around which we were working and present it to a mock meeting with questions and rules of debate. Then comments on each of the contributions would be offered. This proved helpful and a lot of fun as it was done in a friendly fashion. It built the members' confidence and gave us encouragement to participate and speak in public.

One of our state secretaries kept our guidelines on 'How to Organise a Function' proudly displayed on the office wall. Every time a function or meeting was to be organised she would draw members' attention to the guide and encourage it to be used.

Other practical activities included badge making and preparing posters. For a number of years in the 1980s we also ran a small shop attached to our office. Members made goods and offered them for sale. A publications stand displayed leaflets and notices not only of the UAW but other groups – women, union, peace and solidarity groups. A number of members enthusiastically contributed and supported the shop to help raise funds, but also to promote the UAW's activity. Such programs and activity are still of value in equipping women to fully and confidently participate in the community and to give a sense of involvement and responsibility.

Taking into account the composition of the women that the UAW attracted, these activities, especially the practical classes, were most important. Our members were workingclass women, women who have had to struggle and had no opportunity to continue their education – even though they may have wished to do so. One of the features of our work was to provide international experience for our women by sending them on delegations to various conferences and meetings abroad. We adopted the practice when attending international meetings of an experienced member taking a less experienced member to give them training. That is how I gained my international experience, which I have shared and passed on to others.

> ... *rank and file members were involved in organising itineraries, programs and publicity.*

I, as national secretary, spent much of time and energy briefing our representatives in order that they were as well equipped as possible to undertake the task. As WIDF councillor I attended council and other overseas conferences. On return a lot of attention was paid to briefing the membership. This approach was essential for all-round understanding of international developments. Similarly when delegations came to Australia, rank and file members were involved in organising itineraries, programs and publicity. This was all part of a learning process for our members.

I first learned in the union movement that good organisation is essential in getting results. The United Nation's plans and programs of action around International Women's Year and the UN Decade of Women (1976–85) reinforced my approach in this respect. So I encouraged UAW members to develop and work to an action plan. It is vital to determine priorities and have a clear strategy.

We formulated plans between conferences and national committee meetings or at the beginning of the year. We would list the issues and campaigns around which we felt we should give priority. Members were allocated responsibility for a specific area of work, for example women's status, living standards, peace and solidarity, children's needs, older women and organisation or administration. We also had numerous plans for developing the organisation and making it more relevant and efficient. Like many other organisations we were continually faced with being relevant in a changing world.

The voluntary Women's Movement is based on mentoring. Mentoring is about setting an example to others. And it's about providing opportunities for others to learn. It is satisfying to be able to assist others by making available to them what you have learnt. In general, women in voluntary women's organisations are about helping one another. The struggle for equality is advanced only through solidarity with one another. It is sisterhood. It is a conscious desire to help others.

During my life what I have learned from my mentors was crucial to my development. First, my philosophy is that no matter what the job or the responsibility – 'give it a go!' – that's the best way to learn. Life is full of experiences and is the best and most practical teacher. I have always emphasised 'never say you can't do anything'. As women we must compel ourselves to have a go. We can't say we want to be equal then not be prepared to do something.

Nor should we undersell ourselves just because we may not have had an education or haven't had any training or aren't qualified. Have a go. Take up the challenge. If possible take on courses from car maintenance to computers.

> ... *no matter what the job or the responsibility – 'give it a go!' – that's the best way to learn.*

Secondly, I learned that if you always work to a principle you can't go wrong. People will respond to a positive and principled approach. This is important in working with others.

Thirdly, a longtime and highly respected member of the UAW, Mary Wright, who passed away in April 1993, often said: 'We should cherish each and every person like little flowers and give them tender loving care.' This is a great philosophy. Working with people on a voluntary basis requires the utmost consideration and careful, patient work. It is necessary to be appreciative of people's contributions, however modest.

Working in a voluntary organisation requires patience, understanding, compassion, appreciation, commitment and hard work. This I have learnt over many years and have endeavoured to pass on to others.

I pay tribute to the older members who have given and still give of themselves – as branch activists, office support or fundraisers. They all do their bit and are generous in one way or another. I spend a considerable amount of my time keeping in touch with them now they are physically not able to be so active. We owe it to them. They were there when it was even more difficult to work in a women's organisation. They were our pioneers and our mentors. They made a wonderful contribution which too often has gone unnoticed. They should be recognised, each and every one.

Women – Mentors and Models

Edna Chamberlain

Edna Chamberlain is Emeritus Professor of Social Work, University of Queensland. As the first women appointed as professor in the field of socialwork in Australia, she has become something of a role model for younger women entering socialwork. From a Brisbane workingclass family, she studied and worked extensively in Australia and North America, becoming Head of Social Work at University of Queensland in 1973. She was strongly concerned to develop socialwork education at a national and international level, particularly within the Asian-Pacific region, and under her direction the department grew and generated considerable research.

Concerned for the status of women, Edna Chamberlain sought and accepted membership of federal and state government commissions, notably the Australian Social Welfare Commission (1972–75) and in academic administration. As more senior women were appointed in government and academia she appreciated the strength of collective action. She also recognised the value of networking across generations to maintain and extend gains already achieved for women in society. Soon after retirement in July 1986, Edna Chamberlain was awarded the Order of Australia. She received an honorary doctorate in philosophy from the University of Queensland at the December 1995 graduation ceremony.

Reminiscing over more than 70 years yields a lot of data, the yield varying from day to day according to mood and focus. Many women have been connected with me as mentor or model in the context of my career development as a socialwork educator. Shift the context, change the day, or give me more space, and other women of at least equal significance to me would be named. Nor should my focus on women be seen as discounting help received from and passed on to men, nor their (not always benign) influence on my behaviour. Women have played a dominant role in my career, however, and my friendship groups, at least for the latter half of my life, have been predominantly women.

Among the many women who have been important to me are friends whom I first met at highschool or university, or with whom I shared a particular interest, like painting or bushwalking, or who are associated with a period of my life spent in a certain place, such as Melbourne, Victoria or Chicago, in the United States of America. The reasons for starting friendships are legion; their survival depends on mutuality in the interaction. I have been fortunate both in the breadth of stimulation and in the personal and practical supports I have received and still receive from friends.

The reasons for starting friendships are legion; their survival depends on mutuality in the interaction.

Overlapping with these groups of personal friends are colleagues with whom I have worked in initiating community activities, in promoting causes, or simply on the job delivering services or teaching. Generally the relationship was reciprocal. Some, however, were in leadership roles, supervising my activities and offering me advice and support. Those I identify as my mentors and models are women already secure in their own place who have created excitement in me in various ways to grow and achieve. I am aware that many of my mentors and models are no longer wellknown (indeed some have already died) but I should like to acknowledge them as part of a process of linking women through me across the generations.

The status of my family in the 1920s when I was born was upwardly mobile workingclass. Education, even the Queensland State Education Department syllabus of the time, opened doors within a young vigorous society and tantalised within glimpses of other worlds of ideas and imagination as well as geographically and culturally diverse ones. My family was particularly fortunate in the economic downturn of the 1930s as my father retained his job throughout the Depression and we never faced poverty. This was not accidental. My father was a competent fitter and turner who probably had an educational edge on many tradesmen of the day. He was a first generation Australian whose father had migrated from Britain in the closing decades of the nineteenth century. My grandmother died when my father was six years old and my grandfather set about with determination and spirit to provide for his three boys. His expectations of the boys, especially of my father as the eldest, were high. He became a successful restaurateur and in the frontier city of Brisbane had done well for himself in material terms but my father always regarded him as much with fear as with love. Unwilling to stay with his father in business, and hesitant about setting up in opposition, my father chose independence and a trade. He never was entirely free from his father's yoke. My mother understood this and excused any perceived shortcoming of my father on the grounds that he had never known a mother's love.

My mother had been a waitress working for my grandfather. She had experienced deprivations in her early life and was grateful to my father for her home and family. Her schooling had been hampered by poor eyesight. Her severe astigmatism had not been identified and corrected until her marriage. (I was lucky that mine was identified in infancy. There have been undoubtedly psychological repercussions from having 'four eyes' throughout my school years, but seeing and reading gave me the taste and means for other worlds.)

She was my first model of a woman taking the initiative despite personal insecurity and uncertainty of support.

My parents were a devoted couple. They operated in the conventional pattern of the times. His instrumental role complemented her expressive one. My mother was the one who made friends with the neighbours, reached out for social interaction in her church group, and saw to it that her children took up opportunities through school and clubs to extend themselves. She was the battler. She was my first model of a woman taking the initiative despite personal insecurity and uncertainty of support.

Together my parents defined the moral framework within which our family operated; uncompromising honesty in our dealings, the golden rule to guide our social behaviour, tolerance of the foibles of others, temperance in all things, including sexual reticence. My father was a humble man; he counted pride a sin. For years I did consistently well at school. My achievements were made little of at home partly because our parents' sense of justice eschewed comparison with my brother and sister. Once my parents met a relative in the street who commented she had heard I was a high achiever. I glowed as my parents agreed and unaccustomedly exhibited some pride in me. Later I heard my father castigate my mother gently and confess he too had been unable to contain his pleasure. 'And Edna heard us,' he added. 'She must not be allowed to get above herself.' Years later my sister attended my inaugural lecture after my appointment to the chair of socialwork at the University of Queensland and I noted with wry amusement she was still watching on behalf of our parents that I did not get above myself!

In the middle of the 1930s, when I completed primaryschool, the scenario for workingclass girls was a few years in the paidworkforce prior to marriage. Paidwork after marriage was rare and, in fact, precluded by law in many situations.

I attended the State Commercial High School (SCHS), the advantage of which as seen by workingclass parents such as mine, apart from low costs, was that top students in commercial subjects at the Junior Public Examination held after two years of secondary school were awarded positions in the Queensland State Public Service. These positions offered good working conditions and security of tenure (until marriage) which was highly valued in Depression days. The formula must have seemed to my parents to have worked perfectly. At age 15 I duly commenced as a clerk-typist at the then department of agriculture and stock. When I resigned after six years, however, it was not to marry but to start an independent career. I had in the meantime matriculated and had, by parttime studies, completed a university degree in commerce.

I am not sure where the wish for an alternative lifestyle was germinated. I know it was nourished by teachers at SCHS. When Margaret Arundel died a few years ago, I mourned with other members of the literature group she had convened for many years for the Australian Federation of University Women (AFUW) (Queensland). As my teacher in English, she had engendered an appreciation of literature which remains a joy, and encouraged standards in English expression which facilitated my way ahead. She conveyed keen pleasure in my graduation, visited me later in Tasmania, and maintained an interest in my career after my return to Brisbane. My maths teacher, Phyl Staunton, also congratulated me at the time of my graduation and I was able to intimate to her that my two years of study of pure maths in my degree course was a direct result of the interest in problem solving and the high standards she had inculcated. Another teacher I recall with pleasure is Eva Julius who presented us with the facts and fantasy of history with intelligence and good humour. A year later her sister Fanny Julius taught me mathematics for matriculation in an evening class. They were all women of scholarship who not only furnished my mind, they provided a model for living as single women rewarded by their careers rather than married with home and family. These were days when societal values and the absence of childcare facilities necessitated choice even for these comparatively privileged women who had been to university.

> ... they provided a model for living as single women rewarded by their careers rather than married with home and family.

While university lecturers demonstrated appreciation of my work with good marks, none became a mentor. My sole woman lecturer taught pure maths II. Perhaps because of insecurity in her own role she did not seek to encourage me to follow an academic career. In common with my parents and senior officers (all male) in my place of work, my university lecturers saw no answer to the question: 'What is Edna going to do with all this study?' For several years I did not know myself nor care.

I went to the university for the sheer joy of learning. These were war years, however, and students were much preoccupied by the political and ideological issues on the one hand and our own position in relation to volunteering or (in the case of the men) call-up for war service on the other. By the time I graduated I knew it was time to give reality to the dream of an independent career. I had to make it happen in the world which gave a woman few choices and left the running to her if she did not make the obvious one. As well, in the light of an awakened social conscience, I had to find a way of work and life in a world of strife and war to see if I could make a difference. It all came together for me when the Australian Red Cross Society offered scholarships for women graduates to study in socialwork. One woman friend at the university, Kath Watson, interested in poetry and politics, gave me some tools for political analysis. She stood for the Queensland elections in the early 1940s as a Communist candidate. Socialwork did not seem a powerful tool for change to Kath. She sowed the seeds which came to fruition 30 years later when, in response to the radical challenge of the late 1960s, in a presidential address to the Australian Association of Social Workers, I addressed the issues of socialwork and social change. For the present, I had found an acceptable reason to leave home to go to Melbourne to study for a new profession which, like teaching and nursing, offered career possibilities for women.

Though socialwork was seen very much as a women's profession, men without professional qualifications in socialwork predominated in administrative and policy determining jobs in the government bureaucracy and on the managing committees of voluntary welfare associations. Women predominated in the delivery of personal services. Over the coming decades socialwork was to change its definition to encompass social administration, social policy development and social change and, cause and effect, men sought professional education. The phenomenon of male/female imbalance emerged with disproportionate clustering of men in the senior levels of both the bureaucracy and of academia. Many of the women in socialwork in the 1940s assumed and maintained leadership roles, finding individually ways of dealing with the psychological imperatives of marriage and family care. As a profession, socialwork failed to foresee the strength of sociological imperatives.

> ... *disproportionate clustering of men in the senior levels of both the bureaucracy and of academia.*

In the women's world of socialwork I entered in the mid-1940s, a careerpath was open for me, with encouragement to follow through. Encouragement came from the personnel of the Australian Red Cross Society at national headquarters and at Victoria division, and from my academic and field tutors. Joan Tuxen, since retirement a volunteer at the Family Court in the Victorian Court Information and Welfare Program (Court Network) and longtime director of the Victorian Society for the Prevention of Cruelty to Children and Adults (VSCCA), was then director of social services in the Victorian division of Red Cross, and an early mentor. Jocelyn Hyslop, the director of socialwork training at the

University of Melbourne, thrilled me by predicting that I would one day head up a school of socialwork. Alison Player (later Mathews), director of medical socialwork training at the Royal Melbourne Hospital, provided a model of quiet determination in pursuit of whatever she believed necessary for individual patients, for students and for her department. She encouraged me to consider going overseas for further studies. It was 14 years before I took up this challenge. (It was more than 20 years before postgraduate studies in socialwork were available in Australia.)

In the meantime I was assigned by the Australian Red Cross Society to work in the Tasmanian division coordinating their welfare services for returning ex-servicemen. Thus I had the opportunity to participate with a small number of other 'mainland' and overseas trained socialworkers, all young women under 30, who pioneered a professional engagement in community activities, leading on to the introduction of socialworkers to Tasmanian health and welfare institutions and ultimately to education for socialwork in that state. Among these were Rona Hagger (née Clark) (who preceded me at Red Cross), Kate Campbell (née Corven) and Jeanne Whitney (née Bayly) (Commonwealth Social Services), and Dorothy Pearce (first appointed to the Royal Hobart Hospital in the early 1950s). Professional stimulus came from my peers. They were also among my many friends from various walks of life who supported me in good times and bad during my 12 years in Hobart. The good included marriage and motherhood. The worst was the sudden death of my husband. I was 36, my daughter was eight years old.

The good included marriage and motherhood. The worst was the sudden death of my husband.

I had given top priority to my family and saw overseas study now as a way of bringing myself up-to-date before resuming my career. When I chose the University of Chicago it was because of its place in the history of socialwork education. Famous American socialworkers, the Abbott sisters, Grace and Edith, who were associated with setting up the United States Children's Bureau, and Jane Addams of Hull House fame had been Chicago based. Charlotte Towler's book *The Learner in the Professions*, published in 1941, remains a classic. She had conceptualised socialwork as a response to common human needs and had devised a course on human growth and development to underpin socialwork education notable then for the integration of relevant psychological and sociological insights. I saw myself as privileged to attend her last series of 'Human Growth and Development' seminars. Helen Perlman had recently published a text, *Social Work: A Problem Solving Process*, which was to be translated into several languages and influenced the teaching of socialwork world-wide. The suitability of her conceptualisations for socialwork outside the United States was to be later questioned. Nevertheless the warmth with which these and other able women on the faculty welcomed and encouraged me was an important ingredient in my personal development at a time when I was very vulnerable. It was another five years before I became centrally involved with socialwork education and a serious contender for academic advancement. By then the years of protest and chaos on campuses were catching up in Brisbane. The challenges to society in general of disadvantage and discrimination had special meaning for socialwork ends and means. During a sabbatical year (1969–70) at the University of Michigan, in the United States, I was on campus for a Black activists' strike and the anti-Viet Nam war march on Washington. On return to my University of Queensland lectureship, I was catapulted into a vortex of activities and responsibilities assumed in quick succession and held simultaneously by my fiftieth birthday: president of the Australian Association of Social Workers; head of the university socialwork department; dean of the newly created faculty of socialwork; member of the Australian Social Welfare Commission; professor of socialwork. There had always been a sense of solitary endeavour in what I took on. Now there were no mentors. Earlier mentors were women with their feet in a more conservative society. Nor for some of the tasks were models available. I was the first full professor of socialwork in Australia and only the third woman professor appointed at the University of Queensland.

I took something from my predecessor, Hazel Smith, who with spirit and vigour had introduced socialwork to the university. She had sown the seeds for much that was credited to my period as head, not least the moves which led to a separate faculty and the establishment of a chair. Moreover she was a woman with great concern for the needs of children and for the disadvantaged. She early established a tradition of research and practice with Aboriginal people and a commitment to Aboriginal entry to university education. Hazel's early death created a vacuum which I came to fill. It could not be said that I assumed her mantle as our styles were very different but she has a place in the network of women who influenced me.

So, too, does Alma Hartshorn. Again there is a difference in manner and style and in priorities, but we have shared commitments over a long collegial association. We first met in 1948 when we represented South Australia and Tasmania respectively at National Red Cross conferences. Alma was already a senior member of staff when I was appointed at the University of Queensland. Since her retirement and later mine, we have continued to share many community interests.

Looking forward, some of the younger women with whom I have connected are vitally important to all our futures. There were several very talented women in the first series of honours seminars I conducted in 1968 including Stephanie Belfrage (then Fowler), Roisin Goss (then Hirschfeld),

Sue Hurst, Margaret O'Donnell (then McCann) and Jill Wilson. Hazel had encouraged them to consider roles for socialwork based on analysis of issues in terms of violence to humanrights and discrimination. For me there was intellectual stimulation and personal growth in interaction with these and other students leading me to re-examine my own values and perspectives. During the next few years these women appropriately sought tutorships in the department, when it was funded for expansion as a reflection of the Whitlam government emphasis on social justice. Our department gained a reputation for radical social analysis and was in the vanguard of research and teaching in addressing topical social issues. While I took stands in these lively times, I strove for objectivity in my approach and this facilitated negotiation within the university structure for space for innovation in the department. Thus Roisin with sensitivity and imagination was able to work with Aboriginal groups to develop culturally relevant research and welfare practice. Her initiatives and those of her successor (Matt Foley, who became a minister in the Queensland Labor government in the 1990s) when she left to take her law degree, foreshadowed a faculty commitment to Aboriginal entry and the appointment of an Aboriginal tutor in our department, Lilla Watson, to teach from her cultural terms of reference.

Inspired by the emergence of the feminist analysis and a concern for women in welfare, Marg O'Donnell developed linkages through a socialwork student unit set up within the women's shelter. We introduced a course developed by Mary Draper on 'Women in Welfare' which was probably the first of its kind in Australia.

Inspired by the emergence of the feminist analysis and a concern for women in welfare . . .

Jill Wilson, now a senior lecturer in the department, has pursued her career while caring for a young family of four children. My support of her as a staff member with babies on her lap stemmed from my appreciation of her right of choice, echoing the unquestioning way I was received in Chicago with my young daughter in tow.

Roisin Goss has performed her role as wife of the Premier of Queensland with grace and competence. Marg O'Donnell, previously director of the Women's Information Service in Queensland is now director, Alternative Disputes Resolution Division, Queensland Attorney-General's Department. Mary, now a lecturer in sociology at the Royal Melbourne Institute of Technology (RMIT), has been engaged in advising on women's affairs to the government of Victoria. All acknowledge me with warmth when we meet and see our past relationship as having been significant. So too do other University of Queensland socialwork graduates, later in important places, for example Ruth Matchett, Queensland director-general of family services and Aboriginal and Islander affairs, the first woman to be appointed to that level of seniority in Queensland. For better and worse, I was Jan Williams' mentor as supervisor for her postgraduate studies before she found a more rewarding challenge in her role as deputy director, division of community services development, department of family services in the Queensland government. Lesley Cooper and Yvonne Darlington, two of many women to whom I gave encouragement to take on high degree studies, are lecturers, Lesley at Flinders and Yvonne at the University of Queensland after two years at Newcastle. There are women in welfare education who are not University of Queensland graduates, like Wendy Weeks, herself a respected educator in Melbourne, who have paid me the compliment of seeking me out as a mentor. But they are legion, the women I meet around Australia and overseas, some of whom I no longer recognise, who refer to something I said in a lecture or in a conversation as having been meaningful to them, or who comment that I was a role model just because I was a woman coping in a man's world.

> *In the idiom of my times, I travelled alone as an achiever who happened to be a women.*

In the idiom of my times, I travelled alone as an achiever who happened to be a women. Not till the Women's Movement had gathered momentum did individual women like me recognise the need to develop linkages and strategies for support, to counter the male club phenomenon. For example, on my first appearance at a 120 member professorial board, the only other women present, apart from the stenographer, was the then president of the board, the distinguished research professor Dorothy Hill with an international reputation as a geologist. It was clear that her position had been achieved through sheer ability. With her as a model I was inspired to attempt an immaculate performance of my task as head of department without initially appreciating that a good performance presumed knowledge of the politics of the game and strategies for playing. I allowed myself to be appointed to more and more committees to represent women, thus deflecting my energies from efforts to multiply the pool from which representatives could have been selected. The new wave (or, more realistically, ripple) of women who came to play in university administration were more sophisticated. United they were able to draw attention to the status of women in the university and initiate changes. And they learned to lobby.

Janet Irwin, then director of student medical services, was one of this new wave. At the last meeting of the faculty board I attended before retirement she kindly referred to me as having been a role model for women in the academic community. I appreciated her comments though aware of how much more some of my successors, including Janet herself, had given through operating as part of a collectivity. Janet and I had served on several committees together and I have admired both her readiness to go in to bat on behalf of women's issues and her focal role in a network of women on campus and in the community. Late in the day I learned the values of networking.

I gave in a spirit of generosity to those who came after me, however, and many have found ways of using what I brought from my experience, often expanding my insights through sharing their own. There has been a process of networking across the generations encompassing the women who were my mentors and models within the Women's Movement. Like all women the choices they had to make were within the constraints of their times. They are part of a tradition of helping their successors to outdo their own spirit, scholarship or understanding, thus empowering those who came after them, to reduce the constraints and enhance the choices for the women of the future.

> *... a process of networking across the generations.*

Living My Beliefs

Edel Suede

Born in Cavite, a province of the Philippines, Edel Suede emigrated to Australia, arriving on 2 April 1986, after living and working as a missionary and a government contract worker in Papua New Guinea. She is secretary of the Ethnic Communities Council of the Sunshine Coast, Inc (ECCSC, Inc), in Queensland, and also a member of the Multi-Cultural Workers Reference Group, Maroochy Neighbourhood Centre, Maroochydore and acts as convenor for ECCSC, Inc subcommittee on women's issues and the Filipino Australian Sunshine Coast Association Inc (FASCA Inc) subcommittee on welfare.

Edel Suede loves reading, cooking and gardening, as well as enjoying playing tenpin bowling and being a member of a tenpin bowling club. She, with other women, has recently begun a group, 'International Christian Fellowship of the Sunshine Coast', doing craft and *Bible* studies together with other associated activities.

In 1975 I left my home country, the Philippines, going to Papua New Guinea as a missionary. I was involved with the church and wanted to make a contribution by becoming involved in educating people less fortunate than myself. Education was not my only aim: as a Christian, I was concerned to enable people to become Christians, grow in love and be spiritually uplifted.

A missionary with the Asia Pacific Christian Mission (APCM), Alwyn Neuendorf (now retired and residing at Deception Bay in Queensland) came to the Philippines looking for missionary teachers to go to Papua New Guinea. Hundreds applied and only five were accepted. I was one of those who applied, and I was fortunate to be one of the five. From the time I arrived at Dauli, a mission college in Tari, Southern Highlands Province, I became a lecturer at Dauli Teachers College, teaching English, TESL, and social science. I was frequently involved with very young people, teaching religious instruction at government schools and going with the students to outreach meetings. After completing my term with the mission, I worked with the government and taught at two other teachers colleges, Port Moresby In-Service Teachers College and Madang Teachers College teaching TESL, English and education studies. When not teaching, my work encompassed working with women, in particular, for I was active in the community and the church.

My motivation was that I saw a need in others ...

There was a women's group in the church and I worked with them, particularly in *Bible* studies and evening choir work. If problems arose requiring counselling, I stepped in to do this, too. Although I am not a professional counsellor, the women came to me, telling me their problems: family problems, problems with children, problems with the husband's family. I had often been involved with this field when working in the Philippines through the church and also with friends. I majored in psychology at university, then with my masters degree I took on more clinical psychology. My motivation was that I saw a need in others, and there was a responding characteristic in myself: I wanted to help others.

I attended the Philippines Normal University and also the Philippines Christian University. I studied guidance and counselling in addition to other subjects. One of the professors, Mrs Ancheta, an older married woman with no children of her own, treated me like a daughter. I was intrigued by the way she helped people, particularly her students. Amongst my classmates were parttime students and students who were working to put themselves through university, or were simply combining paidwork with study. A number of them were married and I observed that the professor gave help and support to them all. It was notable that although she was a professor and therefore at the top of her field and well-placed in her career, she still had such concern. I thought her dedication arose out of her Christianity. I also believe it was her nature.

When I began teaching, Purification Nadal, the principal of the school at which I taught, was also an inspiration. In her direct work as principal, she inspired me, and I saw that her work did not end there. Outside the school she was supportive to teachers who were experiencing problems within the family, perhaps in relation to husbands, maybe domestic problems, even financial problems. I wondered how she could live as a principal, with high academic achievements and an emphasis on the academic side of her work, yet was also able to relate to people in a very human way. Purification Nadal was popular with all the teachers, not only because she was exceptional academically and in running the school, but because she was helpful, always there when needed, even if it were outside the school. Regardless of the problem, whether it was personal or work-related, she was there.

A third woman who played a significant role in my development was Luisa A Kalagayan, a sister of my grandfather. I have always called her 'aunt'. She was a spinster: having had opportunities to marry, she did not take them up. Rather, she was always helping others and continues to do so. Women in particular are one of her concerns. A reason for this may be that she is an older woman and has a broad experience of the world. For as long as I have known her, she has been able to respond humanely and with a positive and thoughtful way of looking at the particular problem.

> *I became a soundingboard for problems experienced by women.*

The support of each of these women, and being able to observe at firsthand the way they went about counselling, encouraging and uplifting others, meant I had examples before me to follow. This was particularly important when I became a soundingboard for problems experienced by women. It was my work in the church and in the community which brought women into contact with me.

When I was in my early twenties, I was first singled out by being invited to talk to women. At first I wondered: 'What will I talk to them about? My goodness! I am not even married myself.' But then – I was a woman. I did some research and mapped out a talk and enjoyed delivering it and talking with the group. I found the company of older women pleasurable. They impressed me and in turn made me feel useful.

My work in New Guinea reinforced this aspect of my personality and the growth of my character. I lectured at the teachers college, then at weekends or evenings I attended women's groups. The groups were centred around craftwork, perhaps sewing, and in this setting religion was not a sole focus of discussion. Rather, the women talked openly about their aspirations, their daily lives and their problems, and how they could resolve whatever difficulties confronted them.

Housekeeping was a matter of considerable concern to the women attending the craftwork classes, and health issues were important. There was no formal training for homemakers, no mothercraft training, no training in childrearing or personal and marital relations. Some women were one of five wives. Although it may sometimes be difficult for outsiders to understand, many coped well in these circumstances.

I married whilst I was in Papua New Guinea. My husband, Bert Suede, was in the same group of missionaries. Jenny Clarke, originally from Melbourne and one of my godmothers (as in the Philippines we call our witnesses) at my wedding, visited me on a weekend after Bert and I married. She asked me about Filipino culture regarding women's role in the family and society. She also briefed me on the Australian way of life, and I found it both enlightening and helpful. This firsthand information equipped me greatly for my future life, which was to be in Australia.

Because I married, I was not able to return to Dauli, even if I had won a lecturing position there. Port Moresby Teachers College was fully staffed, so I was unable to secure a position. Meanwhile, Pamela Quartermaine (from Perth), who was the superintendent curriculum/inspections with the Teacher Education Division, Papua New Guinea Department of Education, recommended me for the post of librarian at the Port Moresby College. This was an instance where mentoring didn't work as it should, for I declined the position, not knowing that Pamela Quartermaine had played a part in the process. I did not go for the interview. Even with a diploma in library science, and being a qualified librarian with experience, I preferred teaching, not librarianship. I was also concerned about the salary level. Perhaps if I had known of her support I would have taken the matter further, accepting that my foundation in teaching was relevant to the post and being more confident about pressing for a higher remuneration package. Finally, Pamela Quartermaine asked if I would like to work as her professional assistant. I gladly accepted. Eventually (later that year) I won a position at the college.

> *This was an instance where mentoring didn't work as it should, for I declined the position...*

After Bert and I had been married for some time, a pastor came looking for someone who was qualified to be the principal of a school in Cairns. At the time my husband and I were working for the government of Papua New Guinea. The pastor contacted the director of the mission, John Sweeney. Did he know someone who might be interested in being the head of a Christian school in Australia? The director knew us and gave our names to the pastor. The school contacted us. At the time, we had begun thinking of returning to the Philippines then going on to work somewhere else. I was depressed, for I had recently lost one of my brothers, who was very dear to me.

The pastor telephoned us, talking about the school and the requirements for the person who was to act as principal: 'Would you like to take the position?' 'Well,' I said to my husband, 'we'll talk about it.' However, there was a barrier: my husband was a contract worker which meant he ran the risk of losing some remuneration and also had to give three months notice if he were to resign. I also was a contract worker but, being classed as his 'dependant', I would not lose as much.

I was a teacher. I had secured my registration in Australia a year or so before. We approached the school. 'Is it acceptable if *I* come as the principal rather than my husband?' The response was that I was equally welcome as my husband to fill the position. I said: 'Okay. I'll come.' I took the job, with my husband completing his contract in Papua New Guinea then joining me in Cairns. I travelled to Cairns and was principal of Cairns Christian Community School from 1986 until 1988, when I developed an allergy and had to leave the area.

On the advice of a Townsville specialist whom I consulted, my husband and I took two weeks holiday. The allergy disappeared, my skin cleared, and we resigned from our positions in Cairns. Moving to the Sunshine Coast, I began working as a relief teacher, then I lost my patience! I decided to spend more time with the children, for we had been in paidwork all their lives. From 1989 I ceased fulltime paidwork. I wanted to enjoy just 'being there' with my daughter and son, until they reach 18 or 19 years and have finished school.

I wanted to enjoy just 'being there' with my daughter and son ...

Whilst in Cairns I met many, many Filipino women living in Australia. I developed many friendships and found that in Cairns, as had been so in Papua New Guinea, women came to me with problems. In most instances, it was Filipino women, but women from all sorts of ethnic backgrounds came to me at various times. As the problems poured out, I thought: 'Oh, no, not again.' But that was a passing reaction. My next and more lasting desire was to help to the best of my ability.

In Papua New Guinea my work in the community and with associations was different from what it is in Australia, in that most Filipino women living there are married to their countrymen, most of them being contract workers and in the country for a set period only. This meant the problems were different from those arising for Filipinos in Australia. In Australia Filipinos, mostly women, are married to foreigners.

Many of the problems arise where Filipino women have married men who are not Filipino – usually men who are Australian by birth, or European-Australians. I can empathise with these women, although I am not in that position. One of the most significant issues is that Filipino women who come to Australia are generally highly educated, or at least better educated, often, than the men to whom they are married or with whom they are living. These women cannot take a subordinate role. They cannot be 'doormats'. Frequently they want to assist their families living in the Philippines. There is a cultural expectation in the Philippines that family members support each other, financially as well as emotionally and spiritually. If I had the money, I would want to buy houses for my mother and brother if they needed accommodation. Filipinos living in Australia do this for their relatives. I am fortunate, for my family doesn't need monetary support from me, although on one occasion my husband's nephew required some help and to me it was important that we assist. However, some families in the Philippines are not financially secure. There are some husbands who do understand the Filipino culture on this matter and their wives help out by sending money to their families in the Philippines without any difficulties arising in the marriage. Some provide money for their wives to send home regularly. For others, this need creates problems for Filipino women in Australia: their husbands or partners are irritated or become angry about money being sent back to the extended family. The women may not have money to send back, because the husbands object to their being in paidwork or the women are unable to find jobs. In other cases, the husband demands control of the woman's income or at least wants to know what she is earning and what she is doing with her wages. If she is sending it back to the Philippines, this causes strain and arguments, and even a denial of her right to do so. Sometimes the woman may say: 'Oh, well, my husband said that if I work, okay, I don't need to report what I do with the money, so if I send it to the Philippines, that's fine. But not *his* money.'

Some women who seek my help may not have an education, or an education that is superior to that of the man they have married. They may have finished primaryschool or possibly completed schooling at provincial highschool, but they cannot express themselves fully. The difficulty can be in not knowing the words to use. Sometimes I have to read between the lines, working out in my head the essence of what the woman is saying. Many women find it difficult to be direct when discussing their problems, and although they generally find it less difficult with me, searching for the words to describe their plight to me is not easy.

The difficulty can be in not knowing the words to use.

For some women it may be what seems at face value to be a simple problem which has a dark side: the husband refuses to allow them to drive, or to learn to drive. The reason? 'Oh, well, if you drive you'll be going here and there.' It is as if these men need to know precisely what the woman in their lives is doing, every minute of the day. They may be extremely insecure in their relationships, particularly with their wives, and this results in domination of the woman, or suffocating her with their surveillance. I have, fortunately, seen some changes in this attitude, particularly for those who have children and are able to see the necessity for a driver's licence.

In some instances, I have assisted the women to secure shelter in a refuge. I have helped abused women and abused women whose children have also been abused. On one occasion I had to deal with a person who was threatening to commit suicide. Sometimes the responsibility has become overwhelming and I have thought: 'I don't want to do this any more.' My next thought is: 'Someone has to do it.' I couldn't sit by, doing nothing. Other people have said to me: 'Oh, but you don't want to get involved.' I would respond: 'Yes, you're right. I don't want to get involved.' But what can a person do? You *have* to 'get involved'.

When, early in the morning – at about 5.30 am – a man came knocking at the door saying his wife wanted to commit suicide, I thought: 'Well, what does a person do?' Often people who come seeking help do not want to go to a government department. They are reluctant to do so. I sought the help of God. I prayed, saying: 'Help me. Just tell me what to do.' He enlightened my mind, and I went forward confidently to help the couple, who had been experiencing many problems in their relationship. Bert and I went to speak personally to the woman, then talked with the husband and wife together. She came through that trauma, although she and her husband are continuing to experience difficulties in their relationship.

Some women come to me simply because they want to confide in me. Some come because they know I understand the bureaucracy to a degree they do not. I don't ever give advice of the kind: 'Well, you should do this,' or 'you should do that'. For me it is important to say: 'It's up to you to decide what you would like to do. It's your life, so you have to choose.'

I work through the options with the women as we talk, going over the possible consequences of taking any particular step. Often I ask the women to write a list of the advantages and disadvantages of each approach to the problem, then to add up the columns. On some occasions a woman may take the option with the highest number of negative consequences. I have had telephone calls where a woman says: 'I did the wrong thing. I took the wrong path,' or 'I really should have done that'. Again we talk the issues through. This assists her in making further choices – perhaps without taking the least favourable path this time.

> Often I ask the women to write a list of the advantages and disadvantages of each approach to the problem . . .

I ache for all these women, and I have made it my business to seek out resources available – such as women's centres – where they can find support amongst women in a similar situation. I have also made myself aware of government policy and ensure that women have access to relevant government bodies. Yet some women do not want to approach 'outside' organisations or bureaucracy. There is a cultural barrier. They do not want to confide in 'just anyone'; they prefer to talk with someone whom they know personally.

There is a high lack of awareness amongst Filipino women of the government resources available. This is particularly so for those who have recently arrived in Australia, and the first year is the most difficult. Some men will not let their Filipino wives mingle with other Filipinos. Some are suspicious that their wives will learn about their rights, grow increasingly brave, and not simply do what the husband wants them to do. Again, there are others who do not act in this way.

Somehow the problems of the women become my problems. Dealing with the issues takes courage combined with knowledge and learning. When you are in a position such as this, it is important not to let the problems of others weigh you down. It takes a great deal of adjustment and there is a need to separate your personal life from the issues that arise in talking with and helping others. I am fortunate in that there are no problems in my personal life of the kind the women raise with me.

I have been blessed. My husband, Bert and I relate well. We relate well, too, with our two children. The women who seek me out see the way my family operates and this may encourage them to accept that a stable and happy family life is their right, too. They trust me, even though I am not able to give 'answers'. After all, who can?

In 1993 I was elected as the first president of the Filipino Australian Sunshine Coast Association. This association began as a small group in which I was not initially involved. At the time I was going through a period of thinking I would withdraw from helping and advising women. I thought that if I became a member of the group it would increase the number of people coming to me for advice, and simply to talk. Then a group of women telephoned me and came to visit. 'Come on,' they said. 'Please come to the meetings because a president will soon be elected.' 'No,' I replied. They were insistent. I talked with a lot of them. 'Come along,' they said. In the end I went, although I had reservations because I felt that if I became involved I might be elected as an office-bearer and if I take on a job, I want to do it properly. As it was, I was elected president. 'Here I am again!' I thought.

After I completed an 18-month term as president, the group wanted me to continue. I thought it was time to stand back and stand down. The pressure had become too great. They then persuaded my husband to take up the post! Thus the pressure remains, because I am the wife of the president, but it is not a pressure which lies directly on me.

... it was time to stand back and stand down. The pressure had become too great.

Then I was asked to become convenor for welfare with the association. I have built up a great deal of knowledge of governmental organisations and departments and their activities and operations. The welfare role is mainly associated with the problems of Filipino women. Not all the work is problems, however. Nor do all the functions revolve around difficulties. Rather, we meet at social gatherings, lunches and so on. These work so as to increase the confidence of women and the women encourage one another. We share in advice and guidance. Often there are no husbands present. Sometimes one or two attend, but usually it's just women, and we can talk women's issues. The women learn how to react to particular situations and gain from the lives of the other women. We share our experiences. This helps in building relationships between the women, and between themselves and their husbands, their children and their parents-in-law.

I am currently the secretary of the Ethnic Communities Council of the Sunshine Coast, Inc. Working with other ethnic groups is an opportunity

I realise the importance of respecting all cultural backgrounds, especially as Australia is becoming increasingly a melting pot of diverse cultures. Cultural differences are important. Coming from a different culture means that there can be a lack of awareness about how people relate, the importance of particular celebrations, and the way particular days are celebrated. One of our friends invited me and my husband to lunch on Christmas Day. I was pleased to accept, and then learned that some of her in-laws were coming also. This indicated to me that it was a family gathering, so I told her it would be better for us to join them on another occasion. 'But I want you to come,' she said. 'I have told my husband and he said: *Yes*. After all, it is our house.' Again, I agreed. Then I received a call from her saying: 'It has all changed. My sister-in-law wants the lunch to be at her home. But she told us you can come and I'd very much like you to be with us there.' Later she rang to say that she had decided to have us for lunch at her home, and her husband would attend the lunch with his sister and family. I pointed out that it was important for her to be with her husband and his family on this occasion. 'Your relationship is involved. You've got to be present. Forget about us. There are many more times that we can visit for lunch.' She was most apologetic. But I could see that it was a family affair, and it was important for her to be there. Her husband (whom we know as a kind person) was probably thinking: 'Oh, goodness. I'd love her to come. What will I tell my sister and my brothers?' She went. Later she telephoned me saying how glad she was that she did. It was an example of cultural difference. The desire that she had, to be with friends, people of the same cultural background, on an occasion such as Christmas is understandable. At the same time, it is important to 'fit in' to a certain extent with the expectations of the husband's family. This is not about overriding the woman's rights, but about learning to accommodate. Of course, it is important that the accommodation not be one sided.

I have learned to be strong, when necessary . . .

I spend a great deal of time on the telephone. Often I declare I am going out, because if I stay at home the telephone doesn't stop ringing. People may say: 'This will take only a moment,' then remain on the telephone for up to an hour. They may come for a short visit, then stay three or four hours talking over the issues that are concerning them. I have learned to be strong, when necessary, in these circumstances. Otherwise I would have no life of my own, would rarely see my husband and children!

Spending time with women is, however, its own reward. I recognise that often the important issue is to let women talk. Through talking they come to recognise the hills and mountains they have climbed, the depressions that confront them, and their own developing confidence. When I do this work I think, sometimes, about my mother and grandmother. When

I was a young child my grandmother was extremely active in the way I am today. She was comfortable, economically, and made her time available to women who were in distress, women who needed to talk about their lives and their circumstances. My mother had a similar approach to life. She was keenly involved in work with the community.

My father was a businessman who travelled a great deal. I was the eldest grandchild on both sides, so my father's mother and mother's mother played an important role in my life. For the first few years of my life, I grew up with my grandmother on my mother's side. I learned her values and those of my mother. People came to my grandmother's home so that even as a small child I saw that she was important to the community. She was asked to be the godmother of many of the children. In our culture, a godmother is extremely important to the child and to the parents. It builds a relationship between families. The godmother holds an important place in the family of her godchild. Rather than having a bridesmaid as witness at our weddings, for example, we have godmothers and godfathers. I follow in my grandmother's footsteps in this regard, too. I have 50 godchildren in the Philippines, as well as some in Australia. In some instances I have two godchildren in the one family. 'Me again?!' I say. 'Yes, yes!'

At no time can I remember my maternal grandmother not having anyone there, in her home, talking with her, seeking her advice, seeking comfort from her. Those years play back to me, like a record or a film: 'When there are people who are in need, you need to do this, you must do that. You must give your time, your time, that's the most important thing. You give your time.' I say, as if I am speaking to my grandmother: 'Oh, yes. I *am* giving my time!'

With me, too, Christianity is important. I want to practise it, put it in action. The Philippines is predominantly a Catholic country. I was a student at an exclusive school and educated by priests and nuns until I completed highschool. Then I became a born-again Christian. I was already a teacher, by that time, and that was, I think, a driving-force as well. Put love in action. Illustrate, through the way you live, that if Christ loves you, you can show this love to others. This is my philosophy, and it is the force that drives me.

When a person cares, it is important that other people know it. It is important to show that you are willing to spend time with them. Words are easy to say: 'I care.' 'I love.' These words may be overstated, so that people come to doubt them. Time and effort needs to be put in to show what love and caring are in essence, what love and caring are in action.

Words are easy to say: 'I care.' 'I love.'

Once a friend of mine said: 'I don't know why it is that these women come to you although you don't know them at all, and tell you all their problems!' 'I don't know either,' I said. 'Perhaps it is because I do not know any other approach than doing my best to listen, to talk the issues through, and do what I can to help.'

Sometimes I think: 'Oh, maybe that is God's gift to me. It is what is in me.' Perhaps that is what they see in me. It may be that I have a gift for sharing with other women in one way or another. I cannot take them out of the problem, but I can even it out, or maybe halve it, simply by listening. Then they are able to come to a stronger sense of themselves, gain confidence in their own ability to deal with the issues, and move forward.

The Wisdom of Keeping Options Open

Margaret Pewtress

Margaret Pewtress was an inaugural member of the Australian Sports Commission and, as a commissioner, headed the Task Force for Women's Sport which formulated the federal government's National Policy Plan for Women in Sport. She was a chairperson of the commission's Women and Sport Committee which initiated projects and campaigns to provide increased opportunities for women and girls in sport. Her extensive experience in sport primarily came from participation in netball where she has coached club, state and national teams.

Until her death in August 1995, Margaret Pewtress was president of the All Australia Netball Association. She was the chairperson of the World Championship Company, responsible for the 1991 World Netball Championships. In 1989 she was awarded a Medal of the Order of Australia (OAM) for services to netball and in 1994 she was recognised for her outstanding achievement in sport by the Avon Spirit of Achievement Award.

My sixtieth birthday depressed me slightly. I couldn't think of anything positive in connection with being sixty. Other decades had their philosophical resolutions. At 40 I resolved I would never allow embarrassment, or the fear of it, to stop me doing anything. Fifty, children becoming independent, and disposable income meant it was time to do things that had been put aside. Fortunately I was in Asia when I shared my sixty-first anniversary with a group of Muslim women. They set me straight: 60 was a statement that one had lived a life, but from then on one is revered and sought out as a source of wisdom – and no one disputes your views. Well, it hasn't quite been like that; however I am content and enjoying the 'recollection' time of my life.

I had a happy and secure childhood due to the love and caring of my mother, Pearl Tubb, and her mother, my Nanna, Isabel Green. I grew up in Victoria in Albert Park, but Nanna lived in Ballarat, which meant school holidays in the country surrounded by young aunts who let me tag along, and a grandmother who included me in all her activities: cooking, church work, card games (euchre), and most importantly gave me the opportunity to listen, particularly the talk and anger of post Depression days and the start of the second world war. Both my grandparents had a strong sense of social justice; they were gentle non-violent people, but I can still hear Grandpa's passionate anger as he spoke of the role of the British banks during the Depression. Nanna Green had books and when she tired of me I was told 'to read'. It became a lifetime habit.

> I can still hear Grandpa's passionate anger as he spoke of the role of the British banks during the Depression.

My mother was ever prepared to listen to me and, I realise now, she taught me to reason. As life became more complicated and 'real' decisions had to be made, she would listen, ask questions but at the end of the day her reply to the question: 'What should I do?' was always: 'Keep thinking, but it is your decision!' My father was a shearer and I have little recollection of him in my early childhood, but I certainly became aware of his views when I wanted to stay at school after I turned fourteen: 'There was good money to be earned at the Kraft factory.' Later the favoured occupation was a tram conductress.

Both emotionally and financially, Mum supported my desire to stay at school. She took herself in to Swanston Street and became a waitress at Woolworth's. There were ups and downs over the next few years, constant harping from my father, but again strong support from Mum who saw the value of education for a girl.

My primaryschool education was uneventful, but mainly a happy time. Infant school at Middle Park Primary, then off to Ballarat for Grade 3, because of the fear of a Japanese invasion, and then a return, this time to Albert Park Primary until Grade 4, and back to Middle Park Primary.

Several memorable teachers. Miss Smith in Grade 5 made me aware that I was good at maths. She treated us all as individuals and organised wonderful excursions to Melbourne to see films and to explore the historical buildings; she encouraged learning by reinforcing positives.

Sport became a passion in Grades 5 and 6 and one advantage of growing up in South Melbourne in the 1940s was that the streets, the parks and the beach were our playgrounds and there was no gender or sex bias. Boys and girls played street cricket, football, keepings off and Bulldog Drummond. By the time we girls became aware of inter-school sport we had the basic skills and coaches were our only need. They appeared as visiting physical education specialists.

The Miss Eunice Gill who came to teach us physical education one day a week did not impress at first meeting. Her very formal attire – grey culottes and knee-high emerald green woollen socks – and her formal precise manner was a new experience for us. However once she established that she would coach the school rounders and basketball (now netball) teams and we beat Eastern Road she became our hero. Little did I realise that in later life we would meet again in the arena of sports politics: she became my mentor as I learned my way through the power games of sport. Eunice had one of the best analytical minds I have encountered and again I found a listener and a questioner who at the end of our discussions would say: 'Let me think about it and I will get back to you!' It was Eunice who taught me the wisdom of keeping options open when you are lobbying for change, particularly if your view is a minority one. Also, never coordinate into just one group: her theory was it is easy to silence and disenfranchise a single group. Unfortunately Eunice died shortly after her retirement from senior lecturer in physical education at Melbourne University. I miss her clarity of thought.

I miss her clarity of thought.

The other sports specialist in primaryschool was Grace Canole, the swimming teacher, who waited patiently each week at Stubb's Sea Bath for us to arrive. The joy of learning to float, dog paddle and then proper strokes, which allowed you to swim in deep water, after the magical 'Herald Learn to Swim Certificate' was gained. I learned, after I became a physical education teacher, that Grace was the first women to gain the Royal Life Saving Society's diploma of swimming: again I had the good fortune of having a skilled teacher who encouraged and never damned. Every Australian student should be taught to swim in primaryschool. This skill opens up so many social avenues in the Australian lifestyle. It is a disgrace that physical education has been decimated in the state school systems. I found it unbelievable that my own children, in the 1970s, had such poor programs compared to what was available to myself in the 1940s and 1950s.

Middle Park Central provided my education for Form 1 and 2. At the end of Form 2 mandatory decisions were made by the staff with regard to where one went. MacRobertson Girls High School or J H Boyd Domestic College for the girls while the boys were allocated to Melbourne High or South Melbourne Technical. Again, the luck of having a school like Mac-Rob as your local highschool. I hated it at first. The rules, the formality and the constant reminding of tradition all seemed meaningless and there were put downs. My only way of getting there was to walk or cycle. The uniform and book expenses put more strain on mum's finances, so I protected them carefully, on wet days, by covering myself, particularly the felt hat and the book carrier, with a brilliant green cheap plastic poncho. Mary Hutton, the principal, decided to greet the bike riders one morning and I was told: 'MacRobertson Girls do not wear green plastic over-garments.'

THE WISDOM OF KEEPING OPTIONS OPEN

After the initial shocks, and discovering 'the middleclass', the girls from the eastern suburbs, we found our friendship groups. My find was Del Watson who has remained a lifetime friend, again that good fortune that leads to a more fulfilling life. Del and I have shared all our ups and downs, doubts about careers, panics with colic babies and, when we both finally arrived at university in middle age, nurtured each other.

MacRob opened up new horizons for me. The constant reinforcing that a woman had the right to enter all professions without having to sacrifice the expected roles of wife and mother led to new ambitions. The dignity and caring of the principals, Mary Hutton (I discovered she had a keen sense of humour and forgave her the 'green plastic' statement) and Rubina Gainfort, encouraged learning.

Maths and sciences remained my main study stream, I enjoyed their logic, but I also found them easy and hence needed to spend less time on these and thus had time to explore the new love, history. Mary Lazarus took modern history and at last I had found an adult who could lead us to discover why we had had two world wars and what was now happening with the cold war.

Money, or lack of it, was still a major consideration and I felt mum had given me a fair go . . .

As I completed Year 11 decisions loomed. The choices were, return for Year 12 and go on to university to do science or take up a teaching bursary. Money, or lack of it, was still a major consideration and I felt mum had given me a fair go; also a fellow called Bill had become a constant companion; so exit MacRob and enter the education department.

In the early 1950s the scheme for training teachers was sensible. A year as a student teacher in a school before entering teacher's college and I was lucky to be sent to my old school, Middle Park. The principal, Mr Bryant, was an intelligent, caring person. Each of the student teachers spent two months in each area of the school and one of these was acting as receptionist to the head. I learned more in this year than I did in teachers college.

Melbourne Teachers College was fun but, apart from some exciting teaching rounds and the sport, not inspiring. The psychology lecturer, Mr Walters, was memorable. His approach to discipline was very positive: nurture through praise and rewards. He believed you minimised unimportant details such as placing undue value on materialism, and maximised the learning of reasoning. My own experience as a student had made me determined never to use sarcasm as a discipline tool. It destroys enthusiasm.

My early teaching years were varied and mainly enjoyable, although my first appointment was traumatic. Watsonia Primary School sounded ordinary, but it turned out to be unique. It was a school on the old army base. All the families lived in the army huts, 50 shillings rent, and these families had come from Camp Pell, the wartime camp set up in Royal

Park. Public housing had been found for most of the Camp Pell residents, however the leftovers, namely women with young children whose husbands were either in gaol or had deserted them, were herded out to Watsonia, a remote outer suburb. No support services except a primaryschool temporarily erected in the middle of the camp! I quickly learned new skills.

The infant mistress, Mary Rice, was a wonderful woman with 'straight down the line' priorities. First daily tasks were to wash the children – good old Velvet soap – then breakfast. As only one third of students ever attended on any one day, we had plenty of 'free' milk and Mary brought the biscuits and fruit.

The school was vandalised every night and the head had a rule that all female staff would not arrive before 9.00 am and all would leave at 3.30 pm. He and the male staff cleaned up each morning. After one term I was having nightmares and the head demanded I be moved. I have often wondered how an appointments officer had decided to send a 19-year-old first year graduate to such a school. However, it was a lesson in how teachers with commonsense, compassion and good skills will always produce something of worth for children.

Over the next few years I taught in a variety of schools, which included a two-teacher rural school. I realise now that I was fortunate to have so many varied experiences. Life was good, Bill and I were engaged, our social life was hectic and there were not enough hours in the day to fit everything in.

I finally was appointed to a permanent position on the physical education staff and for me this was a great prize. It involved teaching swimming in the summer and visiting schools in the winter as a consultant for the staff. I had kept up all my sporting interests that had been nurtured by my physical education teachers and now, full of enthusiasm, I was the mentor.

> . . . now, *full of enthusiasm,*
> *I was the mentor.*

A further experience came about with the royal tour in the 1950s. It was decided to have a mass display of dance and gymnastics on the Melbourne Cricket Ground (MCG). It was exciting to be involved with the planning and to see the choreography genius of senior staff, such as Merlyne Lee Dow and Joy Longden, unfold. The senior girls' routine was a marching pattern with skilful use of ribbons, while the juniors did a flower dance to Ivor Novello's *Dancing Years*.

Myself and two male teachers, Joe and Paul, worked well as a team. Joe on violin, Paul on saxophone and my singing of the tunes whenever necessary, created quite an atmosphere of fun. Most schools welcomed us and joined in the spirit of creating a pageant; however some of the church schools did not appreciate state school teachers instructing their students. One 'prestigious' establishment made me translate all directions and assistance through the 'madam' in charge of dance. They were hopeless and deserved their final position on the Melbourne Cricket Ground, down behind the point post!

After all this was over I was appointed phys ed teacher at my old school, MacRob. It was quite a shock to be teaching 800 girls in a traditional academic school, and I felt completely inadequate. Furthermore, Bill and I had married and I discovered my salary would decrease by £500 because I was now a temporary teacher, as married women lost all status. What a deal!

The next five years turned out to be the best part of my teaching career. A new principal, Daphne Barrett, had been appointed and she brought new thoughts and ideas with her. She gave total support to my suggestions that phys ed should be an integral part of all students' curriculum – right through to the matriculation students. My commitment was that I would attempt to teach life skills, not just sport and gymnastics. We developed a sport for all policy as well as providing top competitions for the talented sportsgirls. I find it amazing that there is still a keen debate in the 1990s as to where money and resources should be spent – elite or sport for all – either one is useless without the other.

I was a one-person department so had to coerce fellow staff members to help me and this proved easy. First approaches were frequently met with: 'I am no good at sport, I was hopeless at school.' Once they were reassured that all that was needed was supervision, encouragement and commitment, they not only came on board, but most enjoyed a new experience. We had many senior girls who were making their way into state and Australian teams and once they realised sport was valued in the school they became enthusiastic leaders and coaches of junior teams.

The other area where Daphne Barrett gave me support was her participation in the High School Sports Association. Traditionally this was led by the principal of Melbourne Boys High, the impressive and respected former Australia cricket captain, Bill Woodfull. Daphne had dignity, style and charm. She used these attributes well to achieve a much better deal for girls in all areas of sport. I learned a great deal from her. Diplomacy often encases a determination to achieve change.

Staff at the school were becoming increasingly militant over the conservative government's lack of commitment to state education. The big issue was unqualified staff being appointed to fill vacancies. The Victorian Secondary Teachers' Association (VSTA) emerged and there were many debates as to whether to join this comparatively radical union. Again Daphne Barratt showed strength and courage when she announced at a staff meeting that she intended joining the VSTA.

My own recreational activities during these years had mainly centred on women's basketball (renamed 'netball' in 1970). Again it was the interest of a caring teacher that had led myself and friends into the Melbourne Basketball Club. Our phys ed teacher at Middle Park Central was a champion player and at the end of Form 2 she invited some of us to come to her club. When we discovered they played on Saturday afternoons, our immediate answer was: 'Thanks, but no, we follow South Melbourne Football Club on Saturdays.' However, something made us re-think and we told her we would give it a go. Again a new world opened up. We discovered a well-organised club, run by great women who made us welcome, and the atmosphere was friendly and non-threatening.

> ... *something made us re-think and we told her we would give it a go.*

The coach was Anne Henderson, who over many years encouraged hundreds of young women to become involved in netball. All standards were catered for, the social player as well as those with potential to be champions. There was one golden rule and that was that you contributed to the club by not only playing and training, but also umpiring, coaching juniors and attending meetings to join in the decision-making of the Victorian Netball Association. A support network was ever-present, whenever anyone was coerced into jobs she believed she was not capable of doing. In this way I became a national coach and finally the president of the state association.

This experience in administration opened my eyes to what a poor deal women's sport received from community resources. At no time did we have a permanent home, despite hundreds of volunteers providing good sporting experiences for thousands of girls and women each week. For years, we had been putting sixpence aside from each player's game fee, for a stadium fund. Finally the Melbourne City Council agreed to give us land in Royal Park. We put up our money for the building and we would pay a substantial rent – this was 1967 and the lease and rent continues.

Three of us were given the responsibility of negotiating with the Melbourne City Council architect and this became a difficulty. He did not like dealing with women and appeared determined to build what he wanted, which would not have been safe or suitable for our game. The crucial meeting arrived, I was ready to meet him head on, but my wise, wily treasurer Phyllis Cross suggested another strategy. She bought flowers from the flower seller outside the Town Hall and presented them to him with a quick follow-up of how we three women, unskilled in building matters, really needed his advice and support to get the right building. It worked!

I didn't realise I was learning skills that would stand me in good stead for when I was drawn into the wider issues of sports politics.

Life altered with the arrival of my three children, Ian, Stephen and

Elizabeth – quite a shock to go from career and a hectic social life to being mum to three children under five. I enjoyed the break away from teaching and Bill and I decided that until the children reached school age I would stay at home. Initially this sounded great, but I found it increasingly stifling. I decided to study and after gaining entry to Monash University I began doing a single subject a year. I loved it, particularly the histories.

When I returned to teaching in the 1970s I discovered many changes. Students were lively and demanding and the great debate among educators centred on whether each student should be encouraged to develop to their full potential or whether the labelling of students as As, Bs, Cs, etc, was all that a teacher should be expected to do. Fortunately I was teaching in an all-girls technical school, Whitehorse Tech, and the leadership in the school emphasised that every student had worth.

I was able to finish my arts degree, on study leave.

With the support of the principal, Betty Lawson, I was able to finish my arts degree, on study leave. I decided it was time to give up teaching physical education and to teach in the humanities area: history, sociology, English and social education. I enjoyed these years of teaching until my retirement in 1989.

My interest in sport remained, but apart from learning to play golf and being a taxi driver for all my children's sporting activities, I had little involvement and therefore I was surprised when I was appointed as an inaugural member to the Australian Sports Commission. This was the statutory body set in place by the Hawke Labor government to administer the federal government's sports budget. The sports minister, John Brown, appointed a 21 member commission. I was to discover later that when he had invited 17 wellknown male sporting identities to become commissioners, he was advised to appoint some women. He happened to ask one of my netball colleagues did she 'know any *good* women sports administrators', hence my entry into the bureaucratic side of sport.

I was past 50, had acquired many skills and was quietly confident of my ability to communicate and to come to grips with issues. I also believed I had a fair knowledge of Australia's sports system. Any confidence disappeared at my first meeting of the commission. I didn't understand any of the agenda items, the chairman was very imposing and there was definitely a 'bonhomie' between most of the men. We four women remained silent and, as I discovered later, we all felt intimidated.

My reaction was to gather as much information as I could get my hands on before the next meeting. I read all the reports leading up to the formation of the commission and contacted colleagues who were on sports committees to get a feel for why the commission had been formed and who were the key players. I was also lobbied: many people began contacting me with their special viewpoints and grouches. It soon became clear that there were keen debates in the wider sporting community between funding for Olympic and non-Olympic sports and funding for elite sport versus mass participation. During the 10 years I have been on the commission, these two issues have remained at the core of most of the debates.

Negatives can always be turned into positives. I didn't have the confidence to contribute anything to my first commission meetings, but I did listen and observe. There were key powerbrokers and most of the others agreed with whatever viewpoint they expressed. I have learned that there is an advantage in being a women on a very male-oriented committee. Most of the men are extremely conscious of belonging to the 'in group' and frequently this will inhibit them from offering a differing viewpoint. The women don't have this problem. They have nothing to lose and it is easy to be 'true to one's self' and ask the hard questions. The trouble with this can be you become 'the conscience' of the committee and unless you tackle this head-on you will find the weak-kneed males asking you to ask questions for them. I have learned to bargain and negotiate before meetings.

Needless to say, the women on the commission networked and between us we decided we knew as much about the sport system as most of the others and we would speak up. I read my meeting papers carefully. I had established contacts with people who could supply any extra information I needed and on any issues I felt strongly about I would write out my questions, ring my younger female commissioners and share my views.

In 1985 the *Women in Sport Media Report* ('the Crowley report') was tabled in parliament. The Hawke government had set up this inquiry, which was chaired by Senator Rosemary Crowley. The report clearly showed sex and gender inequity in most aspects of sport in Australia. It made many recommendations. The major one was that the Australian Sports Commission (ASC) should establish a Women in Sport Unit, the main task of which was to address problems identified in the report.

This report came onto the commission's agenda and we were expected to make decisions on the recommendations. I naively believed the commission would support and budget for the establishment of a Women's Sport Committee of the Commission. Wrong, and I was amazed at the anger the issue roused. Coupled with this emotion were some of the most stupid arguments, mainly coming from the sycophants who believed they were currying favour with the powerbrokers. Most of the argument claimed that the majority of women's sports were 'minor' and shouldn't expect any better treatment than male minor sports. I learned another lesson here – don't lose your temper when you lose the first round of a debate. I took in the smiles of enjoyment as I claimed: 'It's not fair.' After that meeting I resolved that

Most of the argument claimed that the majority of women's sports were 'minor' ...

'motherhood' arguments were out and cool logic with some help from the women's sport lobby would prevail.

Word spread that the Crowley report appeared to be buried and the women's lobby groups advised everyone to write to Sport Minister Brown asking for some action. There is an adage that once the one hundred and first ministerial is received the public servants alert the advisers. Senator Crowley negotiated tirelessly to keep the issue alive.

The strategy we used at the boardtable was to point out that one of the prime objectives of the ASC charter was: 'To increase the level of participation of Australians in sport.' Yet we had a document that showed 52 percent of the population were, because of attitudes, being discouraged from participating.

By persistence, the day was finally won, but it was tokenism at its worst and I have often wondered had we refused the offer would we have achieved the final goal more easily. A task force was set up – myself as chair, plus two other commissioners, Jim Yates (lawn bowls) and Vicki Cardwell (squash) with a budget of $15 000!! And we were to write a national policy and plan for women in sport. I coopted Wendy Ey who as the South Australian women's sport adviser to the state sports minister had initiated many splendid programs for South Australian sportswomen.

We had fun doing it. At least a lean budget cuts out consultants and endless meetings! The final document made 14 concise policy statements, set targets and documented the strategies to achieve these. We commissioned a cartoonist, Jenny Coopes, to provide a visual for the policy statements. (These created good publicity when the document was launched.) Wendy Ey, Vicki Cardwell and I realised at our last meeting that we were related through phys ed teaching. I had taught Wendy at MacRob and Wendy had Vicki as a student in teachers college.

> *At least a lean budget cuts out consultants and endless meetings!*

By the time the Sports Commission accepted the policy, Graham Richardson had become sports minister and he supported our policy document. The Women's Sport Promotion Unit was established within the ASC and a small budget allocated, but it was enough to allow us to really start to network.

The first network we established was between our committee and each of the state and territory departments of sport and recreation. We had so little money it was essential to initiate projects where we could share costs. At first Queensland, Tasmania and the Northern Territory governments would not send representatives, now they do. The sharing of ideas at these meetings was marvellous. The 'seniors' in this field showed the enthusiastic newcomers how to fund projects and to gain community support.

I spoke anywhere I was asked. 'Women in Sport' was becoming a favourite topic but we were determined that it would not just become 'flavour of the month' issue. We set our goal as mainstreaming the Australian sport system. Many sportswomen were now speaking out; at first, particularly in traditional sports, women had shied away from becoming involved. Increasingly I was being made aware that our new supporters, many of them men, were telling us to stop the negatives (that is whingeing) and to inform and educate people how to solve the problems.

The pro-active stance has produced results. Some folk wanted the unit to tackle the whole sports system – the violence and so on, but the commission's commitment is to national sporting organisations and it appeared wise to tackle their attitudes and practices towards females who are or wish to be involved with their sport. We pointed out that 'user friendly' to women and girls sports would not only benefit with more players but also officials and administrators.

The appointment of Ros Kelly as sports minister solved our budget problems. Ros made it clear right from the beginning that the women in sport issue was to be a priority. I found the reaction to her appointment fascinating. Again the entrenched males who revelled in the masculine ethos of Australian sport found it extraordinarily difficult to cope with a female sports minister.

My involvement with the women in sport issue was a big learning curve for me. I now know how it feels to be a disliked minority. It was an asset to be a mature woman. The insults and the stupidity were easier to cope with and I realised that many of the younger women working on the issue needed strong support. We invited Quentin Bryce, the sex discrimination commissioner, to speak at one of our workshops and she shared with us the difficulties she had faced and how she had coped. This sharing of experiences is invaluable. It encourages and revitalises those working for social change. I have gained more confidence, I no longer dread public speaking and I enjoy being able to support the younger women who are now applying for senior positions in the sports arena. It is a more 'even playing field'.

In 1989 I was asked to nominate for president of the All Australia Netball Association and again decisions had to be made. Bill and I were retiring from teaching and all the plans were being made for golf, leisure and travel. Netball has a huge participation base, it had always been efficiently managed, but politically it was naive and its government funding reflected this. Many players and coaches were pushing for change. However, the structure of the organisation discouraged such moves. The executive director, a brilliant young sports administrator, Noleen Dix, had a vision for the sport and was enthusiastic to get things moving, particularly as we were to host the World Championship in 1991. I approached the critical 'young Turks' and negotiated that if I became president they would take on committee positions and work for change from within.

The five years from 1990 to 1995 have been exciting. Netball has undergone a management restructure and sponsorship, government funding and media coverage have increased. The women who for years have quietly organised the game in every community in Australia have relished the opportunity to promote the sport and many have become confident and skilled in negotiating a fair share of their communities' sports resources.

I have enjoyed being head of a 'business' and particularly seeing the growth of career opportunities for women in our sport. Many are now employed fulltime as coaches and administrators. The increased funding for sport in Australia has opened up many new opportunities, but it has been a hard road for women in the male-oriented sports. There are very few female national coaches or executive directors. Netball's current executive director, Pam Smith, is a well-qualified successful business administrator and politically astute. The sport continues to prosper.

At one stage of my life I became quite resentful of the amount of time being taken up by community involvement. I pinned 'No' on the telephone and made resolutions. Unfortunately once you become 'aware' it is harder not to become involved. I am lucky – my family are all talkers and doers. I believe my sons are SNAGs (Sensitive New Age Guys) and having a daughter is a nice bonus. Bill has encouraged and supported me and his philosophy of 'seize the day' has been motivational.

Thank You, Women, and Whitlam Too

Lenore Coltheart

Lenore Coltheart was born in Brisbane in 1940 and spent her childhood in Canberra. She left school in 1957, worked as a nursing aide and a clerk in Sydney, a receptionist in Brisbane, a typist and a nurse in Darwin, and married in 1961 and 1977. She finally graduated BA Hons from the University of Queensland in 1977 and gained a PhD at Griffith University seven years later. She has two daughters, Clare and Frances; five sons, Joe, Bill, Chris, Jim and Trevor; three granddaughters, Lynette, Madelaine and Alyssa; three grandsons, Lloyd, Matthew and Bodhi, and two books. She was appointed to her first permanent job, as lecturer in politics at the University of Adelaide, in 1991.

A breeze moved the light yellow curtain, the floor gleamed, the house was bright, clean, shiny and silent except for the ticking of the tall old clock. I remember the absolute luxury of that sound in that setting – I never heard the clock or saw the window reflected on a shining floor at my place. Lucille's house was so like her that I felt quite at home, and had no trouble settling down with a pile of books and notes even that first morning – though I did wonder how she would be feeling, exchanging this lovely large house for a tiny housing commission box, in a street without a garden in a suburb without a view.

How I worked there – every morning for three weeks until my exams. The first time I had attempted two subjects, the first time I had taken seriously the idea of actually one day getting a degree, and had told my friends about it instead of being so unsure I would finish each year. Her room seemed to cheer me on and not to disapprove at all, the way my own messy house did, the frowning pile of washing, the flowering basket of ironing with its ability to expand but never contract. At lunchtime each day I returned home to find the children solemnly finishing their lunch, with tea and sandwiches prepared for us, before Lucille Kidney left for her house and I took over my own. Yes, I passed the exams – the best grades I had earned so far. From then I felt like a student – still a 30-something housewife, still with seven children under 10 years of age, still four thousand kilometres from the university, still with no money in the bank after the next pair of school shoes were bought. But I felt like something else as well and stopped feeling apologetic about the fat envelopes from the University of Queensland, or the piles of books and papers on the kitchentable or the ironingboard, the laundry bench or the vast mending box as soon as the last child was put to bed, and while I waited for my husband to come home.

I began to wonder why I felt guilty, and why I needed to keep this apart from my everyday life.

Though I had told hardly anyone, I had been studying for six years by then – one subject a year – and it was only there, in Lucille's sittingroom, that I began to wonder why I felt guilty, and why I needed to keep this apart from my everyday life. The very first year when I was struggling to remember highschool English lessons I had bumped into Charlotte Mohring in the Darwin library while searching for books on my reading list. When I mumbled about not remembering much from school 10 years before, she talked about lessons on Schiller and Shakespeare in her own highschool years in Germany, and teaching them when she had gone to Kenya as a governess in the 1930s. From then I could always count on her for coaching, and for a glimpse into a life so rich and so different from mine.

These were Penguin friendships – a club for women, the Darwin branch started my second year in Darwin, just after I had a second child, the delight of having two tiny healthy sons balanced by the feeling of being trapped in a suburban house, no car, in a city where I knew no one except my husband. I had to force myself to go to the first meeting, and Charlotte was the first person I saw there, rather formidable and seeming quite old to my 22-year-old self – although she would then have been 10 years younger than I am now. I liked her then, and liked her more when I discovered how comfortable it was to visit her, even a group of us with a battalion of small, many-fingered children. She seemed to live a big life – I gradually gathered fragments of it, her growing up in Germany between the wars, her life in Africa which she loved with such intensity, the internment camp where she and her husband met, her home in what became Soviet East Germany – I never realised the pain of that exile though until her tears when, 40 years later, the wall came down. This much broader backdrop gave her a perspective which we seemed able to share, when big problems were discussed and small problems became trivial. There were innumerable conversations and lunches in her garden, and cups of coffee in her house – one big room with half-walls of corrugated iron, the rest flywire, shaded by broad eaves. There Penguins consolidated friendships which have lasted ever since, with problems and achievements shared – the club itself just the framework for that extraordinary support and encouragement these friends exchanged.

When I remember friends at that time I think of the groups we began – Helen and me trying to find out as much as we could about pregnancy and childbirth, reading everything the library held because the only doctors we could go to dismissed our lists of questions with: 'Don't worry, dear, I'll be there.' When we realised after having our first babies how inadequate both the doctors and the library were, we renewed our quest for information and discovered the Childbirth Education Association (CEA). By our next pregnancies we had started our own branch in Darwin, with weekly classes and even brave midwives and physiotherapists who ignored the disapproval of the local obstetricians and taught the classes – each also taking a turn as a student during her own pregnancy. Our babies have now had babies of their own, in the kind of environment which was the vision of those early CEA groups, recognising the right of women to understand pregnancy and birth, and to *give* birth in safe and friendly surroundings, rather than have the baby 'delivered'. Helen Moore and I have laughed about our rather naive approach in those days to the politics of childbirth practices and we have never really weighed up how important that work was. Even when we had both left Darwin, the Childbirth Education Association continued, with teachers paid for their work.

When we realised after having our first babies how inadequate both the doctors and the library were ...

In the same way we women started a Northern Territory branch of the Family Planning Association (FPA), and a family planning education group teaching women about the connections between hormonal activity, ovulation, and menstruation. When outback women wrote to us I went to Katherine, Tennant Creek and Alice Springs to help them start these groups, and then to more isolated places, Port Keats, Yirrkala, Bathurst Island and Groote Eylandt. It was about this time – the early 1970s – we must have begun to wonder why so few services were provided in the Territory for women in the things which were closest to their experiences – pregnancy, childbirth, contraception, looking after a new baby, childcare, early childhood education, for a start.

We were more than ready to start a branch of the Women's Electoral Lobby (WEL) immediately after this was first established in Melbourne and Canberra, and we became much better organised in providing a voice for as many women as possible. Maryanne Beames, who had been a journalist before her husband's job brought them to Darwin, and she had their first child, started a journal – the *Northern Territory Mother*, a collection of articles and letters sharing experiences and also featuring heated debate on issues like population control in developing countries. We organised a conference called 'A birdseye view of the Territory', the first time women from all outback communities, young and old, Aboriginal, Asian and European had the opportunity to identify their different needs and to support all in common. Leith Cameron, Elaine Wise, Gabrielle Kirby, Judith Rivalland, Lynne Reid, everybody – that was a great thing we did!

Meantime I was still studying at snail's pace, and for the first time took a course in which there was a woman tutor. She took the time to write lengthy comments on external students' essays, knowing how important this contact was when it wasn't possible to talk. I plucked up the courage to send a note asking about studying for honours when I finished the degree – I wasn't even halfway there, and had no idea what honours might be. She explained, and at the end of the year wrote a list of books I could have posted to me from the university library to help me follow up ideas I was interested in. The next year Merle Thornton became part of our new political life when she agreed to come to Darwin for another conference we had organised, an invaluable infusion from the Women's Movement in Brisbane, in which Merle had already played a stimulating part.

From 1972 to 1974 it seemed all this work could achieve our aims; could create a voice for Territory women in our political institutions, and secure our achievements by the funding of adequate community services, designed by women to suit the needs of women. It would have taken a cyclone to destroy what we had made together – and that is what happened on Christmas Eve 1974. Though it was another year before that constitutional cyclone when the Whitlam government was dismissed, for us all the gains of those vital years seemed to vanish overnight. While the cyclone raged and my husband and I, my mother, and our seven children were huddled under a table as the house broke up around us, all I could think of was getting the children over to Lucille's house when it was all over so they could still have Christmas. Instead, as the wind began to abate in the first light on Christmas morning, and we could struggle out of the ruined house, a devastating sight greeted us – everything was flattened – every house, every suburb, and no one had a house left to help anyone else.

When the evacuation was underway I was flown with the children to Brisbane, and after five very lonely days in the houses of host families I saw the first familiar face – Leith, who had been in Brisbane on holiday and who had set about finding where her friends had been scattered. It is painful to remember how helpless I felt and acted during those weeks, but Leith, with a very characteristic determination, steered me around, until we had arranged a rented house to have all the children with me again, and found a school for them, and secondhand furniture and clothes. Not satisfied with that, she then took me to enrol for the first time as a 'real' student at the university, then to fix up a kindergarten place for my preschooler, and through a bewildering series of government offices to find out what funding there might be to make this all possible. As I had no job qualifications or skills and was now permanently separated from my husband I urgently needed to be earning money, but could not afford childcare and so needed to be home when the children finished school each day. Leith Cameron found the answer – a Whitlam NEAT grant to complete my degree in a year so I would have a better chance at employment, and delay the childcare problem for the year. As I had done only half the subjects in seven years, to finish in a year should have seemed impossible – I think it was Leith's determination that stopped me pointing this out!

That year I even had support from women I didn't know – I still don't know the name of the benefactress who sent money to the bookshop enabling me to get the books I needed. The best way to acknowledge such generosity was to get through, and I did – with the help of other external students, like Pam Jones, one of those women who always makes you feel you can reach a little bit further to get what you need, and then is so happy when you do. My marks were good enough to get into an honours year – and now I knew it was the bridge to postgraduate study. More importantly to me then were other legacies of the Whitlam government – TEAS, and supporting mothers' benefit. By studying another year I could still look after the children without paying childcare, and earn enough to support us all with some parttime work, and if I did well enough I had a chance of a scholarship to do a postgraduate degree for three years – neatly covering the primaryschool years of all but the youngest of the children.

Though I managed to get a scholarship, I received a letter from the professor of the faculty to which I was applying advising me that someone 'in my position' should not try to do a PhD. I furiously ignored it, and was lucky enough to have Lyndall Ryan (now at Flinders University in Adelaide) appointed supervisor of my research – not only the role model I needed but a firm supporter through every crisis, academic, domestic, financial. Although there were many times I thought I could never manage to finish my thesis, at no time did I feel she thought that, and I did finish. I had no doubt about the importance of the encouragement and support of other women since those early days of needing to find out about childbirth and, when I gained a temporary post in a university where I was the only woman lecturer in the department, formed a group with women in the same situation in other departments. We had lunch together on Thursdays, and if we needed a name used 'Thursday women' in rejection of the 'girl Friday' role which women on the academic, administrative, and general staff all seemed

> *I received a letter from the professor of the faculty to which I was applying advising me that someone 'in my position' should not try to do a PhD.*

expected to fill. Instead we provided for each other the support which male academics seemed to get from the everyday scheme of things.

It was as if the women academics were out of gear with the university system, so we designed our own program, like a monthly seminar series – though we called them 'ovulars' as the papers were given by women, on their research and experiences. The name started as a joke – but when we looked at the origin of the word 'seminar' we decided 'ovular' was just the name we wanted. The ovulars provided a place for women's work in a men's university, a platform to speak from as a woman. When external students came for residential schools they wanted to be part of this so we started the newsletter *Thursday Women*. We campaigned for a Women's Studies course – just one! – and brought back from conferences resolutions for the inclusion of books about women on reading lists in existing courses. We thought how good it would be to be in contact with women on other campuses, and started an ambitious enterprise of compiling a directory of women's studies researchers in Australia. In 1985 the first edition of the *Violet Pages* listed 250 women and their work, but was immediately out of date because almost all those women with academic jobs held them only on short term contracts – just like most of the Thursday Women, who by then were no longer on campus because their contracts were not renewed, or had moved on to other temporary posts.

... an ambitious enterprise of compiling a directory of women's studies researchers in Australia.

The feminist poet Adrienne Rich wrote of the unravelling of women's experiences as fast as women weave them together, explaining why women do not have a history. Perhaps this is why the spinners and weavers are always so busy. It is only in writing down for the first time the generosity of women friends that I recognise how important these busy groups have been in shaping and reshaping threads of connection, and how this kind of support is reciprocal, and enduring.

The problem of being denied the chance to do the work you really want to do is not only women's, and not only the problem of academic women. It is a particular advantage to have a training that enables you to see this is not necessarily the result of your own inadequacy – and to have friends sharing these experiences. The ambivalence of thinking if I was any good I would be able to get a permanent job, and knowing talented and hardworking academics who didn't have jobs either, was brought home to me in my next job, organising parttime teachers for adult education courses. Women students always outnumbered men and it was easy to offer Women's Studies courses.

From those classes a group of women began to run their own discussion groups, and we had the idea of starting a Women's Academy, offering the chance for unemployed women academics to keep up their teaching experience, and to design their own courses, with students able to enrol more cheaply in the non-profitmaking enterprise. The idea seemed so exciting some of the time – and so impossibly difficult at others. The mutual encouragement of the group kept the idea alive – no, that is far too kind a recollection of the persistence of Rhonda, Robyn, and Shirley Jones. We heard of premises we could use and went to an inner Sydney warehouse where we met Eva Cox. Lots of people could have warned us that if there is the slightest hint of an idea warming up Eva will ignite it – but we were not warned, and walked into an enormous old warehouse with a makeover – upstairs was transformed into spaces for a whole range of women's publishing, broadcasting, lobbying, training and consulting enterprises. It was huge – not the ivy-clad walls and dreaming spires of our Dorothy Sayers' whimsies, more the spartan surrounds of the women's college Virginia Woolf described in *A Room of One's Own*. But it was huge – such a contrast to the corners and cupboards in which most of our women's work had been done. It really seemed as if a Women's Academy might happen there, though in the next few months of planning and hard work we all wondered if it would happen. However the excitement of our goal never diminished – we all knew exactly what Dianne meant when she exclaimed: 'This is wonderful – you know, just like the Whitlam years, when you couldn't be bothered going home to get the tea!'

In the midst of Eva's organising a farewell for Edna Ryan who was moving to Canberra, there to continue a lifetime of activism for women, we decided the launch of the academy would be a great farewell gift in honour of Edna, and found our energies redoubled. It was a great occasion, one of those times when the chance comes to celebrate our shared achievements – and we made the most of it. The struggle to establish the academy on a permanent basis has now been taken on by more women – I wonder do they guess how often I think of them, and send them proud and grateful thoughts.

The story of the academy is interwoven with another – this one also fuelled by the work and achievements of a generous women. While the thought of the academy had just grown gradually – and obstinately – and I would have forgotten it if my friends had let me, I remember the exact time and place the idea of a women's library was born. Shirley Jones had given me a lift home and we were chatting in her car outside my house about how to make books written by women more widely available now and in the future – to assist the work women's publishing houses were doing, especially in bringing us writing which had not been kept in publication. We thought of the Fawcett Library in London and how good it would be to have a women's library

We thought of the Fawcett Library in London and how good it would be to have a women's library in Australia.

in Australia – both thinking immediately what a good idea! As that library was named in honour of British suffragist Millicent Fawcett, ours could be named after Australian feminist, Jessie Street. Judy Small had written a song in honour of the centenary of her birth, and a conference and a book were planned, – we would add a women's library. One of the fascinating things about starting the organisation to found the library was how everyone seemed to have the same feeling we had in that car that night – that this really was a wonderful idea. Shirley has worked from that moment for the dream of the library, and has been joined by an army of generous and energetic women. I have earned a reputation for having good ideas that turn out to be a lot of work for others!

That time Lucille Kidney gave me her house to study was 20 years ago. When I think of her gleaming sittingroom now I see there all those women who mean so much in my life, like embroidery threads with which so many good things have been worked. I have learned through them what it is to be generous – to encourage someone else even when you don't share their goals – to give when there is no thought of investment, return, dividend – to clear a path so someone else has an easier way – to help and support without seeking control or influence – and the marvellous feeling when someone else's work is rewarded, when someone else is lucky, when you have a part in someone else's success. The warmth and support of other women and the indifference of government is the constant in this chronicle – it is as if women have a separate state, ancillary to the one men run, where citizenship is dependent not on contract nor on constitutional rights, but on something far more reliable – the incalculable generosity women show the world.

EPILOGUE

Generous Women, Generous Lives

Jocelynne A Scutt

Born in Perth, Western Australia on 8 June 1947, Jocelynne A Scutt trained in law in the 1960s, when there were no visible (and few if any invisible) women in positions of power in the profession. She had the good fortune of a childhood filled with generous women – mother, grandmothers, great-aunts, aunts – (and a generous father), but had to go to the United States of America to find mentoring women in law and academe (Virginia Blomer Nordby and Rosemary Sarri). She appreciates having worked with Lionel Murphy (an unmatchable experience) and being appointed by Neville Wran to the New South Wales Women's Advisory Council in the 1970s, is fortunate in having good friends and wise women outside the law in Australia, and has enjoyed the support of women in the community legal centre movement and in labour law.

'Finding a (male-defined) mentor' has never been a goal. For more than 25 years Jocelynne Scutt has expended her energies on a practical and theoretical critique of the law and legal profession, and working with women to reform them. This has been far more exciting.

Living generously is something women are good at. Edith Morgan, Kay Saunders and Susan Kelly are good at it, despite the sometime lack of support they received in their early years and their years of young womanhood. Joan Kirner, Christine Ramsay, Marj Oke and June Benson are good at it, building on the encouragement they garnered as children and young women. Joyce Apap, Daphne Milward, Natasha Stott Despoja, Mary Owen, Lenore Coltheart and Val Marsden are good at it, although they experienced the hurt of separation from parents, death of a husband or father, the divorce of parents or marital stress and breakdown. Melinda McPherson has known the hurt and confusion of violence inflicted by a person for whom she cared; Carmel Guerra and Joyce Apap have known the conflict arising from living in one culture and having strong familial (or direct personal) links with another; Donna Justo knows well the struggle to overcome childhood taunts and summon up reserves of energy for walking when walking is made difficult; Edna Chamberlain and Joyce Nicholson know how very difficult it was, in the past, to find women mentors, in a field where no women trod. Each of them lives generously despite – or because of – their lived experiences.

Women's mentoring is different from the traditional form of mentoring men have used over the centuries. It has had to be, for women are in a different position of power, authority and control. Jill Lennon, Ruth Lechte, Margaret Pewtress and others make this point. Women's mentoring comes often through collective action, in unions and women's organisations, as Audrey McDonald, Wendy Weeks, Edith Morgan, Marj Oke and others have found, and it can come through women's presence in the church, as Edel Suede knows. And as Lillian Holt and others know, it can come from women about whom we might have ambivalent feelings: 'the woman who is my *hair-shirt* is my mentor', Lillian Holt might say.

The role of mentor is 'swapped about' between and amongst women . . .

Women's mentoring is done collectively, where one woman may promote the concerns and careers of a group or groups of women. Women like Jill Lennon, Melinda McPherson, Wendy Weeks, Carmel Guerra, Margaret Pewtress, Audrey McDonald, Natasha Stott Despoja have had this, through teachers, nuns and lecturers. It is done collectively where a group of women promotes the career of an individual woman or women, Lenore Coltheart's experience. The role of mentor is 'swapped about' between and amongst women, too. This difference occurs because women's careers do not generally match the straight trajectory that characterises male careerpaths. It happens also because the positions of power women may hold are often tenuous, and a woman who mentors today may need mentoring tomorrow.

Women's mentoring comes in the simple and true, strong and affirming words of Lillian Holt's mother: 'That's a strong, intelligent forehead you've got. Use it.' So, says Lillian Holt, 'I went through life thinking I was pretty damned smart, having such a prominent Aboriginal forehead.' It comes in the letters written to Donna Justo by neighbours Joan and Margaret Lockie, on a working holiday exploring the world, encouraging through their messages the traveller's feet and adventurous soul of a young girl from a workingclass suburb. It was there for junior staff member Wendy Weeks, in Canada some 20 years ago, included in debate on 'what should be taught and how; about field education; and about [the university's] responsibility in education and research in the wider community'. It was there for Marj Oke, when her father told her: 'Never *rat*,' and impressed upon her the trade union credentials of Jesus Christ, his father and brothers. It was there for June Benson when her grandmother gave her and her opinions, along with those of her siblings and cousins, 'a fair and equal hearing'. It is encompassed in Daphne Milward's experience of observing her uncle, Doug Nichols, and Stan Davey when they spoke for themselves, their people and the Aborigines Advancement League: 'I followed what they did . . . I was learning all the time and they were great examples.' It lies in the wisdom of Jean Blackburn who told Joan Kirner that if she 'wanted to understand decision-making', she'd 'better understand economics'.

That women live generously is worth celebrating, for there is so much in patriarchal social organisation that is designed to drive wedges between women and to make mean souls of us all. The 'queen bee' edict may interfere with women's encouragement of other women, and may operate specifically to preclude mentoring by women of women. The making of queen bees can be seen early on in their careers. Thus in 1984 Meredith Burgmann attended a conference on women and management, one of the many conferences, seminars, workshops and courses conducted for the past decade or more designed (ostensibly) to 'get women up the ladder' and into management. On 19 April 1984, in an article in the *National Times*, she wrote:

The making of queen bees can be seen early on in their careers.

> The whole assumption of the conference was that feminism is about making it to the top. I questioned some of the women when it was over. All agreed that it had been a really worthwhile experience. They felt well informed and inspired.
>
> I asked if they felt inspired to help other women along the way. After some intelligent introspection they answered quite firmly that they did not.

The queen bee syndrome operates where a woman who has 'made it' *does not* encourage, guide or assist other women, *does not* do her best to ensure that other women are able to march steadily up the ladder after her. (Indeed, she may do her level best to prevent any woman from coming after her thus, ironically, preserving her own token – and essentially both insulting and demeaning – status.) This approach has a number of rationales: women who act in this way may do so because they do not want to acknowledge they are women, for in doing so they fear their male colleagues will recognise they *are* women (which, of course, the men know anyway). Thus, some women seek to 'pass' as something other than women – a hybrid sex, perhaps. It is these women who will fiercely say: 'I'm *not a woman*, I'm a manager . . . accountant . . . barrister . . . judge . . . professor . . . taxation expert . . .' and so it goes. This approach is akin to that recognised by Indigenous Australians and Black Americans within their own community, and articulated in *Race, Gender and Power in America – The Legacy of the Hill-Thomas Hearings*, published in 1995 and edited by Anita Faye Hill and Emma Coleman Jordan. In her contribution, Judith Resnik observes that while being a member of a 'community of color' may give a person 'firsthand understanding of the pain inflicted by those of other colors', sharing the same race as the racially subordinated group does not mean that the experience 'will animate one to work toward righting such injuries'. 'Living within the framework of current social structures,' she writes, 'many who share markers of subordination aspire to escape rather than to remake the meaning of those markers.' Striving to do so, those in the subordinate group can pretend they do not share the characteristics of the group; they deny their colour or race. They act in accordance with 'white' norms, seeking to 'pass' in a white community where racism abounds, by pretending to be white rather than Black. So, too, a woman may seek 'male' legitimacy.

Women who contract the queen bee paralysis may act in this way through knowing nothing of the strength of sisterhood that women have developed through involvement in the Women's Movement. Some women have worked in male-dominated fields for years, and have never stepped outside to see how the rest of the world is made up. A woman may consider herself a 'top flight' scientist who has 'made it' in a man's world. Brains and persistence have placed her in the position she holds, and she can see no other reason for her success. Yet women generally know better than this: women know of the history of the fight by strong and brave women during the nineteenth century to enter universities and to enable women to train and practise in fields and disciplines that were closed to them by man-made laws, regulations, rules and customs. Without these women, the woman scientist, head of department or division, lawyer, banker, boardmember, judge, architect, town planner, medical practitioner . . . would not exist. Women know also of the many women who, once women gained the right to go to university and to enter male-only trades and professions, trained as scientists, architects, mathematicians, geologists . . . Without these women paving the way, no woman today would be in a 'high level' position in science, the law, accountancy, business; no woman would be a professor whether in a 'women's field' or a 'man's field' . . . We also know that *no one* succeeds in any career, whether in the private or public sector, without the support and assistance of others – all along the way. (As the first-ever woman appointed as professor of socialwork at an Australian university, Edna Chamberlain acknowledges and appreciates the support and recognition of highly placed women academics at the University of Chicago, where she went as a postgraduate, following the sudden death of her husband.)

There are many, many talented people (women and men) in the world

– scientists, lawyers, town planners, specialists in English or Australian literature... Why are some – or one – chosen above another or others? How did some manage to 'break through' where others didn't? How did some gain their training, obtain their experience, come into the field of vision of those who selected them, promoted them, encouraged or even mentored them? Yes, we need to applaud the persistence and skills of women who have 'made it', whether in science, medicine, the law, literature, government, business or any other field. Their personal endeavours are key to their achievements. Yet there is not one key alone that turns the lock. And their achievements are not solely theirs. Rather, the work, effort and skills of the many women going before them are the central key to the lock, and their achievements are theirs *and* achievements for all women. Without other women, they would not be there, and that *other* women are not there alongside them is no reflection on the capabilities and talents of those other women.

Just as anglo-Australian middleclass men benefit from sexism, classism, ethnophobia and racism, women in 'top' positions have benefited from their class, their race and their ethnicity. The talented female scientist with a degree from the University of Prague or Moscow is no immediate challenge to the scientist who gained her degree at an Australian university. She may be equally talented as, or more so than, her Australian counterpart, but she has another battle on her hands: to gain proper recognition for her degree, which may well be superior to that of the University of Melbourne graduate.

> *Just as anglo-Australian middleclass men benefit from sexism, classism, ethnophobia and racism, women in 'top' positions have benefited from their class, their race and their ethnicity.*

Yet it is difficult for some women, indoctrinated by the ethos of patriarchy, to come to terms with this. Some women decide not to come to terms with it at all, but do their best to maintain what they see as a position of superiority – the *only* woman 'top' scientist... – without any challengers. Sadly, they have been socialised into regarding other women as a challenge to their position. So long as they are the only one in the 'superior' position, they will be accepted as a marvel: the woman who 'thinks like a man'.

Sadly, such women fail to see that existing as a woman who survives only because her male colleagues class her as a non-woman or admit her (on sufferance) to the 'men's club' denies them their own humanity. It is patronising as well as insulting to be 'accepted' on the basis that an intrinsic part of oneself is ignored, and that other persons of the same sex are despised or regarded as 'stupid' because they 'think like women' (whatever *that* means). Queen bees are also vulnerable, for they 'pass' only so long as the dominant group allows them to do so. And they can be assured that the same old myths and insults that are meted out to other women are used against them, even if only behind their backs.

Some women fall into the queen bee trap in the belief that currying favour with men will assist them in their own promotional prospects, or at least maintain them in a position of superiority to other women. Another approach is to emphasise their own 'respectability', inferring that other women are 'not so respectable' and are therefore 'different', so as not to deprive themselves of a place in the male hierarchy. In *Australian Women*, Rosemary Pringle draws attention to New Zealand research on women in the medical profession:

> Medicine was compatible with stereotypes of woman's role as long as it was contained within the stereotype of 'lady doctor', which implied that women doctors continued to fulfil roles consistent with late-nineteenth-century norms of behaviour acceptable for middle-class women. In contrast, 'medical men' were free to set themselves up as aggressive entrepreneurs. By emphasising respectability, the early women doctors created difficulties for those who came later. While it became perfectly acceptable for women to study medicine, they had difficulty in buying or selling practices and were obliged to take salaried positions or practise within the confines of the stereotype 'lady doctor'.

This meant that women continued to be precluded from the most lucrative areas of medicine, and thus were denied access to the 'highest' status:

> ... status was defined by hospital or university appointments, [but the 'right' to such appointments] was meaningless without a successful private practice. As long as the choice hospital positions remained honorary, there was little opportunity for women to compete without proof of entrepreneurial success.

> *... to gain a foothold in the medical field, women felt themselves constrained to emphasise their own respectability.*

Thus in order to gain a foothold in the medical field, women felt themselves constrained to emphasise their own respectability. They believed that, to succeed in a 'man's profession', they had to maintain an aura of 'ladylikeness'. This meant, in turn, that they worked hard to 'shut out' any women who did not display the same 'ladylike' attitudes or behaviours. Ironically, they also eliminated themselves from 'entrepreneurial' medicine, because the role of entrepreneur was not seen as one for a 'respectable woman'.

Women in the medical profession are not alone, and the medical profession is not the only field where this has occurred. Because of discriminatory patterns of behaviour and sexist attitudes of men in the professions, (some) women believe they *must* show themselves to be 'acceptable' to the dominant group. Yet adopting the 'respectable' approach, or that of 'not rocking the boat', can (the 'queen bees' think) enable them to maintain a position alongside the men. Although they do not realise it, by limiting themselves in this way, 'queen bees' will *never* be 'equal' with their male colleagues. Their male colleagues do not operate under the same self-applied constraints, for they have no need to remain 'acceptable', in the way women do, as 'women within the profession'. The queen bee approach also serves to 'close out' those women who do not want to 'toe the line', seeking rather to do the job to the best of their ability without a show of respectability or being 'acceptable' according to stereotyped notions of women's 'good' conduct.

The queen bee problem can arise anywhere, and journalism is another prospective field. In *Pen Portraits – Women writers and journalists in nineteenth century Australia*, Patricia Clarke documents the growth in journalism practised by women in Australia from the time of Louisa Anne Meredith who arrived from England in 1839 and published nineteen major books in her lifetime. According to known records, she was the first woman in Australia to write a regular column for a major colonial newspaper. 'Publishing for women' developed from this time, and:

> ... on 7 January 1888 the *Sydney Morning Herald* began a weekly 'Woman's Column', sometimes sub-titled 'Woman's Talk to Women', in its Saturday edition. The column differed from conventional women's page material in containing no household hints or society or fashion news. Instead there were long essay-style articles dealing with serious topics of interest such as female suffrage and female employment opportunities.

With the growth of the press, radio and television, more positions have become available for women working as on-air reporters and journalists, producers, editors, columnists and researchers. Many work in full cognisance of the power they have to report accurately on women's issues and the Women's Movement and strive positively within the constraints confronting women in the media to be fair and accurate. Nonetheless, as Zelda D'Aprano observes in *Zelda – The Becoming of a Woman*, some 'female journalists . . . see feminism as an industry'. These women, she says, have 'made a lucrative career out of playing the devil's advocate' in the media. As she puts it, such women are 'used by powerful men in the media to do their bidding'. That 'bidding' is to 'constantly criticise' women and feminists 'in a destructive manner'.

Although women like Edna Chamberlain, Edith Morgan, Joyce Nicholson and Kay Saunders between them had no female role models to emulate and few women mentors, they developed the generosity that we know as women's mentoring. Yet not all women become so. Having no role models to provide a different view of the world and their possibilities within it, leads some women to become 'queen bees'. In *Enterprising Women – Australian women managers and entrepreneurs*, published in 1990, Leonie Still quotes a direct marketing expert who was victimised by a new woman boss who engaged in a malicious campaign leading to a job move for her subordinate:

> It is not easy to form a picture of women in management because I haven't had many women manage me. Inevitably because I have been blazing new directions there haven't been women above me. But the few I have seen in comparable positions or even more senior positions in different divisions have developed an aggressive masculinity... The women in management behave in a male way almost as though they are compensating for being a woman.
>
> They seem to lose their pleasures, if they ever had any, in being a woman. They dress severely and speak harshly to their inferiors. They make management a return punishment program. If they are getting a tough time from their bosses they pass it down.

Interviewed by Leonie Still, the direct marketing manager goes on to say:

> I don't think women know who they are in management. There are few role models to copy. Sometimes you come across gentle men who are well-bred, educated, courteous, compassionate, and determined, and you can accept them as role models. But women haven't an elegant, attractive, well-spoken, well-presented, gracious management role model to follow in their sex. So they seem to over-react...

Without role models, women are 'doing it hard'...

Without role models, women are 'doing it hard', and this can have unfortunate consequences for themselves and for other women. Needing to prove they are 'worthy' of a position no other woman (as far as they can see) has held, they seek to emulate the model of a manager as they imagine a manager should be. This not infrequently occurs in fields that are male-dominated: women too readily believe that they must 'toe the line', 'play by the rules' and 'act tough', for this (they believe) is the way men act. This, they believe, is the way 'managers' (or police, or lawyers, or professors) act. To prove themselves as managers, they must, therefore, act according to the male dictate. This brings in its wake a reluctance to encourage or guide women further down the line. They do not see male managers (or police, or judges, or entrepreneurs) encouraging or guiding *women* into managerial posts. They cannot therefore do it (even *think* of doing it) for that would set them outside the paradigm.

Like Joyce Apap, Joan Kirner, Jill Lennon and others, every woman who works politically for the betterment of women will have experienced at one time or another the joy of supportive women – and the lows of lack of support, even the active working against her goals by another woman, or other women. This happens to every one of us. Every woman who works collectively and individually for women's rights and the betterment of humanity will also have faced, at one time or another, that gulf that yawns before us – the trench of petty meanness into which we might so easily fall. Into which we might, once, have fallen. Into which, unless we guard carefully against it, develop our generosity so solidly to combat it, we might fall sometime in the future. This is the trench where our generous spirit trips up on our historical memory. The memory every woman carries with her, which arises out of women being colonised by dominant values that are not woman-friendly. The memory of the witch-hunt, the future fear of wandering the streets as a 'bag lady', the past categorisation of women as 'mad' because, as Phyllis Chesler's *Women and Madness* showed, and Wendy Weeks learned in the conferences and seminars held at McMaster University in Canada, for a woman to step outside her 'given' role as wife-and-mother (and 'only' wife-and-mother) she *can't* be sane!

This historical memory can frighten us into pretending we do not belong to the collective group 'women', for that group has too often been a dangerous one to belong to. That group has been classed as 'the other', and who wants to be 'the other' rather than 'the one'?

It is this historical memory, too, that can propel us into thinking (falsely) that to 'succeed' we must renounce our female souls and don the mantle of masculine, not feminine, hope. Anita Hill refused to do this. When she appeared before the Senate Judiciary Committee of the United States congress at the hearings into Clarence Thomas' confirmation as an associate justice of the Supreme Court, Anita Hill writes:

> I was required to validate myself and my experience within the experiential realm of the members of the Judiciary Committee. The fact that the senators were all men, all White, all powerfully connected, all insiders, and that I, with no political connections, was a dual outsider by virtue of race and gender, made the likelihood of my success remote – and all the more so as I had only two and a half days to prepare for the hearing.

In 'Marriage and Patronage in the Empowerment and Disempowerment of African American Women' in *Race, Gender, and Power in America*, Anita

Hill explores questions of reallocation of power, the problem and pressures of patronage, and the issue of being a woman in a male-dominated institution, run by men in a world organised to promote the interests of men – powerful men.

... questions of reallocation of power, the problem and pressures of patronage.

'My reality,' she writes, 'was so different from that of the members of the Senate Judiciary Committee that they found it incomprehensible.' What was fundamental in this lack of comprehension was the 'failure' of Anita Hill to be 'attached' to *male* defined and designed institutions:

> They failed or refused to relate to almost every dimension of my race and gender, in combination with my education, my career choice, and my demeanour ... They could not understand why I was not attached to certain institutions, notably marriage, which has traditionally defined the relationship between men and women, and the patronage system, which has often defined the relationship between African Americans and Whites.

Patronage is a key to success in the United States political system, just as it is a key to success in business the world over. Issues must be presented with official endorsement to be seen as 'legitimate'. People putting forward claims must come 'officially endorsed' to legitimate those claims or even the putting forward of them. Women who enter male institutions and who seek to be heard must come with a patron, or they enter at their peril and run the risk of no man hearing them.

'According to the reality' of the Senate Judiciary Committee, Anita Hill points out:

> ... every Washington outsider worthy of interest has a patron to confer legitimacy at official proceedings like the hearings and to navigate the corridors of power. Clarence Thomas had such a patron in Senator Danforth. The fact that I had none, and chose to speak for myself, aroused suspicion.

Yet would she have 'succeeded' with a patron? Anita Hill was not prepared to run the risk of 'selling herself' to gain patronage, and thereby selling herself out. Attaching oneself to a patron has a price: the patron gains a sense of ownership over the patron-ised. Patrons can assist a person to succeed, but at a cost. The cost can come, as it came for Mary Cunningham in her experience at Bendix, in dismissal or forced resignation. It can come through having to adjust oneself to a different approach – one dictated by the patron. It can come through losing a sense of oneself, because success is seen as to be gained only by ape-ing the patron. There is a cultural and social price to be paid, writes Anita Hill, for rejecting patronage and marriage as the basis of one's identity. Conversely, there is a personal price to be paid for accepting these institutions as the 'meaning' of who one is.

The price women pay for adopting powerplays which ape or conform to power paradigms the way they operate within social and cultural institutions imprinted with patriarchal ideology can be enormous, for it can lead to the loss of sense of self. And the return may not be enough, for patronage (as Anita Hill explains) does not necessarily confer insider status. Like patronage, to claim (male-defined) mentoring as the answer to eradicating power differentials between women and men is to look simplistically at the way the world is, and to ignore that we want the world to be a different place.

> *The price women pay for adopting powerplays can be enormous, for it can lead to the loss of sense of self.*

Yet mentoring *can* help us work toward making the world different. Lillian Holt has been given 'a good talking too' by a woman mentor when needed. Susan Kelly found a mentor when, in the depths of despair, she thought to abandon her university studies, just as at a later time she found a mentor in a friend who told her that she had lost her sense of humour. 'You've changed. And I don't like it.' Susan Kelly listened, reorganised her life, and regained her joy and laughter. Daphne Milward was mentored by the aunt who became her mother. Val Marsden found a mentor who set up mock interviews to provide guidance in applying for jobs. Kay Saunders found one in an elderly spinster-of-the-parish with whom she gardened, a 'very independent woman who rejected conventional domestic life . . .' Melinda McPherson, Edel Suede and others found mentoring in the guidance of teachers at school. Christine Ramsay had wise old women to guide her. Lenore Coltheart, Ruth Lechte, Edel Suede and Lillian Holt were mentored by women friends and colleagues, often their contemporaries. Edith Morgan learned 'not to rely on anyone' in her political activism, and waited years until she met the mentoring of women on the local council who engineered, against the odds of crusty old patriarchal dogma, her appointment as socialworker with the Collingwood council: '. . . the "old guard" Labor men on the council didn't even want a socialworker . . .' Joyce Apap's mentors didn't know they were, just as they do not know they have been mentors to thousands of women all over Australia. She identified with Maggie Tabberer, Ita Buttrose and Denise Drysdale, and her experience tells us what we ought to know, but sometimes fail to see: that the role models and mentors who 'work' are not all *the same*; that mentors and role models need not necessarily be feminist icons. For Joyce Apap, Denise Drysdale's joyousness, courage in retort, and refusal to be put down by her male television colleague, in turn gave Joyce strength and courage. She stands strong on the lessons in strength she learned from her 'Denise and the Go Go Girls' television heroine.

Women's mentoring has a built-in multiplication factor. Joyce Nicholson, learning late in life that she is a role model and mentor to so many women, buys every book written by women she can find and hangs on her walls paintings by women artists. Like Joan Kirner, Natasha Stott Despoja appreciates the work of leading political journalists who are increasingly younger women; and works in federal politics to build supportive links between and amongst women. Melinda McPherson repaid some of the mentoring she received from those enthusiastic and encouraging music teachers, by teaching music and encouraging her own students, and now works to expand this repayment through a policy position in the higher education sector. Mindful of the support and mentoring she received, and the lack of networks for young people from minority ethnic and cultural backgrounds, Carmel Guerra mentors through the networks she has worked, together with colleagues, to create and nurture. Christine Ramsay repays her mentoring through encouraging women artists and photographers, and staging one-woman shows and exhibitions of the work of women who have not shown previously, or who have had small chances to do so. Mary Owen mentors – although she has not *believed* she does – and in doing so says 'thank you' for her mentoring. And she lends her name to the huge networking event that is the Mary Owen Dinner, which celebrated its tenth year in 1995 and welcomes as diners, friends, colleagues, networkers – 700 women annually, who have shared the words, the wisdom and the mentoring of Joyce Nicholson, Marj Oke, Edna Ryan, Delys Sargent, Faye Marles...

A very real part of the significance of mentoring for women is our need to acknowledge our mentors, letting them know how much their work and being has meant to us. How much it has made us what and who we are. Jill Lennon recognises this, showing it in her wish to say 'thank you' to her music teacher of old, Sister Margaret. So does Ruth Lechte, in her appreciation of the political activism of Doris Lester and Muriel Lester who, through their opposition to the 'principalities and powers' helped make her a staunch opponent of political and patriarchal manipulation. Like Marj Oke and Edith Morgan, Audrey McDonald knows the importance of appreciating – out loud – our longlived women's organisations, like the Union of Australian Women (UAW), and the thousands of women who have made it, and made its strength. Christine Ramsay thanks a grandmother and 'amah'; Edel Suede thanks a grandmother, an inspiring school principal, a great aunt, examples she had before her, whom she could follow, and did. And like Carmel Guerra, albeit from a different cultural and ethnic background, and from a different generation, Margaret Pewtress was encouraged by a sportsmistress to take up team sports. Like Carmel Guerra, she and her friends were reluctant at first. Then, second thoughts. They became champions, revelled in a new found freedom – and Margaret Pewtress went on to make a mentor of herself for so many sportswomen and others. She encouraged and made feel splendid the women whose lives she touched.

With the certainty of a woman who has herstory in her heart, Lenore Coltheart knows that institutions can be living, breathing spaces. She knows that mentoring can be individual and collective, and that when spaces and places like the Jessie Street Library are established, we are right to claim the space and the place in the names of our mentors and role models. Ruth Lechte has had the wisdom and the glory of knowing mentoring and the strength that comes from recognising wisdom that crosses ethnic lines, and that renounces the notion of stultifying boundaries of race and ethnicity that are set to diminish our humanity. Lillian Holt knows we may be angry at a mentor – who tells us 'what's what' – this morning, and gratefully appreciative of her next week. Edna Chamberlain knows that those we thank today are important alongside others whom we might thank tomorrow: 'Shift the context, change the day, or give me more space, and other women ... would be named.'

> *She encouraged and made feel splendid the women whose lives she touched.*

Women can succeed in ways that do not result in denying 'womanness' or 'femaleness'. Women can be successful and remain true to our own sense of ourselves as women, and retain a pride in our own methods of working. Mentoring can operate in a way that is constructive and productive at myriad levels, rather than being designed to promote only the 'chosen few'.

The women in *Living Generously* show this to be so.

In June, 1993, Ruth Bader Ginsberg was nominated by President Bill Clinton to the Supreme Court of the United States. At her Supreme Court confirmation hearing before the Senate Judiciary Committee, reported in the *New York Times* of 15 June 1993, she said:

> Surely I would not be in this room today without the determined efforts of men and women who kept dreams alive – dreams of equal citizenship in the days when few would listen – people like Susan B Anthony, Elizabeth Cady Stanton, and Harriet Tubman come to mind.
>
> I stand on the shoulders of those brave people.

All women in positions of power stand on the shoulders of those who have gone before them. All stand on the shoulders of women of the past who fought (most often without reward or recognition) for their own rights and the rights of all women. All stand on the shoulders of women of the present who continue the struggle.

All women who survive in a patriarchal world do so by our own strength, through the strength of the women who have marched before us, and by the strength of the women marching alongside us.

Women who recognise this, who understand and appreciate it, cannot but develop a drive to emulate those earlier women and their compatriots. Women who do so are, in turn, women who live generously. Generous women are the women who provide, as far as they are able, room on the steps of the ladder, space on the stairs. They are women who work toward the goal of ensuring that there are so many spaces on the steps and the stairs that we will stand on tiers that stretch for miles.

Generous women are the women who provide, as far as they are able, room on the steps of the ladder, space on the stairs.

Standing alongside one another, we applaud individual talent, individual capabilities, individual wisdom. We can applaud, too, the talents, capabilities and wisdom of us all, working together. In standing alongside each other, we can see so clearly the special qualities each one of us has. Because each one of us is special, we can cheer the qualities of our sisters.

Women who live generously do so because they have received generosity from others. They do so because they have the wisdom to see that generosity and to acknowledge it. Where they can, they offer their shoulders to others. Whatever the pain and the hurt, we who have been encouraged and supported by women know this. And we know that our shoulders, like the shoulders of all women, are strong.

Index

Abbey, Eve 193
Abbott, Edith 289
Abbott, Grace 289
Aboriginal Consultative Group, Vic 96
Aboriginal Legal Service, Vic 92
Aboriginal and Torres Strait Islander
   Cherbourg Aboriginal Settlement, Qld 21, 23
   childcare agency 92
   Cummerangunja mission reserve, Vic 89, 90
   dreaming 238
   girls' hostel, Vic (Northcote) 91
   health service 92
   infant mortality 95
   Land Rights 217
   Lake Tyers mission 92
   liaison officer 96
   men's business 45
   mentoring scheme/program 97
   National Aboriginal and Islanders Day Organising Committee (NAIDOC) 92
   organisations 25, 92, 93
   position at Trades Hall Council, Vic 98
   premature death/life expectancy 95, 99
   Rumbalara transitional village 89
   studies 55
   Tauondi (Aboriginal Community College), SA 21
   women's business 45
Aboriginal Workers (Saunders, McGrath and Huggins) 144, 150
Aborigines League/Advancement League 88, 91-2, 94, 96, 327
Aborigines Welfare Board 92
Aborigines and Torres Strait Islanders 21-30, 35, 45, 84, 88-99, 162, 200, 205, 320
   see also cross-cultural awareness/ training/programs, difference, racism
   and education 89, 90, 95-6, 290, 291
   and employment programs/strategies 91, 95-8, 291
   as elders 25, 27, 55, 89
   and equal pay 95
   and Human Rights and Equal Opportunity Commission enquiry ('the Stolen Children') 99
   and Job-Link program 97
   and NESA (National Employment Scheme for Aborigines) 96
   and native Canadians 94
   and 1967 referendum 94-5
   and paidwork 90, 91, 93, 95-8, 291
   in public service 97
   stereotyping of 96
   as stolen children 23, 99
   and Wave Hill walk-off 95
   and White Australia 23
abortion 195, 251-2
   see also family planning/contraception
Ackerman, Piers 115
Action Research Issues Association 55
Adamson, Nancy 52
Addams, Jane 289
Addison, Sue 111
Adelaide Writers Week 190
Adie, Jaccie 54
Adler, Louise 115
Adoption Reform Movement, Vic 49
affirmative action/equal opportunity 5, 6, 12, 53, 79, 86, 87, 100, 114, 130, 139, 195, 259, 260, 263-4 *passim*, 265-6, 272
African Laughter (Lessing) 194
agedcare 163, 259, 260, 266
   see also women – and aging
Agee, Bill 1-2, 3, 4, 7, 8-9, 10, 12-13
Alcott, Louisa May 32, 37
Alderson, Glenn 55
Alexander the Great 59
Alice in Wonderland (Carroll) 102, 227
All Australian Netball Association 305, 315
Alley, Diane 70
Alternative Nobel Prize 124
Ancheta, Mrs 295
Anderson, Marianne 76-7
Anderson, Sheila 84
Andrew Hood & Son 102
Anne of Green Gables (Montgomery) 64, 102
Anthony, Susan B 337

INDEX

Anzac Day demonstrations 263
Apap, Joyce 16, 112, 167-84, 325-6, 333, 335
Armstrong, Gillian 38
Arundel, Margaret 287
Asia Development Bank 267
Asia Pacific Christian Mission (APCM) 294
Athena (goddess) 59
Atkin, Elsa 265
Atkinson family 90
Atkinson, John 90
Atkinson, Kitty 90
Aunty Rita (Huggins and Huggins) 144
Australian African National Congress (ANC) Support Committee 275
Australian Asian Association 240
Australian Association of Social Workers 288, 290
Australian Book Publishers Association (ABPA) 193, 194
Australian Broadcasting Commission/Corporation (ABC) 25, 38, 93, 149, 196, 197, 259, 263-6
  and Australian Women's Broadcasting Cooperative (AWBC) 264-5
  and 'Coming Out (Ready or Not) Show, The' 197, 264-5
  and *7.30 Report* (television) 115
  and Triple J 207
Australian/Charter of Women Workers' Rights 279
Australian Democrats 199, 204-5, 251
Australian Labor Party (ALP) 33, 68, 69, 72, 100, 104, 110, 111, 112, 114, 149, 154, 159, 162, 163, 196, 200, 202, 206, 253
Australian National Maritime Museum 144
Australian Natives Association (ANA) 240
Australian New National Agenda for Women 280
Australian Psychological Society 119, 129
Australian Red Cross Society/National Red Cross 119, 288, 289, 290
Australian Research Council (ARC) 150
Australian Schools Commission 106, 107, 109
Australian Social Welfare Commission 284, 290
Australian Sports Commission (ASC) 305, 312-6 *passim*

Women and Sport Committee 305
Women in Sport Unit/Promotion Unit 313, 314
Australian War Memorial 144, 153
Australian Women – New Feminist Perspectives (Grieve and Burns) 3, 330
'Awful Truth Show, The' 266
Avon Spirit of Achievement Award 305

Bagley, Serena 150
Bamblett, Alf 95
Barrett, Daphne 310
Barry, Fenella 206
Battle of the Coral Sea conference 151
Beacham, Jenny 108-9, 110-11, 115
Beames, Maryanne 319
Beatrice, Sister 152
Beaurepaire, Beryl 153
Beauvoir, Simone de 47
Belfrage, Stephanie (formerly Fowler) 290
Bell, Janet 263
Bellamy, Sue 264-5
Benn, Connie 48, 49
Bennett, Sarah 68
Bennett, Steve (Stephanos) 68
Bennett, William ('Bill') 58-68 *passim*
Benson, Alice 80
Benson, Ellen 79-80
Benson, Irene 80-1
Benson, June 15, 79-87, 325, 327
Benson, Linda 80
Benson, Malcolm 80-1
Berman, Peggy 252
'Beyond the Legal Mystique' (Wilson) 254
Billabong books, the 47, 61, 227
Bible/Bible studies 208, 294, 295
Book of Ecclesiastes 244, 246, 256
Bicentennial Older Australians Project 259
Binns, Viv 266
Black Beauty (Sewell) 102
Blackburn, Doris 91
Blackburn, Jean 11, 109, 110, 327
Blackburn, Maurice 91
Bligh, Anna 42
Bloomfield, Gwen 259-61, 266
Blow, Reg 96
Blue Stocking Week 203
Bluecollar and beyond – the experiences of non-english speaking background women in the Australian labour force (Alcorso and Harrison) 9

INDEX

Blumenthal, W Michael 13
Blummet, Debbie 42
Bold, Shirley (formerly Evans) 255-6
Bolen, Jill 43
Bolton, Geoffrey 150
Bonner, Del 36
Booth, Anna 11
Borgeest, June 255
Boyer Lectures, The 266
Bradford, Joyce (formerly Evans) 255
Braidotte, Rosie 225
Breaking Through – Women, Work and Careers (Scutt) 254
Bredemeyer, Liz 139
Briggs family 89, 93
Briggs, Gerry 92
Briggs, Lois (now Peeler) 93
Briggs, Margaret 93
Briggs, Sally 92
Brisken, Linda 52
British Broadcasting Corporation (BBC) 264
British Government Office, Vic 93, 94
Brixton Housing Group, UK (Lond) 39
Broad, Candy 111, 115
Brockway, Marion 137
Brophy, Vivienne 192
Brotherton, Pat 127
Brown, Bill 279-80
Brown, John 312
Brown, Freda 278-9, 280
Bruce, Janet 197
Bryant, Gordon 91
Bryce, Quentin 315
Bucephalus 59
Bunn, Felda 36
Burgmann, Meredith 327
Burke, Frances 240
Burns, Creighton 195
Burton, Clare 3, 14
Buttrose, Ita 335
Byrne, Jackie 41
Byth, Val 197

Cairns, Jim 158
Caldercott, Jack 156
Caldercott, Ken 155
Cameron, Bunnie 103, 105, 106
Cameron, Leith 320-1
Campbell, Kate (formerly Corven) 289
Canberra Press Gallery 207
Canole, Grace 307
Cantrell, Annie 255

Capp, Josephine 192
Cardwell, Vicki 314
Carnell, Kate 11
Carr, Bob 149
Carrell, Liz 255
Carruthers, Fiona 207
Carter, Jimmy 13
Casey, Ron 196
Catterns, Angela 207
Central Intelligence Agency (CIA) 158
Centre Against Sexual Assault (CASA), Vic (Melb) 43, 55
Cerutty, Dorothea 47
Chamberlain, Edna 16, 284-93, 326, 328, 337
Chambers v. James Cook University 10-11
Channel 7, HSV 196
Chaplin, Charlie 128
Chappell, Noelene 192
Charles, Amy *see* Amy Cooper
Charles, Henry 90, 92, 94
Charles, Lilly 90
Charles, Stan 90
Charlton, Boy 68
Charter of Rights (older people) 165
Cheney, Ros 263
Chesler, Phyllis 51
Chesser, Leeza 206
Child, Marie 157
Childbirth Education Association (CEA) 319
Children's Book Council 190
Childs, Kevin 252
childcare 50, 51, 103-4, 105, 132-3, 142, 148, 157-8, 205, 209, 249, 250, 272, 277-8, 287, 296, 317-18, 320-1
  see also industrial conditions, paidwork, unpaidwork
Chipp, Don 251
Chopin, Frederick 101
Christ, Jesus 69, 208, 326
Christopher Robin 102
Christie's Beach Women's Shelter, SA (Adel) 40
Chu, Marjorie 234
Chung, Craig 207
Churchill Fellowship 231
Churchill, Winston 231
Cinderella 227
Citizens Welfare Service (CWS), Vic 49
'City Person, A' (Jackson) 5-6
City Women Country Women – Crossing the Boundaries (Scutt) 5

INDEX

Clancy, Pat 276
Clarke, Jenny 296
class/classism/class struggle 5, 33, 47, 50, 74 *passim*, 75 *passim*, 101, 121, 122, 131, 145-6, 147, 152, 157, 162, 167 *passim*, 169 *passim*, 170-1 *passim*, 174-5, 176, 195, 197, 211, 217-8, 220, 221, 227, 236-7 *passim*, 241 *passim*, 274, 282, 284, 285, 286, 308-9 *passim*, 330
  advantages/disadvantages of 109 *passim*, 308-9, 329
Cleary, Percy 73
Clements, Ernie 90
Clinton, Bill 337
cloning effect 2-3, 7
Coady, Cathy 51
Cohen, Bernard 207
cold war 308
Cole, Millicent ('Mill') 101
Coles, Susan 203
colonialism/neo-colonialism –
  Indigenous people and 194 *passim*, 269-70
Coltheart, Bill 317-18, 320 *passim*, 321 *passim*
Coltheart, Clare 317-18, 320 *passim*, 321 *passim*
Coltheart, Chris 317-18, 320 *passim*, 321 *passim*
Coltheart, Frances 317-18, 320 *passim*, 321 *passim*
Coltheart, Jim 317-18, 320 *passim*, 321 *passim*
Coltheart, Lenore 17, 317-24, 325, 326, 335, 337
Common Ground Cooperative 55
Communist Party (of Argentina) 34
Communist Party of Australia (CPA) 34, 154, 155-6, 159, 160
community development/services 88, 155, 290
community health centres 109
community work/politics 103-6, 107, 110, 135, 285
Connell, Bob 110
Connors, Libby 151
consciousness-raising 14, 164-5 *passim*, 272
Convict's Daughter, The (Nicholson) 190
Coolock House, Qld (Bris) 40, 41
Cooper, Amy (now Charles) 90, 92, 94
Cooper, Lesley 292
Cooper, Lyn 89
Cooper, William 88

Coopes, Jenny 314
Cottee, Kay 38
Coulter, John 205
Cox, Eva 192, 264-5, 266, 323
Cox, May 64
Craig, Judy 256
Cribb, Margaret 147
criminal assault at home 31, 34, 40, 41, 49, 207, 212-3, 299
  see also violence against women
Crisp, Kathleen 48
Cronin, Kathryn 149, 153
Crooks, Mary 231
Cross, Phyllis 311
cross-cultural awareness/training/ programs 88, 93, 98-9, 230
  see also difference, non-English speaking background – women and
Crowley, Rosemary 313
Cruysmans, Benedicte 266
culture/ethnicity *see* difference, multiculturalism, non-English speaking background, racism
'Culture and Merit' (Kalantzis, Issaris and Cope) 5
Cunningham, Mary 1-2, 3, 4, 8-9, 10, 12-13, 334
Curlewis, Joan 70
Curthoys, Ann 152
CYSS (Commonwealth Youth Support Scheme) 220-1, 223, 226, 230

Daly, Mary 272
Dancing Years (Novello)
D'Aprano, Zelda 7, 331
Darlington, Yvonne 292
Davenport, Christopher ('Chris') 47, 53
Davenport, Clem 45-7
Davey, Stan 91, 92-3, 94, 327
Davies, John 201
Davis, Flo 276-7
Dawkins, John 204
Day, Helen 41
Deagan, Carole 264-5
death 31, 34-5 *passim*, 95, 111, 127, 299-300
  of brother 131, 297
  of child 111
  of father 94, 127, 325
  of husband 136, 289, 325, 328
  of mentor 305, 307
  of mother/grandmother 24, 115, 244, 285

343

INDEX

of parent 111
by suicide (of uncle/grandfather) 146
D-Generation 202
Delahunty, Mary 115
Depression (1930s) 75, 154, 249, 269, 285, 287, 307
Despoja, Luke 200
Despoja, Mario 200
Despoja, Natasha Stott 16, 199-207, 325, 326, 336
Despoja, Shirley Stott 199-200
Devlin, Bernadette 37
Diana (goddess) 59
Dickens, Charles 102
difference
  cultural 5, 16, 144, 145, 209, 239-40, 269, 296, 298, 300, 302, 303, 320, 336, 337
  sex, race, ethnicity 5, 16, 53, 199, 203, 205, 209, 212, 217, 218, 224, 239-40, 313, 320, 336, 337
Dimousi, Joy 152
discrimination – age, sex/sexism 17, 35, 48, 52 *passim*, 142, 148, 165, 193, 271, 252-3, 254, 265, 290, 306, 313, 328, 331, 333-4
Dix, Noleen 315
Dixon, Elaine 40-1
Dixon, Robyn 115
domestic violence
  see criminal assault at home, violence against women
Donkin, Nance 190
Donovan, Francis 48, 54
Dostoevsky 101
Douglas Nichols Hall 94
Draper, Mary 291
Drummond, Bulldog 306
Dryden, Elizabeth 135
Drysdale, Denise 335
Duff, Catherine (later Englander) 145-6
Duffy, Ann 50-1
Dunlop, Edward ('Weary') 240
Dunlop, Frederick 240
Durack, Mary 190
Durack, Stefany 231
DW Thorpe Pty Ltd 188-9, 190-3

economic rationalism 54, 75 *passim*
education 25, 27-8, 33, 35-6, 37, 39, 40, 49-50, 53-4, 57, 58-9, 61-6 *passim*, 70, 75-8, 79, 81, 82, 83, 84, 85, 89, 97, 98, 100, 101, 103-8, 106-110 *passim*, 119, 121-2, 125, 131, 134, 139, 140, 145, 147-8, 154, 157, 158, 188, 199, 200, 201-4 *passim*, 206, 207, 208, 209, 211, 212, 214, 216, 217-8, 219, 220, 221-3, 224-30 *passim*, 232, 233, 234, 235-6, 245-6, 248, 249, 254, 259, 261-2, 267, 268, 270, 272, 274, 275-6, 279, 282, 284, 286, 287-8, 289-90, 294, 295, 298, 299, 303, 306, 307-8, 317-18, 320-1, 322-3, 328
disadvantaged schools program 109
fear of success 125
political activism re 103, 106-110 *passim*, 199-207 *passim*, 225-6, 231-2 *passim*
Educating Voula (Tsolidis) 226
Education Act 1870 (UK) 2
educational institutions/organisations
  Albert Park Primary School, Vic 306
  All Hallows' Convent, Qld 152
  Aramac Primary School, Qld 21
  Ballarat Primary School, Vic 306
  Bentleigh East Primary School, Vic 70
  Box Hill High School, Vic 160
  Cairns Christian Community School, Qld 297
  Canberra Boys Grammar, ACT 200
  Canterbury Girls High School, Vic 252
  Central School/Elwood Central, Vic 70
  Central School/Richmond Central, Vic 58, 59, 62, 63
  Claremont High School, Tas 123
  'Continuation School', Vic 57
  Council of Adult Education (CAE), Vic 119, 160, 239
  Crown Street Girls School, NSW
  Curtin University of Technology, WA 83
  Deakin University, Vic 97
  Edith Cowan University, WA 79, 86
  Errol Street Primary School, Vic 77
  Essendon High School, Vic 154
  Essendon State School, Vic 154
  Fitzroy Primary School, Vic 109
  Flinders University, SA 292, 321
  Griffith University, Qld 31, 32 *passim*, 37, 38, 317
  High School Sports Association, Vic 310
  JH Boyd Domestic College, Vic 307

INDEX

Kingsley Hall, UK 269
Korowa CEGGS (Church of England Girls School), Vic 243
Lalor High School, Vic 219-20, 221-3 *passim*, 224, 232
LaTrobe University, Vic 209, 212, 213, 215-6, 243
Lauriston Girls School, Vic 243, 255
McMasters University, Can 50-2, 54, 333
MacRobertson Girls High School, Vic 307-8, 310
Madang Teachers College, PNG 295
Manly State School, Qld 36
Melbourne Boys High School, Vic 57, 308, 310
Melbourne Teachers College, Vic 75, 209, 308
Mentone Primary School, Vic 62
Methodist Ladies College (MLC), Vic 47, 188, 268
Middle Park Central Primary School, Vic 306, 307, 308, 311
Moe Primary School, Vic 63, 76, 77-8 *passim*
Monash University, Vic 97, 105, 226, 312
Mooroopna State School, Vic 88
Mordialloc High School, Vic 62, 63, 65
National Union of Students (NSU) 199, 202
Newcastle University, NSW 292
North Lake Senior High School, WA 81
Northcote Secondary College, Vic 209
Northern Rivers College of Advanced Education (CAE), NSW 259
Northland Secondary College, Vic 109
Philippines Christian University, Phil 295
Philippines Normal University, Phil 295
Phillip Institute of Technology (PIT), Vic 53, 55, 220
Port Moresby In-Service Teachers College, PNG 295, 297
Prahran High School, Vic 243
Presbyterian Ladies College (PLC), Vic 247

Princes Hill School, Vic 76
Queensland University of Technology (QUT), Qld 38
Royal Melbourne Institute of Technology (RMIT), Vic 53, 55, 219, 291
Rusden, Vic 212
St John Vianney's, Qld 36
Scoresby Primary School, Vic 67, 70
Scotch College, Vic 188, 189
Selly Oak Colleges, UK 268
Shepparton High School, Vic 88
South Melbourne Technical College, Vic 307
Southern Cross University, NSW 259
State Commercial High School, Qld 286, 287
State Council of Students, SA 202
Stradbroke Primary School, SA 199 *passim*, 207
Students Association of the University of Adelaide 199, 203, 204
Subiaco Primary School, WA 137
Swinburn University of Technology, Vic 119
Tauondi (Aboriginal Community College), SA 21
Thomastown Primary School, Vic 219-20, 227 *passim*
University of Adelaide, SA 199, 203-4, 233, 236, 317
University of Cambridge, UK 145, 147
University of Chicago, USA 328, 289, 291 *passim*
University of Colorado, USA 21
University High School/University Practising School, Vic 62, 64, 65-6, 100, 101, 220, 224
University of Melbourne, Vic 47, 56, 62, 97, 119, 154, 329, 160, 209, 212, 216, 225, 234, 236, 243, 248, 255, 289, 292 *passim*
University of Michigan, USA 290, 325 *passim*
University of Moscow, Russ 329
University of New England, NSW 259
University of Prague, Che 329
University of Queensland, Qld 21, 55, 144, 147, 284, 286, 290-3 *passim*, 317, 318
University of Siena, It 228, 229

INDEX

University of Sydney, NSW 259
University of Tasmania, Tas 92, 124
Watsonia Primary School, Vic 308-9
Whitehorse Technical College, Vic 312
Wodonga College of Technical and Further Education (TAFE), NSW 96
Worawa College, Vic 93
Wynnum State High School, Qld 31, 36
Edwards, Kathy 202
EEO in Thirteen Organisations (Niland and Champion) 9-10
Ellis, Edward S 61
Elizabeth Fry Society, Can 53
EMILY's List 114, 205
employment *see* affirmative action/equal opportunity, industrial conditions, paidwork, trade unions/trade union movement, sexual harassment, unpaidwork
Employment Services Regulatory Authority (ESRA) 100
Englander, Oswald 145-6
English as a second language/remedial English 84, 119, 294-5
Enterprising Women – Australian women managers and entrepreneurs (Still) 332
equal opportunity *see* affirmative action/equal opportunity
Equal Opportunity Board/Equal Opportunity Commission, Vic 88, 96
Equal Opportunity Commission, SA 203
Erika, Sabina 264-5
Ethnic Communities Council of the Sunshine Coast, Inc (ECCSC, Inc) 294, 301
Ethnic Minority Youth in Australia (Guerra) 219
ethnophobia *see* racism
Eunuchs for the Kingdom of Heaven (Heinemann) 216
Eureka Youth League (EYL) 100
Evans, Erin 144, 145, 148, 149, 153
Evans, Gaynor 149
Evans, Raymond 148, 151, 153
Evans, Tyrell Granville 243-4 *passim*
Evatt, Elizabeth 11
Even in the Best of Homes – Violence in the Family (Scutt) 174

Exclusion, Exploitation and Extermination: Race Relations in Colonial Queensland (Saunders, Evans and Cronin) 144, 149
Ey, Wendy 314
Eyers-White, Arna 202
Ewinska, Teresa 53

Factor, June 100-1, 103
Factor, Mary 101
Faine, Jon 196-7
Family Planning Association (FPA) 135-6, 319
family planning/contraception 135, 155-6, 195, 196, 199, 203, 251, 278, 319
Fanetti, Ombretta 212
Faust, Beatrice 192
Fawcett Library, UK 323
Fawcett, Millicent 324
Fell, Liz 263
Female Eunuch, The (Greer) 38, 163, 192, 224-5
Feminine Mystique, The (Friedan) 38, 49, 163, 252
feminism/feminists 44, 53, 110, 112, 114, 121, 134, 155, 187, 188, 196, 197-8, 201, 202, 204, 206, 207, 209, 214, 216, 223, 224, 252, 253, 263, 264-6 *passim*, 268, 269, 270, 278, 280
 anti-feminism/anti-feminists/backlash 115, 203, 207
 and racism/ethnocentricism 151, 225-6
Feminismo (Carlson) 34
Filbee, Gwen 123
Filipino Australian Sunshine Coast Association, Inc (FASCA) 294, 328
Finch, Lyn 150, 151, 153
Finemore, Miles 147
Fire with Fire – The New Female Power and How it Will Change the 21st Century (Wolf) 113, 207
first world war, 1914–18 59, 267, 308, 318
Fisher, Peter 108
Florence, Jenny 197
Foley, Anne 37, 38, 40
Foley, Gary 93, 94
Foley, Matt 291
Follett, Rosemary 11
Fonda, Jane 38

INDEX

Food and Tobacco Workers conference 276
Foot, Rosemary 11
Forbes, Amanda 207
Forde, Leneen 11
Franks, Else 40-1, 42
French Lieutenant's Woman, The (Fowles) 224, 225
Freud, Sigmund 50
Friday, Helen 48
Friedan, Betty 255
Fukuyama, Francis 266
funding/fundraising 37-8, 106-7, 115, 232, 240, 281, 284

Gainfort, Rubina 308
Gale, Faye 11
Garbo, Greta 73
Garner, Helen 206
Gaudron, Mary 11
Gayford, Mollie 147
Gelade, Cassandra 206
Gender Relations in Australia (Saunders and Evans) 144, 150
Gerrand, Valerie ('Val') 54
Ghandi, Indira 37
Ghandi, Mahatma 269
Gibbs, Leah 42
Gibson, Linelle 105-6
Gifthorse, The – A critical look at Equal Employment Opportunity in Australia (Poiner and Wills) 6-7
Gill, Eunice 306-7
Gilmour, Kate 43, 53
Ginsberg, Ruth Bader 337
Girls Friendly Society 146
Glass, Dee Dee 152, 153
Gleeson, Beth 111
Glezer, Helen 192, 195
Glorious Age – Growing Older Gloriously (Scutt) 8
Go Go Girls, the 335
Good Earth, The (Buck) 102
'Good Samaritan, The' 209
Gorky's Mother 100-1
Goss, Roisin (formerly Hirschfeld) 290, 291
Gould, Peg 149
Gould, Suzanne 149
Graff, Linda 50
Graham, Barbara 190
Grassby, Al 226-7
Gravenall, Faye 54
Green, Alison 37, 38

Green, Isabel 306
Green, Massey 74
Green, David 48
Greenpeace 271
Greer, Germaine 38, 100, 163
Gribble, Di 192, 193
Griffin, Pam 96
Gryzb, Helen 83-4
Guerra, Carmel 16, 219-32, 325-6, 336
Gurrindgi people 95
  see also Aboriginal and Torres Strait Islander, Aborigines and Torres Strait Islanders

Hagger, Rona (formerly Clark) 289
Haila, Sou 40
Haines, Janine 205
Hall, Angela 150
Hall, David 48
Hamilton, Susan 153
Hamilton Women's Centre, Can 52
Hampson, Enid 277
Hancock, Emily 133
Handbook for Women Unionists (UAW) 279
'Hansel and Gretel Phenomenon' 122
Hard Act to Follow, A – Step-parenting in Australia Today (Kelly and Whelan) 119
Harmer, Wendy 38
Harper, Jan 192
Harris, Joan 190
Hartshorn, Alma 290
Haslam, Kate 140
Hawke Labor government 312, 313
Hawker, Bruce 149
Healy, Pat 193
Heartache of Motherhood, The (Nicholson) 194
Hegel 50
Heinemann, Ute Ranke 216
Hellman, Lillian 271
Henderson, Anne 311
Hepburn, Audrey 33
Hepburn, Katherine 38
Hera (goddess) 59
Hewitt, Maureen 165
Higher Education Contribution Scheme (HECS)/Higher Education Administration Charge (HEAC) 204
Hilda, Ann 174, 176
Hill, Anita 333-5
Hill, Dorothy 292
Hishon, Miss 36

INDEX

Hogg, Caroline 111, 112, 115
Holmes a Court, Janet 11
Holt, Lillian 15, 21-30, 326, 335, 337
Home, Douglas 93
homebirths 35, 57, 130, 145, 147
Hope, Deborah 14
Horatius 59
House Un-American Activities Committee (HUAC), USA HR – Congress 158
Huggins, Jackie 144-5, 150, 151, 153
Huggins, John Henry 145
Huggins, Rita 144
Hughes, William ('Billy') 68
Hull, Bon 160, 165
Hull House, Chicago 289
Hungarian Revolution 158
Hunty, Shirley de la 152
Hurst, Sue 291
Hutton, Mary 308
Hyslop, Jocelyn 288

In Our Own Hands (Hull) 160
incest
　see criminal assault at home
Indigenous Australians
　see Aborigines and Torres Strait Islanders, Aboriginal and Torres Strait Islander
industrial conditions/entitlements 4-5, 53, 54, 72, 74-5, 132, 141, 145, 195, 230, 243, 249, 277, 328
　see also paidwork, unpaidwork
　enterprise bargaining 141, 249
　equal pay 72, 135, 195, 250, 272
　ILO (International Labour Organisation) Convention 156
　longservice leave 4, 128
　marriage bar/teacher's bond 4, 48, 72, 189, 262, 310, 328
　maternity leave/allowance 277, 278
　permanency 4, 48
　re family responsibilities 55, 72, 249
　seniority system 5-6
　superannuation 4, 243, 249, 259, 260
Innes, Beverly ('Bev') 42
International Christian Fellowship of the Sunshine Coast 294
International Women's Tribune Centre 272
International Women's Year (IWY)/Day (IWD) 50, 51, 160, 164, 250, 254, 274, 278, 280
Irvine, Betty 158

Irving, Kay 255
Irving, Lillian 255
Irwin, Janet 292
Is That All There Is? (song – Lee) 133
Issues Facing Australian Families – Human Services Respond (Batten, Weeks and Wilson) 45, 55

Jackson, Betty 47
Jackson, Margaret 11
Jackson, Robin 5
Jago, Bonnie 277
James, Florence 190
James, Ron 97
Jebb House, Qld (Brisbane) 37
Jersey, John de 153
Jessie Street Library 323-4 *passim*, 337
Johnston, Ross 150
Johnstone, Betty 165
Jones, Pam 321
Jones, Shirley 323-4
Judiciary Committee, USA Senate 333-4
Julius, Eva 287
Julius, Fanny 287
Justo, Alicia Moreau de 34
Justo, Agustin 34
Justo, Donna 15, 31-44, 326
Justo, Francisco 34
Justo, Jo 36, 39
Justo, Juan B 34
Justo, Kahl 32
Justo, Liborio 34
Justo, Luke 32
Justo, Mark 43
Justo, Sarah 34
Justo, Sherrin 39

Kalagayan, Luisa A 296
Keating, Paul 142
Keesing, Phyl 277
Kelly, Bill 127, 128
Kelly, Fran 197, 207
Kelly, Robyn 122, 125 *passim*
Kelly, Ros 315
Kelly, Susan 16, 119-29, 325, 335
Kelly, Vivienne 122, 125 *passim*
Kennett Coalition (Liberal/National) government, Vic 109
Kernot, Cheryl 205
Kidney, Lucille 317-18, 320, 324
Kiers, Deb 111
King, Geoffrey 193

INDEX

Kingston, Margot 115
Kinnaird, Genny 212
Kirby, Gabrielle 320
Kirner, David 103, 112, 115
Kirner, Joan 11, 16, 53, 100-15, 325, 327, 333, 336
Kirner, Kate 103, 112, 115
Kirner, Michael 103, 112, 115
Kirner, Ron 103, 112, 115
Kirsop, Ethel 8
Kitson, Jean 38
Knox, Andrew 207
Koch, Peta 37, 38
Kockocinski, Licia 111
Koori *see* Aborigines and Torres Strait Islanders, Aboriginal and Torres Strait Islander
Koorie Women Mean Business (KWMB) 88
Kramer, Leonie 11
Kruck, Beverley 38
Kudis, Nancy 255

Labour Council, Vic 68
labour movement *see* industrial conditions/entitlements
Lady (Gladys) Nichols committee 88
Lansdowne Press 189
Lasch, Christopher 120
Lawrence, Carmen 11, 53
Lawson, Betty 312
Lazarus, Mary 308
leaders/leadership 156, 180, 204, 268, 281, 310, 312
  male models of 156, 205
  women and 55-6, 79, 113, 119, 120, 151, 285, 288
  see also 'tall poppy' syndrome
Learner in the Professions, The (Towler) 289
Lechte, Ruth 16, 267-73, 326, 335, 336, 337
Lee, Peggy 133
Lee Dow, Merlyne 309
Lennon family 261
Lennon, Jill 16, 259-66, 326, 333, 336
Leonidas 59
lesbian/lesbianism 164, 218, 225, 259-61 *passim*, 263, 266
Lessing, Doris 32, 47
Lester, Doris 277-9, 336
Lester, Muriel 268-9, 336
Levine, Gil 51-2
Levine, Helen 51

Levinge, Cherryl 37, 38
Lewis, Suzanne 150
Liberal Party, Aust 115, 196, 252
Linardi, Fran 226-7, 230
Little, Mavis 150
Little Women (Alcott) 47
Living Museum of the West 100
Living My Life (Goldman) 149
Livingstone, Tess 152, 153
Lockie, Joan 32, 326
Lockie, Margaret 32, 326
Loder, Kaye 141
Loh, Morag 238, 240
Longden, Joy 309
Lovering, Kerry 254

McCulloch, Deborah 138
McDonald, Darren 277-8
McDonald, Audrey 16, 274-83, 326, 336
McDonald, Liz 193
MacDonald, Sarah 207
McDonald, Tom 276, 277-8
McEwan, Melissa 207
McGuinness, Bruce 93, 94
McKenzie, Jan 107
McKenzie, Kirsty 207
McKillop, Mary 261
McLaughlin, Beth 127
McLeod, Di 42
McMahon Coalition (Liberal/National) government 124
McMillan, Jenny 111
McPhail, Margaret 52
McPhee, Hilary 192, 193-4
McPherson, Melinda 16, 209-19, 325, 326, 335, 336
Mabo decision on Land Rights 217
Mackey, Pat 33
Macmillan, Geva 190
Madonna House, Qld (Brisbane) 37
Mahlab, Eve 11, 192, 186, 196, 197
Malcolm, David 142
Mandala Consulting Services 88, 98
Mandela, Winnie 37
Mandell, Tina 50
March, Jo (*Little Women*) 47
Margaret, Sister 336
Marie Stopes Clinic, UK (London) 39
Maris, Hyllus 93
Marles, Faye 336
'Marriage and Patronage in the Empowerment and Disempowerment of African American Women' (Hill) 333

INDEX

Maroochy Neighbourhood Centre 294
Marsden, Val 16, 130-43, 325, 335
Marx, Karl 50
Mary Owen Dinner 57, 194, 336
Mason, Carolyn 42
Matchett, Ruth 291
Mathai, Wangari 272
Mathew, Rae 53
Mathews, Iola 114
Mathews, Race 106, 159-60
May Day 276
media, the 104, 114-5, 190, 197, 203, 205, 207, 331
  see also newspapers/newsletters/magazines/journals, radio/television, paidwork
Medlin, Diana 202
Meir, Golda 37
Melbourne Basketball Club 311
Melbourne Cricket Ground (MCG) 309-10
Mentor Human Resource Group 119
mentoring
  drawbacks of 10-2, 13-4
  elder to child/younger 15-6, 25, 29, 55, 68-9, 190, 197, 206, 207, 315, 317-18, 321
  male/patriarchal/'old boys'/male club' 2-3, 5, 7, 12-3, 113, 205, 213-4, 263, 292, 312, 335
  models of 1-2, 4, 13-4, 15-7 passim, 241, 244, 263-6 passim, 282-3, 284, 337
  reciprocal 15, 114-5, 127-8, 244, 255, 292-3, 308
  through mutual support 15, 55, 48-9, 82-3, 114-5, 127, 190, 193-4, 253, 263-6 passim, 285, 315, 319-21
  through working together 15, 39-42 passim, 52, 54-5, 192, 193, 263-6 passim, 278-83 passim, 285, 292-3
  younger to elder 16, 55, 323
  see also patrons/patronage
mentoring schemes/programs 79, 86, 112-13, 322-4 passim
  re longterm unemployed 265-6
  including persons with disabilities 86
  under Aboriginal employment strategies 97
mentors 15-7, 113, 194-5, 241, 254-6 passim, 268-9, 270, 277, 282-3, 284-5, 287, 288, 290, 296, 336, 337
  'amah' as 235, 237, 242, 336
  aunt as 16, 26-7, 28, 102, 121, 124, 245, 255, 306, 336

  colleagues as 16, 22, 41, 42, 51-2, 83, 99, 139-40, 152, 176-7, 202-3, 205, 231, 240, 289, 321-2, 335
  father as 16, 46-7, 61, 62, 85, 101-2, 187-8, 275-6, 306
  friends as 16, 22, 127, 139-40, 190, 240, 321-2, 335
  grandfather as 306
  grandmother as 16, 32, 235, 237, 242, 302-3, 306, 336
  as hair-coat/shirt 25, 26, 326
  lack of 16, 154-66 passim, 190, 222, 332
  male 1-2, 3, 8-9, 16, 51, 52-3, 150, 205, 284-5
  mother as 16, 22-5, 25, 28, 45-6, 101, 200, 201, 276, 295, 302-3, 306
  as 'surrogate father' 16, 121
  as 'surrogate mother' 16, 25, 81, 105-6, 120-1, 149
  teacher/school principal/academic/supervisor/professor as 36, 37, 51, 81-2, 122-3, 129, 139-40, 150-1, 153, 181-2, 184, 202, 210, 221-2, 261-3, 287, 292, 307, 325, 336
  see also patrons/patronage
Menuhin, Hepzibah 265
Mercer, Jillian 81-2
Meredith, Louisa Anne 331
merit principle 5, 6
migrant experience 167-84 passim, 200, 215, 219-32 passim, 233-42 passim, 294-304 passim, 255, 275, 279, 285
  see also English as a Second Language/remedial English, multiculturalism, racism/ethnocentricism
Mildenhall, Bruce 112
Millar, Kate 263
Millett, Kate 49
Milner, Sally 193-4
Milward, Daphne 15, 88-99, 325, 327, 335
Milward, Karen 93 passim, 99
Milward, Shelley 93 passim, 99
Mitchell, Heather 108, 110
Mitchell, Jocelyn 195
Mitchell, Margaret 32
Mitchell, Roma 11
Mitchell, Susan 14
Mohring, Charlotte 318-9
Mollison, Bill 124, 125, 128
Monday Conference (television) 106
Moore, Bob 106
Moore, Clive 153
Moore, Helen 319

Moore, Sharon 54
Mordue, Liz 52
Morgan, Bill 156, 157, 163 *passim*
Morgan, Edith 16, 154-66, 325, 326, 331, 335, 336
Morgan, Mary Ann 247
Morris, Robyn 40-1
Morrow, Ann 109, 113, 197
Morton, Alma 158, 165
Mottee, Matina 152
Mozart, Wolfgang Amadeus 261
Mulder, Lizzie 42
multiculturalism 35, 98, 220, 226-7
 Jewish culture 100-1
 see also migrant experience
Mung, Heather 107
Munro, Cathy 42
Murphy, Dennis 150
Murphy, Joy 96
Murphy, Lionel K 325
Murphy, Mrs 59
Murray, Bess 90
Murray, Gary 95
Murri *see* Aborigines and Torres Strait Islanders, Aboriginal and Torres Strait Islander
My Friend Flicka (O'Hara) 102
My Place (Morgan) 43

Nadal, Purification 295
Nagata, Yuriko 151
National Australia Day Council 144, 152
National Committee on Violence Against Women 130, 142
National Gallery Women's Association 233, 240
National Party 108
National Policy Plan for Women in Sport 305, 314 *passim*
National State Schools Parents' Organisation 107-8
National Women's Consultative Council 130, 140, 141, 280
Near, Holly 272
Nelson, Nurse 255
networks/networking 2, 6, 9-10, 14, 41, 107, 109, 129, 199, 200-1, 202-6 *passim*, 207, 213, 216, 230, 272, 284, 290, 292-3, 311, 312-6 *passim*, 336
 negative aspects of 14
 see also mentoring
Neuendorf, Alwyn 294

'New Education Fellowship' conferences 71, 75, 76
Newman, Geoff 147
newspapers/newsletters/magazines/ journals 75-6, 190, 191, 196, 207, 252, 253, 280
 Advertiser 200, 201
 Age 114, 115, 195-6, 253
 Australian 207
 Boys' Own Magazine 61
 Broadsheet (WEL) 195
 Connections 52
 Electra 48
 Hecate 149
 Herald Sun 115
 Labor Call 68
 Modern Unionist 279
 National Times 327
 New York Times 337
 Northern Territory Mother 319-20
 Sydney Morning Herald 331
 Thursday Women 322
 Vogue 53
Nichols, Douglas ('Doug') 91, 92-3, 94, 327
Nichols, Gladys ('Gladdie') 91, 92, 93, 94
Nichols, Ralph 93
Nicholson, Joyce 16, 187-98, 326, 331, 335-6
non-English speaking background 9, 86, 109, 215, 217, 218, 219-32 *passim*, 259, 298
 see also difference, migrant experience, multiculturalism
Non-English Speaking Background Immigrant Women in the Workforce (Alcorso) 9
Nordby, Virginia Blomer 325
Norris, Ada 190
Northcote Community Health Centre 57
Northcote Self-help Hydrotherapy and Massage Group 57
'Not According to the Calendar' (Kirsop) 8
Novello, Ivor 309
Nuclear Free and Independent Pacific Movement 268
Nun's Story, The (film) 33

O'Connor, Heather 254
O'Donnell, Marg (formerly McCann) 41, 291

INDEX

O'Donoghue, Lois 11, 152
O'Donovan, Anne 193
O'Grady, Rosemary 202
O'Neil, Lloyd 189
O'Neil, Pamela 11
O'Shane, Pat 11
Office of the Status of Women (OSW) 280
Oke, Brian 77
Oke, Marjorie 15, 57-78, 156, 165, 325, 326, 336
Older People's Action 154, 165
Olle, Betty 158
Onus, Bill 94
Onus, Eric 92, 94
Order of Australia 305
Orton, Maureen 52
Out of School Child Care Association (OSCCA) 137
Outhred, Gwen 47
Outrageous Fortune – People Coping with Major Life Crises (Kelly and Reddy) 119
Owen, David 249, 250, 252
Owen, Mary 16, 243-56, 325, 336
Owen, Rosemary 246, 251, 252 *passim*
Owen, Wendy 251, 252, 255

Paglia, Camille 207
paidwork 4-6, 23-4, 41, 46, 50, 55, 57, 58, 64, 68, 81, 86, 90-1, 99, 104-5, 128, 132, 141, 209, 210, 213, 234, 250-1, 252, 261, 262, 263-6 *passim*, 274, 276, 279, 286, 299, 308, 322, 328, 331
    see also industrial conditions, trade unions/trade union movement, unpaidwork, women
  as architect/town planner 328
  in bank/in business 90, 124, 191, 248, 266, 328
  as barmaid/waitress/'tealady' 4, 145
  in biotechnology 153, 328
  in bookbinding/librarianship/publishing 68, 187, 188-98 *passim*, 296, 323
  as cleaner – industrial/house 4, 23-4, 90, 124, 250, 276
  as comedienne/dancer 115, 201
  as consultant 43, 98, 230, 233, 259, 267, 309, 321
  as director/producer (film, television, radio) 152, 199, 264, 266
  as dressmaker/sewer 124
  as editor/reviewer 187, 189, 190, 191
  as gallery director 239-42 *passim*
  as historian 104, 238
  in engineering/chemical engineer/computer industry 84, 145, 211
  in factory 72-3, 102, 134, 163, 254, 276, 306
  as landlady 132, 236
  in law/courts/judge's associate 84, 90, 210, 211, 260, 288, 325, 328
  in management 4, 6, 97, 129, 187, 190-2, 193, 233, 328, 332-3
  in marketing/publicity 233, 332
  as mathematician 328
  in medicine/community health 85, 90, 135, 260, 263, 292, 328, 330-1
  in non-traditional jobs/male dominated 112-13, 132, 206, 207, 223, 328, 332
  in nursing 59-60, 64, 68, 70, 85, 90, 100, 104, 134, 135, 201, 214, 221, 288, 317
  as parliamentarian/minister/premier 34, 37, 101, 102-3, 110-15, 138, 199, 205
  parttime/casual/job-sharing 37, 50, 52, 55, 72-3, 150, 162-3, 189, 213, 224, 249, 276, 279-80, 321, 322
  as photographer 233, 237, 239
  in policy 140, 224, 265
  in politics – administration/advisor 110, 112, 199, 205
  in priesthood/as missionary 80, 294-7
  in public service/bureaucracy 4-5, 43, 79, 82, 83, 96-99, 130, 137, 231, 260, 263-6 *passim*, 287, 291
  as restaurateur 260, 266
  as scientist/geologist/chemist 233, 292, 328
  as secretary/clerk/administration 4, 90, 91, 93, 96, 129, 133-4, 130, 134, 135, 137, 138, 190, 191, 209, 214, 248, 249, 250, 254, 264, 276, 287, 292, 296, 317, 321-2
  in senior executive service/senior management 5, 113, 254, 291
  in shops/retail trade/door-to-door 90, 102, 124, 134, 156, 250, 255, 259, 276
  in socialwork 47-56 *passim*, 55, 154, 158, 160, 161, 163, 164, 221, 225, 228, 260, 284-93, 328
  in trade/student union 199, 202-4

passim, 250, 265, 274, 276-7, 279-80
  in teaching/lecturing/research/as governess 63, 67, 70, 71-2, 75-8, 75, 81, 82, 83, 100, 104, 105, 108, 109, 119, 124, 128, 134, 150, 161, 210, 211, 215, 216, 218, 221, 223, 236, 259, 260, 261-3, 264, 268, 284-93 *passim*, 295, 296, 297-8, 308-12 *passim*, 318, 319, 321, 322
  in television/radio/journalism/media 115, 119, 190, 187, 197, 199, 207, 221, 248, 259, 260, 263-6 *passim*, 280, 323, 331, 336
  as waitress/tramconductress 286, 306
  as youthworker 119, 220, 221, 223, 224, 226 *passim*, 228, 230-32 *passim*
Palmer, Elizabeth 270
Pankhurst, Emmeline 145
Partridge, Elsie 120-1
Parents' Federation, Vic 106
patriarchal practices/ideas/attitudes 7, 45, 48, 53, 179, 192-3 *passim*, 201, 205, 206, 207, 213, 222, 223, 232, 236, 241, 263, 269, 271, 288, 292, 312, 313, 316, 321, 329, 335
patrons/patronage 150, 240, 333-5
  see also mentors, mentoring – models of
Pavlin, Frank 48
Pearce, Dorothy 289
Pease, Bob 54, 55
Pedler, Robyn 207
Peers, Julie (formerly Stevens) 96
Pen Portraits – Women writers and journalists in nineteenth century Australia (Clarke) 331
Penguin Club 318-19
Penny, Harry 50
People's Palace (Salvation Army), Sydney 276
'perceptual maps' 3
'Persons Campaigns', Can 52
Petersen, Joh Bjelke 152
Pettit, Judith 195
Pewtress, Ian 311-12, 316
Pewtress, Bill 308, 309, 310, 312, 315, 316
Pewtress, Elizabeth 312, 316
Pewtress, Margaret 16-17, 305-16, 326, 336-7
Pewtress, Stephen 311-12, 316
Philipson, Edith 45-7
Philippou, Lydia 141
Pickles, Sue 111

Pill, the *see* family planning/contraception
Pilone, Joan 8
Pizzey, Erin 39
Player, Alison (now Mathews) 289
Podesta, Lesley 230
Pollyanna 102
power 7-8, 113, 165-6, 217, 218, 232, 264-6 *passim*, 272-3, 274, 325, 331
  male structures/models of 2, 13-14, 49, 53, 114, 139, 151-2, 153, 160, 165-6, 205, 217, 218, 222, 223, 292, 312, 316, 329, 331, 332-3, 334, 335
  women and 9 *passim*, 13-14, 15, 17, 113, 191, 205, 326, 331, 334-5
  women using against women 7-8, 182, 199-200, 201-2, 205-7, 242, 265, 333, 335, 338
Powerplay – What Really Happened at Bendix (Cunningham with Schumer) 2, 12
Presbyterian Fellowship 103
Pringle, Rosemary 330
Prior, Thelma 78
Pritchard, Vi 190
Prize and the Price, The (Kelly) 119
Progressive Reform Party (PRP) 251, 252, 253
Proust, Marcel 102
Purlman, Helen 289
Purse, Frank 276
Putman, Robert 266
Pym, Barbara 147

Quartermaine, Pamela 296
queen bee syndrome/phenomenon 7-8 *passim*, 56 *passim*, 267 *passim*, 328-33 *passim*
Queensland Police Service 43
Quinn, Marjorie 54
Quit Campaign 197

Race, Gender and Power in America – The Legacy of the Hill-Thomas Hearings (Hill and Jordan) 328
Race Relations in Colonial Queensland; Exclusion, Exploitation and Extermination (Saunders, Evans and Cronin) 144, 149
Rachmaninov, Sergei 101
racism/ethnocentricism 17, 22, 29-30, 90, 151, 157, 211, 217-8, 328

INDEX

see also Aborigines and Torres Strait Islanders, difference
Raine, Lindy 149
Ramsay, Christine 16, 233-42, 325, 335, 336
Ramsay, Janet 42
rape/marital rape
  see violence against women
Ravlich, Robyn 263
Ray, Margaret 111
Raya Gallery, Vic 234, 239-41 *passim*
Razer, Helen 207
'Reclaim the Night' marches 52
Red Riding Hood/Il Capucco Rosso 227
Redgrave, Lynne 38
Redgrave, Vanessa 38, 271
Reid, Lynne 320
Reid, Maree Ann 150
Reidy, Joan ('Sister Hannah') 107
Relationships Australia (formerly Marriage Guidance Australia) 119
Resnik, Judith 328
Reuther, Rosemary 272
Rice, Mary 309
Rich, Adrienne 322
Richmond, Katy 192
Richardson, Graham 314
Ridgeway, Bessie 47
Rigg, Julie 263
Rivalland, Judith 320
Roberts, Annie 42
Robins, Bernice 201
Robinson, Pam 110
Roiphe, Katie 207
role models 32, 38, 41, 48, 79, 87, 147, 190, 194, 209, 213, 236, 255, 268, 271, 284, 287, 292, 293, 332, 335, 336, 337
  see also mentors, mentoring – models of
  colleague as 83, 321
  aunt as 26, 60, 80, 102
  elders as 268-9
  father as 66-7, 85, 211
  grandmother as 67, 80, 132-3
  lack of 154-66 *passim*, 290, 331-2
  mother as 134, 209, 286
  teacher/supervisor as 134, 147, 209, 222, 262, 263, 321
Rollins, Leslie J 8-9
Room of One's Own, A (Woolf) 323
Rose, Sister Margaret ('The Sphinx') 261-2
Roth, Lillian 25, 30

Rowan, Dawn 40
Royal Australian Airforce (RAAF) 45, 156
Royal Australian Naval Reserve (RANR) 249
Royal Life Saving Society 62, 307
Royal Women's Hospital, Vic 59
Ruby Gaea House, NT (Darwin) 42
Russell, Jean 129
Ryan, Edna 255, 323, 336
Ryan, Lyndall 152, 321
Ryan, Susan 107-8

St John, Ethel 190
Salvation Army Boys Home, Vic 46
Sambell, Ena 190
Sandon, Pamela 113
'Sapphoteria' restaurant 266
Sargent, Delys 336
Sargood, Marian (formerly Evans) 245-6 *passim*, 255
Sarri, Rosemary 325
Saunders, Cecil 145
Saunders, Elizabeth Walsh 145-6, 147
Saunders, Eric 145-6, 147
Saunders, Ernest 145
Saunders, Florence Sizer 145
Saunders, Frank 145
Saunders, Kay 16, 144-53, 325, 331, 335
Saunders, Louise Bass 145
Saunders, Mollie 145
Save the Children Fund 89, 90
Save Our Sons (SOS) 278
Sayers, Dorothy 323
Scarlet Pimpernel (character – Baroness Orczy) 102
Schiller, J C Friedrich von 318
Schubert, Misha 207
Scott, Denise 115
Scott, Joanne 151, 153
Scratton, Joan 48
Scream Quietly or the Neighbours Will Hear (Pizzey) 39
Scutt, Jocelynne A 1-17, 325-38
Second Sex, The (de Beauvoir) 163
second world war 74, 102, 130 *passim*, 132, 144, 151, 188, 189, 249, 269, 287, 306, 308, 318
  Japanese invasion/internment during 151, 306
  reconstruction 74
Selman, Fred 50
Selman, Millie 50

service clubs – Apex/Lions 91
Setches, Kay 53, 111, 114, 115
Seven Little Australians (Grant Bruce) 61
sexism *see* difference
sexual harassment 10, 53, 113, 142, 193, 203
Shakespeare, William 26, 102, 318
Sheldon, Gay 42
Shields, Brooke 210
Shiva, Vandana 271
Shute, Carmel 149-50, 153
Shaw, Sylvie 250
Siegal, Linda 50
Singer, Jill 115
sisterhood 14, 48, 192, 203, 206, 255, 279, 281, 282, 338 *passim*
Sisters in Crime 150
Sizer, Harriet Watts 145
Sizer, Hubert 145, 147
Sloane, Jane 207
Small, Judy 265, 324
Smart, Mary 39
Smith, Dorothy 48
Smith, Hazel 290, 291
Smith, Mary 148
Smith, Miss 306
Smith, Pam 316
Smith, Yvonne 158
Snow, Jennifer 40-1
Social Work: A Problem Solving Process (Perlman) 289
Socialist Party (of Argentina) 34
Social Planning and Research Council, Can 52
Social Security Appeals Tribunal (SAAT) 154
Somma, Penny 191, 192
Sorgi, George 222-3, 232 *passim*
South Melbourne Football Club 311
South Australian Women's Suffrage Centenary Committee 199
South Pacific Commission 270
Spanish civil war 160
Spearritt, Katie 150, 153
Special Broadcasting Service (SBS) 102
Spence, Nancy 109
Spender, Jeffrey 10-11
Spot on Joan Concert 115
Stand and Deliver (film – Escalante) 123
Staying Alive (Shiva) 271
Stanton, Elizabeth Cady 337
Staunton, Phyl 287
Stead, Christina 32
Steinbeck, John 102

Stephenson, Mary Lee 52
Stevens, Joyce 265-6
Stevens, Marg 41
Stewart, Marjorie 270-1
Still, Leonie 332
Storey, Rachel 112
Stott, Jessica (formerly Swinfield) 200
Street, Jessie 324
Stretton, Hugh 53
Subanzski, Magda 115
Sue-Tin family 146
Sue-Tin, Mrs 146
Suede, Bert 296, 297, 300, 301
Suede, Edel 16, 294-304, 326, 335, 336
Summer School for Human Services 55
Summers, Anne 206
Summons, Elizabeth 240
Sunshine Coast Winter-Agency Research Group 42
Sunshine Coast Women's Rape Crisis Service, Qld (Maroochydore) 41, 42
Survival and Celebration (exhibition) 238, 240
Swain, Pam 83
Sweeney, John 296
Symons, Kerry 126

Tabberer, Maggie 335
'tall poppy' syndrome/'tall poppies' 151, 153, 281
Tancred, Peta (Sheriff) 52
Tankred, Fran 40
Task Force for Women's Sport 305, 314 *passim*
Taylor, Elizabeth 102
Taylor, Judy 40
Taylor, Lenore 207
Taylor, Lyra 48
Therese, Mother 37, 127
Third World Women's Conference (Nairobi) 280
Third World Working Women's conference (Prague) 279
Thomas, Clarence 333
Thomas, Helen 81-2
Thompson, Lindsay 104
Thornton, Merle 320
Thursday Women 321-2
Tibbie, Jane 161
Tilbrook, Dale 83-4
Tingle, Laura 115, 207
Tolstoy, Leo 101
Towler, Charlotte 289

INDEX

trade unions/trade union movement 33, 50, 54, 69, 72, 73, 95, 98, 141, 156-7, 159, 161, 200, 202, 250, 274, 275, 276-8 *passim*, 279-80, 281-2
   Australian Council of Trade Unions (ACTU) 98, 276-7, 279
   Builders Labourers Federation (BLF) 158
   Building Workers Industrial Union (BWIU) 276, 277, 279
   Canadian Union of Public Employees 52
   Food Preservers Union (FPU) 73
   Hotel, Club and Restaurant Union (HCRU) 275, 276, 277
   Iron Workers Union (IWU) 78
   Laundresses Union 2
   Liquor Trades Union (LTU) 275
   Metal Workers Union (MWU) 279
   Public Sector Union (PSU) 149
   Seamens Union 279
   Sheet Metal Workers Union 276
   and strike breakers/breaking 161
   Tailoresses Union 2
   Trade Union Education and Research Centre (TUERC) 279-80
   United Automobile Workers 4
   Victorian School Teachers Association (VSTA) 310
   Waterside Workers Union (Wharfies) 276, 279
   women and 50, 275-83 *passim*
   World Federation of Trade Unions (WFTU) 279
Trades Hall, Vic 159
Travellers Aid Society 69
Tree of Man (White) 134
Trotsky, Leon 158
'Truly Civil Society, A' (Cox) 266
Tsolides, Georgina 324-5
Tubb, Pearl 306
Tubman, Harriet 337
Tucker, Marg 92
Tuxen, Joan 288

United Nations Decade for Women, 1975-85 263, 279, 282
United Nations International Women's Year/Year of Women 279, 280, 282
United Nations International Year of the Child 279

United Nations International Year of Youth 202
United Nations Mid-Term Review of Decade, 1985 (Copenhagen) 280
United Nations Women's Forum, Beijing 1995 267, 280-1, 282
United Nations Women's Forum, Mexico 1975 267, 279, 280
United Nations Women's Forum, Nairobi 1985 41, 267, 280
unpaid work 33, 46, 58, 59, 69, 73, 104, 105, 110, 132, 141, 155-6, 189, 209, 244, 249, 275, 288, 296, 317-18, 319
see also voluntary work

Victoria Police Force 251-2
Victoria Women's Council 112, 167, 183
Victorian Council of Social Service (VCOSS) 55
Victorian Council of State Schools Organisation (VCSSO) 106, 109
Victorian Court Information and Welfare Program (Court Network) 288
Victorian Netball Association 311
Victorian Society for Crippled Children 46
Victorian Society for the Prevention of Cruelty to Children and Adults (VSPCCA) 288
Victorian Teachers Education Council 72
Victorian Women's Trust (VWT) 88, 196-7, 219
   Million Dollar Appeal 196-7
Viet Nam war, anti-movement 144, 148, 158, 159, 161-2, 277, 278, 280, 290
violence against women 12, 31, 37, 40, 45, 124-5, 139, 142, 146-7, 148, 153, 164, 203, 207, 212, 213, 214, 231, 269, 273, 299, 325
see also criminal assault at home, sexual harassment
Violet Pages 322
voluntary work 89, 94, 220, 275, 281, 282, 284, 301
see also unpaid work

Wachner, John 149
Wadsworth, Yoland 55

356

INDEX

Wainer, Bertram 251, 252, 255
Walker, Judy 37
Walker, Karen 9
Wallace, Christine 207
Walsh, Elizabeth Duff 145
Walsh, Peter 145
Walters, Catherine 11
Walters, Joan 49
Wannan, Lynne 109
War on the Homefront (Saunders) 144
Ward, Penny 157
Ward, Russel 157
Watson, Del 308
Watson, Kath 288
Watson, Lilla 55, 291
Watson, Sue 221-2, 232
Webster, Marion 197
Weeks, Dion 49-50, 52-3 *passim*
Weeks, Ian 49
Weeks, Karl 49-50, 52-3 *passim*
Weeks, Wendy 15, 45-56, 292, 326, 333
Wenzel, Carolin 263
West, Errol 96
Weston, Alex 57-8
Weston, Elizabeth Grace 57-68 *passim*, 70
Weston, Eva 68
Wheeler, Michael 52-3
White Australia Policy, The 227
White, Lisa 84-5
White, Pat 192
Whitely, Alma 83
Whitfield, Roxanne 81
Whitlam, Gough 105, 106, 159, 162, 196, 200, 250
Whitlam (Labor) government 95, 104, 108, 159, 227, 250, 279, 291, 320, 321, 323
Whitlam, Margaret 106
Whitney, Jeanne (née Bayly) 289
Whitlam Years, The (Whitlam) 226
Why Isn't She Dead (Berman and Childs) 251
Wilderness Society 206
Williams, Jan 292
Wilson, Beth 254, 255
Wilson, Bruce 225
Wilson, Dawn 42
Wilson, Jill 291
Wind in the Willows, The (Graham) 227, 266
Winlaton Girls Training Centre, Vic 48
Winnie the Pooh (Milne) 227
Wise, Elaine 320

Wiseman, John 53
Withers, Fanny 255
Wolf, Naomi 113, 207
women
  see also education, paidwork, unpaidwork
  and aging/older women/middle age 21-2, 23, 24-5, 29, 45, 70, 155-6, 163, 165, 213, 252, 259, 266, 282, 296, 305, 308, 315
  as artist/craftsperson/painter 200, 201, 240, 241, 245, 264, 275, 295
  on boards/committees 106, 107-8 *passim*, 155, 163, 183, 193, 194, 199, 204, 271, 279, 284, 292-3
  as Brownie and Girl Guide leaders 36
  and church/religion 84, 209-13 *passim*, 213, 216, 242, 247, 248, 251, 267, 268, 269, 270, 272-3, 294-304
  and community work 37-8, 41, 43, 53, 60, 295
  as cooks 84, 155, 156, 161, 163, 190, 209, 294
  and development/community development 268, 269, 271
  and disability 31-2, 36, 39, 41, 46, 122, 131, 133, 146-7, 148, 155-6, 158
    astigmatism 286
    dementia 262
    dyslexia 35
    hearing loss 201
    HIV/AIDS 36
    multiple bypass 260
    muscular dystrophy 32, 36 *passim*, 39 *passim*
  as dreamers/as 'earth mothers' 27, 49, 56
  and environmentalism/as environmentalists 60, 107, 142, 267, 268, 269, 272
  and exile/displacement 40, 318-19
  as farmers/rural/outback dwellers 107-8, 110, 265, 267-8, 269, 275, 279, 309, 319
  and financial dependence 69, 146, 162, 163, 205, 213, 252, 295, 297, 298, 299
  and independence 47, 69, 81, 121, 122, 125, 138-9, 147, 148, 166, 187, 201, 212, 223, 245, 251, 255, 260 *passim*, 262, 266, 269, 287, 288, 299

INDEX

Indigenous 270-1
and international perspective 17, 43, 231, 268-73 *passim*, 278-83 *passim*, 284
as invisible/disappearing 134, 193, 194
and Landcare 110
as letter-writers 28, 29, 172, 229, 243, 252, 254, 319-20
and literacy 235
and loss of identity 229-30, 334-5
and management 119, 237, 263-4, 265
as matriarchs 23, 89-90
as mothers/stepmothers 24, 31-2, 46, 48, 51, 80-1, 83, 144-5, 153, 155-6, 163, 187, 189, 194, 201, 209, 228, 243-5, 255, 266, 285-6, 295, 312, 316, 317-18, 319-20
and music 36, 101, 200, 203, 210, 211-2, 233, 261, 262, 264, 265, 268, 309-10, 324
of non-English speaking background 84, 167-84 *passim*, 217-8, 219-32 *passim*, 233-42, 259, 260, 266, 294-304 *passim*
and peace/anti-nuclear movement 37, 268, 269, 270, 272, 274, 277, 278, 281, 282
and politics/political activism 37, 84, 196, 199, 202-7 *passim*, 252-3, 269, 271, 272, 274, 276, 279, 288, 323
and pregnancy 251, 252, 319
and prison 144, 152, 260, 263
as property/trophies 126
as public speakers/commentators 70, 78, 84, 92-3, 109, 113, 114, 115, 119, 192, 193, 194, 198, 203, 217, 279, 281, 296, 314-5
on (job) selection panels 115
and self-esteem/confidence 23, 82, 135, 142-3, 187-8, 190, 194-5, 214-5, 265, 266, 281, 282, 326
as single parents 35, 49, 50, 53, 79, 81, 83, 121, 130, 132-3, 136, 247, 289, 320, 321
as spinners and weavers 322
and spinsterhood/singularity 36 *passim*, 47, 65 *passim*, 133, 147, 170, 255 *passim*, 268-9 *passim*, 270 *passim*, 287, 296, 306-7 *passim*, 335
and sport 60-8 *passim*, 203, 221-2, 244, 245, 246, 268, 294, 305-16 *passim*, 336-7
stereotyping of/sex role conditioning 50, 115, 187, 188, 192, 201, 202, 206, 260-1, 272, 330-1, 333
and substance abuse 31, 119-25 *passim*, 128, 148
and suffrage 270
and TEAS/Austudy 203, 321
as travellers 24, 31, 32, 34-5, 38, 39, 40, 43, 81, 93-4, 96, 134, 137, 192, 209, 218, 222, 226, 228-30, 231, 233, 259-66 *passim*, 260, 262, 266, 267, 268, 270, 276, 289, 318
as VADs 59
and wisdom 15, 120-1, 126, 144, 231, 246, 271, 305, 337, 338
working with women 45, 55, 86, 115, 195, 264-6 *passim*, 268-73 *passim*, 274, 277-83 *passim*
as writers/poets 28, 31, 38, 39, 152, 187, 189-90, 191, 194, 238, 243, 245, 247, 248, 264
Women in Canada (Stephenson) 52
Women and Leadership conference 79
Women and Madness (Chesler) 50, 333
Women in Social Work conference, Can 51
Women in Sport Media Report, The ('Crowley Report') 313-4
Women Working Together – Lessons from Feminist Women's Services (Weeks) 45, 55
Women's Academy (Sydney) 322-3
Women's Advisory Council (WAC), WA 138, 139
Women's Advisory Council (WAC), NSW 274, 280, 325
Women's Bureau, Department of Industrial Relations 254
Women's Health Cooperative, Vic 160
Women's Health Policy Unit, Qld (Brisbane) 42
Women's House, Qld (Brisbane) 37
Women's Information and Referral Exchange (WIRE), Vic 175-6
Women's Information Referral Exchange (WIRE), WA 130, 138-9, 140
Women's Information Service, Qld 291
Women's Information Switchboard, SA 138
Women's Liberation/Movement 7, 144, 148, 149, 278
Women's Movement 7, 11, 14, 17, 37, 38, 45, 53, 57, 69-70, 139, 142, 162, 164, 165, 196, 199, 201, 217-8, 252, 254, 256, 274, 275, 278-9, 280-1, 282-3, 292, 320, 328, 331

women's groups/organisations 154, 280, 296
- Australian Federation of University Women (AFUW) 287
- Gorgeous Girls, The 199, 207
- Karrakatta Club 2
- Koala Club 152
- National Council of Women (NCW) 2, 57, 69, 70
- National Gallery Women's Association, Vic 233
- Older Women's Network (OWN) 165
- Rural Women's Network 113
- Union of Australian Women (UAW) 57, 69-70, 154, 158-9, 274, 275, 277-83 *passim*, 336
- Women of the West 112, 173-5, 176
- Women on Campus 202
- Women's Caucus of the Canadian Schools of Social Work 52
- Women's Christian Temperance Union (WCTU) 70, 145
- Women's Electoral Lobby (WEL) 130, 135, 136, 137, 138, 150, 192, 195, 243, 253, 255, 256, 319
- Women's International Democratic Federation (WIDF) 278-9, 280
- Women's International League for Peace and Freedom (WILPF) 69
- Women's Suffrage League 2
- Young Women's Christian Association (YWCA)/World 267, 270-2 *passim*

Women's Policy Unit, Qld 42
women's refuges *see* violence against women
Women's Room, The (French) 225
women's services 41-2, 230
Women's Studies 54, 55, 56, 209, 216, 217, 322-3
Woodbridge, Pauline 40
Woodfall, Judith 196
Woodfull, Bill 310
Woodward, Lois 191, 197
Woolf, Virginia 265, 323
Workers' Compensation Board, SA 254
Working Women's Centre (WWC), Melbourne 243, 250, 253-4
Workman, Vic 276
World Netball Championships/World Championship Company 305, 315
Wran, Neville 274, 280, 325
Wright, Mary 283
Wright, Tom 276

xenophobia/ethnophobia *see* racism

Yates, Jim 314
Yerbury, Di 11
Young People, Social Justice and Multiculturalism (Guerra) 231
young women 17, 113-4, 147, 199-207 *passim*, 230, 231, 267, 269, 271, 289, 290, 313, 315
Youth Affairs Council of Victoria/Ethnic Youth Issues Network 219, 228, 231
Yorta Yorta people 89
- *see also* Aborigines and Torres Strait Islanders, Aboriginal and Torres Strait Islander

*Zelda – The becoming of a woma*n (D'Aprano) 7, 331
Zervos, Kominos 230

Cover Illustration

'A Garden Full of Fairies' by Alison Brown forms part of the series 'Acceptance', completed in collaboration with patients and staff, Cancer Unit, The Royal Women's Hospital, Melbourne.

Cynthia Holland, Social Work/Project Coordinator, Royal Women's Hospital, writes: 'This series is a tribute and a dedication to all those women diagnosed with gynaecologic cancer. With rare insight and fortitude, they have given us strength and inspiration to carry on against all odds. The six "Acceptance" paintings are snapshots of a kaleidoscope of dreams, aspirations and memories now living on . . .'

The painting is reproduced with thanks to Alison Brown and the women, staff and Social Work Department of The Royal Women's Hospital, and the Ethel Hermann Trust, Melbourne.

Every effort has been made to trace copyright holders, but in a few cases this has proved impossible. The publishers would be interested to hear from any copyright holders not acknowledged here or acknowledged incorrectly.